The challenge of Japan
before World War II and after

The challenge of Japan before World War II and after

A study of national growth and expansion

Nazli Choucri
Robert C. North
Susumu Yamakage

London and New York

First published 1992
by Routledge
11 New Fetter Lane, London EC4P 4EE

Simultaneously published in the USA and Canada
by Routledge
a division of Routledge, Chapman and Hall, Inc.
29 West 35th Street, New York, NY 10001

Typeset in 10/12 Times by
Falcon Typographic Art Ltd, Fife, Scotland
Printed and bound in Great Britain by
Mackays of Chatham PLC, Chatham, Kent

British Library Cataloguing in Publication Data
  The Challenge of Japan Before World War II and
  After: a study of national growth and expansion
  I Choucri, Nazli   II North, Robert C.
  952

ISBN 0-415-07589-0

Library of Congress Cataloging in Publication Data
has been applied for.

ISBN 0-415-07589-0

With the collaboration of
Dale L. Smith

Contents

Illustrations

TABLES

Acknowledgements

We are grateful to colleagues, former students, and current students for helpful contributions and suggestions at various stages of this study. In particular, we would like to thank Anne Tickner, Richard Samuels, Ronald Dore, and Peter Brecke for a careful reading of earlier drafts.

Throughout this study we undertook considerable experimentation, formulation, and reformulation of approach and analysis. We are especially grateful to Richard K. Ashley, Brian Pollins, Raisa Deber, and Linda Kahn for their contribution to early formulations. Hayward R. Alker Jr and Nobutaka Ike have made especially important observations and suggestions at various stages of the conduct of our research.

Raun Kupiec and Seong-Ho Lim helped with statistical and bibliographic work. Sung Joon Roh and William Stanley were especially helpful during the completion of the final version of this study. Elizabeth McLaughlin typed numerous drafts of the manuscript.

Dale Smith participated in parts of this study. We are especially appreciative of his collaboration.

We acknowledge, with gratitude, support from the National Science Foundation in the conduct of this study (grants No. Soc. 74–18551 and No. Soc. 74–19510).

Nazli Choucri
Robert C. North
Susumu Yamakage
1992

Prologue
National growth, expansion, and conflict: The case of Japan

This book is concerned with national growth, the expansion of a country's activities and interests, and the extension of its power beyond national boundaries. It explores the sources and consequences of these activities on conceptions of security and on propensities for international competition and warfare.

Our purpose is to ascertain through systematic analysis of Japan over 100 years the extent to which territorial expansion is less an inevitable consequence of growth than an outcome of the demands and requirements of states and their economic, political, strategic, and security needs – and also the extent to which territorial expansion, once accepted as a security imperative, may create its own demands and requirements for even further expansion. Our basic proposition is that expansion may take on many guises and many modes; however, the demands generated by expansion – of any type – can create new interests and imperatives and demand for further growth and expansion. None of these issues is unique to Japan nor to Japanese history. They are central to politics among nations and especially to major power interactions.

The Challenge of Japan: Before World War II and After belongs in a sequence of studies pertaining to the dynamics of international conflict and integration. At the core of these studies is a theory of national expansion (*lateral pressure*) presented in what we have called a conceptual model designed for testing relationships among national growth, national expansion, and international conflict (Choucri and North 1975: 14–25; North 1990: 9–25).

Early phases of the ongoing study focused primarily on psycho-political aspects of conflict and international crisis (perceptions, expectations, affects, decision making, and other 'black box' functions). The first book-length report to emerge from these investigations was *Crisis, Escalation, War* (Holsti 1972). This was followed by *International Crisis: The Outbreak of World War I* (Nomikos and North 1976), which moved from capital to capital throughout the summer of 1914 by way of close, almost 'hour-to-hour' analyses of diplomatic documents of the period between late June and early August 1914.

Meanwhile, a study of interactions between national growth and international violence had been initiated and reported upon in *Nations in Conflict* (Choucri and North 1975). Quantitative evidence presented in this investigation suggested that the outbreak of war can often be traced back to uneven growth, development, and expanding activities and interests among and between states. According to this perspective, many ordinary social activities may combine to set these processes in motion; and thus in pursuit of seemingly legitimate purposes, states and empires often lock themselves into escalating competitions, rivalries, and antagonisms in ways such that disentanglement becomes exceedingly difficult short of war.

The long-term pursuit of these investigations provided us with national, international, and global perspectives that had been beyond our reach earlier; but even as we proceeded, new insights uncovered new issues which in a number of respects appeared to challenge conventional wisdom in the field of international and global politics. Among the unconventional aspects of analysis were the admission of population density and growth – *in combination with* technological (and economic) advancement and resource accesses – as elementary contributors to national expansion and international conflict: see the earlier book *Population Dynamics and International Violence* (Choucri 1974).

By the mid-1970s the largely independent thrusts of these two sets of investigations – the *cognitive and affective* and the *growth and developmental* (demographic, technological, and resource access functions) – presented a clear challenge: how, if at all, could these quite distinct approaches be integrated conceptually to elucidate conflict processes and their relevance to national decision and policy making within the international and emerging global systems? An answer to this challenge was presented in *War, Peace, Survival: Global Politics and Conceptual Synthesis* (North 1990).

THE JAPAN CASE

Keeping the long term in mind, we have examined the course of events before and after World War II in order to ascertain the extent to which Japan's basic population, technology, and resource access profile (or structure) between 1868 and 1945 was similar to and different from its postwar profile and to compare and analyze the country's responses to domestic needs and demands and to changes in the external environment.

Within a major power context, the history of Japan over the past century provides an opportunity for identifying transformation in national profiles and distinctive manifestations of outward expansion, distinguishing various forms of leverage and their outcomes and testing lateral pressure hypotheses. As in other societies, population, technology, and resources have been important factors in Japanese history, but this study documents the powerful influence of these factors in a country that industrialized, acquired and lost an empire, and found an effective economic and political alternative to territorial expansion and international violence – within a century.

The Japan case offered an important attractive feature. Bounded largely within slightly more than a century, the country's uneven growth and development in terms of its 'master variables' – population, technology, and access to resources – provided almost unparalleled possibilities for observing, analyzing, and to some extent explaining the dramatic changes that occurred in the state, its society, and patterns of behavior during years leading up to World War II and, even more radically, elucidating the postwar transformation that occurred over the next half century.

In the course of these events Japan transformed itself from a developing country to an industrializing, expanding power, to a state annihilated by a world war, to reconstruction and reconstitution, growth, economic expansion – to become possibly the dominant economic power of the twenty-first century. None of this can be understood without reference to the interplay between domestic growth and expansion and the configuration of the international system, relations with other states, and the ensuing modes of interactions.

Preliminary analyses of this transformation revealed in addition that Japan belonged to a relatively small number of countries with a particular 'profile' – a relatively large population, a rapidly advancing technology, and a severely limited resource base. By examining the broad, underlying processes of change, we seek to uncover the relationships of patterns of national growth and modes of international expansion and propensities for competition and conflict. And, in relations among nations the characteristic nature of the international system at any point in time may shape and influence both the pattern of growth and the modes of expansion.

HISTORICAL PERSPECTIVE

Growth, expansion, competition, and power politics have been traced to ancient Egypt, Assyria, Persia, Rome, China, India, and other civilizations of the past. The pursuit of power and wealth seemed to be a given feature of international relations. Centuries later, the effective employment of power was the central theme in Machiavelli's advice to the Medici. So, too, in the wake of European feudalism, mercantilist writers treated wealth as an element of power and proposed that the larger and more economically developed of the new nation states would possess more leverage in the emerging international system than their less developed competitors (Heckscher 1935: vol. II, 17). At issue were the sources of power and of wealth and the consequences of the pursuit of one end or the other.

With the opening of sea routes to the Far East and discovery of the Americas, there was a widespread consensus that overseas expansion and widespread exploitation of the new lands would provide the primary source of economic growth for the countries of Europe. During the sixteenth century, Portugal and Spain established extensive overseas empires. The Low Countries, England, and France soon followed suit, and competitions among them contributed to hegemonic struggles. During the latter part of the nineteenth century, German leaders in and out of government pushed the expanding activities and interests of their newly unified regime into Africa, the Middle East, and parts of the Pacific. Meanwhile, the United States had extended its sovereignty from the Atlantic seaboard across the Appalachians into prairie regions of the Middle West, into Mexican territories from Texas to California, and eventually to Cuba, Puerto Rico, and the Philippines.

EXPANSION AND WAR IN THEORIES OF IMPERIALISM

Throughout the twentieth century there has been considerable speculation, writing, and empirical research about the influence of economic activities on expansionism, colonialism, and war.

Early in this century, the British liberal, John A. Hobson, wrote a then radical landmark book developing the concept of imperialism as the pursuit by 'the great controllers of industry' of markets for the goods they could not sell at home and fields of investment for their capital surpluses (Hobson 1902). Contending conceptions and explanations of imperialism were subsequently put forth, leading to alternative views and assessments. A half century later, Quincy Wright saw imperialism as 'the art by which a politically organized people' subject and govern other peoples whom they consider inferior because of differences of geography, culture, economic development, military strength, and the like (Wright 1955: 183).

Wright interjected control and domination to the concept of imperialism. By contrast, Hans Morgenthau, often identified as 'the founding father' of the realist school, thought states pursued power as an end in itself and defined imperialism as the struggle for power. He distinguished, however, between power 'adjustments' ('leaving the essence of power relations intact') and increases aimed at 'the overthrow of the status quo' involving a 'reversal of the power relations between two or more states' (Morgenthau 1967: 41–2). On the other hand, William Langer, much like Hobson, construed imperialism as a disposition of one state to establish economic or political control – directly or indirectly – over another state, nation, or people. Included among imperialist objectives were access to resources and markets, cheap labor, and opportunities for the investment of surplus capital. He conceded, however, that the concept had fallen into 'bad repute,' in part because it had been used in so many different ways (Langer 1956: 67).

Another, perhaps more important reason for the increasing reluctance by conventional Western theoreticians to pursue studies of imperialism stemmed from the writings of V. I. Lenin, who explained twentieth-century expansionism, colonialism, imperialism, and war as outcomes of the 'highest' stage of capitalism. Transforming J. A. Hobson's theory of economic imperialism within a Marxist framework, Lenin located the capitalism of his time within

> that stage of development in which the dominance of monopolies and finance capital has established itself; in which the export of capital has acquired pronounced importance; in which the division of the world among the international trusts has begun; in which the division of all territories of the globe among the great capitalist powers has been completed.

From this perspective he saw World War I as an imperialist struggle among great capitalist powers for a redivision of the world, its resources, markets, and opportunities for the investment of 'surplus' which could no longer be invested profitably within those states themselves (Lenin 1939: 89). Thereafter Soviet 'communists' and Western (and increasingly the Japanese) 'capitalists' regularly denounced each other as imperialists – each side relying on its own definitions (and, to the extent feasible, expanding its own activities, interests, and holdings, or at least defending whatever it had accumulated).

ECONOMIC ACTIVITIES AND WAR

In *War and the Private Investor*, published some twenty-five years after Lenin's *Imperialism, the Highest Stage of Capitalism*, economist Eugene Staley concluded from an empirical study sponsored by the Social Science Research Committee at the University of Chicago that the influence of economic activities – and foreign investment in particular – on international conflict and war tended to be greatly overstated. 'Private investments seeking purely business advantage,' he wrote, 'have rarely of themselves brought great powers into serious clashes.' Staley thought that the cart had been put before the horse. The foreign investment issue had served government interests more often than the interests of private investors and had been 'considerably more useful as an aid and protection to navies' than navies had been 'as an aid and protection to foreign investments' (Staley 1935: 80–100). With respect to raw materials Staley concluded in a subsequent study that nations are essentially interdependent and that conflicts over resources were the outcome of 'economic nationalism,' 'the quest for power,' and 'the abuse of monopoly power' (Staley 1937: 234–43). Not all demands and complaints 'advanced in the name of raw materials,' Staley thought, could 'be accounted for on the basis of genuine conflicts of interest.' On the contrary, it seemed clear that in some cases 'raw material demands are consciously used as pretexts for the furtherance of other real purposes' (Staley 1937: 9).

However, in a subsequent volume published as World War II was breaking out in Europe, Staley appeared to have modified his view somewhat. 'If one way of using the world's resources makes peace more secure while another stokes the fires of conflict,' he wrote, 'there is no doubt about which the people of today should prefer' (Staley 1939: 98).

Also writing in the 1930s, Norman Angell (1936: 5) set out to debunk the notion that war could be explained by 'the need of industrial people for raw materials' (or for 'expanding populations'); 'or out of the desire of capitalists for the expansion of profits, for opportunities of exploitation; or out of a need to dispose of surplus production which the home market cannot absorb.' Drawing on Japan and its ongoing activities and those of Nazi Germany and Fascist Italy for his debunking operation, Angel put forward an essential rationalist (and circular) argument to the effect that since none of these courses of action *could* have brought about the outcomes for which they were allegedly undertaken, clearly they could not be accepted as evidence of Japanese motivations or as factors contributing to war.

UNRESOLVED ISSUES

Neither the waging nor the outcomes of World War II settled the issue. The question remained: do – or do not – population pressures and/or economic growth and expansion contribute to war?

Writing twenty years after Japan's surrender, Kenneth Boulding, an economist with many years' experience in studying the antecedents of war, also took issue with the proposition that Japanese expansionism during the 1930s and 1940s could be explained by population pressures and such considerations as the need for access to and control over raw materials and markets and higher levels of favorable trade. 'Surely, the desire for military expansion showed itself in Japan long before population growth and industrialization had created a substantial need for foreign markets and sources of supply,' he asserted. Boulding saw the overpopulation argument as 'little more than a convenient myth which served to stimulate the laggards at home to lull the gullible abroad' (Boulding and Gleason 1965: 3–4).

Boulding considered Japan's expansionist policies to be 'imperialist' but motivated less by economics than 'by a powerful nationalistic sentiment or pride,' by precedents set by Western imperialism, and by a belief that they were a 'chosen people of the Orient destined to rule the less favored' (Boulding and Gleason 1965: 9, 13).

The Sino-Japanese War of 1894, the Russo-Japanese War, and World War I, Boulding conceded, had 'proved immensely profitable to large business organizations'; the conquest of Manchuria in 1931 'was almost fantastically cheap'; although the zaibatsu had been disinclined to cooperate with the military, there 'may have been less reluctance as the opportunities grew for profiting from expanding military expenditures'; and 'strong economic dissatisfaction undoubtedly contributed to rural support of the ultranationalists' who led the country into war during the 1930s (Boulding and Gleason 1965: 6–7, 9–13).

Another explanation which the 'statistical realities' failed to confirm, according to Boulding, was the assumption that Japan's military expansion was the result of its difficulties in international trade, in finding, for instance, markets for its exports or sources of supply for its imports. Much had been made of restrictions imposed on Japanese imports during the early 1930s, particularly by the United States through the Fordney–McCumber Act of 1922 and the Hawley–Smoot Act of 1930, which provided further tariff increases, 'but left raw silk, the critical item, on the free list.' In spite of these restrictions, however, 'Japan's exports to the United States improved after 1931,' and the United States remained Japan's largest single buyer until 1934, when it became a close second to China (including Manchuria and Kwantung Province) – and even then its purchases in the United States remained 'fairly close to those of China' (Boulding and Gleason 1965: 4–6).

In Japan, according to historian Peter Duus (Duus 1984: 128–9), most parties to the debate (especially scholars 'under the influence of Marxist-Leninist theories of imperialism) have assumed 'a necessary and intrinsic relationship' between their country's socioeconomic development and its 'policies of expansion abroad.' Duus thought the time was ripe 'to reopen the question of what role, if any, economic matters played in Japanese expansion' into Korea and other East Asian territories. Also writing in the 1980s, however, Japanese economist Takafusa Nakamura (1983: 40–3) put forward views that were largely in accord with Boulding's. Both authors underscored the consideration that Japan's acquisition of colonies did not 'necessarily' produce benefits for the Japanese economy as a whole and that insofar as Japan's military conquests and political controls may have expanded trade with Manchuria after 1931, these gains were surely offset by a retardation of trade with other countries – thus revealing the Japanese militarists as 'responsible for creating one of the very conditions they cited as justification for their activities' (Boulding and Gleason 1965: 6).

Nakamura (1983: 40) attributed Japan's 'imperialism' to 'power politics' rather than to economic factors. At the time when the country was opened to the world in the mid-nineteenth century, 'the Western powers were quite strong economically and militarily and were expanding throughout the world both as traders and as colonists.' Thereafter, as a neophyte modern state, Japan had no choice but to resist the great powers, as expressed in the popular Meiji era slogan *fukoku kyohei*, 'a rich country and a strong army.' Nakamura concluded that Japanese imperialism was not necessarily rooted in 'the search for profits by "monopoly capital"' and that in the case of Japan it was 'difficult to find instances of a resort to war for the expansion of economic markets or to obtain resources.' He conceded that the 'opening of the Pacific War in 1941' was a response to the US embargo on oil exports to Japan and that 'the goal of the war was to secure oil from Southeast Asia,' but this could be seen as 'more a military than an economic motive.'

Perceiving Japan as bent on achieving military parity with Russia and the United States as well as hegemony in East and South Asia 'preferably economic but achieved by force if necessary,' political scientist Bruce Russett (1972: 45–51) saw a US policy of 'gradually tightening economic measures' – including embargoes on fuel oil and scrap metal – forcing Japan into a Hobson's choice between giving up its ambitions in China and Southeast Asia or risking war. Along similar lines, historian Paul Kennedy (1987: 300–1, 342–3) emphasized that as Japanese industry recovered from the shock of the late 1920s, the nation's economy became increasingly dependent on outside resources for raw materials – iron ore and pig iron, coal, copper, and, above all, petroleum. This contingency then strengthened the influence of high-ranking army and navy officers, contributed to Japanese military expansion into Manchuria and China, and by the summer of 1941 persuaded the imperial leadership that 'unless they gave in to American political demands or attempted to seize the oil and raw materials supplies of Southeast Asia, Japan would be ruined economically within a matter of months.'

Who was right: those who emphasized cultural factors and nationalism and dismissed demographic, economic, and resource availability factors as myth or misplaced materialism? Or those who hinted at an obverse perspective?

Editing a self-assessment of Japan's destructive expansion by the Japanese in *The Fateful Choice*, James Morley attempted to have Japanese scholars describe how, in the wake of Germany's victories in western Europe in 1940, 'the Japanese expansionists decided to move southward against the colonial empires in southeast Asia rather than northward against the Soviet Union – a choice which brought Japan ultimately into direct conflict with the United States' (Morley 1980: x). The underlying question raised by Morley (and Japanese authors) was, what went wrong in the course of Japanese policies and actions leading to the attack on Pearl Harbor? Explanations, all of which appear relevant to one degree or another, ranged from domestic terrorism, fascist responses to a perceived communist threat, flaws in the nation's struggle for democracy (including dysfunctional communications, both domestic and external, of Japanese leaders and bureaucrats), relations among big business, the political parties, the bureaucracy, and the military, and so forth (Morley 1971: 105, 139–78, 423–58). In an 'overview' chapter, Edwin Reischauer underscored 'the gap between relatively traditional social and ethical attitudes' and 'rapidly evolving economic and political institutions.' Conceding that uneven growth in any society, 'producing new imbalances,' can be evolutionary in the longer run, Reischauer argued that resulting imbalances may become 'dangerously pronounced when growth has been artificially forced, as in Meiji Japan, by a strong leadership utilizing the experience and patterns of more developed societies' (Morley 1971: 509).

Drawing upon the analyses of his colleagues as well as his own knowledge of Japanese economics, history, and politics, Morley called for the development of a generalized 'Pathology of growth, a study of the kinds of difficulties societies are likely to encounter as a result of various choices made in the growth process.' With respect to its 'pathological' aspects, he thought, 'as well as in its healthy aspects, Japan's modernization is a rewarding object of study' (Morley 1971: 29–30).

THE GROWTH AND EXPANSION OF POST-WORLD WAR II JAPAN

The phenomenal recovery of Japan after World War II, the surge of economic activity, and the eventual emergence of Japan as a major economic power all signal new modes of international activities and new strategies and priorities. The transformation of Japan's internal characteristics and external behavior since the war is a central aspect of this study. History provides few precedents for economic dominance globally in the absence of commensurate military power. That Japan remains within the United States' strategic alignment is well understood. Less clear are the eventual outcomes of bargaining and leveraging as today's dominant military power attempts to share the burden – and cost – of security with Japan, the emerging economic power.

Students of Japan have examined and explained the nation's rapid economic growth since World War II from a variety of perspectives. Each of these is distinctive in its assumptions and scope of inquiry, and each purports to provide a unique and persuasive explanation of Japan's remarkable economic performance.

For the most part these undertakings fit into three major groupings according to their basic assumptions and approach to the problem: (a) the shaping influence of Japan's unique cultural attributes and social values (Hadley 1970; Vogel 1979; Moroshima 1982); (b) economic analyses derived from the neoclassical growth paradigm (Kaplan 1972; Patrick and Rosovsky 1976; Murakami 1987); and (c) the intense interactivity between the power of economics and the power of politics, notably the state (Gershenkron 1962; Krasner 1978; Johnson 1982; Yamamura 1986; Katzenstein 1988). In this connection, the strong 'statist' implications of writers in the third group have been applied successfully to a wide range of specific issues areas, including the semiconductor industry, and bargaining strategies used by governments and businesses in their dealings with each other (Okimoto 1984; Friedman 1988; Samuels 1987).

Our interest in Japan's rapid economic growth is somewhat different – with the result that while we do not fit neatly into any one of these groupings, we draw upon them all to one degree or another.

GROWTH, EXPANSION, CONFLICT, AND NONVIOLENT ALTERNATIVES

The overarching concern of this study is with conflict, violence, and the outbreak of war, which, as dependent variables, are international (or global) events, and also with *alternative modes of expansion that are more competitive and peace-prone than conflictual and warlike*. In both instances, however, we proceeded from the assumption that 'causes' of war and alternative modes of expansion are in considerable part rooted *within* states (demands for resources from the outside as responses by national leaders and others within a state to external events – including decisions and actions initiated from within other states). This means that we cannot examine the outbreak of war (or alternative modes of expansion) without probing into economic, demographic, military, and other essentially 'behavior' variables mediated by bargaining and leveraging by leaders, bureaucrats, and citizenry on various organizational levels and contributing to war (or peace).

In many ways Japan since the Meiji Restoration provides an excellent opportunity for identifying distinctive manifestations of outward expansion and war, including the different types of leverage and their results and testing lateral pressure hypotheses. For all countries, population, technology, and resources remain important factors in national history, but among nations Japan appears to be unique insofar as the country industrialized, acquired and lost an empire, and developed an effective economic and political alternative to territorial expansion and *possibly* war – all within the span of one hundred years.

This study is designed to ascertain – through systematic comparisons of variable changes within and between states – the logic and dynamics of a nation's growth, expansion, conflict, warfare, defeat, reconstruction, and the generation of new conflicts and alternatives to expansion through violence, threat, and war. What are the sources of this sequence? Are they demographic, economic, political, nationalistic, or a combination of these and other phenomena? Are the levers of change ascertainable? Are expansionism and warfare the 'inevitable' consequences of national growth or the indeterminate outcomes of the options, means, and imperatives that leaderships select in their pursuit of economic, political, and strategic 'security'? Can nations, through their leaders (and/or the populace at large), change established patterns of behavior?

In comparing the profiles (or fundamental structures) of Japan before and after World War II, we found the country characterized during both periods by growth and development, strong resource demands (but limited domestic resources), and the expansion into the international environment of national activities (public and private). But during the latter period a profound transformation occurred, not only in the Japanese profile but also in the mode of Japanese expansion. The critical dimensions of this transformation are illuminated by Japan's pre-World War II obsession with territorial conquest and its postwar skills as applied to technological management and innovation, trade, and direct foreign investment.

Are these more recent manifestations of expansion favorable for long-term peace – or are they precursors of bitter competition, coercion, and possibly war?

MODES OF INVESTIGATION AND GUIDELINE PRINCIPLES

The analyses in this book are anchored in statistical and econometric modeling of the processes of lateral pressure and embedded in an historical analysis. Our objective is to specify some of the key features of the theory of lateral pressure in order to understand (test, estimate, and simulate) how a nation's growth, expansion, and pursuit of economic, political, and strategic security can lead to escalations of violence and the spread of war, and how changes in the mode of lateral pressure may generate changes in patterns of international activities.

Additionally, the historical chapters, probing into some of the complexities of Japanese bargaining, decision making, and leveraging, provide a context for interpretation of, and a source of support for, the quantitative analyses. In this way we combine aggregate statistical inquiries – over long periods of time – with reconstructions on 'micro-levels' of how leaders, bureaucrats, and militant interest groups influenced the course of events from the Meiji Restoration to the end of World War II and how since then Japanese growth, expansion, decision making, leveraging, and expansion have taken new and different turns.

Although demographic and economic as well as political and military factors (variables, measures, indicators) are included in both the historical analysis and the quantitative inquiry, for the most part they are put to uses which are helpful to our purpose but which a demographer or an economist might not find congenial. Our intent is less to adhere to the disciplinary conventions of economists, historians, or demographers than in an interdisciplinary fashion to draw upon the data they usually employ for the particular purposes of their respective disciplines and to use these materials to explore our own propositions about national growth, expansion, and the propensity for conflict and war.

This book proceeds with four working guidelines that are subjected to empirical analysis and possible modification or even rejection.

First, international conflicts are almost invariably the *outcome of many different factors* – a 'causal' network extending backward, so to speak, from whatever decision, event, or condition appears to have triggered the outbreak. Within the network of contributing factors, moreover, there may be close associations and intense interplays between economic demands, expectations, rewards, or shortages, on the one hand, and feelings of nationalism, patriotism, pride, national prestige, and sense of tradition, on the other. At any given point in the sequence of these contributing factors, however, some may be more important than others, and numbers of them – notably the 'softer' essentially affective and cognitive variables – may be difficult to measure. Motivations and intentions, moreover, are often mixed, even contradictory, and exceedingly elusive.

Second, the security of nations, like many other fundamental issues in human affairs, *is not unidimensional*. Military security cannot be pursued without minimal measures of economic and political security any more than economic security can be attained without some level of political security and protection from outside attack, or political security obtained without economic capabilities and territorial integrity.

Third, in a figuratively shrinking world, it appears increasingly evident that a country's policies, activities, and outcomes are conditioned not only by its economic, political, and military capabilities but also by the numbers of *people*, by their *knowledge and skills*, and by their access to strategic *resources* – and even those resources which they demand but might be able to do without.

Fourth, theories of expansion and 'imperialism' need not be a monopoly of Marxist-Leninists, any more than expansionist and 'imperialistic' policies and behaviors are monopolies of bourgeois capitalism. *Expansion may occur in many 'modes,'* some more exploitative and/or conducive to international conflict than others.

The text is in five parts.

Part I presents the theoretical basis and framework of the study in terms of expansion, or *lateral pressure* (Ch. 1), and structures, or *profiles*, and capabilities (Ch. 2).

Part II contains an historical analysis of modern Japan's early growth and expansion through World War I and a model of the country's lateral pressure during that period. Comparisons of Japan with European powers are conducted here.

Part III covers many relevant events during the interwar period, including the Pearl Harbor decision, models Japan's lateral pressure between the two world wars, compares patterns of pre-World War I and pre-World War II lateral pressures, and presents a simulation of paths to war and counterfactual inquiry: exploring 'what would have happened if . . . ?'

Part IV analyzes Japan's lateral pressures during World War II and after. This part provides a new postwar model of lateral pressure and simulates Japan's subsequent growth and expansion.

Part V discusses the transformation of Japan, projects major trends into the early twenty-first century, and considers alternative prognoses.

Part I

Lateral pressure and Japan

Chapter 1

Conflict and contention
A theory of lateral pressure

The theory of lateral pressure seeks to explain the relationships between domestic growth and international behavior. The most fundamental characteristics of nations – their 'master variables' – are population, technology, and resources. Since states differ in levels and rates of change of population characteristics, of resource endowments, and of technological capabilities, patterns of international activities vary accordingly. In this chapter we consider the international interactions generated by a state's master variables, that is, how various distinct profiles tend to condition the transactions and foreign relations of states, patterns of competition and conflict, and sometimes even war.

The theory of lateral pressure addresses some *generic* features of national growth, international activities, and propensities for international conflict. Japan is a distinctive case in that patterns of growth and development have changed substantially over the past 100 years, as have propensities for expansion, imperialism, and violence. This case illustrates the transformation of both domestic structure and politics and international activities and behavior – and the change from military competition and expansionism to forms of economic competition, expansion, and related activities.

CAUSES OF WAR

In the book *Nations in Conflict* (Choucri and North 1975), we presented an initial conceptual framework derived from the premise that international conflict and warfare among nations are generated from at least three major processes: (a) domestic growth and the external expansion of activities and interests; (b) competition for resources, markets, superiority in arms, and strategic advantage; and (c) the dynamics of crisis. This approach had the advantage of considerable parsimony; while implying cognitive, affective decision-making and associated components, the framework made no specific use of them. Since such national attributes as population, technology (knowledge and skills), and access to resources were used to define the parameters for state activity within the international environment, however, human cognitions, affects, and decision making, as well as organizational capabilities, both empirical and cognitive, were implicit within the framework. In this chapter we render these factors explicit and show how they contribute to the broader processes of growth, competition, and conflict.

There is never a single 'cause' of war. Violence is more likely to emerge from a wide but seemingly convergent network of many factors which contribute variably to the probability of inter-state war. Rarely, however, if at all, are the master variables (population, technology, access to resources) or economic variables (trade, for example, or investment) the proximate 'causes' of war, but *in combination* – interacting over time – these and other factors constitute a *process* which can create the conditions, or set the stage, for distrust, hostile feelings, and an escalation of negative inducements leading to crisis and war. Closely associated with such empirical considerations are desires for prestige, national pride, patriotic reassurance, and other intangibles.

If war is viewed as part of a complex social, economic, and political process rooted in the past, then an abbreviated sequence of 'causation' may help us to understand the processes leading to inter-state war:

- *population, resources, technology*, lead to
- *uneven growth and development*, lead to
- *differential capabilities*, lead to
- *demands*, lead to
- *differential expansion of activities and interests*, lead to
- *intersections of spheres of influence*, lead to
- *leverages (positive and/or negative)*, lead to
- *escalation and crises*, lead to
- *war*.

These are stark linkages, stated in a rather simple-minded way; but to the extent that they may prove helpful in the search for a better understanding of the antecedents of international crises and war, their simplicity serves as precursor to more complex, formal, and quantitative modes of inquiry in subsequent chapters of this book. To that extent, therefore, their use may turn out to be justified. Clearly, they are not unidirectional (the direction of influence may be reversed at any point); there may be feedback dynamics; and there is nothing inevitable about even the most simple of these linkages. To the extent that variability at any juncture can affect subsequent events in the chain, outcomes can be predicted or explained only in terms of probability. This framework evokes all three 'images,' or levels – man, the state, and the international system (Waltz 1959) – and seeks explicitly to articulate the linkages among them (North 1990).

This capsule representation is adequate only for summary purposes. Many other complex and important phenomena are implicit in it, including several that are elusive and difficult to identify empirically. Each phase in the sequence is mediated and, to a large extent, driven by human affects and cognitions, which are often difficult to deal with rigorously. Every change in the master variables is conditioned by cognitions and affects, and vice versa. Indicators of hostility, for example, can be seen as triggering actions or negative leverages in inter-state relations. The exercise of leverage and other manifestations of influence are relatively overt and tend to be relatively ascertainable, however, as compared with motivations, intentions, values, goals, and other somewhat elusive affective and cognitive phenomena, which are likely to be difficult or impossible to identify. Although easily professed, they are often distorted in action or honored in the breach (in crises and war, for example, both sides commonly present themselves as innocent defenders and their adversaries as ruthless aggressors). Despite the obvious oversimplification, a great deal can be learned through use of this framework, provided its limitations are kept in mind.

BASIC INTERACTIONS: POPULATION, RESOURCES, AND TECHNOLOGY

The theory of lateral pressure is rooted in *interactions* among the fundamental attributes of states. The individual human being – interacting with physical and social environments – is the only truly definitive actor on all levels of organization (Sprout and Sprout 1965: 11). All small group and corporate actors, including states, are viewed as coalitions (or coalitions of coalitions).

Each individual is motivated by biological needs (food, water, air, living space) and psychologically generated wants, desires, and aspirations (security, affiliation, affection, achievement, and so on) (Maslow 1970; Sites 1973: 43). These needs and wants tend to be interdependent; that is, access to food, water, and other resources depends on a degree of security; security depends upon resource access; both of these needs depend on organization, and so forth. Aggregated to the state level, individual needs and wants are manifested in terms of demands for security. *The larger the number of people in a community, organization, or society, the greater will be the volume of needs, wants, and demands.*

People and populations can be seen as operating to narrow or close gaps between perceptions of 'what is' and 'what ought to be.' In efforts to satisfy their needs, wants, and desires, people make demands (Easton 1965: 38–9) upon themselves, upon the physical environment, and upon other people in order to narrow or close these gaps – to ameliorate or satisfy their needs, wants, and desires. If the individual lacks an adequate capacity for obtaining the desired results, four theoretical possibilities emerge: (a) to increase personal knowledge and skills; (b) to bargain and to apply leverage, or otherwise 'persuade' someone else to provide what is wanted; (c) to seek the active support or collaboration of others (notably, to join a coalition or 'bargain and leverage' others into the formation of a coalition); or (d) to adjust priorities and do without (Riker 1962; Schelling 1966).

Constraints of the physical and social environments, together with the level of technology (knowledge and skills) available, establish limits of human well-being and achievement but do not determine successes or failures within these boundaries. Technology, including organizational as well as engineering and other essentially mechanical knowledge and skills, pushes back these limits – though not without some costs in resources, toxic wastes, and the like.

People – and states, through their human components – increase their knowledge and skills by drawing on the mechanical, organizational, and other technologies available in the society for the development of specialized capabilities (agricultural, commercial, financial, industrial, military, and so forth). Through technology, people obtain new resources and find new uses for old, relatively abundant resources. *The more advanced the level of technology, however, the greater will be the amount and the wider the range of resources required (for motive power, structures, tools and machines, raw materials for transformation into products, and so on).* Historically, however, the higher the level of technology, the greater have been the amount and range of resources that people have *thought* they needed beyond those required for survival.

All the phenomena indicated so far are mediated and to a large extent driven by human affects and cognitions, which are often difficult to investigate quantitatively or with analytical rigor.

The volume of demands may be expected to rise with population increases and advances in technology, for example, and population changes and technological developments in turn are driven by feelings, perceptions, expectations, and decisions. *Technology* (knowledge and skills) *contributes to increased capabilities* (including further learning), but *if population grows in advance of technological development, capabilities will be constrained.*

Demands combine with capabilities to yield actions, but actions will be constrained by the nonavailability of appropriate resources. In the absence of appropriate capabilities (and/or resources), however, extremely high demand (implying high motivation) can often substitute for limited resources and capabilities, as demonstrated by Viet Cong successes in confrontation with the United States during the 1960s (Choucri and North 1975: 284; Ashley 1980: 13).

A country's basic capabilities and bargaining and leverage potentials are constrained by its profile; however, the ability of its leaders and bureaucrats to extract and allocate resources and develop specialized capabilities (industry, finance, commerce, research and development, military, navy, and so forth) also contributes in major ways to the nation's position in the global configuration of power and its capacity for dealing with other nations effectively.

The capabilities of a state will be affected by the proportional finan-cial allocations that are made to various national goals and functions – production, research and development, domestic security, education, the military, and so forth. The ability of a developing society to industrialize will depend upon agricultural productivity (characteristically, investment in industry depends upon an agricultural surplus) and the relative amounts that are allocated to light and heavy industry, research and development, toolmaking, the acquisition of foreign exchange, and the like. In Japan the period of the Meiji Restoration provides a classic demonstration of successful – and rapid – industrialization.

Two basic sets of functions performed by the individual human being seem adequate to account for the emergence of state and other forms of organization and for both the domestic and external activities of nations. These are the information – (and decision making) and the energy (and other resource) processing functions, which are inexorably intertwined. Like other organizations, a state tends to survive according to the extent that it is effective in obtaining and managing resources, winning compliance from the populace, and organizing materials, labor, knowledge, and skills productively (North and Choucri 1983: 450). Possibilities for control are limited ('plastic'), however, and no regime can be sure of compliance. In subsequent chapters we shall see how the inability of the Japanese government to prevent 'politics by assassination' contributed to Japanese militarism and expansionism prior to World War II.

The acquisition, transformation, and application of resources involve bargaining at almost every step.

BARGAINING, LEVERAGE, AND COALITION FORMATION

The technology of human organization depends on people's willingness to cooperate – more or less voluntarily – as well as upon the ability of some individuals or groups to 'persuade' others to act (or to refrain from or cease acting) in certain ways.

Bargaining, as defined by Thomas Schelling, refers to verbal and/or nonverbal interchanges used in situations where the ability of one par-ticipant to gain particular ends is dependent upon the choices, decisions, and actions another participant undertakes (Schelling 1966: 5–6). Three critical elements are inherent in a bargaining move: a *contingency* (if . . ., unless . . .); a *demand* (an indication of the response that is expected from another participant); and an inducement, incentive, or *leverage* (the advantage, reward, penalty, coercion, or punishment that is awarded, threatened, or inflicted in order to 'persuade' the other participant to close the 'bargain').

Bargaining and leverage – positive (rewarding) and/or negative (threatening, coercive, punishing, violent) – can lead to cooperation, conflict, or some combination thereof. From this it follows that bargaining and leverage strategies and sequences are inherent in organization and institution building (the formation of coalitions and coalitions of coalitions – including states) and also in conflict escalations, crises, and war.

STATES, POLITICAL REGIMES, AND CAPABILITIES

Historically some coalitions of coalitions – notably those evolving into states – have established political regimes, including full-fledged governments consisting of rules, regulations, laws, bureaucracies, lawmaking and administrative roles, offices, and authority figures and empowered by sanctions (leverages) founded on legitimized force. Between levels and sectors of such supercoalitions of coalitions, almost all political and economic processes involve both vertical and horizontal bargaining and leverage.

In order to hold the underlying coalition of coalitions together, maintain itself, and further its interests, a regime must possess at least minimal extractive (taxing, and so on), allocation, and regulatory capabilities (Almond and Powell 1966: 90–212). Regulation, which is a specialized form of bargaining and exercise of leverage, amounts to the development of institutions and protocols for the performance of judicial, security, extractive, and distributive supervisory functions. An important tool for mediating between extraction and allocation functions, for regulating the interactivities of economy and polity, for setting goals and implementing purposes, and for applying domestic and externally directed leverage is a state's budget (Modelski 1972: 78), which, along with the personal capabilities of leaders and bureaucrats, represents an aggregation of power and a source of national or imperial credibility (North 1981: 6).

With allowances for motivation and will, an individual's status and influence under such a regime are determined by the share of those capabilities, and bargaining and leverage potentials that prevail within it. In developing capabilities and acting on a day-to-day basis, every coalition (and coalition of coalitions) is dependent upon access to resources and information, and no collective activity can be accomplished without the organization of both. In a general way, this means that every activity involves both political and broadly economic (though not necessarily market) components and allocations. Intertwined in many complex collective activities, they are often difficult to distinguish (North and Choucri 1983: 447).

In order to sustain itself, a state must maintain both power-as-capability ($power_1$) and power-as-influence or leverage ($power_2$). Measurable in terms of GNP (or GNP per capita, military expenditures, troop levels, armaments, or other indicators), $power_1$ is virtually synonymous with economic, political, military, or overall capability. Power$_2$, in contrast, is the influence one state (or other actor) can exert on another, which implies a retrospective assessment. During the Vietnam War, for example, the United States had more economic, political, and military *capability* dimensions than did North Vietnam or the Viet Cong. In the end, however, the United States did not have a sufficiency of power$_2$ (effective influence, leverage, 'persuasion') to achieve its goal in the struggle. (A third use of the word refers in these pages to country actors: the 'great powers,' the 'superpowers,' and so forth.)

In the realist tradition, states are usually viewed parsimoniously as acting to maximize or optimize power – much as 'economic man,' commercial and industrial organizations, and whole economies are assumed to pursue the maximization or optimization of wealth. Theoreticians do not always make the different meanings of power explicit, nor are they often clear about the sources of capability and influence, unevenness in power distributions, or the mechanisms whereby a weaker state (power) may overtake a more capable or influential one.

Both categories of power encompass intensely interactive economic, political, and police and military components, which derive in complex ways from the country's population, technology, and resource-access levels (and rates of change). Combining ballots (or mere compliance) with extractions (tax and other levies), national leaders and bureaucrats transform these aggregations into regulative, police, military, and other capabilities and operations. In order to perform such basic functions, regimes use combinations of positive and negative leverages in tacit, if not explicit, expectation of compliance and, when demanded, active support from the populace in return (Iklé 1964; Snyder and Diesing 1977).

States draw on power$_1$ in order to enhance power$_2$ and use both sets of capabilities to maintain domestic law and order and to strengthen national security in economic, political, and military terms. These realities contribute to the double-sided security dilemma or paradox, wherein one country's moves for economic, political, and military self-defense may be interpreted by its adversary as a threat, and a conciliatory move by either side can be perceived by the other as a deception or as evidence of a weakness to be exploited.

Any assertion that a state has *decided* or *acted* probably means that (a) an organization is being reified; (b) an individual, a 'strong leader' perhaps (Bueno de Mesquita 1981), is being treated as a surrogate for the state; or (c) the decision and action are outcomes of group decision-making – bargaining and leverage among leaders establishing a coalition in support of an option (Cyert and March 1963: 97–99ff). In lateral pressure theory we rely primarily on (c), which seems to provide a useful approach for Japanese discussions leading to the Pearl Harbor decision. During 1940 and 1941 the Imperial and Liaison conferences provided special arenas for the reaching of such decisions by top Japanese leaders. Whatever their dispositions, ideological orientations, and personal preferences, however, all leaders must use their power and personal charisma to bargain and exert leverage in order to obtain domestic support for the initiatives they want to implement. At the same time, the rank and file in a society can be expected to bargain and apply whatever leverages are available to them in order to obtain at least some minimal support and other positive responses from the leaders and bureaucrats who govern them. Between the early 1920s and the decision to attack Pearl Harbor, political and economic bargaining and leverage patterns underwent some tortuous transformations, as subsequent chapters will reveal.

UNEVEN GROWTH AND DIFFERENTIAL CAPABILITIES

Unevenness in domestic growth and development *within* states conditions national capabilities of all types differentially. Unevenness in growth and development *among* states contributes to overall power differentials and determines international configurations of power, which contribute, in turn, to international competitions and conflicts and to the determination of their outcomes.

Bargaining and leverage activities provide critical linkages within and between states. The concept of linkage is used in several different ways – between variables, between actors, between issues, and the like. Here the word is used as a recurrent sequence of behavior that originates on one side of a boundary between two systems and that becomes closely associated or connected in some way with phenomena on the other side in the process of unfolding (Rosenau 1969b: 44–5). Linkage networks function within, across, and between organizations, including states. In political interactions, at all levels, a large proportion of linkages are provided by bargaining proposals, the application of leverages, and various exchanges of goods and services.

People in a society tend to rely upon the state and its regime to ensure – domestically and externally – some amount of economic, political, police, and military security. Access to such protections is uneven, however, both within and between states. *Within states*, such asymmetries – together with differentials in the distribution of capabilities and leverage potentials – contribute to the formation of classes, interest groups, and élites. Acting through state regimes and bureaucracies, these groups rely upon their ability to tax and allocate resources and other benefits, such as prestige, status, and access to knowledge, skills, information, decision making, and so forth, in order to win compliance, maintain law and order, and protect the state (Almond and Powell 1966: 190–212). Democratic, authoritarian, and totalitarian regimes differ according to their domestic asymmetries (the extent of unevenness of access to decision-making, for example) and the nature and extent of 'control' that leaders and bureaucrats maintain over information, resource, and related distribution processes.

Externally, the ability of the state to ensure some level of economic, political, and military security is constrained by its capabilities (economic, political, and military) relative to those of other nations. Complicating this reality is the security dilemma; for example, the possibility that measures undertaken to maintain reasonable levels of economic, political, and military security may be interpreted by some other state (or states) as threats to its (or their) own security. In this book we are concerned specifically with Japan's national growth and development, its relative capabilities, and the way Japanese 'bargaining' and applications of 'leverage' in the pursuit of raw materials and markets from 1870 down to the present have had profound effects within Japan and between Japan and other countries.

MANAGING DEMAND

In efforts to satisfy their demands, people tend to use domestic resources first, if only because such resources are likely to be more readily available and less costly to obtain than those from elsewhere. Insofar as needed resources are not domestically available, however, or are cheaper when obtained from abroad, two main courses of action are at hand: a new technology may be developed in order to obtain the domestic resources at lower cost (or to find substitute resources at home); or, whether through trade, territorial expansion, or both, efforts may be made to obtain resources from beyond home frontiers (Choucri and North 1975). A third possibility, when raw materials or manufactured goods are cheaper abroad, is to 'protect' domestic sources through subsidies or tariffs, but such arrangements are often dysfunctional in the long run.

There is also the possibility that a society may reduce its demands, but this option is exceedingly difficult to implement, especially if the population continues to grow, without acquisition of alternative, resource-efficient technologies – although low-technology, low-capability countries may suffer severe deprivations under such circumstances. Countries such as Japan, with large and growing populations (relative to their domestic resource bases), combined with advanced and rapidly developing knowledge, skills, and capabilities, tend to generate spiraling demands and pressures for expansion in one mode or another.

MANIFESTATIONS OF LATERAL PRESSURE

Any tendency for human beings to expand their external activities – whether for economic, political, military, scientific, religious, or other purpose – has been referred to as lateral pressure (Choucri and North 1975: 16–19; Ashley 1980: 24, 37–43), a concept that is not unlike the idea of outward expansion used by economist Simon Kuznets (Kuznets 1966: 334–48). Lateral pressure includes *all* of a country's activities undertaken and *all* its interests beyond national frontiers. Lateral pressure is essentially a *behavior* variable in a variety of different *modes*.

The expanding activities and interests referred to as lateral pressure can be either governmentally instigated (diplomatic missions, loans to other countries, the establishment of military bases, or movements of troops) or privately implemented (commercial enterprises or investment programs, cultural tours, religious undertakings, attendance at foreign universities, vacation travel). Historically, lateral pressure has been manifested through exploration and discovery, settlement, trade, conquest, missionary activities, investment, the search for cheap labor, and so forth. Critical to a country's foreign policy are those interests that are considered vital enough to require defense when threatened.

The activities of private individuals, corporations, and other collectivities often contribute to a country's lateral pressure and as such can be aggregated at the state level as 'national' actions for purposes of parsimony.

Any activity that contributes to a country's economic, political, or military *power outreach* can be accepted as a clear manifestation of lateral pressure. The activities of private individuals, corporations, and other collectives often contribute to a country's lateral pressure and, as such, can be aggregated at the state level as 'national' actions. Between 1868 and 1941 Japanese lateral pressures were manifested in part by import and export activities, but increasingly by military conquest and the acquisition of colonies. Although the initiative for the country's expansionist activities and interests tended to be taken by the Japanese government, support was drawn from 'various interest groups and for different reasons' (Lockwood 1954: 534). What became 'an obsession of successive Japanese governments' with the strategic security of the country's frontiers could not be separated from a state policy to further 'the exploitation of less-developed peoples and territories' to the economic advantage of a country with more advanced capabilities (Peattie 1984: 11).

We conceive of lateral pressure as a generic phenomenon that can be traced back to ancient empires of the past and even to expansionist pre-state societies. Historically, it helps to explain the expansion of Egypt, Rome, China, and other ancient regimes as well as those of Portugal, Spain, the Netherlands, Britain, France, and other more recent empires. The 'westward' movement of the English colonies and the United States and the 'eastward movement' of the Russians are also examples of lateral pressure. To the extent that its relative capabilities allow, any state in the international and global systems can – and may be expected to – generate a certain amount of lateral pressure. For conceptual clarity, it is important to distinguish between the *sources* of lateral pressure, the *manifestations*, and the *consequences*. Although we use lateral pressure as a behavior concept, a state may be visualized as generating domestic 'pressures' (construed as motivation) that are not realized or manifested. Such a state, for example, can be constrained by others from engaging in the desired or intended activity, as we shall see with respect to Japan at various times since the Meiji Restoration.

Lateral pressure is not contingent upon particular forms of economic activity – like the Marxist-Leninist concepts of imperialism contingent upon 'bourgeois capitalism' or class conflict – but upon generic growth, rising demands, and increasing capabilities. Although the concept of lateral pressure has some elements in common with Lenin's theory of imperialism, the two concepts are different in important ways. The demands generated in a capitalist economy often contribute to lateral pressure, but capitalism is not a necessary condition for the expansion of a country's activities and interests. Pre-capitalist and socialist as well as capitalist nations have generated lateral pressure, and since World War II the USSR – notably – exerted lateral pressures, 'positive' and 'negative,' in Europe, Asia, Africa, the Americas, the Arctic and Antarctic regions, the oceans, and inner and outer space (North and Choucri 1983; Choucri and North 1989).

The lateral pressure concept also differs from the Western concept of imperialism in that no intent of economic, political, territorial, or military expansion, domination, or exploitation is necessarily implied. Each manifestation is open to evaluation according to its own circumstance and merits. Often it is perceived and assessed quite differently by its agents, by those sensitive to it, and by detached observers. The usefulness of the concept is that it can explain expansion when territorial conquest is not involved.

The strength of a country's lateral pressure will depend in large part upon the relationships (or ratios) of the master variables – population, technology, and resource availabilities – that constitute its *profile* at any given phase of growth and development.

STATE PROFILES AND INTERNATIONAL BEHAVIOR

Uneven growth and development within and between states contribute to differences in their size, which economists and political scientists identify as a major factor in determining their relative capabilities and potentials for influencing each other. Used in this context, size is assessed in a number of different ways. Sometimes it means territorial extent, sometimes economic capability, sometimes political or military power and influence. One way of assessing the relative size and capabilities of states is to compare their profiles, that is, the relationships between their respective levels and rates of change of population, technology, and resource availability (the extent and richness of their territory, for example, and/or the extent and strength of their trade networks). For explanation see elsewhere (Choucri and North 1989; North 1990:119–32).

Two sets of profiles are relevant for the study at hand: those that are characteristic of high-capability states at or near the 'core' of the international system (identified as the industrial powers); and low-capability societies (the Third World or developing states of today), which have been targets, historically, for deep penetration and domination, and often exploitation and conquest, by more powerful states *en route* to becoming empires. The important point, however, is that significant changes take place *within* profiles and, as a consequence, in relationships *among* states.

None of these profiles should be taken literally. In using population density and per capita indicators (GNP per capita, imports and exports per capita, and so forth), we are relying on averages that hide distributions and thus can be dangerously misleading. Profiles, moreover, are 'horizontal' representations, high-speed snapshots, so to speak, of relationships at one cross-section of time, whereas each of the major dimensions (population, technology, territorial size, and so forth) is subject to almost continual change (each at its own rate) – Japan constituting a spectacular case.

Commensurate levels and rates of growth or development in population, technology, and resource access: Profile alpha

Countries with populations, technologies, and resource accesses that are large and advancing commensurately – technological advancement maintaining a substantial lead over population growth – are typically high-lateral pressure states, the most powerful and influential in the international system. This profile allows, perhaps even necessitates, outward-oriented activities. In pursuit of economic, political, and strategic security in keeping with their growing populations, increasing commercial and industrial capabilities, and rising demands, such countries may be expected to extend trade, diplomatic activities, and strategic 'defenses' further and further beyond their original boundaries.

During their colonial periods, the British, French, and other Western European empires expanded their activities and interests over much of the globe. By the early twentieth century, however, having reached their apogee, Britain and France were increasingly challenged by a newly united Germany and, in terms of population growth, technological advancements, and demonstrated capacities for expansion, by the United States and Japan.

Growing population, advancing technology, inadequate resources: Profile beta

The growing population of a *beta* society is large (relative to its territory), and its technology is advancing commensurately, but access to resources is perceived as significantly impeded because (a) the domestic resource base appears to be too limited or inadequately endowed; (b) trade capacities do not seem to provide adequate resources from abroad; and (c) efforts to expand trade and/or its resource base (by exploration, conquest, purchase, or other means) have not been taken or have been assessed as inadequate.

Because of its rising demands for both consumer goods and raw materials for its manufactures, a society with this profile may be expected to feel economically insecure and under continuous pressure to expand its trade or, if that recourse is impeded or otherwise insufficient, to expand its territory by one means or another. Britain, France, and other empires of the past approximated the *beta* profile prior to and during early stages of their imperial expansion.

Essentially a developing country at the time of the Meiji Restoration, Japan began emerging as a *beta* country in the early part of the twentieth century.

Dense population, advancing technology, and expanded resource access: Profile gamma

A *gamma* society differs from a *beta* country to the extent that although its domestic resource base remains severely limited, it has achieved relatively secure access to external resources. A high-volume, reasonably balanced trade network has been established and remains effectively secured. Former *alpha* countries, such as Britain, France, and (to a lesser extent) Germany and Japan, having lost their empires, are examples of *gamma* countries today.

Since World War II, Japan has been notably successful in pursuing a *gamma* course by further moderating population growth, further developing its industrial technology, and further expanding its imports, exports, and investments worldwide.

Low density, advancing technology, secure resource access: Profile delta

A state in which population has remained low, relative to advancing technology and access to resources can be seen as having achieved a 'moving' equilibrium (or steady state). Its *delta* profile may be presumed to have come about because – in addition to its limited population growth – (a) the territorial base is resource-rich, and/or (b) an effective trade network has been maintained, and/or (c) technology has been used in considerable part for production (as opposed to consumption) and available resources have been managed in ways that have created new resources. A central consideration here is that the moderately low population (as compared with *beta* countries) facilitates high levels of per capita consumption at relatively low absolute levels of acquisition and production. Having for generations maintained a strong merchant marine, sustained a far-flung and diversified trade network, and avoided involvement in war (unless invaded) since the Napoleonic era, *delta* nations have tended to possess few (or no) colonies.

Sweden is a notable representation of a *delta*-profile country, as is Norway; but both countries historically were *alpha* profiles. Their transformation to the *delta* profile evolved over time as *alpha*-related activities of these states could no longer be sustained, given the changes in their profiles during this process.

The world's low-capability societies fall into three major categories. The states with 'high' population, 'low' technology, and 'low' access to resources (*epsilon*) and those with 'sparse' population, 'low' technology, and limited access to resources (*zeta*) are characteristically poor, developing, and vulnerable. By contrast, some states are sparse in population but have abundant resources, are rich but still 'developing,' and are importing technology (*eta* profile), such as Saudi Arabia and other oil-rich states.

Historically nearly all countries in the three categories were colonies of Western imperial powers during the nineteenth and early twentieth centuries. Taiwan (Formosa), Korea, China, and other targets of Japan's territorial expansion were historically characterized by *epsilon* (and a few localized *zeta*) profiles. With technological advancement a low-capability society can be transformed into a high-capability category (an *epsilon* state into a *beta* or *gamma*, for example) (Choucri and North 1989). And different national profiles necessitate different development strategies and modes of interaction with other states (Tickner 1986).

THE SECURITY DILEMMA AND INTERSECTION OF INTERESTS

A security dilemma becomes manifest when one nation, in seeking to enhance its own economic and/or political and/or strategic security, undertakes activities that are perceived as threatening to the economic and/or political and/or strategic security of another nation. Such activities may have domestic origins arising from some complex combination of public and private demands, but sooner or later, if sufficient capabilities are available, they are likely to extend into the external environment. To the extent that this occurs, lateral pressure is clearly manifested.

The global configuration of power constrains or otherwise influences the behavior of states in a number of fundamental ways. If the capabilities, bargaining potentials, and lateral pressures of two countries are grossly unequal, the stronger may penetrate the weaker – economically, politically, militarily, and in other ways – and thus impose a relationship of domination and exploitation with or without conscious intent (North and Choucri 1983). Japan's subjection of Taiwan (Formosa), Korea, and Manchuria is a clear example of this tendency.

As people in a society extend their economic, political, military, or other activities and interests beyond national frontiers, the feeling may develop among leaders and citizenry alike that these 'national interests' must be defended. The critical factor in determining the relative importance of a nation's expanding interests and activities is the amount of cost (in resources, capital, human lives, and the like) which a society is willing to incur. *When the expanding activities and interests of two high-capability, high lateral pressure countries intersect – perhaps collide – a range of possible interactions and relationships is available,* with probable choices and outcomes (depending to a considerable extent on the strength of the demands, the relative capabilities, and the types and levels of leverage employed by the two nations). *Insofar as the activities of either nation are perceived as threatening by the other, the two may be caught in a security dilemma wherein reciprocations of negative leverages are generated.*

The expansion of Japanese activities, interests, and power into Formosa, Korea, Manchuria, much of China, Southeast Asia, and islands of the Pacific is a prime example of lateral pressures – and the employment of high levels of negative leverage (a specialized manifestation of lateral pressure). By contrast, even though Japan has remained critically dependent upon foreign resources and markets, its post-World War II lateral pressures generated by Japan have been confined almost wholly to trade and financial, technological, cultural, and other more 'positive' manifestations of outward expansion. Nonetheless, competition with other powers remains, as industrial countries increasingly seek to contain or constrain Japan's economic outreach.

The expanding activities and interests of Europeans began intersecting with those of the Japanese as early as the mid-sixteenth century when the Portuguese and soon after them the Dutch and English (sailors, explorers, merchants, and missionaries) began penetrating the Japanese islands in search of raw materials and goods to trade and souls to save. The first intersection of Japanese and Russian activities and interests occurred somewhat later, as Cossacks, displaced peasants, and fur traders pressed eastward from European Russia across Siberia and northeast along Pacific island chains to Alaska. Chance encounters occurred when castaway Japanese seamen were picked up by Russian vessels, but during the late eighteenth century Russian expeditions were making concerted efforts to penetrate and 'open' Japan. A hundred years after that, expanding Japanese and Russian activities and interests collided in Korea, Manchuria, and elsewhere in East Asia with increasing frequency.

The expanding activities and interests of the United States did not intersect with those of the Japanese until the mid-nineteenth century – after 100 years of 'western movement' by Americans across the Great Plains, into Indian, Spanish, and Mexican territory, as well as into land claimed by the British and Russians, and eventually across the Pacific.

ECONOMIC CONFLICT AND STRATEGIC CONCERNS

Fundamentally, the tendency to expand activities and interests – whether public or private – involves bargaining and leverage activities undertaken in efforts to increase the probability that demands will be met. Such leverages, which may be accommodating, threatening, coercive, or violent, can be expected to shape further relations between the nations involved. The exercised leverage can be viewed as special manifestations of lateral pressure applied by one country – more or less consciously and purposefully – to another country in order to influence its policies or actions. It is always possible, of course, that activities undertaken by one country, A, for other purposes will be *perceived* by another country, B, as leverage purposefully applied to B in order to influence its policies or behavior in one way or another.

Trade is often viewed as a positive tie between states, but trading relationships can also be divisive. Albert Hirschman distinguished between the supply effect (power-as-capability) and the influence (leverage) effect. The supply effect results from policies that obtain gains from trade, especially the importation of strategic goods; trade directed to nations from which there is minimal danger of being cut off; and the control of trade routes. The influence effect, on the other hand, involves leverage which a country can exert over its trading partners by making them trade-dependent. Such leverage can be acquired by developing a monopoly of exports and directing trade to countries requiring these goods; directing trade to smaller, poorer countries and those with low mobility of resources; creating vested interests in power groups within a trading partner's domain; and exporting highly differentiated goods calculated to create dependent consumption and protection habits (Hirschman 1945).

In general, a country of greater size or relevant dimensions is likely to possess more 'carrots' and a larger 'stick' than countries of lesser size (Bergsten 1975: 184). The more efficient and the more technologically advanced economies tend to enjoy more favorable terms of trade, higher rates of profit, greater possibilities for the accumulation of wealth, and a range of derivative benefits as compared with states with less developed technologies and economies (Gilpin 1981: 138). Any such success achieved by one state has the possibility of appearing threatening or injurious to another state. Trade activities can contribute to conflict, but they are seldom the proximate 'causes' of war, which tends to emerge from accumulations of unmet demands, diverse manifestations of pressure, and escalations of negative leverages over substantial periods of time.

TRADE AND SECURITY

Issues of commerce and issues of security, while distinct, tend to be intensely interactive and interdependent. Usually the proximate events triggering international crises and war, which are influenced by trade rivalries, are likely to be more political or strategic than economic. In general, countries possessing secure access to extensive import markets enjoy advantages that are not available to countries whose access is more limited. If an import-dependent country cannot find markets, that country's access to basic resources and foreign goods will be severely constrained. This helps to explain why nations with sufficient power and leverage potential commonly seek protection for their major trade routes and access – 'guaranteed' by one means or another – to resources and markets that are considered critical to their national security and welfare. Nations differ, of course, in the market shares of their particular exports and the ease with which their exports can be substituted. This latter condition affects the degree of monopoly power which the exporting country can exercise. Even with the absence of monopoly power, however, a country with a comparatively large share of a particular export market is likely to possess superior leverage relative to countries with substantially smaller shares.

Whatever actions are taken by a society to maintain or alter its economic situation may be expected to have effects upon its own politics and strategic position and also upon the economy, polity, and strategic security of other countries – just as political stability and strategic security affect the economic strength and well-being of all nations so involved. Shifts in economic activities tend to alter the relative productivity of economies and thus contribute to changes in international distributions of economic, political, and strategic capabilities and bargaining and leverage capabilities. The raising (or lowering) of trade barriers is likely to benefit some interests or sectors of a society and damage others. So, too, protectionist measures which appear to benefit A (or some sectors of A's economy) in the short run may – by damaging the trade position of its partner, B – lead to retaliation against A. In the long run such measures may damage A merely by weakening B's trading capabilities. Objecting strenuously to the protectionist policies of Britain, the United States, and other countries, especially during the 1930s, Japan nevertheless maintained protectionist policies of its own. Many of these and related problems of the pre-World War II era have reappeared in the wholly different context of recent postwar years.

Japan's limited territory and the country's tightly interrelated import, export, and strategic needs and policies – interacting with those of Great Britain, the United States, Russia/the USSR, and other countries – contributed in major ways to Japan's colonial expansion and reliance on armed force until the close of World War II. Import tariffs imposed by the United States, Britain, and other Western countries during the 1920s and 1930s – and by Japan itself – provide examples of economic measures, intended largely for economic purposes, which had unintended consequences in the long run. As indicated by Boulding, Nakamura, and others, neither these activities, nor the search for resources and markets, nor any number of comparable activities can be said to have *caused* World War II in the Pacific, but we assert in this book that they did *contribute* in major ways to an overall *process* that made the outbreak of that war increasingly probable. Viewed from our perspective, a comparison of Japan, the United States, the USSR, and other powers before and after World War II, reveals how much has changed – and how much has remained more or less 'the same.'

Severe domestic and/or external constraints on a country's participation in foreign trade may be expected to strengthen the probabilities that negative leverages will be relied upon. This proposition is likely to be especially relevant for a country characterized by advanced technology combined with a population that is large (and growing) relative to its territory and domestic resources. When such constraints are alleviated, the probabilities for peaceful relations may be enhanced, but the demand for external resources may be expected to continue rising with population growth and advances in technology. There are important lessons to be learned through a comparison of international events, relationships, and trends centering on Japan before and after World War II.

INTERNATIONAL COALITIONS AND ALLIANCES

States and empires do not stand still relative to one another in population, technology, territory, resources, military capability, or strategic advantage. Compared with each other, some are growing, while others are declining, and thus the condition of the international system is perpetual change. *A nation may find itself at a relative disadvantage in the world competition for resources, markets, prestige, or strategic superiority. In this eventuality such a nation's leaders will look for means of improving the nation's relative position.* This may involve increases in military or naval capabilities or improvements in heavy industry. One method of increasing capabilities is to secure favorable alliances. Such bonds normally imply the pooling of some capabilities for the maintenance of shared interests. In defense alliances the partners are able to complement one another's military capabilities.

The effect of alliance upon an adversary can be such as to increase hostilities, competition, and military allocations. In the quantitative analysis of this book we will see how Japan's army and navy allocations were responsive to those of the perceived adversary. The interactions between alignments and arms races are often precursors to greater hostilities.

Alliances, treaties, and other international compacts are often concluded to end or moderate conflicts of interests or to enhance national capabilities. But although these arrangements may ameliorate conflict, they may also create it. Whenever some compact is achieved between two nations not previously allied, it is likely to damage relations between at least one of the parties and any rivals, unless comparable compacts are made with these. Under such circumstances the alignment of one group of nations may encourage other nations to create a competing bloc. Although relationships improved between Britain and France after 1904 and between Britain and Russia after 1907 as a result of alliances, none of these three powers achieved alliance with Germany. In such a case the amelioration of conflict among only some powers may be suspected of contributing in the long run to conflict among all the powers.

Broad alliance patterns (including distribution of capabilities within and across alliance boundaries) may define the structure of the international system. From the viewpoint of a nation's leaders, a strong or strategically placed ally may be viewed as organic to their own national power. A leading power may seek an alliance to prevent a growing power from overtaking it in some area, or a growing power may seek an alliance in order to overtake a stronger power. There is usually a price for alliances, however, since international compacts impose some constraints upon a nation's activities.

MILITARY COMPETITION, ESCALATIONS, AND WAR

Crises and outbreaks of war are usually best explained by escalations of negative leverage, resulting from threatening or violent *collisions* between the expanding activities and interests of two or more nations (or from the attack of a high-capability, high-lateral-pressure nation against a low-capability, low-lateral-pressure country). In subsequent chapters we will examine Japan's position both as target of supply and influence capabilities of other countries and as a practitioner of supply and influence policies of its own, and we will assess the extent to which these various phenomena contributed to Japanese involvement in violent conflicts.

Generally – but not invariably – the proximate causes of war emerge from escalations of negative leverages. Exchanges commonly start at a low or intermediate level of threat or coercion. Deterrence refers to a situation in which one country relies upon leverage of one kind or another to 'persuade' its adversary that the costs and risks of a particular course of action are likely to outweigh the desired benefits. Coercive diplomacy amounts to the employment of limited force to strengthen a nation's leverage in negotiations that are in progress (George and Smoke 1974; George et al. 1971). Often deterrence and coercive diplomacy work, but either can escalate into an arms race, crisis, or war. In subsequent chapters we shall see how the escalation of negative leverages propelled Japanese leaders into a war which they were not confident of winning.

An escalation occurs when one country, A, makes a move perceived by its adversary, B, as threatening or injurious, which elicits a raising of the ante – a more threatening or injurious countermove from B, which A then responds to with its own increase in threatening or violent activity. Once such an action–reaction process has been generated, each side may be expected to exacerbate the trend as long as the probable outcome is assessed as more beneficial (or less costly) than the probable outcome of a de-escalatory or conciliatory move.

Conversely, once an arms race, crisis, or other escalation is put in motion, any effort to de-escalate may be inhibited by a corollary of the security dilemma: *if either adversary should be disposed to make a conciliatory move, the other may interpret the effort as a subterfuge or as a sign of weakness inviting exploitation.* We have termed this corollary the *peace paradox*.

Some, but not all, conflicts, crises, and other threatening exchanges of leverage between states lead to war between the countries involved. Many, if not most, of these conflicts are waged by limited means for limited objectives rather than for the total destruction of the adversary, but sometimes the massive-scale exchanges of violence approach a level of all-out warfare (cf. Schelling 1960; George and Smoke 1974; Smoke 1977).

The waging of all-out war is undoubtedly beyond bargaining as the term is used in the vernacular. But with the addition of the negative leverage concept, the escalation of a limited war to all-out war and the determination 'to crush' the enemy's 'resistance and [to] control its behaviour regardless of its wishes' do not seem to 'pass beyond' Schelling's own definition of a bargaining situation. It is one in which the ability of each side to achieve its objective depends upon the decisions and actions of the other (Schelling 1960: 5). If the attack on Pearl Harbor was the first leverage of high-level violence applied to the United States by Japan, the dropping of nuclear bombs on Hiroshima and Nagasaki was the unprecedented negative leverage – the ultimate means of persuasion – applied to Japan by the United States.

We examine the course of events in Japan before and after the attack on Pearl Harbor in order to ascertain the extent to which Japan's profile (or characteristics) between 1868 and 1945 was similar to or different from its postwar profile and to compare and analyze the country's responses to domestic needs and demands and external policies during the two periods. Many changes have taken place since 1941. After defeat in World War II, Japan became an officially disarmed nation, and its system of government underwent a remarkable transformation. The country was soon recognized as a bona fide member of the community of nations and essentially as an ally of many of its former enemies. Yet, despite a slowing down of Japanese population growth, the structure of domestic attributes remained in many respects remarkably similar to the structure that had been characteristic of the earlier, pre-World War II period, and many of the basic needs, while possibly less acute, continued to multiply and were generally comparable to what they had been before. Expansion of Japan's activities after World War II was strictly in economic terms, reflecting a shift in 'mode' of international behavior rather than an absence of expansionist tendencies and activities.

With the end of World War II, Japan began an economic, political, and military transformation from a *beta* to a *gamma* profile; but, as becomes evident in this study, the nation's population, advancing technology, and resource requirements continued to condition its demands, interests, policies, activities, and relations with other countries. The question that arises is this: can Japan's *gamma* profile, successful at the present time, be sustained as other powers – the industrial states and the newly industrialized countries – pressure for 'concessions' and adjustment of Japan's international economic strategies? And, by extension, what are the prospects for a viable *gamma* profile under these conditions?

Chapter 2

The profile and capabilities of Japan
A critical century

The profile of Japan over the last 100 years provides an almost classical example of a country with a large and growing population and a rapidly advancing technology combined with a relatively constricted territorial base. As with other countries with comparable characteristics, Japan must continue to rely upon the acquisition of critical resources from beyond its own borders. This basic fact has provided the dominant motivation underlying all foreign policy strategies for Japan, from the Meiji Restoration to the present. The strategies and activities have been different at different points in time, illustrating the way Japan sought to adjust to the constraints of the country's basic profile.

Like many, but not necessarily all, 'core areas' that have become the nucleus of territorial empires of the past, Japan was characterized in the late nineteenth and early twentieth centuries by levels and rates of population growth and technological development that, accelerating in advance of ready access to critical resources, led to the expansion of activities and interests beyond the home islands. From the start, these expanding activities included trade and finance, but from the perspective of many Japanese, such activities were constrained by the difficulty of developing enough markets to produce the foreign exchange that was necessary to obtain the resources required to meet domestic demands and to produce goods for export. Scarcities of any kind and other nonavailabilities of resources (such as labor, knowledge, skills, and so forth) tend to be measurable in terms of rising costs. Under such circumstances Japan in the late nineteenth century seemed to be caught in a vicious cycle of limiting processes and attendant constraints.

A nation's basic capabilities, power, influence, and status in the international system derive in large part from some dynamic combination of the three 'master variables' – population, technology, and access to resources – which define the parameters of its possible behavior. Basic human demands increase with the number of people, but a society's ability to meet them is constrained by the availability of resources. In principle, technology (knowledge and skills) can make more resources, but technology requires appropriate raw materials for its own purposes. The activities of a country like Japan, which is characterized by a growing population and an advancing technology relative to the size and resources of its territorial base will be constrained unless access to outside resources (and markets to help pay for such resources) can be obtained in one way or another. Reducing the constraints imposed by the 'master variables' remains a major determinant of Japan's policies and domestic politics.[1]

POPULATION GROWTH AND RISING DEMAND

According to censuses begun in 1721 by the Tokugawa shogunate, population growth in Japan remained relatively stationary for a time at around 26,065,000.[2] The first adequate census was not undertaken until 1920 (Smith and Good 1943:47–8). Increasing throughout the nineteenth century at the rate of about 0.08 percent annually, the number of people is believed to have reached somewhere between 27 and 30 million when the country was opened to the West, and by 1868 the total was perhaps about 34 million. With a national territory of approximately 370,000 square kilometers, Japan had a density of about 90 persons per square kilometer at that time. Throughout the latter nineteenth and early twentieth centuries, Japanese population growth was unprecedented among industrialized countries (Moulton 1931: 22).[3] Between 1874 and 1937 the nation doubled in population (and hence in density) – from nearly 35 to 70 million.[4] By 1976 Japan's population was slightly over 113 million and the density of 303 persons per square kilometer as compared with 322 and 335 per square kilometer in Belgium and the Netherlands respectively, 95 in the People's Republic of China, 11 in the USSR, and 23 in the United States. The population of Japan over the span of 100 years is shown in Figure 2.1.

A country's population density provides a rough indicator of its demands for basic resources relative to domestic availabilities, whereas national income (or GNP) per capita can be used as a rough indicator of the level of technology (knowledge and skills). If differences in data estimates within and across countries are kept in mind, Japan's population density (92 per square kilometer) and national per capita income ($15) in 1875 can be compared as follows: Russia (14/$40); Germany (78/$94); United Kingdom (105/$123); and the United States (6/$133). All income is reported in 1906 US dollars.[5] Long-term trends are also illuminating – see Table 2.1.

Although by 1980 Japan's population was denser than ever (314 per square kilometer), the country's level of technology – as roughly indicated by its per capita GNP – had advanced remarkably ($8,975) as compared with other countries: USSR (12/$4,564); Germany (247/$13,399); the United Kingdom (230/$8,213); and the United States (24/$11,247).

Table 2.1 Population density and per capita income

	Japan	Russia/ USSR[a]	Germany[a]	Great Britain	USA
1875	92/$15	14/ $40	78/ $94	105/$123	6/ $133
1905	122/$27	22/ $63	112/$136	138/$200	[b]11/ $278
1928	162/$57	7/ $104	134/$205	192/$275	16/$1,092
1938	184/$69	8[b]/ $125	148/$259	200/$359	17/$1,018

[a] The national income estimates for Soviet Russia and Germany for the years 1928 and 1938 were adjusted from Mitchell (1980), in addition to the other sources suggested in the References Bibliography. These estimates are highly uncertain and must be viewed with caution.
[b] 1939

Throughout the pre-World War II years period Japan's transformation from a developing (*epsilon*) profile to an industrializing *beta* profile (large population relative to domestic resources, advancing knowledge and skills as measured by national income per capita) seems clear -- although German, British and notably US technology led by considerable margins. By 1980, however, 35 years after losing its empire, Japan -- as measured by its GNP per capita -- appeared as a *gamma* nation well on its way toward overtaking Britain and Germany (which had also lost their empires) and in terms of

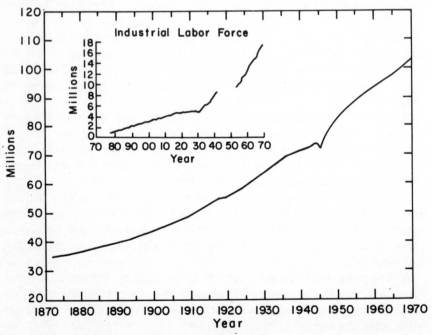

Figure 2.1 Japan's home population, 1870–1970

product (and in spite of its population density), challenging the low-density United States.

TECHNOLOGICAL ADVANCEMENT AND ECONOMIC GROWTH

Until recently, Japan at the time of the Meiji Restoration was characterized as primarily an agricultural country, with 'small-scale industry rising from traditional foundations' (Lockwood 1954: 25). During the 1980s, however, this more conventional view was challenged by studies combining qualitative historical material with data on wages, prices, estimates of yields, and sample household budgets, suggesting that the Tokugawa period was further developed economically than previously thought. One trouble with the new assessments, however, was that at least one study appeared to use two distinct concepts – *standard of living* and *quality of life* – interchangeably (Hanley 1983: 183). Constrained by inadequate natural resources, a mountainous terrain, and land only about 20 percent arable, Japan 'lacked all of the customary prerequisites for economic development' (Kennedy 1987: 206). A defensible conclusion seems to be that Japan's standard of living around 1850 was comparable to that of many countries of the industrializing West at corresponding levels of development (Hanley 1983: 223; Yasuba 1986: 217, 223–4).[6] A stronger conclusion holds that 'Japan entered the modern era far better equipped for economic expansion than contemporaries realized or than a superficial assessment of her assets would suggest' (Allen 1981: 168).

A rough indication of Japan's status at the beginning of the Meiji period and the course of its development over the remaining years of the nineteenth century is provided by the technologies (knowledge and skills) that were introduced from the West at that time. During the latter half of the nineteenth century such innovations occurred in roughly the following sequence: banking and finance; sea transportation and railroads; mining; and textiles (Nakamura 1983: 60–3). Over decades following the Restoration, agriculture provided major contributions to capital formation (Rosovsky 1961: 4–6), to growth in other sectors of the economy, and to early stages of modernization (Allen 1981: 4–5).

In 1870 there were almost no factories in Japan using mechanical power. With new fiscal capabilities introduced from the West, however, the building of transportation facilities, the application of Western mining techniques, and the construction of factories rapidly expanded. By 1905 a total of 4,335 plants with nearly 287,000 horsepower were employing nearly 600,000 workers (Thompson 1946: 238). Leading Japanese industries included textiles, metallurgy, commerce, and finance, all requiring raw materials, new markets, and opportunities for investing the capital that was becoming increasingly available.

Most of Japan's early growth was the outcome of an expansion of the country's basic economy. With population increases, there were added demands for cereals, fish, and raw cotton, which was used in the manufacture of Japanese clothing. In earlier times the production of raw silk had developed as a peasant household industry, wherein the mulberry trees were grown by farmers and their families, who also 'reared the silkworms in sheds attached to their houses and reeled the silk on simple instruments' (Allen 1981: 66–7). With the opening of Japan to the West, followed by rapid industrialization, the demand for cotton and silk expanded. As a consequence of this growth, combined with rapid industrialization, Japanese demand for other goods and resources spiraled.

In general, Japanese agricultural (or primary) investment consisted of residential and nonresidential construction and land improvement by the farming population, expenditures for farm machinery and equipment, and inventories. Prior to World War I – the period of early and impressive agricultural achievements – residential construction in the countryside appears to have been minor, since employment in agriculture did not expand, and only replacement construction was undertaken.

FOOD DEMAND

Traditionally, rice occupied a place in the Japanese diet that was even greater than that of wheat among the English (Schumpeter 1940: 125). Figure 2.2 shows trends in the volume of rice production. Although the land available for cultivation remained severely limited, land available for cultivation continued to be a critical factor in the development of national capabilities. The area used for rice cultivation in 1898 was 2,800,000 acres and grew somewhat in subsequent years. However, during the 1920s Japan relied more and more on imports of rice from Taiwan (Formosa) and Korea (Allen 1981: 118). By the early 1960s land allotted to rice production had reached an all-time maximum of 3,300,000 hectares, an increase of 17 percent since 1900. During the same period, the population of Japan grew from 43 million to 93 million, an increase of 116 percent.[7] Beginning in the late 1960s, however, the land area devoted to rice production dropped back to pre-1900 levels. As consumption of wheat, poultry, beef, and other Western foods increased, the annual per capita consumption of rice fell to below 80 kilograms (from 120 kg in the late 1950s). Demand for traditional food was meeting significant constraints, and new patterns of crops were emerging.

The only other significant food source produced in Japan has been fish, which traditionally constituted the main source of animal foodstuffs for the population. Deep-sea and coastal fisheries have been supplemented by the breeding of fish in ponds and pools in the countryside. Throughout the twentieth century, fish catches have exhibited a trend similar to that of rice production. Since 1928 the landings of fish have more than tripled, from just over a million metric tons in the 1930s to over 10.5 million metric tons in 1973. A decline in fish catches during the late 1930s was largely the result of war devastation (Schumpeter 1940: 163).

INDUSTRIALIZATION AND ENERGY AVAILABILITY

Originally sold as fuel for ships, coal was used increasingly for railroad and industrial consumption and was also exported. During the 1890s as much as 50 percent of Japan's coal was exported, but by the early 1900s this proportion had been reduced to about 30 percent (Nakamura 1983: 62). Bituminous coal was relatively plentiful in Japan and sufficient for ordinary purposes, but coking coal and anthracite had to be imported (Schumpeter 1940: 228, 237). Figure 2.3 shows Japan's production of coal to have increased at a fairly steady rate from the 1870s to the 1930s.

Although the increase looks impressive, the absolute amount was low in comparison with more favorably endowed countries. In the late 1930s and early 1940s, when Japan's coal production reached an all-time high level of 56 million metric tons per year, Great Britain was producing well over 200 million metric tons per year. The postwar decline in coal production was sharp, but a recovery ensued. Beginning in the early 1960s, however, production declined – gradually at first, then steeply in the late 1960s.

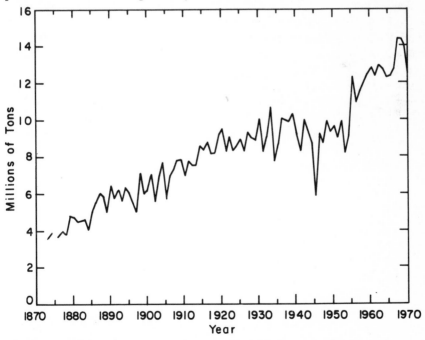

Figure 2.2 ˜ Japan's rice production, 1870–1970

By 1975, largely because of the increased use of petroleum, Japanese coal production was as low as it had been during the earliest phases of expansion, at the 1912 level, or during the post-World War II decline. The inset in Figure 2.3 also shows the coal deficit in Japan (production less imports).

The first major electrical engineering works in Japan began producing motors in 1892, and the manufacture of electric bulbs and accessories started in 1896. A firm producing electrical communications equipment was established four years later. Demand for power expanded rapidly, and an 'explosive boom' in power-generating firms soon followed (Nakamura 1983: 175). The General Electric Company of the United States acquired interests in Japan and began to produce the Mazda lamp. Water-power resources were systematically harnessed, and power stations were built throughout the country. Between 1893 and 1913 the capital invested in electrical supply companies increased from 2.6 million to over 60 million yen (Allen 1981: 86). Graphically represented in Figure 2.4, electric energy generated in Japan shows a trend similar to that of steel. Electricity production was negligible in amount until about World War II, leveled off after the war, and then rose rapidly during the postwar recovery.

Interestingly, the shift in the source of electricity in Japan illustrates part of an ongoing dilemma, namely, the continued need for assured access to

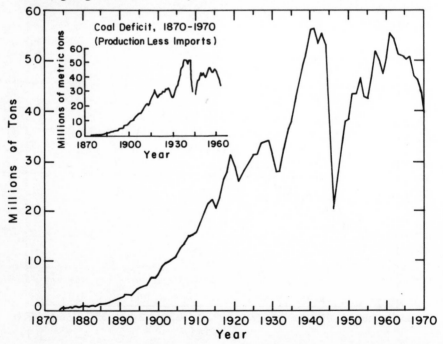

Figure 2.3 Japan's annual coal production, 1870–1970

energy. Over the century Japan shifted from hydroelectric sources, to coal
and oil-related steam, and then to nuclear power. Except for hydroelectric
power, all other sources are imported.

The first Japanese petroleum enterprise was undertaken in the seventeenth century, when primitive methods were relied upon, and it was not
until 1868 that the first Western-style oil company was established (Uyehara
1936: 144). Japan's limited petroleum reserves have been referred to as the
country's 'greatest strategic weakness' (Schumpeter 1940: 428). Over the
long haul, the country's crude petroleum production has followed the same
pattern as coal production, but with a time lag. The postwar increase in
crude petroleum production began in the late 1950s and continued into the
1960s, when annual production exceeded 700,000 metric tons for a number
of years. With an estimated 10 million metric tons in the ground, Japan's
crude petroleum reserves could not have lasted more than 12 years with
production levels as high as those in the 1960s. Imports were essential.

Although gas use began in Yokohama and Tokyo during the early 1870s,
the development of the gas industry did not really begin until 1897, when
incandescent gas lamps were first imported. From that time forward,
demand for gas expanded rapidly, and by the outbreak of World War I
some 84 gas enterprises had been established. During the war, the Japanese
gas industry experienced something of a crisis (Moulton 1931: 90), yet
natural gas did not become significant as an energy source until the 1950s,

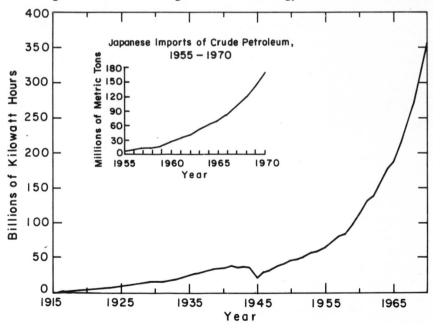

Figure 2.4 Japan's total electrical energy generated, 1915–70

when annual production reached 100 million cubic meters. After nearly two decades of rising production, a leveling off occurred in the 1970s. Despite periodic respites, Japan remained overall an energy-poor country.

MINERALS AND METALS

Metals had been mined in Japan since ancient times, but during the latter part of the 1900s the Ministry of Industries developed and managed leading mines and later sold them to private interests. With the introduction of foreign copper, iron, and steel materials immediately after the Meiji Restoration, domestic metallurgy fell into temporary decline – although copper was Japan's fifth most important export at the turn of the century (Nakamura 1983: 62). The first ironworks using European methods were established under governmental management in 1900. Initially, these works fell short of the results expected, but production steadily increased and soon began to show yearly profits. Thereafter a number of private firms, encouraged by rising demand as well as governmental initiative, were established in quick succession. Even then, the capacity of state and privately owned enterprises met only about 47 percent of the pig iron and 34 percent of the steel that were in demand (Uyehara 1936: 128–29).

For the 100 years of Japanese growth and development surveyed here, iron ore presents a pattern that is similar to that of coal production in the country. Inadequate for the country's needs (Moulton 1931: 60), iron ore production was gradual until the 1930s and erratic during much of the pre-World War II decade as a consequence of an extended financial crisis. Immediately prior to and during Japanese involvement in World War II, iron ore production showed a phenomenal increase from under 500,000 metric tons in 1940 to 1,718,000 metric tons three years later. After a decline immediately following the war, a new start-up took place and around 1960 production rose to levels that were high – but not as high as the peak levels reached during the war. A decrease during the 1960s was as marked as the increase had been during the earlier recovery.

Although negligible in amount as compared with Western European production, Japan well before World War I was producing sufficient quantities of steel to build railroads and successfully to challenge China and Russia in war, but steel plants planned during World War I were not completed until the end of the war or thereafter. Various earlier investment plans were realized after the war, but as demand fell off at the same time, the new capacities were excessive. Shipbuilding followed a similar trend (Nakamura 1983: 177–8).[8] Figure 2.5 shows trends in Japan's merchant marine.

With the outbreak of World War I, iron and steel prices rose so high that by 1918 some 250 factories had been put into production, but overexpansion led to postwar contraction. In response to such recessions in heavy industry, the Japanese tendency was to adopt protective measures and to engage in cartel-like behavior, leading to idle capacity due to the postwar decline in demand.

Despite these setbacks, steel production recovered during the 1930s and by the outbreak of World War II had tripled. With the country's defeat in 1945 production fell sharply, but by the early 1950s the country's earlier wartime capacity had been reestablished, and production underwent a meteoric rise thereafter. Between 1952 and 1969 Japanese steel production rose by a factor of ten; with the quadrupling of oil prices in the decade of the 1970s, production again dropped off sharply. Figure 2.6 shows pig iron production, and Figure 2.7 shows steel production.

The production of other minerals (manganese, chromium, nickel, vanadium, copper, and lead) exhibited similar trends. For a considerable time earlier in this century, Japan ranked third in the production of copper, which was the only metal providing Japan with an important place among world producers (Moulton 1931: 57). Previously negligible, zinc production took a sharp upturn during World War I. After the war, production dropped, but it underwent a rise thereafter. More recently, production has leveled off at about 250,000 metric tons annually.

Dependence on external sources of raw materials is seen in metal as well. During the prewar period imports of iron ore came from China. In the postwar years imports came from Australia. And throughout the prewar and postwar periods, imports of scrap iron and steel came from the United States.

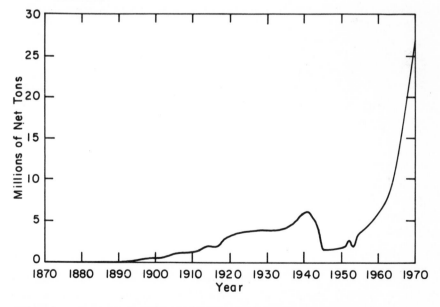

Figure 2.5   Japan's registered merchant marine tonnage, 1870–1970

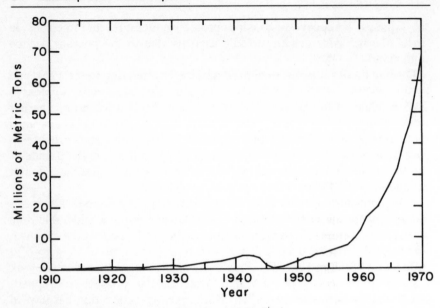

Figure 2.6   Japan's pig iron production, 1910–70

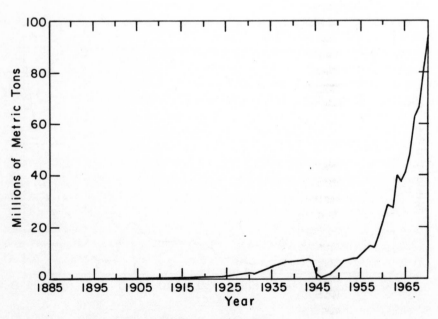

Figure 2.7   Japan's steel production, 1885–1970

NATIONAL INCOME AND PRODUCTIVITY

The measurement of levels and rates of growth of Japan's national income and GNP is still a matter of research and controversy. For early phases of the Meiji regime there are no reliable figures, but national income for 1875 has been estimated at 0.54 billion yen. The growth rate from 1879 to 1913 was probably in the neighborhood of 3.3 percent per year. The growth rate for Meiji Japan was probably as fast as that of many Western countries in the same period. This remarkable performance can probably be accounted for in great part by commitments of the regime to economic growth through technological development, education, and drastic monetary and fiscal measures; and by the opening of a closed country to international trade, exposing an insulated economy to the effects of competition, international specialization, and attendant comparative advantages (Maddison 1969: 31–33).

With corrections for inflation, GNP and, more specifically, GNP per capita are commonly used indicators of a country's level of technological and economic development. (Energy consumption per capita is also a useful indicator of technological development.) Early GNP data for Japan remain controversial. According to one recent estimate: 'Japanese per capita GNP in 1874–1878 was $140 in 1965 prices or $180 in 1970 prices' (Ohkawa and Hayami 1978: 27). Citing Ohkawa and Hayami (1978: 27) and Kravis *et al.* (1978: 216), Yasuba gave Japan's GDP per capita for the 1870s as $280 as compared with $720 for the United Kingdom at that time (Yasuba 1986: 221).

According to Nakamura, Japan's economic growth rate during the Meiji era was 'around 3 percent or, more cautiously' – because of revisions of earlier findings by Ohkawa and others – 'between 2.5 percent and 3.5 per cent,' with recent research pointing to the lower rate (Nakamura 1983: 1). These estimates compare with 4.6 percent for the United States (average of 1869–1913), 2.1 percent for Britain, 2.7 percent for Germany, 1.5 per cent for Italy, 3.0 percent for Sweden, and 3.2 percent for Denmark (Nakamura 1983: 2). By 1913 Japanese national income had reached 4,556 billion yen; by 1945 it was 75,214 billion, and by 1976, 140,221 billion. GNP was 474 billion yen in 1946 and 164,540 billion in 1976. In a study of Japanese growth patterns between the beginning of World War I and 1960, three economists concluded that in 1914 the nation was 'not dissimilar to present underdeveloped countries of the same income level' and that between that year and 1960 its economy was 'transformed from that of a typical underdeveloped country to that of an advanced society' (Chenery *et al.* 1977: 276–7). This view was supported further by detailed analysis of the Japan case in a cross-national context (Minami 1986). Figure 2.8 presents national income and income per capita.

However disruptive the 1973 oil crisis had seemed at the time, the effects on Japan of the second crisis resulting from the sharp increases in oil prices from the end of 1978 to 1980 soon appeared to be worse. Following another initial deterioration in terms of trade and a significant decline in real income, the Japanese economy suffered 'a stagnant trend in domestic final demand and a need for inventory adjustment.' Along with these effects came a slowing down in economic growth, which was first felt during the spring of 1980 and lasted until the early months of 1981.'[9] But the recovery was quick.

IMPORTS AND EXPORTS

For Japan 'the history of exports is very much the history of which industries were the star performers of their eras.' Between 1885 and 1910 the rise in the proportion of exports to total production from 6 percent to 20 percent reflected the

> strong growth of the industries that were the major exporters. Until the mid-1920s, when they were replaced by heavy and chemical industries, silk reeling and cotton textiles remained the country's representative industries. During these decades, Japanese trade was characterized by the importing, processing, and exporting of raw materials with value added' (Nakamura 1983: 35)

And Minami argued: 'Exports also made it possible to expand import capacity. This contribution is especially important for countries that must depend upon imports for natural resources' (Minami 1986: 253).

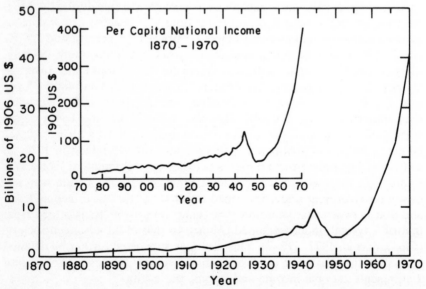

Figure 2.8   Japan's national income, 1870–1970

Because of national seclusion policies that had prevailed for generations, the people of Japan at the time of the Meiji Restoration lacked experience in the conduct of foreign trade, and as a result, it seemed logical that the rapidly developing commerce of the country was carried on in large part by foreign residents for a considerable period of time (Moulton 1931: 252). It was only after the establishment of the Yokohama Species Bank in 1880 and the Bank of Japan two years later that Japanese merchants began taking over the management of foreign trade. Even then, the Japanese economy continued to run a small international payments deficit until the Sino-Japanese War of 1894–1895. After the war, as Japan went on the gold standard, exports expanded and 'a virtual balance on the trade account was maintained.' Exports included such primary products as silk thread, tea, marine products, coal, copper, and increasingly such traditional products as matting, ceramics, and silk garments (Nakamura 1983: 29).

Throughout the early decades of this century, Japan relied heavily on the export of silk and other textiles to obtain foreign exchange for the purchase of Western machinery and manufactured goods. Japanese exports increased substantially throughout most of the past century, but imports tended, overall, to increase more rapidly, with the result that the country often suffered balance of trade and payments deficits.

With the Russo-Japanese War (1904–5) foreign exports underwent notable increases, and during World War I another upsurge occurred – although corrections have to be made for inflation in the latter instance (Uyehara 1936: 210–16). Needed by the Western Allies for the transportation of troops and military supplies, Japan's shipping enterprises grew 'by leaps and bounds' (Schumpeter 1940: 828–9, 873–8), and strong exports and rising price levels led to large trade surpluses. The end of the war exposed serious problems, however. From the early years of industrialization, Japan had needed to import large quantities of raw materials for domestic consumption and in support of the country's export industries. After World War I the trade account was reversed, and 'species reserves began to dwindle.' The import–export relationship became a process that soon operated as a national trap.

Throughout the 1920s a number of exceptional rice crops gave Japan's foreign trade a welcome boost. In the 1924–5 period net rice exports were valued at 116 million yen, whereas the net rice imports had been reduced to just over 13 million yen by 1930 (Moulton 1931: 417). By the end of the decade, however, about 20 percent of the country's rice consumption was being imported, largely from Formosa and Korea. Except for the years 1909, 1915–18, and 1935, in fact, Japanese exports during pre-World War II decades were never sufficient to pay for imports (Nakamura 1983: 29, 35).

With the development of rayon, the Japanese silk industry suffered a serious setback, which contributed to a marked decline in demand for silk and the disruption of the delicate relationship between exports and imports (Moulton 1931: 417). In 1929 the silk-reeling industry accounted for 42 percent of the textile employment, as contrasted with 28 percent in 1935. Measured in product value, the fall was 'much greater,' since rayon weaving, knitted goods, and woolen industries accounted for 19 percent of textile employment as compared with 9 percent in 1929 (Allen 1940: 7). These changes were reflected in Japanese imports during the 1930s. Throughout the 1920s, excesses of imports over exports were largely paid for by borrowing from abroad and by depleting the gold and foreign balances which had accrued during World War I (Schumpeter 1940: 873–8).

With the Great Depression of the late 1920s and the worldwide collapse of the gold standard in late 1931, a controlled foreign exchange system was instituted by the Japanese government. The yen fell substantially, and during the rest of the 1930s exports expanded (Nakamura 1983: 29–35). In 1938 and 1939, however, the apparent excess of exports resulted from capital exports to Manchukuo (Manchuria) and North China, which were then under Japanese occupation (Schumpeter 1940: 828).

Since the most important increases in exports took place in manufactured goods, it was in this way that the Japanese economy, after a severe drop-off during the postwar years, began to bridge the gap between national demands and capabilities. The record of Japan's exports of finished goods tells the story. From about one billion yen worth of finished goods exported in the 1940s, Japan exported 5 billion yen worth in 1961. The foreign exchange generated by these exports was more than enough to meet payments for imports of food and raw materials. Production of these goods remained heavily dependent upon high levels of raw materials imports, however, and any interruption of the flow of such resources into Japan would have a significant negative impact on the country's economic condition. The import–export loop (or the trade trap) has remained a characteristic feature of the Japan profile over the past century. Figure 2.9 shows trends in total trade, and the insets show imports of raw materials and exports of finished goods.

As compared with Germany, Britain, and the United States, Japan's level of imports and exports (relative to its population) tended to be low until after World War II. Like Germany and Britain, Japan's imports tended to exceed exports – see Table 2.2 (in 1906 US dollars for comparability).

During the immediate post-World War II years when Japan was importing more than it was exporting, the country's trade balance remained negative for considerable periods of time. By the late 1960s, however, Japan had achieved maturity as an industrial state, had access to expanding markets, and the balance of trade remained positive – although a temporary gap appeared with the oil shock of 1973.[10]

Table 2.2 Per capita exports and imports (*1906 US $*)

	Japan		Germany		Britain		USA	
	Imp.	Exp.	Imp.	Exp.	Imp.	Exp.	Imp.	Exp.
1885	0.8	1	59	58	67	49	35	44
1905	5	3	114	91	87	63	46	64
1928	9	8	107	93	90	64	59	79
1938	8.1	8.2	77	74	79	46	61	46

Note: These figures must be viewed with caution; they are estimates at best.

Primarily because of steady growth in exports and a slowdown in the growth of imports, however, the trade balance recovered from a deficit of approximately $1.8 billion in the first three months of 1980 to a surplus of about $3.4 billion in the same quarter of 1981. This turnabout was explained in large part from yen depreciation, a successful diversification of export markets, and 'the non-price competitiveness' of Japanese products. Largely responsible for the recovery, however, was 'a dramatic increase in investment in Japanese securities made by foreign investors.' Petrodollars and dollars from pension funds and trust funds of Europe and the United States were thought to account for a large

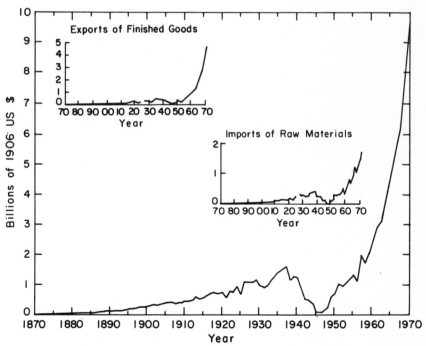

Figure 2.9 Japan's total trade, 1870–1970

proportion of these investments (Economic Planning Agency 1981: 42–7). Again Japan succeeded in effecting a remarkable recovery.

Successful adjustment policies following the oil crisis lead to the reestablishment of a positive balance, the expansion of trade surplus, and an attendant embarrassment in relations with other industrial polities, most notably the United States. Japan's economic performance was faring simply too well. As often observed, 'the great expansion of world market relations has obviously enhanced the role of economic power as an instrument of statecraft' (Gilpin 1975: 28–9). The trend toward global interdependence has greatly increased the possibilities for a strong economic power to exert influence effects upon other countries (Keohane and Nye 1977: 23).

GOVERNMENT REVENUES, MILITARY CAPABILITIES, AND EXTERNAL EXPANSION

Opened to the West and to the world in the mid-nineteenth century, Japan – as 'a neophyte modern state' – was perceived by many of its leaders as having 'no choice but to resist the great powers,' which were seen as strong both economically and militarily. 'Military preparedness was absolutely essential to Japanese independence, and in order to join the ranks of Western powers it was necessary to employ the same policies of international power politics used by Western nations.' Under these circumstances, militarization was considered not only 'unavoidable' but requiring 'unreasonable' sacrifices on the economy. (Nakamura 1983: 37).

During the better part of a decade following the Meiji Restoration, the emperor and his regime undertook the financing and mobilization of armed forces in order to consolidate power, reform domestic institutions, and mount effective domestic and foreign policies. At that time the country's military and naval establishments 'lacked almost everything' (Ono 1922: 8–9). In the course of integrating the military forces of numerous local clans, the suppression of domestic disturbances, and carrying out minor interventions in Taiwan and Korea, the principle of 'a whole nation in arms' was formulated, the conscription law was revised, the terms of service for reserves were extended, and the army and navy were reorganized and expanded (Ono 1922: 39–40).

Soon, having achieved new levels of economic and political growth and integration at home, Japan began expanding its activities and interests beyond the home islands. During the 50 years beginning with the Sino-Japanese War of 1894–5, Japan despatched troops abroad 'more than ten times', including 'the Boxer Rebellion, the Russo-Japanese War, World War I, the Siberian Expedition, three times in connection with the Shantung Expedition, the Manchurian Incident, the Second Sino-Japanese War, and the Pacific War' (Nakamura 1983: 37). Throughout the Meiji period, scarcely any economic change took place without indirect, if not direct, connections with wars or preparations for war. Japanese financial records of the time reveal a strain imposed on the country's economy by the heavy expenditures for armaments and war (Lockwood 1954: 34–5). With a rapidly growing national economy, however, Japan seemed able to afford tremendous expenditures on the military from its own revenues while still providing scope for further such expenditures. Figure 2.10 shows trends in government revenues. The larger the government revenues, over time, the greater, in principle, is the basis from which allocations to the military can be made.

Measured in terms of military expenditures per capita, Japan started from a low base as compared with the Western powers (including Germany) but increased over the years, especially during the 1930s (as would be expected) – see Table 2.3.

As depicted in Figure 2.11, the history of Japanese military expenditures shows substantial percentage increases leading up to the Russo-Japanese War (1904–5), during the Siberian expedition of the early 1920s, at the time of the Manchurian Incident (1931), and during World War II. Untangling the various sources or causes of allocations to the military is a difficult task indeed. In subsequent chapters we examine the historical and political factors pushing for more investments in the military and quantitatively try to untangle some major influences. A common theme among major powers is the effect of bureaucratic pressures generating inertia in allocations – resulting in greater military expenditures from one

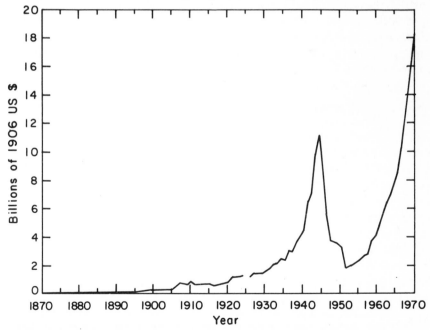

Figure 2.10 Japan's government revenues, 1870–1970

year to the next. Similarly, in Japan last year's allocations to the military influence this year's investments.[11] The insets show the army expenditures and navy expenditures. Expenditures are depicted as rising slowly (largely in response to US and European demands) from a low base. These trends stand in contrast to military expenditures and programs during the decades since World War II. The postwar Japanese constitution expressly

Table 2.3 Per capita military expenditures, 1875–1980 (1906 US $).

	Japan	Russia/ USSR	Germany	Great Britain	United States
1875	0.27	1.08	2.90	4.14	3.64
1905	7.88	2.55	5.25	10.21	9.36
1921	3.24	n.a.	0.37	14.31	25.12
1928	2.18	n.a.	2.05	7.69	10.05
1938	27.88	n.a.	5.20[a]	15.65	18.27
1980[b]	84.00	893.00	347.00[c]	391.00	765.00

[a] This figure (for 1936) is the last available under the Nazi regime and may not be trustworthy. Further, all the figures should be viewed with caution.
[b] The 1980 data are in constant (1983) dollars.
[c] This figure represents West German data only.

restricts the country's military establishment to defense capabilities. Despite spectacular postwar technological and economic growth, Japan was still characterized (with allowance for unprecedented access to foreign resources and markets) by a profile that was remarkably similar to that of several prewar decades.

THE EMPIRE AND ITS COLONIES

Referring to the Japanese colonial empire as 'more strategic than economic in nature,' William Lockwood concluded that Japanese expansionism 'provided the metropolitan country with control over a large food base, created a ring of defense barriers around Japan proper, and afforded bases for further expansion into East Asia' (Lockwood 1954: 51). In fact, as Lockwood's statement betrays, economic (food and also other raw materials and markets required in order to pay for imports) and strategic goals were tightly intertwined; economic capabilities provided a foundation for building military capabilities, and vice versa; and each subsequent stage of military expansion yielded resources that contributed to the next economic stage, and vice versa (cf. Gann 1984: 504).

Derived from a combination of economic, political, and military capabilities, Japanese leverage potentials contributed to the conquest of low-capability neighbors, to the economic, political, and military penetration of these societies, and to the success of the Japanese in the enforcement of their will therein.

From the beginning the Japanese relied on their colonies not only for revenue and the maintenance of their own self-sufficiencies but also as contributors to the economic security and general well-being of the home islands (Peattie 1984: 31). One of the first concerns of Japan's colonial regimes, beginning with the one imposed in Taiwan, was 'to establish a rationalized agricultural tax base' which could provide the metropolitan nation 'with a regular source of revenue' (Myers and Saburo 1984: 420 ff.). This was only a beginning; in due course Taiwan and Korea, Japan's two major colonies, became 'agricultural appendages to solve Japan's food problems' and increasingly a source of fuels and other raw materials for Japanese industries and of markets for the generation of foreign exchange, which was badly needed for solving Japan's balance of payments problems (Ho 1984: 347, 348). By the late 1920s and early 1930s Japan relied heavily upon the minerals, hydroelectric power, investment opportunities, and cheap labor in Korea, especially in order to shore up its own economic security during the global economic crisis of the time (Peattie 1984: 30–3).

In the establishment of the various colonial administrations, the activities of bureaucrats and the Japanese armed forces were closely coordinated. Although they seldom had to rely upon the regular military forces for

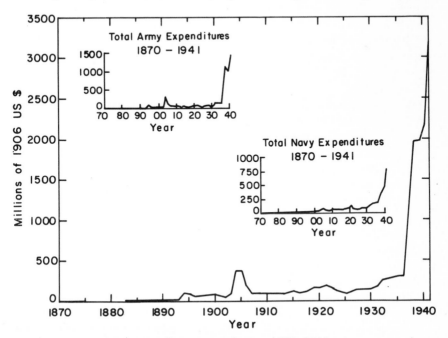

Figure 2.11   Japan's total military expenditures, 1870–1941

assistance, Japanese administrators knew they 'could count on instant, loyal, and overwhelming military support and were therefore much less likely to temporize in dealing with colonial populations' (Peattie 1984: 27). In addition to their routine peacekeeping duties, police in the colonies, drawing on the Meiji police system, were often responsible for enforcing public welfare, controlling public rallies, managing food programs and fire protection, and maintaining surveillance over people suspected of 'dangerous thoughts.'

Drawing on their early experiences in colonial administration, the Japanese authorities adopted the *pao-chia* system, previously employed by the Chinese in Taiwan, for use there and in other colonies. This system grouped ten or so households into *chia*, and a comparable number of *chia* were grouped into *pao* under leaders approved (in use by Japan) by local police officers, who had to report regularly on the residents for whom they were responsible and their arrivals and departures. The system was also responsible for the enforcement of public health measures and under special circumstances to assist in police duties, and able-bodied *pao-chia* members served in local militia units (Chen 1984: 213–17, 220 ff.).

Changes in Japan's colonial area over the years were made in step-wise fashion with increases in 1895 (Taiwan and the Pescadores), 1905 (South Sakhalin and the Kwantung Leased Territory), 1910 (Korea formally annexed), 1919 (Pacific Mandated Islands), and 1931 (Manchuria, proclaimed independent as Manchukuo, but Japanese controlled). Subsequently, as the colonial empire became more and more a staging area for Japanese economic, political, and military domination over East and Southeast Asia, the Greater East Asia Co-Prosperity Sphere was announced as the blueprint for a 'new order' southward and westward as far as India.

Having emerged late in an imperial era characterized by the growth, development, and eventual decline of the Portuguese, Spanish, British, Dutch, French, German, and Belgian empires, the empire of Japan – like the empire extending deep into Latin America and across the Pacific that was dreamed of by many Americans during and after the Spanish–American War – may have been constrained from the start, the costs of empire having escalated rapidly by the early twentieth century and skyrocketed during and after World War I and World War II.[12] In any case, what the Japanese gained initially and at low cost from the acquisition of Taiwan and Korea was subsequently outbalanced by the expense of acquiring and 'modernizing' Manchuria and in due course wiped out by the profitless attempt at conquering China and extending the Greater East Asia Co-Prosperity Sphere to the borders of India and the approaches to Australia.

Critical changes in costs of controlling empires have commonly been explained by rising expectations on the part of colonial subjects (often attributable to rising technologies, educational opportunities, consumer goods imported by the imperial rulers, the training in more advanced weaponry of colonial troops who later turn against the imperial administration, the depletion of colonial resources, the expense, as in the Japan case, of conquering new territories to help pay the costs of administering the old, and the generation of debt and inflation in the imperial regime). Figure 2.12 shows the size of the Japanese empire, and the inset records the history of budgetary allocations for the administration of overseas territories.

NEW MODES OF INTERNATIONAL EXPANSION

With the end of World War II and the rapid disintegration of the British, French, and other colonial empires, the lateral pressure of industrialized and more advanced developing countries was manifested in terms of expanding commerce, finance, foreign investment, and technological and military assistance. In this partially transformed world of the later twentieth century, Japan recovered slowly, at first, but during the 1970s and 1980s developed into a major economic power. Meanwhile, under the postwar 'Peace Constitution,' the country had committed itself to a restricted 'defense' program which freed a certain amount of revenue for non-military purposes.

During the early postwar years, Japanese firms focused primarily on the domestic market. In those years the country had no advantage in foreign markets, and foreign exchange controls constrained investments.

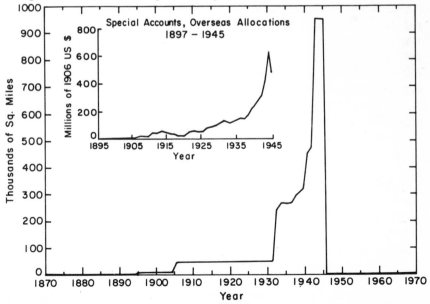

Figure 2.12 Japan's colonial area, 1870–1970

Japanese trade expanded steadily, however, and in the 1970s a liberalization of governmental policies unleashed a growing volume of foreign investments, which soon replaced foreign trade as Japan's major manifestation of economic expansion – and lateral pressure – abroad.

International comparisons of cumulative foreign direct investments show the extent of Japanese expansion in terms of average annual percentage growth rates – see Table 2.4.

Table 2.4 Cumulative foreign direct investment: average annual growth

	% 1971–5	% 1975–81
Japan	37.9	19.1
United States	10.7	10.6
West Germany	21.7	15.2
United Kingdom	6.8	17.1

Source: Itoh and Kiyono 1986: 65

As might be expected, Japan's foreign direct expansion reflected the country's continued demand for raw materials and natural resources. Large investments in mining in Asia and Latin America and in petrochemicals in the Middle East illustrate this continued demand (see the insert in Figure 2.13). Further, foreign direct investments in manufacturing industries increased rapidly between 1971 and 1981.[13] The continued dependence on foreign trade is illustrated by Japan's concentration on commerce in North America (largely the US–Japan link). The most salient feature of the direct investment in the commerce sector is the role of the 'general trading companies' (*sogo-sosha*), where advantage lies in long experience in trade.[14] Consistent with arguments of Kojima (1973a; 1977a) and Ozawa (1979), Itoh and Kiyono summed the Japanese position as follows: 'export expansion made unit cost for direct investment low, while direct investment promoted further exports' (1986: 81). At the beginning of 1986 Japanese companies accounted for 6.8 percent of the world's total foreign direct investment, in the same league as German (8.1 percent) and Dutch (8.6 percent) but still far behind British (18.1 percent) and US (36.1 percent) multinationals (*The Economist* 5 December 1987: 15). We shall note in Chapter 17 the magnitude and scope of Japan's investments internationally relative to those of other powers.

Thirty-five years after the end of World War II, in 1980, Japan's imports and exports per capita were valued at $1,067 and $1,085, close to those of West Germany ($2,865 and $3,012), Britain ($1,925 and $1,957) and the United States ($1,096 and $985) (all in current US dollars). Clearly Japan has demonstrated its capacity to withstand the oil shock and sustain its technological and economic growth.

Japanese exports of technology have increased substantially in recent

decades. Figure 2.13 also shows the remarkable extent to which Japan
has marshaled its physical and human resources and channeled the output
into the sale of high-technology products (and the inset shows Japan's
foreign direct investments). By contrast, the pattern of foreign investment
in Japan was irregular. The relatively low level of foreign penetration of
the Japanese market has been due primarily to the country's restrictive
policies, which have been confronted with something less than equa-
nimity by the United States and other exporting countries in the international system.

While conflicts and contention between Japan and members of the
Western alliance surface along trade dimensions, the fact remains that
Japan's successful technological drive has come to intersect with American
hegemony and the traditional US dominance of the postwar period. From
a global perspective Japan has challenged the United States 'even in
the highest of high-technology goods' (Krasner 1986: 788). This challenge has placed the United States in a dilemma between 'diffuse reciprocity' and 'specific reciprocity.' The American support for 'diffuse
reciprocity' through international negotiations and agreements stresses
multilateralism and dilutes the potential role of an immediate competitor
for US technological dominance. The contentions, challenges, alignments,

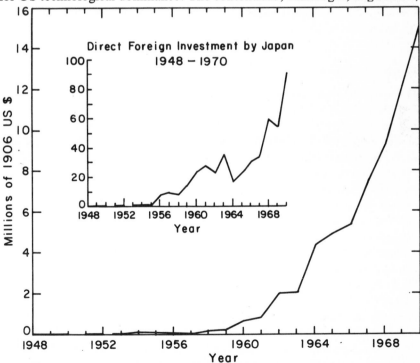

Figure 2.13   Japanese exports of technology, 1948–70

and resolutions are evolving as the parameters of interaction and collisions take shape.[15]

As set forth in the *Basic Policy for National Defense* adopted by the cabinet in May 1957, Japanese leaders since then have tended to pursue policies for ensuring relationships of solidarity and concert with all foreign countries, Western countries in particular; stepped-up cooperation in various United Nations activities; continued contributions to political stability and economic development through diplomatic efforts and economic cooperation to resolve or ameliorate disputes or confrontations anywhere in the world; sustained efforts toward global disarmament. Nonetheless, some lines of policy debates in Japan argued that the country should 'maintain an appropriate military capability to deter any aggression' and to provide a credible defense in the face of 'aggression.' Supporting Japan–US security arrangements was an essential component of the strategy. The extent to which Japan could pursue these policies into the future, maintain current limitations on its military establishment, and resist growing pressures from abroad as well as from its own industrial interest (and arms industry) to rebuild its defense capabilities to match today's major power standards depended upon a wide range of considerations – some domestic, some emerging from Japanese relations with the United States and other industrialized countries, and some imposed by global conditions.

TRANSFORMATION OF PROFILE

The issue of 'long swings' has been noted by many scholars of Japan, and recognition of the prevalence of cycles remains. But there is substantial divergence of views regarding the nature and phasing of cycles in the country's economic history, and there are differences regarding the underlying variable that is the subject of periodicity. Among these are the growth rate of capital formation (Ohkawa and Rosovsky 1973), the rate of economic growth (Ohkawa 1979), the growth rate of real output in manufacturing industry (Shinohara 1979), the growth rate of bank debts (Fujino 1966), and the rate of growth of GNP (Minami 1986). A review of the assessment of others, the different periodization on 'long swings' shown in the history of Japan, and the degree of divergence and convergence among assessments was summarized by Minami (1986: 46) in terms of major economic indicators and their fluctuations; it is extended and presented in Table 2.5. Our own perspective is that underlying the 'swings', by whatever definition, is *an inherent and determinant process of growth*. We have reviewed in this chapter the pattern of growth in all of Japan's indicators, and in Part Three we stress that the postwar growth trends were exponential, confounding statistical analysis and the estimation of parameters. In essence we had to deal with *changes* in the variables.

Table 2.5 Trends in Japan's economic performance

Period	Direction	Economic variable
(1) 1885–96	(upswing)	Expansion of railway Use of electricity Growth of modern spinning industry Reparations from China
(2) 1897–1903	(downswing)	Gold standard causing negative balance of payments
(3) 1904–18	(upswing)	Expansion of exports with investment opportunity
(4) 1919–28	(downswing)	Postwar financial crisis Monopoly and growth of zaibatsu Increased wage differentials
(5) 1929–36	(upswing)	New austerity policy Worldwide depression
(6) 1937–56	(downswing)	Wartime economy Post-World War II recovery
(7) 1957–69	(upswing)	High economic growth period Income Double Plan Consistent balance of payments surplus
(8) 1970–5	(downswing)	International monetary disorder Oil shock Postwar inflation
(9) 1976–80	(upswing)	Untightening monetary policy (1977) Expansionist policy (1977)
(10) 1981–	(upswing)	Global preeminence

Source: adapted from Minami 1986: 47–50

From 1976 on, the strong momentum of growth in the Japanese economy provides an inherent basis of economic competition, even possibly conflict, with other countries. Scholars generally recognize the strong momentum of growth in the Japanese economy and the inherent basis, even strong probabilities, of conflict with other countries (Krasner 1986: 788 Minami 1986: 45–50). This growth and attendant sources of discord continue to remain unresolved issues in Japan's relations with the industrial countries, most notably the United States.

This study – and this chapter – proceeded from the initial assumption that Japan at the time of the Meiji Restoration could be identified as a developing country characterized by a population that was growing at least somewhat in advance of the level and rate of change of its technological advancement – a country approximating what has been identified in Chapter 1 as the *epsilon* profile (a population in advance of technology and large and growing relative to accessible resources). From this base we postulated that over subsequent decades the introduction of Western knowledge and skills *was combined with* – and contributed to – continuing population growth, which resulted in (net) increasing pressures on resources and the transformation of Japan's dimensions into an approximation of the *beta* profile (technology 'equal to' or in advance of population growth, associated with the exacerbation of pressures on limited resources).

A *beta* nation lacks the territorial resources base of a colonial empire such as Britain or France prior to World War II or of an expanded continental power such as the United States or Russia/the USSR. In addition, a *beta* country lacks the developed trade network – the relatively available resource and market accesses that characterized the *gamma* profiles of Britain and France after the loss of their territorial empires in the wake of World War II. From the early twentieth century until the end of World War II, Japan, with an increasingly acute *beta* profile, can be seen as struggling to enhance its capabilities and status by acquiring an empire of its own. When that strategy failed, postwar Japan – rebuilding itself in a more compatible international environment – rapidly transformed itself in a *gamma* direction and in the course of three decades emerged as a notably successful trading state.

During its pre-World War II development and expansion as a *beta* state, Japan penetrated – extended its activities and interests into – and seized control over less developed, *epsilon* regions of East Asia, including Taiwan, Korea, the Liaotung Peninsula, Manchuria, and parts of China proper, as well as Southeast Asian territories extending to the borders of India. Like Japan, these countries were for the most part densely populated,[16] but they were economically, politically, and militarily weaker, and they possessed resources that the Japanese needed.

During the post-World War II period, Japan's international strategies relied almost exclusively on economic interaction, foreign investments, and market acquisition and control. Assuming the characteristics of a *gamma* profile, Japan successfully relied on trade and investments abroad to secure access to critical resources and inputs to industrial processes. Relations with the former colonies changed by necessity, as did interactions with the industrial states. By the mid-1980s Japan had become the world's largest creditor, a role that Great Britain held in the nineteenth century and the United States earlier in the twentieth century. This transformation obscures some of the more persistent features of the Japan profile and the attendant predicaments generated.

Part II

Emergence of Japan

Chapter 3

Growth, development, and early expansion

CRITICAL VARIABLES THAT TRANSFORMED JAPAN

In terms of the theory and model presented in Chapter 1, the critical variables to be tracked through the historical narrative of this book include *population, technology,* and *resource demand.* With a limited territorial and resource base combined with rising demand, Japan relied increasingly on the search for and acquisition of external resources and markets. In order to obtain greater control over markets and raw material *imports,* the Japanese government – emulating Britain and other Western powers – established a colonial empire, which required higher *military expenditures* and the modernization of its army and navy along Western lines. *Lateral pressure* – the expansion of Japanese activities (including negative leverages) – contributed to intersections and collisions with the activities and interests of other nations.

From the middle of the nineteenth century changes in these variables have contributed to a transformation of Japan from a developing (*epsilon*) to an industrialized nation – a *beta* profile between the two world wars, and a *gamma* profile more recently. Associated with these developments have been major changes in the country's social, economic, and political relationships.

Prior to the Meiji Restoration, Japan had been ruled by a hierarchy of territorial lords (daimyo) – supported by a warrior class (samurai), but dominated by a series of shoguns (dictators of the Tokugawa family) – which constituted the effective regime while rendering nominal allegiance to the emperor (Lockwood 1954: 3). Underlying and supporting this hierarchy were the peasants, who carried on rice cultivation, the chief source of wealth in the economy.

For more than two centuries all foreigners other than the Chinese, the Koreans, and the Dutch had been excluded from the Japanese empire, and Japanese citizens were prohibited from leaving the country under penalty of death. To a large extent, this policy developed as a response to vigorous efforts made by Spanish and Portuguese missionaries in the late sixteenth and early seventeenth centuries to propagate the Roman Catholic faith, which tended to threaten indigenous values and institutions. Despite this isolation, however, many Japanese had maintained a continuing intellectual interest in the West and a persistent desire to learn as much as possible about the outside world, and by 1850 Japan had gone through an informal apprenticeship which China would not experience until well into the future – an advantage that helps to explain the country's successes with the new technology (Smith 1955: 1–3).

LATERAL PRESSURES AND THE 'OPENING' OF JAPAN

The country which had been first and most persistent in trying to reopen Japan was Russia. The eastward movement – which provides an historical background for the adversarial relationship that developed between the two countries – can be traced back at least as far as the mid-sixteenth century when Cossacks pressed into western Siberia. Then, during the 'times of troubles' early in the seventeenth century, peasants fleeing political disorder, privation, and bondage to the soil accelerated the eastward migrations – some pushing into wholly new territories and subjugating the inhabitants. Propelled largely by the search for furs, many of the more adventurous made their way to the Pacific coast, to islands beyond the Asian mainland, and eventually to Alaska and southward into California. Although led for the most part by private individuals, the fur trade was largely controlled by the government (Lensen 1959: 14–15). In spite of the initiative and daring of individual Russians, the mounting of numerous government expeditions, and the development of a complex administration, however, the colonization of Russia's eastern regions progressed slowly, and for a long time, except for the fur trade, these vast expanses of sparsely populated territory were viewed as 'economically insignificant' (Malozemoff 1958: 1).

Largely an outcome of resistance from the Chinese to the south and the explorations of Captain Vitus Bering (a Dane in Russian service who sailed initially to find out whether or not Asia and America were joined), Russian activities and interests expanded to Kamchatka (where the first Japanese seen by a Russian was mistaken for an Indian), the Aleutians, and Alaska. Meanwhile Russian clashes with the Chinese along their common border led to the Treaty of Nerchinsk (1689), whereby Russia relinquished claims to lands between the Stanovoi Mountains and the Amur River, and for the next century-and-a-half penetrations along the frontier were rare – although Russian commercial caravans continued to carry goods to Peking and return with tea, and a Russian Orthodox mission maintained a precarious existence in that city (Treadgold 1962: 537–8).

During the latter part of the eighteenth century, the return of Japanese castaways picked up by Russian ships in the Far East was used as justification for two separate voyages launched under ukases of Catherine the Great with the hope of 'opening' Japan to Russian commerce. The second expedition reached the island of Hokkaido, where it was detained. Eventually, after months of waiting (and exchanges of gifts), the Russians were told that only unarmed vessels, like those of the Dutch, were allowed – and only to visit Nagasaki. The expedition, being armed and having provided no advance notice of its arrival, could have been detained permanently. But since the Russians had come to repatriate Japanese castaways, they had been unaccustomed to Japanese laws, and had suffered considerable hardships. They were therefore excused this time and allowed to depart, on the condition that they would not return (Lensen 1959: Ch. 4).

The appearance of Perry's 'black ships' and the 'emergence of foreign relations' helped to precipitate the movement which was to culminate in the imperial restoration of December 1867 (Moulton 1931: 9). American interests in whaling and encounters with Japanese fishermen represented early forms of intersections of interests. From a Japanese perspective of the time, the appearance of the US warships threatened Japan's status as an independent country and raised the fears of possible military defeat and colonization (Crowley 1971: 3).

Initially Japan was a target – rather than an agent – of penetration. The return of Perry in early 1854 led to the Treaty of Kanagawa, which opened the ports of Shimoda and Hakodate to US ships for supplies and for trade and provided for shipwrecked sailors to receive help and protection. An American consulate was to be established in Shimoda (Storry 1960: 90–1). Once made, the breach was soon enlarged. Within four years the Japanese government was compelled to confer rights of trade on British, French, and other foreigners. In this connection five ports were made available for trade, and nationals of other countries were given extra-territorial rights. In 1863 and 1864 the bombardments of Kagoshima and Shimonoseki by an allied fleet of British, Dutch, and French warships and one American vessel (Yanaga 1949: 32) demonstrated to those clans most hostile to new Japanese policies the irresistible force of Western naval power (Allen 1981: 23).

Foreign aggression and penetration also exposed the old regime's vulnerabilities. Within a decade and a half of Perry's first appearance the shogunate, 'weakened by internal decay and financial ineptitude' and under attack from some of the clans, fell and brought with it the collapse of the centralized feudal structure. With support from the victorious clans, a new young emperor assumed the throne in 1868, promised reforms, and pledged the pursuit of appropriate knowledge and skills throughout the world in order to provide the foundations for a Japanese Imperium (Lockwood 1954: 8–9).

POPULATION GROWTH, TECHNOLOGICAL CHANGE, AND ECONOMIC DEVELOPMENT

Chapter 2 reported Japan's population growth rate during the first Meiji decade at about 5 percent and higher thereafter. The pressure on domestic resources was even greater than might have been expected from these numbers, however, because of population densities (92 persons per square kilometer). Combined with the new knowledge and skills flooding in from the West, this upsurge in population growth provided impulses for unprecedented reform and development. Technologically, the country was soon growing at a rate between 2.5 and 3.5 percent annually during the same period. During the Meiji what amounted to a technological and economic revolution produced new attitudes and institutions which transformed an *epsilon* (developing) nation into a *beta* society (essentially an industrial state with a limited resource base).

The Meiji 'revolution' was less the outcome of a rising commercial class bursting feudalistic bonds to establish its dominance in a mercantilist state than a group of able young samurai-bureaucrats taking the lead in pursuing restoration and subsequent reforms and winning support from 'a few court nobles and from influential merchants in Kyoto and Osaka' (Lockwood 1954: 9–10). Lacking the self-confidence, status, and freedom of movement for leadership of a true revolution, the landowners, merchants, and industrial groups dominating both the rural economy and village government supported the warriors and also gave them a kind of direction – transforming 'what might have been a struggle to reorganize the feudal system into a movement to destroy it.' As for the shogunate and the *han* or daimyo governments, their disposition was to resist such radical changes where possible and to 'exploit them where it was not' (Smith 1955: 15–16).

During the next decade the new restoration bureaucrats around the imperial throne undertook sweeping reforms which abolished traditional restrictions on internal trade and movement, property rights in land, and freedom of entry in new occupations. Through the land tax reform of 1873, a unified revenue system was established in the form of a fixed money tax, which was extracted from landowners in proportion to the value of their land as recently assessed. Within this framework Meiji statesmen soon created such infrastructure as banks (indeed a whole new fiscal system), railways, steam shipping, postal and telegraph systems, and electric power.

Composed of many who had bitterly opposed the shogun's policy of coming to terms with the intruding foreigners, the restoration government, once established, moved in the same direction. Recognizing that Japan's military vulnerabilities and economic backwardness were likely to make the country an easy target for further Western incursions, the new leadership concluded with reason that only the adoption of Western methods in industry and war could enable the regime to secure the nation's independence and eventually the abrogation of the 'unequal treaties' that had already been submitted to. Beyond this, Japanese leaders saw how Britain and other Western nations appeared to have become rich and powerful through skillful navigation, trade, competition, and the penetration and occupation of distant (and weaker) lands. Recognizing Japan's limitations, however, they set out to develop the country's capabilities with the prospect of eventually establishing a European-style empire of its own 'on the edge of Asia' (Jansen 1984a: 62–4). With longer-range possibilities in mind, they focused their attention on adjacent islands as well as on Korea and China. Defense and the adoption of Western technology, material equipment, and methods became immediate priorities (Allen 1981: 32).

GOVERNMENT AND TECHNOLOGY

Promoting and diffusing Western knowledge and skills, the Japanese government was active in promoting technological change favorable to economic growth. Initially, the regime set out to borrow British and American techniques of mechanization and extensive cultivation. These methods were not appropriate for the small scale of Japanese agriculture, however, and the regime turned more and more toward German, Dutch, and other approaches that had been developed on the European continent. Fostering improvements in quality and better selection in the search for silk, tea, and other export products, the regime promoted meetings and associations of farmers, improvements in seeds and fertilizers, artificial incubation for the production of silkworms, and new methods of rice production (Maddison 1969: 21–2).

In pursuit of a utilitarian system of education, the government proceeded to emphasize practical training. Taking as a model the highly centralized educational system of France, the Japanese established a national department of education. The country was divided into eight university districts, which were then subdivided into 256 secondary school districts, each of which encompassed 210 elementary school districts, and attendance was made compulsory for all children upon reaching the age of 6 years. Elementary schools and their curricula were patterned after the US model, and when Tokyo Normal School was opened in 1872, an American educator from Honolulu was invited to become an advisor to the Minister of Education as well as a teacher. A year later a vigorous program was undertaken to transplant US educational practices into Japan. In 1877 three separate educational institutions were merged to form the University of Tokyo, and soon graduates of this institution extended into the field of the higher civil service, filling many important positions in the government and diplomatic service, in essence leaving only legislative institutions open to graduates of other universities (Yanaga 1949: 100–5). A central purpose was to modernize and industrialize as rapidly as possible.

Once set in motion after 1868, the growth of Japan's productive powers 'went forward with cumulative momentum and almost uninterruptedly for three generations.' Although there was nothing inevitable or inexorable about the process that unfolded, neither was it confined to any single aspect or sector of economic life; a wide range of economic enterprises were linked together (Lockwood 1954: 151). Domestically and externally, moreover, Meiji leaders tended to see economics and politics, business, and government as inextricably intertwined, and they were increasingly aware of European expansionism in Asia and the race among Western powers for concessions in China. As an agricultural nation, Japan could not compete in the world market or withstand the encroachments of Britain, Russia, or the United States. The country needed a sound economic and political base at home in order to compete successfully abroad (Duus 1984: 132–4).

Yet it would be wrong to assume that all parts of the Japanese economy were brought equally or quickly under direct Western influence. Japan suffered for a time because the country's monetary system and the parity between gold and silver differed from those that were currently prevalent, and several branches of the economy were slow to adapt. The new foreign trade was damaging to some of the older industries, and peasant agriculture and a number of small-scale manufacturing industries remained peculiar to Japan (Allen 1981: 63). Imports and exports were almost entirely in the hands of foreigners.

Trade and payments remained in deficit for a time, and between 1853 and 1881 the outflow of gold may have been as high as 220 million yen (Smith 1955: 24). At the same time, with the new access to Western technology and capital goods and the advantage of good sea communications, Japan had much to gain from international specialization, and the opening of commerce encouraged efficient allocation of resources and created new opportunities for profit. In addition, the Japanese benefited from the fact that China and India were unprotected by significant tariffs and other trade restrictions until the 1930s (Maddison 1969: 27–8).

INDUSTRIALIZATION AND INFRASTRUCTURE DEVELOPMENT

A fundamental problem confronting Japan in its transformation from an *epsilon* to a *beta* state was the process of capital formation. Characteristically, a rapidly developing society must find ways of obtaining capital from its agricultural base and applying it to the growth and development of its economy. Only through the government's power to tax (and to borrow) could the capital be obtained for the construction of the factories, railways, and shipyards that were needed, but the relatively low productivity of the economy, the competing claims on resources, and 'the political dangers of cutting too deeply into consumption' limited the government's extractive capacities (Smith 1955: 68). Linked to trade issues were unequal treaties that had given foreign powers extraterritorial jurisdictions within Japan and various tariff advantages (Nish 1974: 186).

During early years of the Meiji era, the overwhelming majority of the Japanese population had been engaged in agriculture, which had not made much progress in earlier generations. The country's rural society was divided into peasant proprietors, who worked up to 75 percent of the arable land, and tenants. Along with certain labor services, proprietors paid heavy taxes – sometimes 40–50 percent of total yield – through their village to the local lord. Beginning in the late Tokugawa era, however, demand for agricultural products began to increase, in large part as a result of population growth and expanded urbanization. In their efforts to meet the new levels of demand, farmers began reaching for new technologies

> including the general adoption of commercial fertilizers that permitted double and sometimes triple cropping; a large increase in the variety of plants under cultivation; an enormous extension of irrigation and some land reclamation, allowing a shift from dry to more productive paddy rice cultivation; and finally, helping all these, the growth of agricultural science (Rosovsky 1961: 61)

Taking responsibility for encouraging and facilitating these developments, the government sent experts to Europe and the United States to study farming systems, established agricultural schools and colleges, and sent instructors into rural areas to provide advice and guidance (Allen 1981: 64–5). Since savings from agriculture were comparatively large and requirements for investment relatively small, surpluses could be siphoned off for the development of nonagricultural sectors (Rosovsky 1961: 84–5).

The government, meanwhile, had been taking energetic steps to improve transportation and communications, to establish new industries, and to modernize the army and navy. The first Japanese-built steamship was completed in 1866, and steamer service was established between Yokohama and Nagasaki shortly thereafter. Connecting Tokyo and Yokohama, the first Japanese railroad was built in 1870–2 with the aid of a British loan. By 1893 the country's first 2,000 miles of railway, first 100,000 tons of steam vessels, purchased abroad for the most part, and first 4,000 miles of telegraph lines were in place. The first modern silk filature had already been opened in 1870 under a French expert as superintendent; cotton spinning mills were built or reequipped with machinery from England and elsewhere; experimental factories were built for the manufacture of sugar, beer, cement, glass, chemicals, and a variety of Western-type products; and the mining of coal, copper, and precious metals was vigorously promoted (Lockwood 1954: 14–15).

ECONOMIC DEVELOPMENT AND FOREIGN TRADE

'Opening Japan' was in its essence an economic transformation linking Japan's economy with the world economy, brought to the Far East by the lateral pressure of the great powers in the West. Unequal treaties provided Western merchants with 'free trade' and extraterritorial protection, but foreign products did not penetrate into the Japanese market as much as Westerners had expected. Such nontariff barriers as the exclusive distribution system within Japan, in conjunction with Westerners' dependence on Japanese agents, protected the Japanese market from the influence of foreign competitors. Thus, however unequal, treaties of commerce allowed the new Meiji government to pursue autonomous economic development policies.

In order to initiate and maintain industrial modernization, Japan – like most *epsilon* and other developing countries in the industrial era – required foreign exchange to obtain foreign goods and resources through trade. To obtain machinery, merchant vessels, warships, munitions, and other equipment needed for its program of Westernization, the government required foreign currencies at the same time that rising demands for textiles and other consumer goods were obtaining foreign loans with interest payments to be met. At the same time, in view of the underdeveloped state of the country's economy, foreign exchange was scarce, and pressures on the balance of payments rapidly increased. Throughout the 1870s the government established factories for the production of glass, cement, and other building materials and actively participated in export transactions, purchasing domestic stocks of rice, tea, silk, and other products, selling them abroad, and relying on the proceeds to finance the imports that were so urgently required. While the government promoted the establishment and growth of the more capital intensive industries, private firms expanded old enterprises and organized new ones in the pursuit of opportunities that resulted from the opening of the country to foreign trade (Allen 1981: 34).

Since the opening, Japan's major trading commodities had been silk and tea for exports, and cotton and wool fabrics for imports. The Meiji government's industrialization policy transformed Japan's industrial structure, and hence its trade patterns. Industrializing Japan began to export coal in addition to the traditional exporting goods (silk) and to import raw cotton, metal products, and machineries. In geographical terms, the Japanese began to depend more on Asia, most notably China and India, as well as on the United States. This trade structure remained basically unchanged for decades.

EXPANDING ACTIVITIES AND INTERESTS

Japan's entry into the international society induced the government to attempt the establishment of a 'modern way' of relating to neighboring countries and to define Japanese territory as a sovereign state. These efforts allowed the country's activities, interests, and influence (leverages) to expand beyond national frontiers.

During the early months of 1872, Japanese envoys sent to Korea to negotiate a treaty and open the country from seclusion (Yanaga 1949: 85) were rebuffed and several Japanese subjects in Korea were attacked. The issue was brought before the Council of State, and steps were taken toward forcing a Korean capitulation. When word of this proposal reached them in Korea, however, the Japanese envoys – fearing 'not only for their own political power but also for the future of their country' – returned home forthwith 'and finally won support for the reversal of the decision.' In October 1873 the emperor ordered the government to concentrate on internal growth and drop the idea of a military expedition to Korea (Borton 1955: 88–9). Despite this, or rather in order to discharge frustrations that were intensifying within as well as outside the leadership, the government dared to conduct a military expedition to Taiwan in 1874. Meanwhile, in 1876 a commercial treaty was concluded between Japan and Korea after minor hostilities in the previous year. In due course similar agreements were reached between Korea and the United States, Britain, and France, and in 1884 a Treaty of Friendship and Commerce was signed with Russia (Malozemoff, 1958: 16).

Long at issue had been Japanese claims to the Ryukyu Islands (claimed also by China and briefly by the United States, which was later asked by the Chinese to intercede in their dispute with the Japanese), the Bonin Islands (claimed for a time by Britain and also briefly by the United States), the Kuriles, and Sakhalin Islands (claimed also by Russia). With time on its side, Japan had established *de facto* control of the Ryukus (although Chinese claims were renewed during World War II by Chiang Kai-shek). In 1880 the Bonins were incorporated into Greater Tokyo, and thereafter they remained a part of the capital district until occupied by US forces after World War II. In Japan's earliest treaties with Russia the Kuriles had been divided between the two countries, whereas the status of Sakhalin had remained unsettled and thus contributed to a series of incidents between the two countries (Hosoya 1971: 340). During negotiations in the 1870s, Japan agreed to cede the whole Kurile chain to Russia and renounced its claims to Sakhalin, which the tsarist government established as a place of exile for its most hardened criminals (Malozemoff, 1958: 10). The latter settlement remained in force until after the Russo-Japanese War (1904–5), when Japan acquired the southern half of Sakhalin through the Treaty of Portsmouth (Borton 1955: 158–62).

WESTERN LATERAL PRESSURE AND INTERSECTION IN EAST ASIA

The penetration of China, Korea, and other regimes of the Far East by the expanding activities and interests of various Western powers had accelerated after the Opium War of 1839, and in the course of a few decades a long-isolated China, which had seen itself as the center of the universe and the only 'world order' that really counted, found an age-old relationship reversed: the ancient Middle Kingdom, suzerain and receiver of tribute from lesser societies, was becoming a tributary to a 'barbaric' but technologically superior West (Teng and Fairbank 1961: 138–9). In many respects, among all the Western powers it was tsarist Russia whose activities and interests tended to impinge upon those of Japan most directly.

Initially the eastward expansion of Russian activities and interests had been manifested by trappers, fur traders, Cossack bands, and peasants in search of a better livelihood. Although encouragement of trade was part of the government's program, 'there was still a sort of aristocratic contempt of commerce in general as a guiding motive in foreign affairs,' according to David Dallin, and a 'marked feeling of superiority in St Petersburg over "merchant nations," like England and France, which occupied territories and built empires for the benefit of moneymakers.' Toward the end of the nineteenth century, however, Russia entered a period of modernization, and the Tsar, 'heir to a long line of leaders who in a chain of wars had pushed the borders of the once small principality farther and farther out,' became the formal agent for economic expansion as well (Dallin 1950: 15–16).

In 1881 a department of trade and industry was established as a branch of the Ministry of Finance and entrusted with supervision of all of the empire's commercial and industrial affairs. Increasingly thereafter the department's growth constituted an indicator of Russia's economic modernization. Appointed Minister of Finance in 1892 was Sergei Witte, who in the course of a meteoric career had served as manager and then director of the Southwestern Railway Company, a private enterprise, where he combined his knowledge of mathematics and economic theory to design an innovative freight rate system which 'nearly doubled' the value of the line's assets. As Minister of Finance, Witte played a dominant role in the construction of the Trans-Siberian Railroad, proceeding on the assumption that promotion of the country's prosperity was the crucial purpose of the new railway. More specifically, he saw the line 'developing the dormant resources of Siberia with the help of the industries of European Russia and in turn providing new markets for the latter' and, of even greater significance, linking Europe and the Far East 'in an intensified exchange of goods' – with Russia functioning as the dominant carrier of the East–West trade. In this capacity Russia would be able to capture Chinese markets from Britain and effect a radical change in economic relations among the European states (Von Laue 1963: 32–5, 46–8, 82–4, 92–5).

In the course of his career Witte came to the conclusion that in most cases railway building for strategic purposes was 'pure fantasy' and should be undertaken only for economic reasons (Witte 1921: 75). The possible and highly useful connections between economic and strategic considerations were not lost on him, however. The railway, he asserted, would assure the Russian navy 'all the necessary prerequisites' and a solid base in Pacific ports. The navy, in turn, would control all international shipping in Far Eastern waters. There was one more prerequisite to Russian control of its eastern accesses, however. After a visit to China, Japan, and Vladivostok, when work was beginning at the eastern terminal of the Siberian line, the crown prince identified an additional demand that required satisfaction; Russia was 'in absolute need' of a port on the mainland that would be ice-free, open all year, located to the southeast of Korea, and 'connected with our possession by a strip of land' (Dallin 1950: 34–5).

As events unfolded in East Asia, the political and strategic implications of the Trans-Siberian Railway (and its branches and connecting lines) often overshadowed, sometimes obscured, and occasionally were indistinguishable from its economic implications. For many Japanese the building of the railway – after an improvement in Russo-Japanese relations following settlement of the Sakhalin issue – marked a revival of Russia's interest in Eastern Asia, Russian penetration of Korea and Manchuria, and intensifying intersections of Russian and Japanese activities and interests in East Asia (Hosoya 1971: 340).

DEVELOPMENT OF MILITARY CAPABILITY

Along with efforts to modernize agriculture, initiate industrialization, and develop export capabilities, the Japanese government also undertook the reorganization, armament, and training of its armed forces according to Western standards. With the abolition of other feudal institutions, the samurai lost many of their special privileges and became a social class in name only, and the concept of a modern army based on universal conscription was substituted for the old armies of hereditary warriors. Enacted in 1870, the first conscription law provided for three years of active service and two years in the reserve (Borton 1955: 84–5). Modeled on that of Germany, a new general staff office directly responsible for the emperor was established by imperial ordinance in December 1878, a few years *before* von Moltke succeeded in enacting a comparable change in Germany (Matsushita 1956: 7–10). During the following year army organization and training methods were changed over from the French to the German system. The influence of Germany, which had been pursuing its own unification and modernization during the previous decade or so, was marked – especially after the Prussian victories of 1870 and 1871.

By the 1880s, while German engineers and scientists were helping to 'Westernize' Japanese industry and Japanese education, German military officers were 'Westernizing' the Japanese army (Iklé 1974: 269–74). The cost of military investments to the Japanese economy was high, contributed to 'terrible difficulties in finance, and made it extremely difficult to keep finance in harmony with the national economy.' The effects were felt in terms of taxation ('extraordinary expenditures' set out of people's income or property), public loans (involving 'serious expansion of finances'), and the meeting of receipts and outlays (resulting in 'great disturbances in the monetary world' with alternate 'activity and dullness' in the economic cycle). Observers at the time noted that military expenditures tended 'to absorb the production capital out of people's purses and to dissipate it unproductively' (Ono 1922: 252–3). Yet military expenditures also boosted economic performance.

Japan's military had been designed primarily to meet domestic security needs in its various aspects. It was in the mid-1880s that Japan transformed its armed forces into a capability for protecting the state from foreign threats. The army's organizational structure altered from the garrison (*chindai*) system to the division system in order to facilitate the conduct of operations abroad. The equipment was upgraded accordingly. And the Ministry of War was reorganized into two ministries: the Army Ministry and the Navy Ministry. By 1890

one . . . detects within the cabinet and the services a subtle change in the meaning of 'national defense.' Before this time it meant . . . to guarantee domestic tranquility and convince the powers that Japan had an effective government. With the promulgation of the Meiji constitution in 1889, one senses that this axiom was being supplanted by 'national defense requirements of an empire. (Crowley 1974: 14)

The Meiji constitution introduced into Japanese politics the confrontation between the government and political parties. The newly established Diet, whose majority was occupied with antigovernment forces, called for 'small government' (Nakamura 1989: 8). Although the navy construction plan of 1890 was not as expansive as the government publicized, the Diet did not approve it (Muroyama 1984: 191). China's naval buildup and an anticipated depreciation of Japan's navy pressured the government to submit a naval expansion plan each year despite the controversy (Muroyama 1984: 193). Militarily speaking, however, both army and navy were ready to wage war at least in Korea and the Liaotung Peninsula by 1893 (Crowley 1974: 14).

JAPAN'S EXPANSION AND THE SINO-JAPANESE WAR

Although Japanese expansion in Korea intersected with that of Russia, it was eventually with China – with long-standing claims in the region – that Japan collided and fought what amounted to a colonial war.

Autocratic and corrupt, the Korean court had broken into contending factions, one led by the father and regent of the young king with support from China, the other controlled by the family of the queen and supported by the Japanese, who had been waiting for an opportunity for settling permanently the question of which country was to control Korean affairs. Toward the end of 1884 a palace revolution broke out against the pro-Japanese faction in Korea, whereupon Japan sent troops to reinforce its legation guard in Seoul, and China countered with a similar move. Japan and China almost came to blows, but the Japanese premier and Chinese viceroy Li Hung-chang negotiated the Li–Itoh Convention whereby both sides agreed to withdraw their forces and to notify the other side if further disturbances impelled either side to dispatch troops into Korea (Borton 1955: 204).

In the course of these developments Korea, China, Russia, and Japan each leveled charges of intrigue and intervention (or intended intervention) against one or more of the others, thus increasing Korea's political entanglements, generating further Japanese fears of Russia, and spurring Russia to develop a basic policy in Korea with regard to China (Malozemoff 1958: 27). Having failed so far in their efforts to obtain ice-free ports in the Baltic and Black Seas, the tsarist government was particularly anxious – Vladivostok being icebound in winter – to secure a naval base in Korea or, alternatively, in the Gulf of Pechili (Lobanov-Rostovsky 1933: 193).

In June 1894 the Tonghak, or Eastern Learning Society, undertook a rebellion in Korea, purportedly to expel Western influences from the country. The king of Korea formally requested a Chinese intervention, whereupon the Chinese Ministry of Foreign Affairs (Tsungli Yamen) notified the Japanese chargé in Peking of China's intention of sending troops to restore peace in their tributary state. Alarmed by what they perceived as threatening Russian penetration of East Asia 'in which its own designs were not concealed,' Japan demanded from China 'a share in the control of Korean affairs' (Treadgold 1962: 542). Convinced that the time for decision had arrived, Japanese leaders notified China of preparations to send troops under provisions of the Li–Itoh Convention of 1895 and suggested a Sino-Japanese commission to deal with the situation there (Yanaga 1949: 243–4). With China's refusal to participate in a joint action, Japan undertook direct measures. A Japanese mixed brigade was dispatched to Korea, followed by 1,200 troops convoyed by three warships, which Chinese warships fired upon *en route*.

The Korean government requested both countries to withdraw their troops, but no understanding was reached, whereupon Li Hung-chang appealed to Russia for mediation. The Russian minister in Peking saw this offer as an opportunity for increasing his country's prestige in the Far East and for preventing an 'inevitable' and undesirable, open conflict in Korea, but the Japanese Minister of Foreign Affairs asserted categorically that Japan would not evacuate Korea without a guarantee that new hostilities would not break out when its troops were withdrawn (Malozemoff 1958: 53).

Despite some anxieties that Britain might intervene to prevent hostilities or support China (Nish 1974: 189), Japan declared war on 1 August, and in mid-September Japanese forces captured Pyongyang, which was the Chinese stronghold. Port Arthur fell in late November, and Japan destroyed Chinese naval forces, and captured the port of Wei-hai-wei in China proper. In the Treaty of Shimonoseki China 'definitely recognized the full and complete independence and autonomy of Korea,' paid a large indemnity, and ceded to Japan the island of Formosa (Taiwan), the Pescadores (strategically located between Formosa and China), and the Liaotung Peninsula (Reischauer 1964: 135–6).

From a Japanese perspective the war had been a success. Within the space of a few months one of the strongest nations in the Far East had been defeated, and the indemnity received by Japan was more than enough to pay for the effort. The beginnings of an empire had been established stretching from the Ryukyus to the Liaotung Peninsula, acquisitions which seemed to provide 'a natural bridge to further expansion southward.' In addition, Japanese control over the Liaotung Peninsula helped to contain Chinese and Russian interests there, provided new security against encroachments of these two empires in Korea, and created a temporary vacuum in that part of the Far East, which Japan lost no time in filling. Soon the Japanese were operating the Korean postal and telegraph systems, together with the railway from Seoul to Pusan; taxes were being assessed according to Japanese law; and the Korean army was being officered and drilled by the Japanese. The Korean kingdom thus found itself 'at the mercy of a rapidly expanding Japanese Empire which had become the predominant force in Asia' (Borton 1955: 207).

WESTERN INTERVENTION: NEGATIVE LEVERAGES TO CONTAIN JAPAN

Banding together only a week after conclusion of the Treaty of Shimonoseki, however, France, Germany, and Russia 'secured what the Japanese were to remember bitterly as the "Triple Intervention."' Applying leverage through their ministers in Tokyo, these three countries urged Japan to relinquish its claim to the Liaotung Peninsula, including the harbor and fortress of Port Arthur, maintaining that possession of this territory would be seen as a threat in Peking and a disturbance to peace in the Far East – a formulation that the Japanese would 'take to heart and put to good use in later years.' Adding insult to injury, from a Japanese perspective, the same three powers soon began extorting extensive pieces of Chinese territory from the enfeebled Manchu empire. The French took control of Kwangchow Bay, the Germans seized the city of Tsingtao and the nearby Kiaochow Bay area, and the tsarist government occupied and obtained a lease on the Liaotung, which had been denied to the Japanese (Borton 1955: 219).

Predictably, Russia's role in the Triple Intervention 'brought to the surface the basic conflict in the objectives Japan and Russia were trying to achieve on the continent,' and anti-Russian feelings were exacerbated among the Japanese public (Hosoya 1974: 352). The participation of Germany in the intervention was particularly rankling, however, and memories of it became a factor in Japanese decisions and policies during World War I (Iklé 1974: 272).

By the century's end Russia was being viewed increasingly in Europe and elsewhere as an upcoming power in the Far East. Although the Russians had been expanding slowly eastward across Siberia since the seventeenth century, Russian activities and interests in Asia had not become a major concern until after the Crimean War. Over the years it had become 'a law of Russian history,' however, that whenever Russia was checked in Europe, its drive in Asia intensified (Lobanov-Rostovsky, 1933: 47). In 1854 the Amur Valley was seized and foundations were laid for the city of Khabarovsk, thus strengthening Russia's Far Eastern defenses as conflicts resulting from the Crimean War spread into the Pacific. Later, during an Anglo-French occupation of Peking in 1860, the Russians, acting as intermediaries, promised to secure for China a withdrawal which they knew the British had decided upon, and thus Russia, through the Convention of Peking, obtained title to the Manchurian coast east of the Ussuri River and south of the Korean border (Morse 1910: I, 613–14).

Many Russians had their eyes fixed on the rest of Manchuria, but Witte had a broader vision. Manchuria, he thought, was not worth 'all the trouble.' Russia must proceed 'along the road of history,' he thought, whereupon 'the more inert countries of Asia' would fall prey to 'the powerful invaders' and be 'divided up between them.' The only survivors would be countries 'like Japan' with a capacity for acquiring 'speedily' those acquisitions of Western culture that were 'necessary for self-defense.' The problem confronting countries with superior capabilities was how 'to obtain as large a share as possible of the inheritance of the outlived oriental states, especially of the Chinese colossus.' Both geographically and historically, he concluded, Russia had 'the undisputed right to the lion's share of the expected prey' and thus 'the absorption by Russia of a considerable portion of the Chinese Empire' was 'only a matter of time.' Witte thought that the absorption should occur 'naturally,' however, 'without precipitating events, without taking premature steps, without seizing territory,' in order to avoid 'premature division of China by the Powers concerned, which would deprive Russia of China's most valuable provinces' (Witte 1921: 122).

Meanwhile, preliminary surveys of proposed stretches of the Trans-Siberian Railway looping through Russian territory northward around Manchuria to Khaborovsk would be extremely expensive because the roadbed would have to be protected from floods. Having previously envisaged no more than a feeder line into China, Witte now proposed to build the main line straight across Manchuria – a route which, with the recent Japanese victory over the Chinese and the continuing presence of Japanese troops in Korea and Port Arthur, now appeared to be even more mandatory. The construction of this more direct link would not only save well over 300 miles of track but would also strengthen Russia's strategic position in the Far East 'immeasurably.' Thus, despite warnings that the proposed line was too far outside Russian territory and would cause 'complications,' Witte negotiated with the Chinese government for a Manchurian right of way with connections to existing Chinese railways. His manifest interest lay in 'forestalling European competition in the construction of Chinese railroads in or near Manchuria' and the early channeling of Chinese trade into the Siberian trunk line. In addition, his intention was to secure for Russia (and its French financial backers) an economic monopoly in China (Von Laue 1963: 150–1).

Beyond this, by persuading Germany and France to join in demanding Japanese withdrawal, tsarist diplomats managed to convince the Chinese authorities that for Russia effectively to uphold Chinese integrity, which the Russians claimed to champion, communications between China and Vladivostok as well as European Russia needed to be improved and safeguarded (Morse 1910: III, 80–1; Witte 1921: 89). These negotiations resulted as a series of agreements for the construction across Manchuria of the Chinese Eastern Railway, which became an exceedingly important factor in Japan's relations with Russia and China and in Far Eastern diplomacy at large. The line was to be financed through a Russo-Chinese bank and operated by Russians and Chinese jointly for 80 years, although the Chinese retained an option to buy back the line after 36 years. Provisions were made for the exploitation of natural resources required for railway construction and maintenance of the line.

Eighteen months after the conclusion of these arrangements, the tsarist government obtained from China a 25-year lease on the Port Arthur and Dairen areas for a naval base, and an extension of the Chinese Eastern Railway concessions was obtained in order for the Russians to build a spur system (the Changchun, or South Manchurian Railway) to connect Dairen with the main line.

These and further expansions of Russian activities and interests were to be impeded, however, and in part undone by the Japanese, who felt that except for Russian (as well as German and French) interference, their recent victory would have left them in full control of the Liaotung Peninsula (Pooley 1915: 109–10). From this time forward Japanese military leaders tended to interpret the country's security development more and more in territorial terms (Jansen 1984a: 67–8).

Chapter 4

Intersections with major powers

JAPAN'S ENTRY INTO MAJOR POWER COMPETITION

From the last decade of the nineteenth century until the outbreak of World War I, the major powers of the world were characterized by growth, competition, and the expansions of their activities and interests. In Europe a rapidly growing *beta* nation – Germany – was challenging Britain – an *alpha* empire and the global hegemon. Defeated by Germany in the early 1870s, Britain's traditional enemy, France, was moving closer to the hegemon, its former adversary. In the United States, Americans were watching their own country's 'manifest destiny' unfold offshore in Cuba, Hawaii, Puerto Rico, elsewhere in the Western hemisphere, and as far away as the Philippines (and into China). Minor intersections with Japanese interests in the Pacific were probably harbingers of more violent collisions to come. European leaders on both sides were already cognizant of the United States as a candidate major power; they tended to underrate US capabilities which, on a number of dimensions, were overtaking those of both Germany and Britain.

Japan was moving into fast company. US Admiral Alfred T. Mahan saw already taking shape in the Far East, as in Europe, 'a fresh instance of the multiform struggle between land power and sea power' (Mahan 1900: 24 ff). Japan's first advance, the pacification of Taiwan by military force, could be compared with the commitment of French military forces in the 1880s to put down Black Flag rebels in Tonkin or the United States army expedition against Filipino insurgents following the Spanish–American War (Peattie 1984: 18–19).

Previously the inclination of various European powers to expand their activities and interests in the Far East had been 'restrained only by the belief in Chinese military power,' which was greatly overestimated. In 1880, when Russian forces, expanding into Central Asia, clashed with Chinese troops in Kulja, the German minister in Peking had been quoted to the effect that the Russians 'would not easily overcome the Chinese,' who were 'so numerous . . . had many arms and munitions,' and knew 'very well' how to use their artillery (Lobanov-Rostovsky 1933: 192).

During the Sino-Japanese War the Russian Minister of Foreign Affairs had written a memorandum to the Tsar stating that at the conclusion of those hostilities Russia must decide whether to pursue a passive or an aggressive policy in the Far East. If the decision favored a passive policy, then China would be the 'ideal ally,' Russian frontiers would be 'secure,' and it would be 'some time before China could recover sufficiently from the war to be dangerous' (Malozemoff 1958: 62). As China's weaknesses were exposed by Japanese successes, however, European inhibitions vanished, and China began to suffer disintegration 'at the hands of greedy coloniz-ing powers' (Lobanov-Rostovsky 1933: 192). With the outcome of the Sino-Japanese War freshly in mind, moreover, Europeans and Americans were favorably impressed by Japan's rapid strides toward modernization and the dispatch with which the country had defeated China, secured an indemnity of 300 million yen (Nakamura 1983: 38), and undertaken the economic exploitation of Taiwan (Thompson 1959: 64). Meanwhile, the Japanese had successfully demonstrated to themselves that their country had an army strong enough to protect itself 'and to conquer territory from neighbors who did not have modern armies' (Thompson 1959: 112). Their acquisition of Taiwan had given them a sense of pride and a feeling that they and their country had achieved a position of equality with Westerners (Duus 1971: 134). Among many Japanese, moreover, there was a disposition to conclude that their use of military force – their negative leverages – had yielded highly desirable returns at relatively modest cost.

At the same time some Western leaders were beginning to resent the appearance of 'a new competitor in the game of cutting up the Chinese melon' (Reischauer 1964: 133). Under the surface, moreover, some Japanese, sensing that in Western eyes their skins were still perceived as yellow, began to feel pangs of self-doubt – along with revanchist dispositions toward the Russians (Duus 1971: 134). And Meiji leaders, soon enough, found their recent successes being scrutinized by foreign powers, circling like wolves whose expansion into economic, political, and strategic security areas essential to Japan had somehow to be preempted (Jansen 1984b: 62–63).

In Japan there were feelings of deep indignation against the actions of the three powers – France, Germany, and Russia – which had deprived the country of the full fruits of its victory over China. Their resentments against Russia were especially bitter, however, and indeed, between the end of the Sino-Japanese War and the outbreak of the Russo-Japanese War (1904–5), it was the collision of Russian and Japanese activities and interests that tended to shape the course of events. From a Japanese perspective, Russia – with its fleet nearby at Vladivostok – was perceived to be in earnest and to possess ample leverage for enforcing its will in Eastern Asia. For the time being, however, the Japanese Emperor determined that his subjects must 'bear the unbearable' (Storry 1960: 126–127).

Despite the Triple Intervention and related setbacks and in part because of them, Japan's 1895 victory over China had greatly strengthened the domestic power, prestige, and bargaining and leverage potentials of the Japanese oligarchy, stimulating further economic development and winning unified support for the country's 'aggressive entry into the arena of Far East imperialism' (Lockwood 1954:19). During the war a new kind of patriotism (*Nihon shugi*) had arisen, and now the official acquiescence of the leadership to the demands of the three European powers had consequences with immediate and far-reaching effects. Public indignation was aroused against the government and the contents of the treaty, and national opinion concentrated on how to strengthen Japan's position in the world at large (Borton 1955: 211). Since it now became more necessary than ever for Japan to develop army and naval capabilities sufficient for maintaining its newly established influence in its own environs, both the government and people of the country were soon applying themselves to the energetic expansion of their military capabilities (Ono 1922:80).

LATERAL PRESSURE: EXPANSION OF JAPANESE ACTIVITIES AND INTERESTS

Having achieved unity and independence at home and footholds abroad, Japanese leaders now undertook a concerted program of economic and political expansion, and 'familiar slogans of markets, national security, and imperial destiny' evoked an 'immediate response in the quickened national consciousness and the commercial ambitions' aroused by the country's recent 'triumph on the stage of world politics.' The £38.1 million indemnity which Japan had obtained from China as a result of the Shimonoseki settlement provided a reserve of gold and sterling which facilitated a shift to the gold standard in 1897, and treaties concluded subsequently with Western powers terminated extraterritorial privileges for foreigners in Japanese territory, and income taxes were increased. In addition, loans were raised at home and abroad, and – with the inclusion of loans for the capitalization of state railways – the national debt increased from 207 million yen in December 1894 to 539 million yen. Some of these funds were invested in revenue-raising public works, but the greater part was used for the financing of war preparations (Allen 1981:50). In the late 1890s exports began to stagnate, there was a deficit in the balance of payments, and in 1900 a recession occurred (Nakamura 1983:31).

INTERSECTIONS: JAPANESE AND THE EUROPEANS IN EAST ASIA

By the end of the nineteenth century, meanwhile, several European powers had been expanding their economic and political activities into China and other parts of Asia and competing among themselves for the lion's share of advantage. It soon became clear, moreover, that with the victory over China tsarist Russia had become Japan's major rival in northern Asia. Whereas Great Britain, France, Germany, and other countries were expanding their activities and interests from treaty ports into the interior, Russia advanced overland, seeking to check British influence along Russian frontiers from Turkey to Korea and to acquire warm-water ports on the Pacific coast (Witte 1921: 82–4, 90, 97–100; Lobanov-Rostovsky 1933: 226–7).

Russia's 25-year leases on Dairen and Port Arthur in March 1898 were regarded as a major threat by the great powers, especially Britain. Political leaders in Japan offered the Russians a free hand in Manchuria in exchange for Japan's free hand in Korea. Russia rejected this offer, but in April the tsar's minister in Tokyo, Rosen, concluded an agreement with Foreign Minister Nishi, recognizing Japan's preponderant economic interest in Korea, and guaranteeing that Russia would not obstruct these interests. Japan was unable either to block the Russian advance or to establish an exclusive sphere of influence in Korea. Nevertheless, this entente seemed to stabilize Russo-Japanese relations. But by 1900 this seemingly stable situation was threatened.

The safety of British, French, US, Russian, and other diplomatic legations in Peking was seriously threatened in 1900 by the Boxer Rebellion, a movement – 'spontaneous and cruel' – emerging from the humiliations and defeats long suffered by China at the hands of the great powers (Dallin 1950:62–9). This outbreak 'acted as an alarm which sent all the powers scurrying once more to their diplomatic stations to insure their already considerable holdings and to guarantee their control over any future division of spoils.' Leaders in each of the major powers felt drawn into participation through fear of injury to their own nation's interest and as a warning to rivals against further violation of such interests (White 1964:2). As the uprising reached serious proportions, the imperial Chinese leaders decided to support the Boxers, a move that gave the rebellion the appearance of 'a holy war against all foreign influence on Chinese soil' (Dallin 1950:62).

Perceiving the spiraling conflict as a common threat, the powers – including Japan (and the United States) – temporarily set aside their rivalries and dispatched an allied military force in order to relieve the beleaguered legations. In view of its proximity Japan agreed to supply about half of the forces (Borton 1955: 28–34). A total of 170,000 men and 300 cannon were sent to the East, and on the sea 29 battleships, 22 torpedo boats, 4 converted cruisers, and a number of transports were committed. Each of the powers had its own national purpose, however. The Japanese, for example, saw possibilities for new military advances on the mainland from which they had been expelled a few years previously, whereas the Russian government saw the rebellion as an opportunity for facilitating its own designs in Manchuria and northern China (Dallin 1950:63).

The tsarist government at this time had 50,000 troops in Manchuria, the strategic rail line from Peking to Tientsin and north was under Russian control, and in early November 1900 the Chinese government announced that land at Tientsin had been ceded to the Russians. In the wake of this news, Germans, French, Belgians, Austrians, and Japanese scrambled for further concessions (Langer 1950: 711).

Acting boldly under these circumstances, the tsarist government entered into a secret treaty with China, which was pursuing a conservative, antiforeign policy, and undertook a military occupation and economic and political penetration of Manchuria (Ono 1922:58). Whether Russia had undertaken an offensive or the Chinese had initiated hostile acts of their own was not entirely clear to Japanese observers, but the dispatch of Russian troops onto the scene and Russian occupation in Manchuria were taken as a clear sign of Russia's intention to advance southward.

RUSSIA AS THE THREAT

Foremost among Japanese concerns was whether or not the tsarist regime would accord Japan's 'special position' in Korea the recognition and respect that was sought (Borton 1955: 234). By the early years of the twentieth century more than three-quarters of Korea's foreign trade was being carried on with Japan, and Japanese settlers, living largely in the towns where they controlled most of the shipping, promoted railway construction and served as advisors to the government, already outnumbered any other foreign group in the country (White 1964: 78–9). Increasingly, under these circumstances, the Japanese assessed Russian railway building and related activities in Manchuria, as well as the intrusion of Russian enterprises into Korea, as an escalating threat to Japanese national interests. By the time the conflict had subsided, the view from Tokyo was that a large section of Manchuria was occupied by Russian troops.

In the meanwhile, the Korean king, having taken refuge from the Japanese at the Russian legation in Seoul, had granted to a Vladivostok merchant and his heirs an exclusive timber concession in the Yalu River region of Korea which provided a base for expanding Russian interests in that country (White 1964: 32–3). Witte opposed such Russian 'adventures' in Korea and declared that it might be advisable to give up Korea altogether rather than risk a war with Japan. Other Russian leaders took an opposing view, however, and, as Witte saw it, 'took into their hands the direction of our Far Eastern policy.' The Russian Foreign Minister, Alexander Bezobrazov, formed 'an industrial corporation for exploiting the forest in the Yalu River Basin' (Witte 1921: 120-4). Japanese observers in Korea reported some 2000 troops 'of various origins' – 'Russians, Koreans, and Chinese, the latter largely ex-Boxers, discharged soldiers, or bandits' – being concentrated in Manchurian territory directly across the Yalu (White 1964: 44).

After the settlement of the Boxer affair, Russian evacuation from Manchuria became a key question in the Far East. Specifically, the proposal of the Russians that China provide them with a monopoly of concessions in Manchuria, Mongolia, and Chinese Central Asia in return for evacuation from Manchuria was a great shock to the Japanese government. Japan's strong protest to Russia had been turned down by the tsarist government until Britain joined the protest in April. 'In support of the new hard line, various elements in the Japanese government became increasingly attracted to the idea of strengthening Japan's hand by seeking an alliance with Britain' (Hosoya 1974: 360).

ANGLO-JAPANESE COALITION AND ESCALATING LEVERAGES

Recognizing that 'Russia standing alone would be a dangerous foe' and that 'a coalition of European powers would be disastrous for Japanese ambitions,' the Japanese government began negotiating with Britain. In January 1902 the two nations concluded the Anglo-Japanese Alliance, which provided both countries with new bargaining and leverage potentials and created a new configuration of power in the Far East (Reischauer 1964: 38-9). Temporarily checking tsarist expansionism in Korea and elsewhere, this agreement helped pave the way for a Japanese victory in the Russo-Japanese War and the substitution of Japan's influence for some of Russia's economic and political penetration on the Asian mainland (Hershey and Hershey 1919: 259; text in *British State Papers* 1902).

While brooking no interference in its expanding activities and interests on the Asian mainland, Japan was nevertheless willing to concede that Russia had special rights and interests in Manchuria and 'to recognize that it would be far less expensive to win Russian acceptance of its demands by negotiation rather than war,' which would have the further advantage of gaining time for completion of the Japanese military and naval expansion programs. With these and related considerations in mind, Japanese negotiators proposed that each of the two countries should respect the zones and special interests of the other, but Russian counterproposals were only partially satisfactory to Japan. The practical options became clear. Japan could settle for 'restricted hegemony over Korea, exclusion from Manchuria, and the continued menace of Russian naval bases on both flanks of Korea at Port Arthur on the west and Vladivostok on the northeast.' The other alternative was to rely upon warfare as a leverage for displacing Russia from Manchuria and establishing itself as the chief power in northeast Asia. The premier, high-ranking military officers, and Japan's admiralty were not convinced that the country could defeat tsarist forces, but in general the public 'believed that a war with Russia was inevitable and the sooner it was over the better' (Borton 1955: 234–6).

On paper, Japan did not appear to be a match for Russia. In terms of national income per capita (in 1906 dollars), but with allowance for data uncertainties, Japan at this time ($27) ranked below Russia ($63), to say nothing of Germany ($136), Britain ($200), and the United States ($278). Japan's military expenditures per capita were comparable ($7.88) to Russia ($2.55), Britain ($10.21), and the United States ($9.35). On the other hand, with 149 persons per square kilometer, Japan was generating more population pressure on resources than Britain (135), Germany (113), or the sparsely populated United States (10) or Russia (22).

Retrospectively, it appears, however, that the tsarist government, disposed to avoid a showdown at this time, was willing to abandon its economic activities and interests in Korea and take other adjustment measures in its relations with Japan. But this was 'not what Japanese decision makers understood Russian intentions and moves to be,' according to Hosoya. 'Japanese leaders felt increasingly that, owing to intensification of Russia's aggressive policy, Japan's national security was on the verge of being destroyed' (Hosoya 1974: 371).

In fact, although Russian capabilities were generally viewed at the time as much superior to those of Japan, the tsarist government had the disadvantage of pursuing hostilities at the far end of the Trans-Siberian Railway – several thousand miles of single trackage – which was difficult to operate in winter (Reischauer 1964: 138). At the beginning of the war an uncompleted section of the line skirting Lake Baikal required the conveyance of troops and supplies by ferries, which were unreliable when ice on the lake was thick. The Russian navy was dispersed, some ships being based in the Baltic Sea, some in the Black Sea, others at Vladivostok, and others at Port Arthur (White 1964: 145–50). Russian planning and military activities were also hampered by domestic revolutionary activities. Meanwhile, by carefully timing their attack, the Japanese established a new pattern of modern warfare – 'first crippling Russian naval strength in the Far East, and then declaring war' (Reischauer 1964: 138–9).

Facing what they foresaw as a diplomatic impasse, the Japanese broke off negotiations on 6 February 1904. On the same day Russian troops crossed the Yalu into Korea, and a Japanese fleet departed from the naval base at Sasebo bound for Port Arthur, where the Russian fleet was attacked at anchor with its lights undimmed. Two days after the opening of hostilities, a Japanese rescript proclaimed a state of war – taking the French, the German, and even the Russian government by surprise, none having been 'fully aware of Japan's determination to go to war to settle the issues' (Storry 1960: 138–9). Within three months Japanese troops succeeded in driving Russian forces out of Korea, and Russian naval forces were crippled by Japanese warships. In March 1905 the Manchurian city of Mukden fell to the Japanese (Borton 1955: 240).

Japan had counted upon surprise, proximity to the war arena, and short-term superiority in the immediate availability of troops to wage a short, quick war calculated to bring the Russians to the negotiating table at an early date. With the siege of Port Arthur, which dragged on until January 1905, the Japanese began to suffer from the erosion of their early advantages, and by spring the strains of war began to tell upon them. Fortuitously for Japan, in May Admiral Togo won an important naval victory in the Straits of Tsushima, which nearly destroyed a Russian fleet that had sailed around Africa from the Baltic, and a stalemate was reached (Duus 1971: 132).

Map 1   The Russo-Japanese War, 1904–5

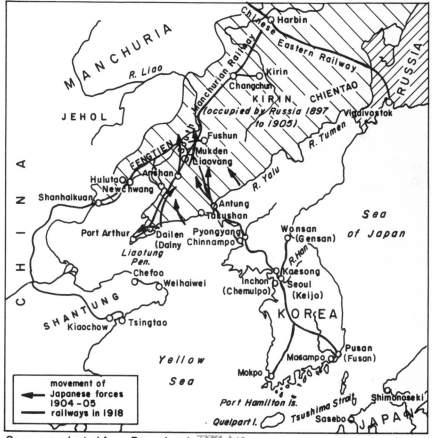

Source: adapted from Barraclough 1978:243

DIPLOMATIC BARGAINING AND LEVERAGE: THE TREATY OF PORTSMOUTH

In connection with their double-pronged military drive into Manchuria and Korea, meanwhile, the Japanese had undertaken a vigorous diplomatic campaign as leverage in support of their military campaigns and to ensure optimal political rewards among the outcomes. This diplomatic initiative included efforts to safeguard continued support from Britain and the United States; to preserve the image of Japan as the defender of foreign rights and interests in China; to portray Japanese demands for compensation as a just reward for defending these rights; and to sustain the fiction, borrowed from Russia, that they, the Japanese, were acting in defense of Chinese sovereignty. In their efforts at strengthening US support, Japanese diplomats laid the foundations for President Theodore Roosevelt's subsequent role as mediator between Japan and Russia in the reestablishment of peace (White 1964: 155, 157–69).

Concluding hostilities between Japan and Russia, the Treaty of Portsmouth (5 September 1905) provided for the Russian recognition of Japan's economic, political, and military interests in Korea, which became a Japanese protectorate. All foreign troops were to be withdrawn from Manchuria except Japanese railway guards, and the tsarist government yielded to Japan all Russian territorial advantages and special concessions in southern Manchuria, along with Russia's Dairen and Port Arthur leases, the section of the Russian-built South Manchurian Railway between Port Arthur and Changchun, and Russian coal mining and other rights and privileges associated with the rail line. Southern Manchuria thus became a Japanese sphere of influence. In addition, Japan acquired half of Sakhalin, where valuable oil and minerals were later obtained (MacMurray 1921: I 522–8). The treaty also provided for noninterference by the signatories in whatever measures China might take in Manchuria for commercial and industrial developments there (Borton 1955: 243).

By their readiness to accept Japanese demands at Portsmouth, the Russians in effect acknowledged the emergence of Japan as a continental Asian power. Yet the conclusion of the treaty was not welcomed by everyone in either St Petersburg or Tokyo. The war had been fought by both sides not only for the achievement of national interests that often tended to be as vague as they were grandiose, but also with forces that proved to be matched evenly enough so that neither side could advance far beyond its own limited objectives. Consequently, each side was forced to be satisfied with the attainable rather than the ideal (White 1964: 310–17).

Publication of the terms of the treaty elicited responses in Japan ranging from dutiful, if unenthusiastic, acceptance to public indignation and violent opposition. Having heard nothing but reports of success for a year and a half, the best knowledge of most Japanese was that their forces had defeated the Russians in 'three or four great battles in Manchuria,' and had succeeded in capturing a fortress and naval base 'so strongly defended that, like Singapore in later years, it was rumored to be almost impregnable,' and that their navy had swept the Russian fleet off the sea. To the Japanese populace it was much less evident that the war against Russia had been much more costly than the Chinese war had been (Thompson 1959: 113) and that war expenditures had left finances in an insecure, if not precarious, position (Ono 1922: 146). Nor were they aware, since they had not been told, that the country was not in a position to insist on the indemnity from the Russians that many Japanese had come to regard as 'indispensable' (Storry 1960: 142–5; also White 1964: 282–309, 310–29).

JAPAN'S NEW (UNCERTAIN) STATUS IN EAST ASIA

Overall, even though the Japanese had gained less from the war than their sacrifices seemed to justify, they appeared to have obtained a number of substantial advantages nevertheless (Storry 1960: 142–5). Japan had not been required by the major powers to relinquish what it had won by conquest and treaty but was – for the time being, at least – 'applauded . . . for the overwhelming victory' (Yanaga 1949: 314). The country now possessed a sphere of influence encompassing both Manchuria and Korea, was well advanced toward a controlling influence over Eastern Asia (Borton 1955: 243), and 'in the eyes of the world' had won recognition as a full-fledged member of the community of nations (Yanaga 1949: 14).

Japan's foremost concern immediately after the war with Russia was with the establishment of its interest in Manchuria. At the end of 1905, China and Japan concluded an agreement confirming Japan's control over Russia's vested interests from the prewar days. Meanwhile, the United States intended to apply the 'open door' policy to Manchuria. Specifically, Washington was interested in joint management with Tokyo of the South Manchurian Railway, but Foreign Minister Komura barely managed to succeed in establishing Japan's monopoly in the form of a semigovernmental corporation. The Japanese government was eager to extend Japan's interest in other aspects as well. Although beyond the railway zone, the coal mine at Fushun near Mukden came under Japanese control. Moreover, the railroad connecting a town on the Korean border with Mukden, which was originally built during the Russo-Japanese War for Japanese logistics, was to be upgraded as an integral part of the South Manchurian Railway.

As might be expected, the 'applause' in other countries died down as the full significance of Japan's 'triumph' over Russia began to be recognized. During and immediately after the war, Japan tightened its grip over Korea, which was reduced to a Japanese protectorate and by 1907 to colonial status. In 1909 the assassination by a Korean of Hirobumi Itoh, former premier and one of the great Meiji leaders, provided the Tokyo government with a pretext for the outright annexation of Korea (Storry 1960: 144). By achieving military victories over China and Russia, together with the adroit exploitation of rivalries among other powers, Japan had step by step succeeded in winning an empire which encompassed colonies nearly equaling the area of the home islands themselves. 'The growth of armament which accompanied this process, and the strategic gains which it conferred, would enable Japan a decade later to emerge from the Washington Conference as the predominant naval power of the Pacific' (Lockwood 1954: 533). For the pre-World War I years, however, the Japanese victory was not sufficiently decisive to provide the country with undisputed hegemony in the Far East, nor to produce a stabilized configuration of power, nor to yield much more than what had been referred to as a system of 'balanced antagonisms' in the East Asian region (White 1964: 310–29).

JAPAN'S ECONOMY AFTER THE RUSSO-JAPANESE WAR

It was much harder for the Japanese government to set up postwar economic policy in 1905 than in 1895 (Nakamura 1989: 27). The war with Russia left Japan a large sum of national bonds and foreign loans, and was settled without any reparations. Nevertheless, public investment helped improve various social capital such as railways, telecommunications, and public works. Moreover, demobilization shifted many skilled workers from arsenals to private factories so as to develop industries in wider scale (Sawai 1989: 217). Especially, the development of small and medium-sized factories met the increasing need for machines by producing price-competitive products (Sawai 1989: 247). The market for industrial products was not totally dominated by imported goods; instead, industrialization took place at a rapid pace.

Japanese exports expanded steadily after the Russo-Japanese War with increases in raw silk, silk piece goods, and cotton yard and piece goods. By 1914 these four exports accounted for more than half of the country's total – with raw silk representing about 30 percent. Japanese imports underwent corresponding changes. During the early 1880s almost half the country's imports were manufactured goods, whereas imports of raw materials had remained relatively small. By 1913 the import of raw materials had risen to about a third of total trade, whereas manufactured exports had declined to less than a fifth. Semi-manufactured goods constituted about a sixth of total imports. As a result of successes in food production from agriculture and fisheries, however, food and drink imports accounted for a smaller proportion of the total than they had in the early 1880s (Allen 1981: 96–7).

For a considerable part of the Meiji era, Japan faced serious payments difficulties. Despite the growth in export strength, the country's foreign

Map 2 Japan's expansion abroad, 1868–1918

Source: adapted from Barraclough 1978:243

indebtedness rose from 467 billion yen in 1896 to 1,970 billion yen at the close of 1913 – an increase attributable in part to military expenses and in part to private capital formation (Lockwood 1954: 254–7). During the 1903–13 period Japan borrowed heavily from abroad, largely in the form of bond issues, with the result that outside capital helped the balance of payments and supplemented domestic saving (Maddison 1969: 29–30). By the early months of 1915, however, 'it became clear that the country was on the threshold of a period of unexampled prosperity.' Through the inability of former suppliers to meet current demands because of World War I, markets in Asia and elsewhere were thrown open to Japan; 'contracts for munitions began to be placed with Japanese manufacturers by Allied Governments'; and there arose a strong demand for Japanese shipping – a trend that persisted until the spring of 1920 (Allen 1981: 100).

Japan's overall position among the powers had changed since the opening years of the century, but, in view of the country's defeat of Russia, not as much, perhaps, as might have been expected or its leaders might have hoped. As indicated by national income (1906 dollars) per capita, Japan ($38) was close behind Russia ($47), but still trailed Germany ($148), Britain ($197), and the United States ($307). In terms of military expenditures per capita, Japan ($1.98) had pushed slightly beyond Russia ($1.91) but still lagged behind Germany ($9.07), Britain ($9.50), and the United States ($9.61). Japan's growing population continued to exert pressure on its domestic resource base. With a population density of 136 persons per square kilometer, Japan in 1914 was more thickly populated than Britain (146) and Germany (125). The United States at that time had only 13 persons per square kilometer – and Russia had roughly 27.

COMPETITIVE LEVERAGING OF JAPAN AND THE GREAT POWERS

Not all Russo-Japanese exchanges of leverage were coercive or violent. As European powers leased more enclaves in China, such alienation of Chinese territory was perceived by the Japanese as putting their own country in a seriously disadvantageous position in terms of national defense. Under these circumstances it became a necessity for Japan to expand its capabilities and 'develop a real military power' in order to maintain its position in the Far East and effectively assert itself in Far Eastern affairs (Ono 1922: 80).

Although Russia had been weakened by its recent defeat at the hands of the Japanese, German expansion in China provided the two countries with a common interest there, with the result that Tokyo and St Petersburg, recognizing a stalemate in their own rivalries, negotiated a series of secret agreements (1907, 1910, 1912) which reserved southern Manchuria for Japanese and northern Manchuria for Russian expansion. Subsequently, during World War I, Japan secretly sanctioned a number of minor Russian advances in Outer Mongolia in return for Russia's recognition of Japanese spheres of influence in Manchuria, Shantung, and eastern Inner Mongolia (Price 1933: 35–8, 107–8). At the same time the Japanese were expanding their concern for the coal mines, iron mines, and iron works held in Central China by the Hanyehp'ing Company, which had received a number of Japanese loans since the turn of the century (Tiedemann 1955: 52).

Japan's position in power politics was strengthened by the revision of Anglo-Japanese Alliance (1905) and the entente with France (1907), in addition to the above-mentioned series of Russo-Japanese treaties. True, they were in some degree the reflection of the shift in the European power balance against Germany, namely, the Triple Entente, but Japan was expected to exercise its influence in the game of power politics.

In 1907 the Japanese government adopted the Imperial National Defense Policy. Classified as top secret, and revised a few times subsequently, the document spelled out the most fundamental defense policy of prewar Japan. There were three major points. First of all, Japan identified its potential (or hypothetical) enemies: Russia in the first place, then the United States, followed by France. Secondly, the army was to consist of twenty-five divisions in peacetime; the navy of eight battleships and eight cruisers were the major power symbol. Finally, the army was supposed to conduct a preemptive attack against the Russian army mainly in northern Manchuria, while the navy was to control the western Pacific and destroy American navies coming to the area. The military administration and institution were revised on a large scale in 1907 and 1908 in particular. The military buildup soon followed.

Japanese leaders became increasingly adept at playing the great power game. A few years later, taking advantage of the war in Europe in which the major powers were fully occupied fighting each other, Japan began to extend its power into China proper.

Chapter 5

Comparisons of profiles
Japan and the major powers

Lateral pressure theory, previously examined with respect to major European powers prior to the outbreak of World War I, is particularly relevant to Japan in terms of growth and expansion during the decades following the Meiji Restoration. To draw out some of the key similarities and differences between Europe and Japan, we compare certain basic attributes and relate them, however tentatively, to some of the behaviour patterns that seem to have led to major wars. Our focus is on population, national territory, aspects of technology and production, and trade – those attributes that we see as contributing to the tendency of nations to extend their activities, spheres of influence, and territorial possessions beyond their home territory.[1] Of concern also is the extent to which each nation was constrained in its efforts toward expansion, and thus how likely it was to perceive its demands as generally satisfied or unsatisfied.

COMPARISONS OF PROFILES

Nations in Conflict reported on a formal investigation of relations among Britain, France, Germany, Russia, Austria–Hungary, and Italy between 1870 and 1914, focusing on their growth and expansion and the thrust of events leading into World War I. During this period, all six of the powers were increasing the levels of their demands and improving their capabilities, but from different bases and at unequal rates of change.

As their lateral pressures developed, Britain and France found their activities and interests colliding in various parts of the world (much as they had collided in the eighteenth century and thereafter) – although these intersections, for the most part, were not as intense as those between Britain and Russia. Increasingly, moreover, Britain and France began resolving such conflicts diplomatically, through positive rather than negative leverages, and the conclusion of treaties.

During these years, the tsarist empire extended its activities and interests into the Balkans, the region of the Dardanelles, the Turkish territories of Ardahan, Kars, and Batun, to Bukhara, Khiva, Krasnovodsk, Kokan, and

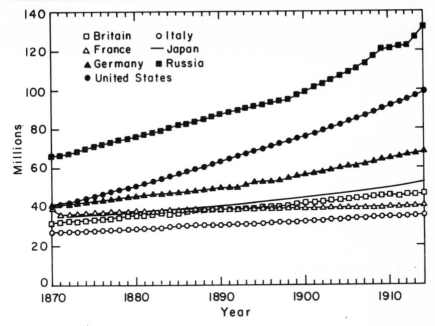

Figure 5.1   Home population, 1870–1914

Merve. The Russians also penetrated northern Persia and other parts of the Middle East, Korea, Manchuria, and the island of Sakhalin, which they occupied and claimed (Choucri and North 1975: 181). In the west and southwest, however, they were constrained by Britain, in particular, and increasingly by Germany, whereas the path eastward led for the most part through sparsely populated, largely underdeveloped territories – except insofar as they were increasingly blocked by the expanding Japanese.

Throughout the nineteenth century, the United States, which was not under scrutiny in *Nations in Conflict*, had been expanding its activities and interests southward into Spanish lands (Florida), westward through Indian territories, and southwestward into Mexico (resulting in the acquisition of lands from Texas to California). US activities and interests also collided for a time with English and Canadian interests, but after the War of 1812 conflicts in this sector were largely settled through diplomacy. Following its purchase from Russia, American activities and interests began penetrating Alaska, but the main US thrust was still westward into Hawaii, to Japan ('opened' to the West as a result of the arrival in Tokyo harbor of naval vessels under Commodore Perry), into the Philippines (seized from Spain along with Cuba and Puerto Rico), and, via the 'open door,' missionary activities and a modest amount of gunboat diplomacy, well into the interior of China (where Russia, Britain, France, Germany, Portugal, and Belgium had already acquired leases, concessions, and other advantages

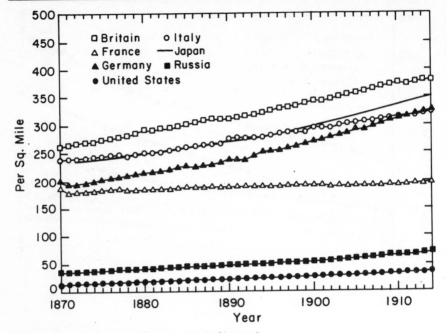

Figure 5.2 Population density, 1870–1914

through the use of various leverages – positive and/or negative – on various levels of negotiation, coercion, and relatively small scale violence).

It remains a matter of great controversy whether Japan can be compared to other major and lesser powers (Minami 1986: 421–2) and during which time periods. Here we show trends descriptively, tied to strict chronology and focusing largely on the European powers. We include the United States wherever appropriate. Later on we consider how Japan ought best be compared to the European powers before World War I.

Population

The population levels of the major powers and Japan are shown in Figure 5.1. Japan can be located roughly between Britain and Germany. If we measure population density, we get the same location of Japan relative to these powers, but we observe a much starker delineation of population pressures on home territory. (See Figure 5.2.)

Both population and technological advancement contribute to increases in demands, which, in combination with national capabilities, contribute to lateral pressure. All of the major powers experienced some advances in technology, as measured by the production of iron and steel.

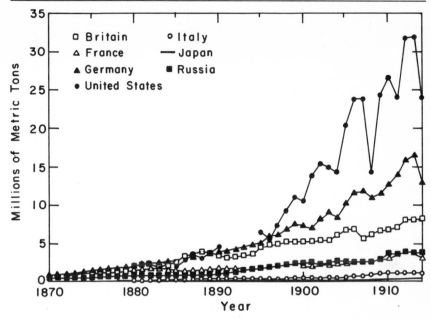

Figure 5.3 Steel production, 1870–1914

Iron and steel production

Compared to the European powers and the United States, Japan was
clearly at a disadvantage. Japan's iron production did not begin substantially until the turn of the century. By contrast, the other powers' iron and
steel production had grown markedly. Britain was ahead. During the latter
part of the nineteenth century, however, in the course of about 30 years,
Germany experienced 'what England required over one hundred years to
complete – the change from a backward and primarily agrarian nation to a
modern and highly efficient industrial and technological state' (Pinson 1954:
219).[2] Figure 5.3 shows the levels of production of Japan and the major
powers between 1870 and 1914. Differences among the powers in *rates of
increase* in iron and steel production were also diverse; Germany and Italy,
starting from vastly different base levels, increased at mean annual rates of
5.0 and 9.1 percent respectively, followed by Russia (5.6 percent), France
(4.2), and Britain (1.2). By comparison, Japan was a newcomer to iron
and steel production.

National income

Since iron and steel production is an incomplete measure of technology, we
have used national income as a broad indication of the level of technological
advancement and per capita national income as an indication of the population–technology relationship. As can be seen from Figure 5.4, all powers

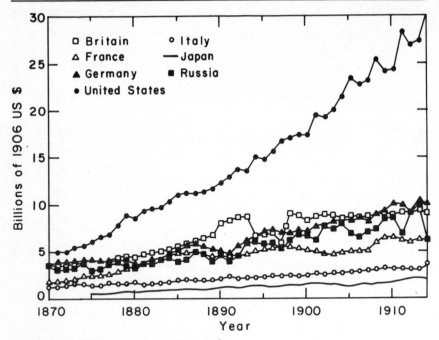

Figure 5.4   National income, 1870–1914

experienced increases in national income during this period. Compared with the European states, Japan was clearly lagging. The level of income was the lowest among the powers. Although German national income was initially somewhat higher than that of Britain, the latter's income rose steeply, surpassing Germany by 1878 and retaining the lead until 1906. However, to one degree or another, all the European powers suffered declines at some point. Compared to the European powers, Japan's *growth* in national income was impressive, with an average annual rate of increase of 3.85 percent for the period before World War I. The other powers showed relatively more modest growth: France ranked first (3.04 percent), followed by Italy (2.84), Germany (2.49), Britain (2.42), and Russia (2.32).

The growth of per capita national income for the great powers (and the United States) is shown in Figure 5.5. Japan's income per capita was, at that time, much lower than that exhibited by the European powers. In the long run, Britain and Germany showed similarly high rates of growth and levels of national income, although Britain greatly surpassed the other nations in the level of national income per capita. Japan exhibited a growth rate of income per capita of 2.8 percent between 1875 and 1913.

Trade and merchant marine

Demands generated by population growth and technological advances can generally be met by developing national capabilities, increasing domestic

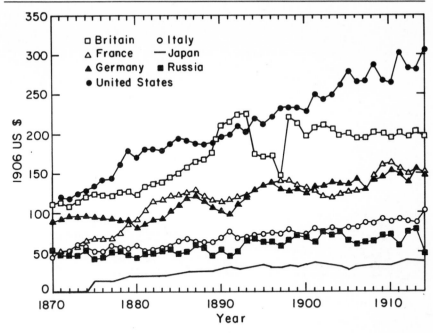

Figure 5.5 National income per capita, 1870–1914

resources (agricultural yields, mineral deposits, water power), acquiring new territories, or developing trade. With limited national resources of its own, Japan also lagged behind the great powers in trade – see Figure 5.6 showing the trade rankings. In terms of two indirect indicators of trading capacity – merchant marine tonnage and number of commercial ships – Britain ranked first, surpassing by far both France and Germany, the next two ranking powers.[3] In merchant marine tonnage, Germany surpassed France in the early 1870s and retained a substantial lead throughout the entire period (1870–1914). Britain dominated throughout, however, whereas Japan, once again, remained far behind – see Figure 5.7.

Colonial expansion

The expansion of the major powers during the nineteenth and early twentieth centuries was characteristically colonial, defined by territorial acquisitions. Territorial expansion measures only one type of lateral pressure, however, and as an indicator it leaves much to be desired. Figure 5.8 shows the growth of colonial territory (measured in total area) for Japan and the five European powers.

Britain and France were clearly the most expansionist of the powers (if measured only by territorial gains), and thus the most likely to be reasonably satisfied with the status quo – which presented them with

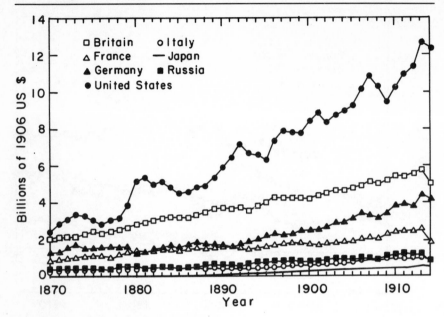

Figure 5.6   Total trade, 1870–1914

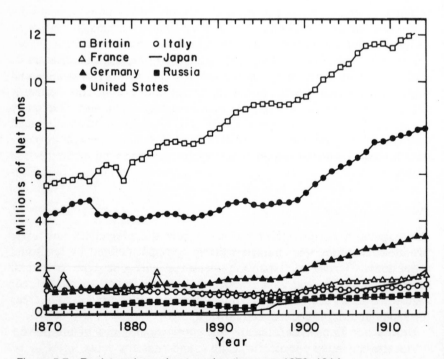

Figure 5.7   Registered merchant marine tonnage, 1870–1914

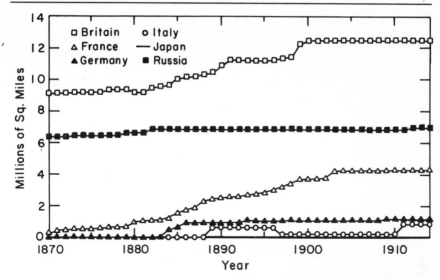

Figure 5.8 Colonial area, 1870–1914

opportunities for continuing acquisitions (Louis 1967: 10–11). The size of
the British empire far exceeded that of the French, but the rate of French
territorial growth – which started from a much lower base – surpassed
that of Britain. Although Germany and Italy expanded their respective
colonial territories, the possibilities open to them fell considerably short
of the advantages enjoyed by Britain, France, and, to some extent, Russia.
Russia's rapid movement eastward, in combination with considerable
advances in technology and production, suggests that the tsarist regime
might have been relatively satisfied had it not been countered and blocked
by Japanese expansion.

Military expenditures

As a country grows in population, technology, industrial production, and
other attributes and capabilities, military expenditures are likely to increase
more or less commensurably. Domestic interests and bureaucratic processes
may push for greater allocations to defense and to the military. Yet a
nation's extension of interests and activities beyond its home territory also
stimulates increases in military expenditures. In the European cases apprehensions of competition and rivalry led to increased military preparedness,
and domestic factors and bureaucratic politics further shaped the escalating
expenditures for armament. Figures 5.9, 5.10, and 5.11 show the levels
of army, navy, and total military expenditures for the six major powers
and Japan. The impact of the Russo-Japanese War of 1904–5 is clearly in
evidence for Japan's total allocations to its army and navy. When compared
with the European powers, however, Japanese military expenditures were
relatively modest.

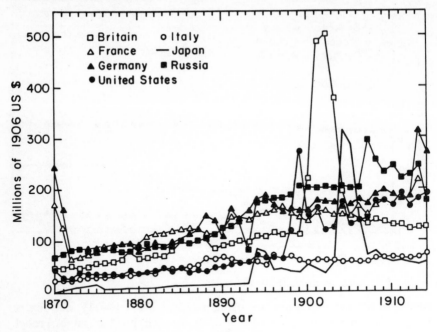

Figure 5.9   Total army expenditures, 1870–1914

JAPAN AND GERMANY

It has been with Germany that Japanese scholars have tended to compare their country most frequently, and it was German success at expansion that the Japanese government tried most often to emulate. Both societies had 'achieved national unification and appeared on the stage of international politics about 1870,' and the 'comparative lateness of these events' placed both countries 'in such a state of rivalry with the more advanced countries as to stamp certain common features on their modern institutions and politics' (Hayashi 1971: 461–2). In both cases, 'the power of the modern state was created not so much to accomplish the self-governing objectives of civil society as to concentrate the nation's strength to meet' what were perceived as threats from abroad. As a consequence, the state, in both cases, 'assumed a strong leadership role, therefore opening a gap between the "governors" and the "governed," and giving the state officials the character of a "ruling class."' Germany emerged as Europe's typical 'bureaucratic state,' and in this regard Japan viewed Germany as a viable model, making official life a conspicuous feature of the Meiji system. To a large extent, national unification in both countries was accomplished through military measures.

At the time of the Franco-Prussian War (1870), when a newly integrated Germany struck out against France and gained control of the industrial complex of Alsace and Lorraine, the two countries, France and Germany, were relatively equal in both population and national income. During the next 30 years, however, Germany's birth rate became the highest in Europe, that of France the lowest, and the German economy expanded at almost twice the rate of the French. Impressed by Britain's imperial successes, in the meantime, many Germans came to believe that what 'was and is valid' for Britain was valid for them (Langer 1956: 289–322).[4] By 1914 German overseas possessions totaled an expanse approximately one half the size of Australia but only one-tenth the size of Britain's colonial territory (Choucri and North 1975: 183). Such German successes were not lost on the Japanese.

Japan's victories over China in 1895 and Russia in 1905 paved the way for the rapid expansion of Japanese activities and interests on the Asian mainland and, during the 1930s, for the increasingly frequent intersection of these activities and interests with those of the United States, the USSR, and other powers. With respect to their resistance to the post-World War I Versailles system, the Japanese were 'a step ahead' of the Germans in that the Manchurian Incident was precipitated two years before the collapse of the Weimar Republic in 1933, 'and parliamentarism was destroyed as an outcome of the murder of Premier Inukai' a few months later (Hayashi 1971: 467–8, 471).

POWER TRANSITIONS

By the end of World War I (and after the Treaty of Versailles), the United States had joined Britain and France as a full-fledged *alpha* power. Russia, on the other hand, drained by its wartime experience and disrupted by revolution, was in chaos and could be described as having regressed (temporarily) in the *zeta* direction (low population density, 'primitive' technology, limited access to resources). Germany, having lost not only the war but also its 'empire,' was reduced to disrupted *beta* status (relatively advanced technology, still, 'dense' home population, limited access to resources). For its part, Japan during this period had developed from an *epsilon* state (a developing, low-capability society) toward a *beta* profile. In this connection, moreover, it is important to note that although the Japanese had enlarged their colonial territory (and hence their resource base), the territories they had acquired before, during, and as a result of the war – Taiwan, Korea, Kwantung, numerous Pacific islands – were themselves densely populated overall (although generally not as densely populated as Japan), had limited access to resources, and were technologically and economically underdeveloped. Only a certain amount of resources could be extracted out of their empire.

These comparisons with the major powers illustrate differences in power and capability as well as relative positioning on power transitions. Drawing

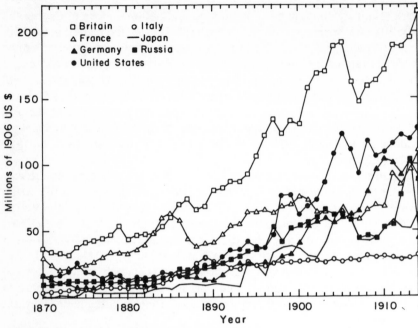

Figure 5.10   Total naval expenditures, 1870–1914

upon these comparisons as well as the historical narrative of the previous chapter, at least two conclusions can now be drawn.

First, during the period of major power expansion in *Nations in Conflict* on almost all indicators of profile, Japan was consistently on the lower end. In these terms Japan was considerably less outwardly oriented than the major powers. The domestic pressures, nonetheless, were building rapidly. This suggests that Japan's profile in the period of expansion (in its *beta* phase during the interwar years) most closely approximates the expansionist profile of the European powers *prior to World War I*.

Second, Japan's lateral pressure and early configuration of expansion were shaped by internal factors, the master variables; but the most serious intersections came as the expanding activities and interests of the major powers advanced eastward. In relative terms, at least, well-established Western lateral pressures and expansions collided with Japan's own, more recently generated lateral pressure. From a European perspective Japan had not yet become a major power, whereas perceived from Japan the Europeans refused to recognize the emerging status and power of the Japanese. Thus the comparisons in this chapter show that on a set of empirical indicators Japan was far from fully attaining the basic requisites of international power. At the same time, however, Japan's domestic growth and external victories over China (1895) and against Russia (1905) paved the way for more expansion and greater conflict. By the outbreak of World

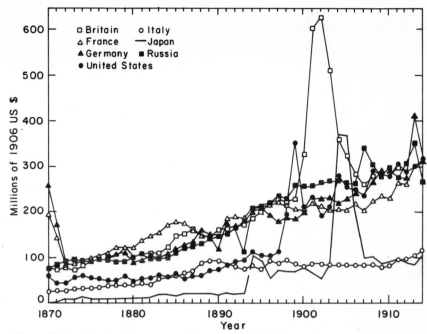

Figure 5.11 Total military expenditures, 1870–1914

War I in Europe, Japan had effectively completed the transition from a developing (backward) *epsilon* state toward becoming an industrializing, newly powerful and expansionary *beta* power. The defeat of Russia a decade earlier had been a powerful test of newly acquired capabilities. By 1914 the transition appeared complete. And the immediate postwar years set the stage for new challenges and new risks.

Chapter 6

A model of lateral pressure
From the Meiji Restoration to World War I

In the context of the discussion in earlier chapters, we now turn to a quantitative inquiry into the processes of expansion, competition, and conflict. The conceptual model guiding this analysis derives from the framework presented in Chapter 1, which in turn is a further specification of the lateral pressure model developed in the World War I study (Choucri and North 1975) focusing on the major European powers. As indicated, the focus of the World War I study was on the *interactions* of the major European powers in their dealings with each other, whereas our treatment of the Japan case amounts to a case study – a study of the special circumstances of growth and transformation of a country with a rapidly advancing technology combined with a population that was (and still is) large (and growing) relative to the extent of its territory and resource availabilities.

In many respects, Japan of the 1870–1941 period was roughly comparable to Britain, France, Germany, and the Low Countries during early phases of their commercial and industrial growth (prior to and during initial decades of their respective efforts at territorial expansion) rather than during the height of their colonial acquisitions. The comparisons in Chapter 5 are designed to follow the historical narrative. In terms of dynamic processes, however, it is insightful to consider the issue of phase: at which points in time did Japan exhibit the pattern of growth and expansion characteristic of European power expansion leading to World War I? This chapter presents the quantitative analysis for the Japan case prior to World War I and then compares briefly the results with data from the European powers.

Japan has been the subject of some of the most important and innovative work in quantitative economic history. The country's development has provided a rich record for economists and economic historians seeking to explain the structure and driving mechanism leading up to the Japanese 'miracle'; contending 'lessons from Japanese development' are put forward, subject to contending analytical specifications and estimation procedures (Kelley and Williamson 1974; Minami 1986).[1] The thrust of their work is on economic activity; politics are exogenous and evaluation of the instruments of politics or of force, such as military allocations, territorial expansion, or conquest, are restricted to secondary, and often minor, consideration. There are major differences (as well as similarities) between the economic historians' view of the Japan case and ours, as there are in methods and modes of inferences.[2] Our purpose is to show the way internal growth, and its attendant economic demands, contributed to expansion and, in turn, how expansion led to conflicts of interest, military competitions, and arms races.[3]

As with other quantitative analyses of Japanese economic history, our approach entails model building, pretesting, estimation of simulation equations, simulation, and extensive use of counterfactuals: what would have happened if . . . ? Our task is not primarily to explain sources of Japanese economic growth, however, but rather its consequences internationally. The economic component is necessary, but not sufficient, to provide a rich explanation of international activities.

Our view of economic growth during the Meiji period, and attendant initial international behavior, is indebted to Kuznets in *Modern Economic Growth* (1966), Rosovsky (1961), Ohkawa and Rosovsky (1960), and the Yasuba (1986)–Hanley (1983) debate.[4] Kuznets drew attention to technological change, sustained per capita growth, transformations of industrial structures, and enhanced international contacts. We incorporate the three initial conditions in our simple growth equations. The fourth condition – the implications for international interactions – carries the burden of our analysis. Rosovsky highlighted the importance of World War I in changing the economy of Japan; to some extent we accept the inference, and use 1914 as a breakpoint, consistent with our European case studies. Further, however, we will compare model structure and behavior before and after World War I. Consistent with Kelley and Williamson (1974) we emphasize endogenous forces, and specify further interaction among jointly dependent economic and political variables. And the Yasuba–Hanley debate casts light on the impacts of the Tokugawa development on the Meiji period.

Five attendant problems are encountered in any modeling effort that must be resolved on theoretical and methodological grounds. First is the plausibility test: how reasonable is the implicit structure, how explicit can it be rendered? Second is the data issue, not in the conventional sense of availability, but in the conceptual sense when the historical record does not provide observations consistent with our modern standards. Third is the model-building strategy, modular versus integrationist. Ours has been a conscious equation-by-equation specification and pretesting toward the development of an integrated system of simultaneous equations. Fourth is the estimation (replication) of the historical record, as a requisite for simulation and counterfactual analysis. Fifth is dealing with historical 'breaks.' Large-scale discontinuities (such as World War II) require respecification and estimation, as the 'real world' experiences dramatic transformations.

The model of lateral pressure presented in this chapter is generic in the sense that it seeks to capture characteristic features of the Japan case from the Meiji Restoration to World War II. The idiosyncratic features are estimated by comparing the model's performance before and after World War I. (The quantitative results are presented for the Meiji period alone, and then, in a subsequent part of the book, for the interwar period.)

MODEL OVERVIEW

In order to operationalize the broad conceptual framework in Chapter 1, we developed and estimated a system of simultaneous equations explored initially for the case of the major powers of Europe prior to 1914 (Choucri and North 1975: 25, 169). Using the resulting coefficients, we

Table 6.1 The Japan model: pre-World War II

Component of the model	Description and rationale	Measure
Growth and economic capability	National productivity resulting from economic performance, population activity, and domestic resource exploitation	Exports of finished goods
Resource demand	Demands for raw materials resulting from interactive effects of population growth, technological development, economic productivity, and domestic resource exploitation	Imports of raw materials
Military capability	Expansion of military establishments; these grow as a result of internal and external pressures and as a consequence of the pursuit of national objectives and of scarce and valued resources	Army expenditures Navy expenditures
Expansion in trade mode	Resource demands resulting in expansion of behavior outside national boundaries in search for external control and resource acquisition	Proportion of colonial imports to total imports
Expansion in territorial mode	Extension of behavior outside territorial boundaries results in control over alien territories; such control occurs to the extent that there are demands to be satisfied and capabilities to pursue these demands	Colonial area Government expenditures for administration of controlled territories

then simulated the entire system over time. The simulations became the foundation for policy experiments designed to identify the most likely consequences of alternative policies (Choucri and North 1975: 164). The model is presented in Table 6.1. In five components and listed in the first column of the table, the model represents (a) *the process of growth and economic capability* (b) *resource demand*, (c) *military capability*, (d) *expansion in the trade mode* and (e) *expansion in the territorial mode*. Each of these components is influenced (and highly interactive with) exogenous factors and other components. See Appendix II.

The point of departure (or driving mechanism) is growth. In contrast to economic historians who seek to explain growth (with GNP or national income as critical variables to be explained), we use economic output measures in the case of Japan as explanations for the outcome of growth, namely, exports of finished goods. Growth, then, is represented by the variable indicating *exports of finished goods*.

The second component is *resource demand*. Few countries have been as strapped as Japan with respect to raw materials within its territorial boundaries, and greater growth has led inexorably to more resource demand.

The third component is *military capability*, represented by army and navy expenditures.

The fourth component is indicated by the ratio of *imports from the colonies* to total imports. This component ties growth to expansion in yet other ways.

The fifth component represents expansion in the territorial mode, specified by the *colonial area* acquired by Japan, and by the government's *expenditures for the administration of controlled areas*.

The model is anchored in three master variables: population, technology, and resources. *Population* factors have generally not been as central to the economic historians' analysis of the Meiji Restoration and developments until World War I (Kelley and Williamson 1974), and the impacts of the population characteristics inherited by the Tokugawa period have not been adequately assessed. In fact, Japan supported *a smaller rate of population growth than other powers of the period*, and questions remain regarding the extent of the impacts driven by population factors (Minami 1986). In our model population is a leading exogenous variable affecting demand for raw materials and expansion.

Central to lateral pressure theory, *technological change* is an even more elusive factor to the extent that direct measures are generally difficult to operationalize. In our analysis, technological change is implicit in the model prior to 1941 (indicated by national income). For the postwar period later on, we develop and use explicit measures of the technology variables. Economists acknowledge that 'by far the larger part of the observed increase in output per head is a consequence of "technical progress" rather than of increased capital per head,' (Solow 1960: 89). Summarizing the evidence, Solow demonstrated the importance of technical progress relative to other factors in the production function (1960: 97). Historians generally agree regarding the role of technological change in Japan during the post-World War II period, but considerable uncertainty prevails on the nature of the technological factor during the Meiji period and the interwar decades. Kelley and Williamson (1974: 24, 26) found that technical change during the Meiji period played a significant role in facilitating rates of capital accumulation, and placed emphasis on the role of technical change in agriculture, which goes a long way in explaining the Japanese model of agricultural output. And Minami (1986: 426) states boldly: 'Technological innovation has played a decisive role in the modern economic growth of Japan and will continue to be important in the future.'

An essential feature of the lateral pressure thesis as applied to the Japan case is *resource* constraints. Economic historians raise added queries about the real limitations of such constraints. Kelley and Williamson found that offsetting effects and dynamic countervailing forces show that relaxing land constraints creates more rather than less urbanization pressure (1974: 28). Our model highlights a related set of effects, namely, resource constraints create pressures for conditions that would relax those constraints, thereby creating 'feedback effects' and enhancing the impacts of resource constraints themselves.

The system of simultaneous equations in Table 6.2 was developed iteratively, guided by the conceptual model outlined above, through a series of partial analyses and exploring the properties of the individual subsystems, or components of 'reality.'[5]

System of simultaneous equations: growth, resource demand, and trade

The first equation specifies *growth and trade* in terms of the key master variables.[6] The equation representing *growth* treats it as determined by the size of the industrial labor force in proportion to the total labor force, the production of coal (a key raw material), the previous year's balance of trade (indicating prevailing trade burden or absence thereof), the proportion of colonial imports to total imports (jointly dependent variable), and, most importantly, imports of raw materials (a jointly dependent variable that obviously shapes and constrains production possibilities). The dependent variable is viewed as a critical output of the growth system, namely, exports of finished goods. This variable connotes industrialization and manufactured products. The existence of domestic pressures (from resource constraints or from the labor market) generates demand for resources whose acquisitions are essential inputs into the further manufacturing of goods for exports.[7] Even in the pre-'miracle' period, the strong export performance of the Meiji period was characterized by, and reflected, considerable economic strength.

Table 6.2 The Japan model: growth and expansion from the Meiji Restoration to 1941

(1) Exports of finished goods $= \alpha_1 + \beta_{11}$ (imports of raw materials) $+ \beta_{12}$ (% of industrial labor forces to total labor) $+ \beta_{13}$ (production of coal) $+ \beta_{14}$ (previous year's balance of trade) $+ \beta_{15}$ (proportion of colonial imports to total imports) $+ \mu_1$

(2) Imports of raw materials $= \alpha_2 + \beta_{21}$ (exports of finished goods) $+ \beta_{22}$ (proportion of colonial imports to total imports) $+ \beta_{23}$ (population of Japan proper) $+ \beta_{24}$ (previous year's balance of trade) $+ \mu_2$

(3) Army expenditures $= \alpha_3 + \beta_{31}$ (Russian military expenditure) (dummy variable of Russia as a potential enemy) $+ \beta_{32}$ (colonial area) $+ \beta_{33}$ (proportion of colonial imports to total imports) $+ \beta_{34}$ (previous year's army expenditures) $+ \beta_{35}$ (government revenue) $+ \mu_3$

(4) Navy expenditures $= \alpha_4 + \beta_{41}$ (US navy expenditures) (dummy variable of US as a potential enemy) $+ \beta_{42}$ (British navy expenditure) (dummy variable of Britain as a potential enemy) $+ \beta_{43}$ (imports of raw materials) $+ \beta_{44}$ (colonial area) $+ \beta_{45}$ (proportion of colonial imports to total imports) $+ \beta_{46}$ (previous year's navy expenditures) $+ \beta_{47}$ (government revenue) $+ \mu_4$

(5) Colonial area $= \alpha_5 + \beta_{51}$ (military expenditures) $+ \beta_{52}$ (imports of raw materials) $+ \beta_{53}$ (imports of food per capita) $+ \beta_{54}$ (population of Japan proper) $+ \mu_5$

(6) Colonial imports $= \alpha_6 + \beta_{61}$ (tonnage of merchant marine) $+ \beta_{62}$ (national income) $+ \beta_{63}$ (military expenditures) $+ \beta_{64}$ (colonial area) $+ \beta_{65}$ (food imports per capita) $+ \mu_6$

(7) Government expenditures on colonial administration $= \alpha_7 + \beta_{71}$ (government revenue) $+ \beta_{72}$ (proportion of colonial imports to total imports) $+ \beta_{73}$ (colonial area) $+ \mu_7$

Deflator: Wholesale Price Index (1870–1970). Sources of the Japanese price indices include the Asahi Shimbun Index (1868–1900), the Bank of Japan Index (1901–65), and the International Monetary Fund Index (1966–76). Differences among the base years were standardized.

Instrumental variables were used to estimate the following independent variables: imports of raw materials (11, 43, 52), proportion of colonial imports to total imports (15, 22, 33, 45, 72), exports of finished goods (21), total military expenditures (51, 63), colonial area (32, 44, 64, 73), and the previous year's army (34) and navy (46) expenditures. Figures in parenthesis refer to the coefficients in the model equations.

Instrumental variables (IV) were selected from among a wide range of instruments, checking also for multicolinearity and autocorrelation among IV's.

Instrument list: Rice production, wheat production, government expenditures (special account), railway length, total exports, and total imports. In addition to the variables listed, all the exogenous variables that are not independent variables in the respective equations are used as instrumental variables.

It is not uncommon for quantitative economic history studies of Japan to distinguish between industrial and agricultural activities, and to posit a two-sector model (Lewis 1954; Jorgenson 1961; Fei and Ranis 1964; Ohkawa and Rosovsky 1968; Kelley and Williamson 1974). For analysis concerned with the structure of economic activity this 'dualism' is relevant as it draws attention to differences in production processes, factor intensity, and technological characteristics. The differentiation relevant to our purpose is delineated by territorial boundaries, that is, those activities generated internally; and these impacts have obvious cross-border impacts. In contrast to the economic history literature on Japan, our emphasis is on the sources of expansion, the implication for armament, and the resource allocation for territorial and related aggrandizement – all serious precursors to war.

The second equation focuses on *resource demand*, with imports of raw materials as the dependent variable. Recall that imports of raw materials served as an explanatory variable in the first equation – reflecting the interdependence of import demands and export performance. The model suggests that the criticality of raw materials imports is due, to a large extent, to domestic industrial requirements and the requirements of manufacturing goods. This growth, modeled in the first equation in terms of exports of finished goods, is a critical element in determining requirements for raw materials. Thus, the first explanatory variable in the resource demand equation, namely, the *exports of finished goods*, incorporates the growth processes (represented by overall specification of the first equation). *Resource demand* is also a function of colonial imports, the previous year's balance of trade, and the population of Japan.[8]

The linkages between the imports of raw materials (equation 2) and the exports of finished goods (equation 1) are central to the relationships at hand and essential features of Japan's realities, then and now. These are *jointly dependent* where a positive feedback loop reinforces the linkage, tying growth in one variable to the growth of the other. Exports are essential for obtaining those inputs necessary for industrial activity, and, because of domestic resource limitations, raw materials imports are essential inputs for the production and the export of finished goods. Any interruption in the supply of one affects the other, and because of strong feedback linkages, the effects are mutually reinforcing.

Military capability

The third and fourth equations in Table 6.2 represent the growth of *military capabilities*, which are indicated by army expenditures and navy expenditures. These capabilities are engendered by, and associated with, economic growth and demand for resources.

Each equation stipulates that Japan take into account the capabilities of its adversaries as annual budgetary decisions are made. A form of the 'Richardson process' (Richardson 1960a: 13–36) is specified as an outcome of *domestic growth* and *resource demand*, reinforced by perceptions of threat and feelings of tension. The equations are adjusted to changes in perceived adversaries by inclusion of an adversary variable, to help determine the effects of the opponents.[9]

Each equation is designed also to capture the institutional influences that shape military expenditures through the exercise of bureaucratic processes. In view of the influence of Japanese navy and army ministers in the decision process, these aspects of the bureaucratic process are of particular relevance. Playing an important role in this process are Japan's colonial holdings, which serve two functions in the model; they provide sources of raw materials and create at the same time a 'need' or 'necessity' for increasing military capabilities – and, in the longer run, the 'need' or 'necessity' of even further raw materials, (and hence further territorial expansion, greater military capabilities, and the inescapable incurring of higher costs).

The independent variables in these equations are colonial area and the ratio of colonial imports to total imports. Imports from the colonies are also an input into the imports of raw materials modeled in equation 2. Imports of raw materials are included as an explanatory variable only in the navy expenditures equation. (Other influences, not specifically represented, are included indirectly through the error term.)[10]

The economic historians' view of military expenditures in Japan, and attendant military 'adventurism,' stresses the forgone private investment associated with government war financing (Kelley and Williamson 1974). Wars tend to draw resources away from private investment, and hence detract from growth. Our model highlights a related aspect, namely, the militarist consequences of growth. The post-1905 economic performance of Japan could be interpreted as due largely to the absence of military investment; indeed, war financing seemed more consistent with our specification, namely, as an outcome of the extensive economic growth and 'lateral pressure.'

Colonial expansion

The *process of colonial expansion* for Japan during this period of study reflects complex relationships, with attendant bureaucratic and political rationales. There were at least three aspects of expansion, each represented, in turn, by an individual equation. First is external expansion through direct *territorial acquisition* – extreme applications of negative leverage (equation 5). Second is use of colonies as a source of critical raw material *imports from colonies* (equation 6). Third is the allocation of financial resources for colonial expansion, the budgeting of governmental resources targeted for direct expansion overseas and for the *administration of acquired territories* (equation 7). For Japan before World War II, these three aspects of expansion are depicted by individual equations (with attendant dependent variables).

Territorial expansion, the most direct form of expansion, is measured by colonial area (equation 5). It is determined by military expenditures (representing the capability for expanding territorially), imports of raw materials (representing the resource demand impelling such expansion), and imports of food per capita (indicating the home population demand for food not satisfied by domestic resources and the home population of Japan proper). (The error and intercept terms incorporate those influences, such as colonial expansion on the part of competing powers, which are not modeled directly.)

Imports from the colonies are a form of commercial leverage (equation 6), based on territorial acquisition. Such imports are specified as a function of national income, merchant marine tonnage, food imports per capita, military expenditures (a product of the expenditures for the army and the navy), and, most importantly, of course, colonial area.[11]

The final equation in the model is government expenditures for overseas territories (equation 7). It is shaped by government revenue, colonial area, and imports from the colonies. Budgetary allocations for territorial expansion are critical, as they indicate the extent of financial resources disbursed specifically for this objective.[12]

The model integrated

To summarize, the model represents highly interrelated sets of relationships that specify the process of lateral pressure. Lateral pressure in Japan was manifested in several modes; motivation for expansion emerged from a variety of sources – the possibility of outwardly expanding activities being traced to several sets of capabilities. Figure 6.1 shows the components of the model path integrated in a system of simultaneous equations.

METHODS AND DATA

The Japan case during the Meiji period and before World War I has been modeled as a set of simultaneous equations whose parameters were jointly estimated.[13] The *Nations in Conflict* model was much simpler in specification, formulation, and intention.[14] The current formulation of the model takes account to some extent of the constraints imposed by limitations in the availability of a complete data set for the entire period from 1870 to the present for all variables. Having differentiated the whole period into two segments, 1868–1914 and 1915–41, we examined each of the segments separately and in great detail. The break with World War I was designed mainly to help comparison with the European powers and to assist in identifying the nature, extent, and source of system change.[15]

The data for the estimation of the equations are annual observations of each of the variables. These figures are obtained from various Japanese government publications as well as some non-Japanese sources. For more 'political' variables, such as identification of adversaries, more complex, history-based analysis was required in order to represent historical perceptions as metricized (quantified and scaled) variables.[16] The sources used for the figures for the years indicated are listed in Appendix I.

AN OVERVIEW OF RESULTS

The system of simultaneous equations shown in Table 6.2 was estimated by the two-stage least square (2SLS) method with generalized least square (GLS) corrections for the three separate sets of observations for pre–1914, 1915–41, and the entire period until 1941. This chapter reports principally on the results for Japan during the period from the Meiji Restoration to World War I. The detailed results are in Appendix II.

The overall characteristics of the system of equations as a whole can never be observed in any one of the equations individually – therefore the simultaneities, feedback relations, and interdependence of influence must be explicitly recognized and specified accordingly.

Our point of reference is Figure 6.1, which presents an overview of the model and all the hypothesized *theoretical* linkages with the independent and jointly dependent variables. We represent the analogous *empirically* determined coefficient estimates for the system of simultaneous equations in Figure 6.2. Of related interest, discussed in Parts Three and Four of

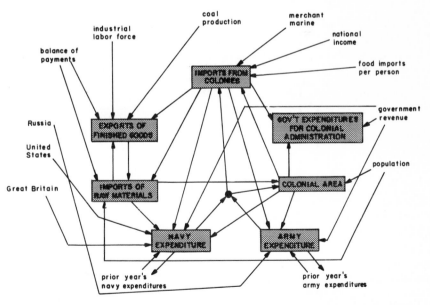

Note: The darkened circle represents total military expenditure.

Figure 6.1   The Japan model leading to war, 1914 and 1941: overview of the system

this book are the emergence and 'decay' of individual linkages – where in the system, and when, do various influences become more significant and when do they 'die off'? The related coefficients (in Appendix II) are indicated for each individual equation to highlight the finding that, despite the existence of certain individual nonsignificant influences, the explanatory variables, together, account significantly for the variance in the individual jointly determined variables.

The following patterns stand out during the period up to 1914:

(a)   Domestic population (generating demand) exerted pressures for imports of raw materials.
(b)   Military expenditures (military capability) and merchant marine (commercial capability) were important determinants of imports from the colonies.
(c)   Government revenues provided significant impacts and pressures on expenditures for colonial administration.
(d)   Navy expenditures were influenced largely by navy commitments earlier, by imports from the colonies, and by government revenue. (It was only in the later period that the United States became a significant adversary with powerful impacts on Japan's navy expenditures.)
(e)   Of Japan's adversaries, only Russia exerted a significant influence upon Japan's army expenditures. Its impact was strongly positive, contributing to increases in Japan's allocation to the army.

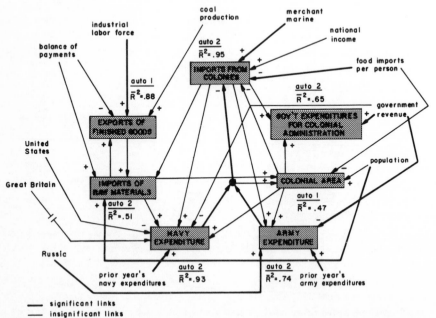

Figure 6.2   Robust linkages, to 1914

(f)   Internal bureaucratic pressures for increasing both naval and military expenditures were of considerable significance.

A CLOSER LOOK

At this point we present the results in detail, equation by equation.[17] The system is thus fully integrated.

Japan's growth, generating *exports of finished goods*, is very well accounted for. Over 80 percent of the variance in exports of finished products until 1914 is accounted for. A significant factor is the input of raw materials, as is the industrial labor force. The other explanatory variables are not statistically significant during this period.

Resource demand, represented by *imports of raw materials*, is explained somewhat less successfully. Only 51 percent of the variance until 1914 is accounted for. The exports of finished goods are a significant determinant of imports of raw materials. Japan's population is also a statistically significant variable, as is the balance of trade.

For *army expenditures*, the equation explains 74 percent of the variance during this period. The significant factors are total government revenue, the previous year's army expenditures and notably Russian military expenditures.

Navy expenditures are successfully explained; over 90 percent of the variance for the period until 1914 is accounted for. The effects of bureaucratic processes (last year's budgetary allocations) in conjunction with the reaction to enemies' allocations provide strong pressures for naval expenditures. Some influence of the US navy is discernible (but the coefficient is negative, which means that there may be a lag and/or a directly inverse relationship in this period).

This analysis strongly indicates that Japanese military expenditures were affected by military expenditures of adversaries, as well as by bureaucratic inertia and budgetary constraints. Colonial acquisition and the trade-related features of the colonies were also important. With powerful statistical evidence of the interplay between domestic and foreign factors, it is difficult to see how, once set in motion, the pressures toward more and more military investments could have been resisted effectively by the Japanese leadership; the leverages and pressures were too elusive and powerful to be readily controlled (let alone reversed).

The colonial expansion process shows some strong thrusts. Japan's *colonial area* was acquired in a series of spaced lurches. This pattern suggests that Japanese pressures for territorial expansion accumulated over time with population growth and technological advancement. Then, once a colony – a new resource base – was acquired, a period of consolidation, adjustment, and investment ensued. In time, however, the productivity of the new territory was insufficient to cover the costs of conquest, the levels of investment, and the demands generated by the colonial populace and its efforts at development – a situation that provided the motivations and pressures for a new expansionist 'lurch.' In any event, the equation for colonial area failed to explain or represent adequately the process which brought Taiwan and Korea under Japanese control during the earlier period. For the years before World War I, about 47 percent of the total variance in colonial area is explained by variables in this equation, but none of the independent variables was found to be a statistically significant 'causal' factor during this period. The abrupt acquisition of territory appears not to have been driven by abrupt and equivalent functions in any of the explanatory variables.

By contrast, *imports from the colonies* are explained well. As high as 95 percent of the total variance is accounted for. The negative coefficient for food imports appears to reflect a rise in imports from the colonies. This is relevant for demonstrating the effects of domestic constraints (and the pressures of demand) and the importance of the colonies for meeting demand. These relationships capture the demands for furthering Japan's reliance on colonial imports. During this period, merchant marine tonnage generated a positive influence on acquisition from the colonies, providing the capabilities needed. However, military expenditures also imposed countervailing, negative influences. There is a dampening effect of military expenditures on imports from the colonies during wartime, when military expenditures are particularly high – and/or an increase in imports from the colonies following the conquest of new territory. (Recall that imports from the colonies influenced army expenditures as well as navy expenditures.)

Government expenditures for colonial administration are well accounted for; 65 percent of the variance is explained by the variables in the equation. Japan's government revenue alone appears a powerful and statistically significant factor. The financial resources available (from both inside and outside the colonies) thus seemed to provide the basis for colonial administration expenditures. Interestingly, total area of the colonies was not by itself enough of a determinant of government allocations for colonial administration.

In this period, the predominant forms of lateral pressure were associated with the extraction of raw materials from the colonies and the export of finished goods to external markets. The salient features of the Japanese system during the years between 1868 and 1914 are the domestic pressures generating strong demand for expansion. Other forms and manifestations of lateral pressure took shape and became apparent during subsequent decades. Even with the benefit of hindsight, it is difficult to view this period in isolation from subsequent events, and the pressures and dispositions leading to war in 1941.

What have we learned so far about the Japan case and about comparison with the major European powers during this period?

COMPARISONS WITH THE EUROPEAN POWERS

Despite differences between the European and Japanese cases, useful comparisons can be made to highlight further the generic features of lateral pressure. Despite the more detailed specifications of the Japan case compared with the model in *Nations in Conflict*, some important inferences can be made.[18]

Colonial expansion

Nations in Conflict showed that Britain's colonial expansion was best explained by population density and military expenditures (and by the constant term representing earlier levels of expansion). National income per capita was significant in the earlier but not in later decades, suggesting that Britain went through a transition from strictly lateral pressure processes due to growth, to lateral pressure leading to military competition. Military expenditures and armament competition became especially significant in the latter period. The data show a similar pattern in the case of Japan, but *the pattern takes place later in time*, during the interwar period. German expansion was also influenced by population density, the constant term, and national income per capita; but for the most part only population density and the constant were significant. The fact that military expenditures were not significant seems to indicate that German colonial expansion was not propelled by military competition.

In the Japanese case military expenditures (and militarism) appear to have contributed more strongly and directly to the expansion of the colonial area than in the European cases. Military expenditures played only a minor role in explaining British territorial expansion and did not provide significant explanation of German colonial expansion. Home population and national income were not direct predictors of Japan's colonial expansion during the pre-World War I period. (However, population does indeed have a positive impact on imports of raw materials during subsequent decades.) There are feedback loops in the case of Japan, as we will discuss later on, that are more discernible than for the European powers.

Japan's colonial expansion is best explained by military expenditures and by imports of raw materials. Indeed, for this period imports of raw materials are the main predictor of colonial area. It is noteworthy that for both Germany and Britain the significance of the constant term reflects the impact of expansion that had occurred prior to 1870, but for Japan this term is not significant, reflecting the absence of colonial expansion prior to the period under study.

Military expenditures

In *Nations in Conflict* Britain's military expenditures were determined by expenditures in previous years, military expenditures of nonallies, population, and national income, and, to a lesser extent, by intersections with other powers. Over time there is an observable transition from processes of growth of lateral pressure, colonial competition, and intersections prior to 1890, to processes of armament competition and arms race behavior after this juncture. The German case was more stark; throughout the period, population in conjunction with national income, military expenditures at $t-1$, and the constant term shaped military expenditures.

For Japan military spending (army and navy) appears to combine lateral pressure with arms race behavior. However, only the previous year's naval spending is a strong and significant determinant of navy expenditures, and the coefficient for the impact of US naval spending is actually negative. These results probably reflect the importance of Japanese military rivalry with Russia during this period, which is indirectly included in the model through the adversary variable.

British naval spending was primarily a function of past naval spending, with intersections and population times national income as possible additional variables which were not quite statistically significant. These results suggest that British naval expenditures were primarily the product of internally generated and bureaucratic processes. Germany's naval expenditures were explained by population and national income – the constant term was positive and significant – reflecting 'pent-up' lateral pressure and pressures for naval spending in years prior to the period investigated. Differences aside, however, the influence of domestic factors, bureaucratic in the British case, and growth and lateral pressure in the German case, appear to have been very important in shaping naval spending for these two powers.[19]

Trade and security links

Japan's success in securing colonial territory and resources appears to have a dampening effect on army and navy spending. Imports from colonies tended to push for more expenditures; and the influence of government revenue becomes negative, reflecting constraints on financial resources. Army expenditures at $t-1$ and Russian military expenditures remain positive and significant throughout. We infer that Japanese competition with tsarist Russia during this period seems to be more important than budgetary constraints or bureaucratic processes.

Overall, trade competition with potential rivals appears to have been more important in the Japanese case than in the European case. If anything, in terms of their direct and indirect impacts on military expenditures, variables contributing to lateral pressure such as population and national income appear to have had some dampening effect at some points in time. It is possible, however, that US, British, and Russian military spending, which appears to drive Japanese military spending, may have been a response, in part, to Japan's own colonial expansion. If this were the case, what emerges in the model as military competition may in effect be an indirect outcome of Japan's own lateral pressure.

The Japan case is distinctive in showing a strong positive feedback relationship between exports of finished goods and imports of raw materials; continued success in exporting finished goods played an important role in diverting Japanese lateral pressure away from at least one form of military expression. This positive loop essentially reinforced, for a period, the 'downward escalator.' But it also created pressures for expansion and militarism that become statistically significant in subsequent periods.

Domestic growth and bureaucratic factors

Domestic growth was important for both Japan and the European powers. Among variables contributing to lateral pressure in the British case, population density and national income, as well as their interactive effects, are both strong positive predictors of colonial expansion. Colonial expansion, in turn, had a significant and positive impact on intensity of intersections and, through influence on intersections, upon military expenditures as well. Population and national income pushed military expenditures upward and had a positive impact on alliances and counteralliances. In the case of Germany, national income and population density also had a positive effect on colonial area. Population and national income exerted a positive impact on military expenditure, and indirectly on intensity of intersections.

Bureaucratic processes were powerful contributors to expansion for both Japan and the European powers. Naval and army spending in Japan was strongly and positively influenced by the previous year's spending. Last year's allocations provided an important element in the 'upward escalator.' Although British spending appears to have been more responsive to past spending than that of Germany, for Germany domestic pressures (population and national income) were most critical.

For Japan, growth of the industrial labor force exerted a strong impact on exports of finished goods, which in turn had a negative impact, via raw materials imports, on naval spending. This set of relationships shows the 'dampening effects' at work. Growth in government revenue enhanced army, navy, and colonial expenditures. And national income, clearly a growth variable also, had a positive influence on imports from colonial sources. The results suggest that high levels of colonial imports necessitate a larger army establishment to secure colonial areas while reducing the need for naval forces (primarily useful for securing alternative sources of supply). Russian military spending and US naval spending both had strong positive influences on Japanese army and navy spending. During this period, the influence of the Russian military dominated throughout. (We interpret the negative sign on the US navy coefficient, noted above, in the context of and in conjunction with events in subsequent decades, as reported below.)

The European and Japanese cases both shared a tendency for bureaucratic process to affect the level of military spending. The positive and driving impact of domestic growth on colonial expansion is also a shared feature. Later on we will refer again to the trade – security link for Japan, derived from key and statistically significant negative coefficients between external expansion and militarism.

Part III

Expansion, competition, conflict

Chapter 7

Gains from World War I
Japan as an emerging power

Immediately following the outbreak of World War I, Japanese leaders had difficulty deciding whether to remain neutral, to join the Allies, or to side with Germany. During the deliberations that took place, however, the Anglo-Japanese Alliance – together with Germany's part in forcing the retrocession of the Liaotung Peninsula – became an issue, and in the end Japan decided in favor of the Allies.

Soon after this decision had been conveyed to the Western powers, France and Russia, acting through the British government, urged that Japan dispatch three army corps to the European theater; and after Turkey sided with Germany in October, Britain joined the other two powers in appealing for Japanese military assistance. Japanese leaders estimated that at least ten corps would be required to shift the balance significantly – a contribution that would make the homeland vulnerable. Thus, although further requests were received, the Japanese government was adamant, and no Japanese land forces were ever committed to the European theater (Yanaga 1949: 358–59).

Japanese agriculture flourished during World War I, and imports of food decreased for a time; but the most striking wartime outcome was the country's industrial and commercial development. As a result of demands from home and foreign markets, investments of capital increased before and after the war, larger enterprises were undertaken, and management methods were improved. The skill of Japanese workers was enhanced, and the volume of output grew rapidly. Of various manufacturing industries the greatest developments took place in shipbuilding, machine production, and chemical, electrical, and gas enterprises (Uyehara 1936: 16–17, 24, 31, 54, 211, 213, 239).

Japan's primary concern in World War I (and in the peace settlement thereafter) was to improve its economic and political position on the Asian continent and its strategic advantage in the Pacific (Borton 1955: 281). The Russo-Japanese War was remembered as a collision with Russia which had greatly enhanced Japan's influence on the Asian mainland, and now the great war which had originated in Europe seemed to offer extensive opportunities in Asia at low cost.

Britain would have preferred to see its Japanese ally stay out of the war, but there was a widely held belief that Japan's naval assistance was necessary if German naval strength in the Pacific were to be destroyed (Grey to Green, 14 August 1914, in Gooch and Temperley 1926–1938: XI). In fact, Japan's overriding success in World War I could be explained in large part by the government's commitment to domestic economic growth combined with (and partly attributable to) efforts at institutional reform, technical and educational advancement, drastic fiscal measures, and the exploitation of wartime opportunities for international trade 'with all the technological gains and economies of specialization involved' (Maddison 1969: 33).

BARGAINING AND LEVERAGING

Because of the war, Japan was able to make further gains in bargaining and leverage potentials at minimal political and military expense. With the Western powers busily competing with each other, the Japanese saw a golden opportunity for settling the China question in a manner favorable to themselves (Tiedemann 1955: 53). During early years after the Sino-Japanese War, Japan – in view of its own limited economic, political, and military capabilities – had opposed the penetration and parceling of China by the great powers. The government therefore was well disposed toward Sun Yat-sen and other reformers and revolutionaries in China and elsewhere in Asia (Tiedemann 1955: 52). For a time Japan played the role of an 'energetic younger brother scolding and goading into life the lazy, corrupt, and backward elder brother.' As an outcome of the Russo-Japanese War, moreover, Japan acquired new prestige and leverage potentials in Asia. Later, however, having replaced Russia in southern Manchuria, Japan lost no time joining Western nations in the exploitation of China and competing for the spoils – a policy shift that introduced a contradictory element in Japanese relations with other Asian countries. Pursuing an image of Asian renaissance, extreme nationalists and other dissidents from China and elsewhere undertook hegiras to Tokyo at the same time that Japanese entrepreneurs and government policy makers alike were expanding their activities and interests on the Asian mainland and thus strengthened the conviction in Tokyo that 'Japan had the right to shape the future course of China's development' (Storry 1960: 143–7) and that of other Eastern countries.

During the early years of World War I, however, Japanese leaders quickly took control of German possessions and other interests in China and the Pacific Ocean, and reinforced their country's new position on the Asian mainland by compelling China to accept the Twenty-One Demands. Even after subsequent modification under pressure from other powers, the demands granted Japan special commercial, mining, and extraterritorial legal rights in China proper and special rights in Manchuria (MacMurray 1921: II, 1231–4; US Department of State 1924: 99–103; Tiedemann 1955: 123–7).

According to the treaty that was finally concluded, the Japanese lease of Port Arthur and Dairen and the Antung–Mukden railway agreements were to be extended to 99 years; and Japanese were granted the right to reside and travel in south Manchuria, engage in business and manufacturing, and lease land outside the treaty ports for trade and agriculture. China conceded a right of Japanese subjects to open mines in locations specified by the Japanese and a priority to Japanese capital if China required financial assistance for railroad building in Manchuria, whereas Japan agreed to supply financial, military, or police advisors in south Manchuria when needed. Although these and other advantages were much less than the Twenty-One Demands had specified, Japan obtained advantages from China which continued to further Japanese expansion on the Asian continent (MacMurray 1921: II, 1231–4; Yanaga 1949: 360–1).

In shrewd bargaining during the war, Japan – in return for its support of the Allies – obtained British backing for Japanese claims to German rights in Shantung and numerous Pacific island groups north of the equator (US Department of State 1922: II, 595); secured comparable understandings with France and Russia; and, through the Lansing–Ishii Agreement of November 1917 (superseded by the Nine Power Treaty of April 1923), won US approval of the proposition that, because of its geographical propinquity, Japan enjoyed special interests in China (Reinsch to Bryan, 30 September 1914, in US Department of State 1914).

During the latter stages of World War I, Russian leverage and spheres of influence in the Far East were seriously weakened. On the Western front imperial Russian armies were beginning to collapse, and during the spring of 1917 anti-tsarist forces overthrew the old order. By autumn Lenin and his Bolsheviks had toppled the middle-of-the-road government of Kerensky. Although the Japanese were no more prepared for this turn of events than their Western allies, they were determined from the first that the new leadership in Petrograd should not be allowed to deflect Japan from its own Asian policies. At the same time they were not prepared to see the relationships they had developed with the United States, Britain, and France threatened by the Russian Revolution and subsequent developments.

RUSSIAN REVOLUTION AND SIBERIAN EXPEDITION

When the Bolsheviks first came to power, they publicly repudiated the 'imperialist' treaties and relationships that had been established by the tsarist government in the past. Within a few months, however, Soviet leaders reversed themselves, deciding to hold or reconquer territories acquired by their predecessors – although technically on a federative rather than an 'imperial' basis.

Although Japanese leaders were cool to an Allied suggestion that they undertake a military expedition westward into European Russia, they responded with some enthusiasm to a proposal by Britain, France, and (somewhat later) the United States to join an armed intervention in Siberia and to contribute arms and ammunition to the Czechoslovakian Corps (some 50,000 soldiers of the Austro-Hungarian army, who, as prisoners of war, had volunteered to join tsarist troops against the Germans) that was currently fighting its way eastward on a long march 'home.' Having agreed to send 7,000 of its own troops to Siberia, Japan promptly dispatched three and a half divisions to the Amur Valley and later reinforced them to an aggregate of about 72,000 (White 1950: 278; Morley 1957: 213–32, 260–4). Outnumbering all other Allied forces combined, these troops gave Japan de facto control of the whole region as far west as Lake Baikal (Borton 1955: 287).

Despite misgivings within the United States and other Allied countries and criticism in the Diet (Hosoya 1971: 84), Japanese troops remained in the Russian maritime region until the autumn of 1922 (White 1950). The immediate Japanese purpose was to obtain control over the railway systems of eastern Siberia and Manchuria, but presence of these troops on the Far Eastern mainland enhanced Japan's influence at the peace conference after the war. Relations between Japan and the USSR were not established until the Treaty of Peking was concluded on 20 January 1925 (Eudin and North 1957: 131–5, 319–20). Overall, the prolonged Japanese intervention appeared to discredit, for the time being, the employment of military forces to promote Japanese business and financial interests and thus to favor the relatively liberal era which developed in Japan during the 1920s.

THE VERSAILLES 'BARGAIN'

Only 50 years after the Meiji Restoration, Japan participated in the Versailles Conference 'as one of the great military and industrial powers of the world and received recognition as one of the "Big Five" of the new international order' (Reischauer 1964: 141). With the signing of the treaty on 28 June 1919, Japan obtained recognition of most of its objectives in the Far East (Borton 1955: 295), including all former German rights in Shantung, and was granted League of Nations mandates over the Caroline, Marshall, and Mariana islands, which Germany had bought from Spain and in 1914 had lost to Japan. The mandate areas were not a large gain territorially (830 square miles), but they provided a Japanese presence over wide stretches of the Pacific and served the country well during the early phases of World War II. Subsequent to the conference, Japan returned the Shantung Peninsula to China but retained the economic privileges that had been granted to Germany along with the right to establish a settlement at Tsingtao 'under the usual conditions' (Yanaga 1949: 372).

INDUSTRIALIZING JAPAN

World War I and its outcomes substantially enhanced opportunities for the export of products from expanding Japanese industries (notably textiles) and relatively favorable access to resources on the Asian mainland (Chenery *et al.* 1977: 226–77, 289, 292). As an ally of the Western powers, the country was able to take advantage of demands for processed goods in Asian, Latin American, and African markets as well as those of Europe and the United States. At Britain's expense, for example, Japan greatly increased its share of textile markets in China and India and profited from trading with smaller, poorer nations which under war conditions became dependent on Japanese trade. As a result of this expansion Japan's foreign assets in 1919 exceeded its outstanding debts by 1,300 million yen, an almost complete reversal of the country's 1913 balance. Although Japan's new gains were not the result of the direct application of military and naval leverages, the country had once again obtained important advantages from participation in war that might not have become available through normal peacetime diplomacy.

By the first postwar decade, Japan's profile had completed a number of notable changes. In 1920 the first official census in Japan revealed a population of 55,391,000 (as compared with a 'legal' population for the year, calculated from registration rolls and other sources, of 57,919,000) – up from an estimated 35 million in 1872. Population growth contributed to a continuing demand for resources, but the greater share could be attributed to Japanese industrialization, which was proceeding at a rapid rate. National income per capita for 1920 was $39.9 (1906 dollars), which was high for Japan but low compared with $169.4 for Britain and $746.0 for the United States. As an industrialized nation, Japan ranked low on the major-power totem pole.

Japanese leaders became increasingly aware of an economic dilemma, moreover. Since the country had not kept up with many of the new technologies and fields of production that its Western allies had developed under pressures of war, its plants were outmoded and its commerce relatively restricted. Increasingly the United States and Europe were reentering foreign markets, whereas Japanese manufacturers and entrepreneurs still found themselves unable to match their competitors in readjusting prices downward from wartime inflationary levels. Gone, too, was a considerable amount of the foreign exchange accumulated during the war, eroded by military expansion in East Asia, as well as by expanding domestic consumption (Tiedemann, 1984: 6). If old industries were to be modernized and new industries introduced, and markets expanded, however, capital – scarce in Japan – would be required in large amounts.

Japan was fortunate to have industrialized in an era of liberal trade policies and general world economic prosperity. With trade access to vital resources in many parts of the world, the country's export markets continued to expand, and Japan's early successes with foreign trade were further enhanced by the effects of World War I on international economic conditions.

Later, during the 1920s, Japan's trade composition was significantly altered as a result of the country's rapid technological advancement and economic growth. Export trade shifted from semimanufactures to finished manufactures, while imports were increasingly dominated by raw materials – a change that greatly intensified Japanese reliance on complex trade patterns. In contrast to bilateral configurations, the trend was toward multilateral trade. Surplus silk was sold to the United States – and cotton manufactures and factory goods to China – for the settlement of balances in Europe from machinery purchases and in South Asia from imports of raw materials. This import–export mix continued to be an essential feature as more exports were required to purchase more resources in order to produce more goods for export to buy more resources.

Over the long run a fateful meshing occurred between Japan's exports and an unusual feature of the Meiji constitution.

CONSTITUTIONAL MONARCHY AND THE 'LIBERAL INTERLUDE'

The Meiji constitution, promulgated in 1889, making Japan the first constitutional state in Asia, brought a party government system into the country three decades later. True, the constitution was seemingly opposed to parliamentary democracy, but it made it inevitable for the cabinet to compromise in some degree or another with the Diet, Japan's equivalent of the Parliament, from the first decade. The constitution unambiguously postulated the sovereign authority of the monarch, but it made enacting state organs such as the two chambers of the Diet (the House of Representatives and the House of Peers), the Privy Council, the cabinet, and the Office of General Staff mutually independent and diffusive.

Although all executive, legislative, and judicial authority was combined in the person of the emperor, he himself never exercised these powers except on advice. No signature of the emperor on a political document was valid unless the prime minister and other cabinet members had signed it. There were other constraints on the imperial power including the Diet and the Privy Council. Although the consent of the Diet was required for the enactment of law, many critical issues could be handled by governmental decree. As a further check on cabinet and Diet, constitutional amendments, emergency decrees, treaties, international agreements, and declarations of martial law had to be approved by the Privy Council, but the council was politically neutralized by the initiative of an elder statesman (genro), Kimmochi Saionji.

Although the emperor was the supreme commander of the armed forces, he could act only on cabinet advice. The army and navy ministries were originally restricted to officers on the active list. The military could wreck a cabinet by withdrawing – or refusing to provide – an army or navy minister. In 1913, however, this rule was abolished, and military intervention, even in a tacit form, became largely impeded. Moreover, generals and admirals joined political parties, acquiring extraordinary leverage within the government if they chose to use it (Tiedemann 1955: 36–9, 114–20).

A new party government system had been instituted in 1918 when Takashi Hara emerged as 'the first commoner and the first professional politician of the new generation to become Premier' (Reischauer 1953: 148). Two parties tended to be especially influential during the first 10 or 12 years following the end of World War I – Hara's party, Seiyukai (the Political Friends Party), and Kenseikai (in 1927 renamed Minseito, or the Democratic Party). Events during much of the 1920s seemed to bear out the idea that modern industrialization was a strong force shaping and responding to social pressures. Lesser entrepreneurs and rural landowners had their own reasons for supporting the parliamentary government, since it furnished them with the only institutional basis for directly influencing political power. Small and medium-sized business people, including textile industrialists, were well represented in the Diet, while the large industrialists, through secret financial assistance, continued to exercise powerful leverages within (and through) the political parties (Ishida 1968: 309–10).

More specifically, the Diet provided great Japanese business establishments, known as the zaibatsu, with a convenient arena for increasing their political leverage through judicious provision of financial aid to the parties. During the 1920s professional bureaucrats, generals, admirals, and representatives of such firms as Mitsubishi and Mitsui tended to dominate party leaderships, and some served as premiers. In terms of domestic politics, however, it remained uncertain whether business interests and partisans of party cabinets and constitutional government had sufficient leverage to constrain the political influence of the military establishment (Borton 1955: 307).

Although the trend of the early 1920s favored liberalism, a number of rightist movements also took root. Shortly after the war the Japan Nationalist Society expanded into a nationwide organization with a million members, and in 1922 the League for the Prevention of Communism was established to counteract radical tendencies. Other rightist organizations included the League for the Study of Statecraft, the Radical Patriot Party, and the Patriotic Workers' Party. Most such organizations vigorously opposed the rising influence of democratic, liberal, and socialist elements in the postwar society and were opposed to parliamentary government, the League of Nations, and proposals for disarmament. As the Japanese government began undertaking tougher measures against radical leftist activities in the mid-1920s, some rightist groups concluded that their efforts were no longer needed.

A process of national integration was accomplished in effect by a combination of carrot-and-stick policies. The general suffrage from 1925 reflected the conciliatory measures, and the National Security Act of 1925 reflected the stronger measures.

As the prewar oligarchy disappeared and extragovernmental groups grew increasingly influential, the Diet and party system were clearly useful for the balancing of political forces. In position and perspective, the great bureaucrats of the country and high-ranking military and naval officers, relying on support from political coalitions in the Diet, became, seemingly, the new oligarchs (Reischauer 1953: 147). Influenced by their own interpretations of Western democratic thought, Japanese businessmen of the time disfavored the taxes required to sustain large naval and military capabilities. There was also an inclination among them to believe that the development of a large export trade and the acquisition of economic concessions through diplomatic means were 'less costly and more profitable than colonial expansion by war and conquest' (Reischauer 1953: 149). During much of the 1920s, which could be characterized as the 'heyday' of party politics, internationalism, disarmament, and pacifist views, the power and prestige of the military were seriously undermined (Yanaga 1949: 508–9). Cabinets were formed and dissolved, but until party government collapsed in 1932, the Japanese regime – relying upon party power and leverage potential – tended to represent the dominance of business and economic interests over the other groups that reflected ruling factions in Japan (Reischauer 1953: 148–9).

MILITARY COMPETITION AND THE WASHINGTON CONFERENCE

In spite of the postwar tendency toward more democracy, the intentions of the United States and other Western democracies were still suspect in Japan. The virtual arms competition between the USA and Japan during World War I was recognized by both states. By 1921 Japanese leaders faced the possibility of a genuine arms race with the United States. During World War I, Japan's continental policies had been perceived in the United States with a resentment and an apprehension that were not allayed by the Japanese government's postwar policy, which was designed to include an expansion of the country's industrial capacity combined with the 'fulfillment of national defense.' Although anxious for an accommodation with the United States, which was contemplating an impressive naval program including 10 battleships, 6 battle cruisers, and 100 submarines, the Japanese government announced its intention to maintain supremacy over the US fleet in the Western Pacific by constructing 16 capital warships (Crowley 1966: 26).

Proposed by the United States, the Washington Conference on Naval Disarmament and Far Eastern Affairs (12 November, 1921 to 6 February, 1922) included Great Britain, Belgium, the Netherlands, Italy, France, Portugal, China, Japan, and the United States. In view of their anomalous role in World War I, the Japanese in their bargaining at the Versailles Conference had employed the leverage they had with remarkable effectiveness, obtaining Allied recognition of their continental expansion program, which had been facilitated by the war and which had progressed to a point where the country was almost capable of extending hegemony over all of Asia. When an invitation to participate in the Washington Conference of 1921–2 was received in Tokyo, however, many Japanese viewed it with suspicion, believing it to be a way by which Britain and the United States would divest Japan of its influence over Manchuria and Mongolia, wreck the country's proposed naval expansion program, and thus deprive the country of all the gains won with great effort and sacrifices (Yanaga 1949: 416).

Soviet Russia, whose own activities, interests, and commercial holdings in the Far East tended to intersect with those of Japan, China, and several of the Western powers, was not invited to the conference (Eudin and North 1957: 135–7).

The concept of 'adversary' incorporated in the model presented in the previous chapter seeks to represent these real antagonisms. Historically Great Britain, as an insular power, had relied upon its navy not only for protection of the home islands but also to exert leverage on the European continent, support British expeditionary forces abroad, and further the expansion of an already extensive overseas empire (Choucri and North 1975). Similarly, as a rising insular power, Japan, prior to the Russo-Japanese War and thereafter, had been aggressive in developing its naval capabilities not only for defense of the Japanese home islands but also as an instrument for the expansion of Japanese activities and interests on the Asian mainland and, in due course, in the Pacific mandates. In effect, a US–Japan competitive arms buildup had taken place during World War I. By 1920 Japan was approaching a 60 percent ratio with the British fleet, thus threatening to equalize Anglo-Japanese naval capabilities in the South Pacific. If Japan were to obtain a 70 percent ratio with the US fleet under such circumstances, Britain might well commit itself to an arms race in order to safeguard the security of New Zealand and Australia.[1] The fear in Japan was that such an outcome might precipitate an Anglo-American alliance that could threaten the security of the Japanese home islands and of the empire itself (Crowley 1966: 27).

Even prior to the termination of World War I, a naval race began among the major powers. A major purpose of the Washington Conference of 1921–2 was to cool the great-power naval competition following World War I. On grounds of 'fairness' as well as national security, however, Japan demanded a 10:10:7 naval ratio for the three leading naval powers, whereas the United States and Great Britain insisted on a 5:5:3 distribution. According to existing data, however, Japan's per capita military expenditures at the time were $2.85, as compared with $25.00 for Britain and $28.00 for the United States (in 1906 dollars).

Most antagonistic to the Washington Conference and its outcomes were the Russians. In a series of protests the Soviet government, as well as the Communist International, denounced the conference for attempting to settle Far Eastern problems without Russian participation and took special umbrage at discussions of the Chinese Eastern Railway, in which the Soviets had commercial, financial, and managerial interests inherited from the tsarist regime. Pending a conclusion of discussions between China and the Soviet Union on this issue, the Soviet government claimed that its rights to the railway should remain in force and could not be set aside by a conference to which the Russians were not a party (Eudin and North 1957: 135–7). Negotiations proceeded in stages.

Ultimately, the Five Power Naval Treaty established a 5:3:3 ratio which reserved Japan's right to retain a newly built battleship. (Yanaga, 1949: 422–3). Later, in a Nine Power Treaty, Japan and the other signatories pledged to respect the sovereignty, independence, and administrative and territorial integrity of China; to provide China with the fullest opportunity to develop and maintain a stable and effective government; to facilitate the establishment and maintenance of the principle of equal opportunity among the nations for pursing commercial and industrial enterprises in China; and to refrain from seeking special rights and privileges within Chinese territories (Crowley 1966: 28–9). Japan agreed to restore Shantung Province to China, stipulating consistency with the 1915 and 1918 treaties. The Anglo-Japan Alliance was terminated.

In terms of its practical effects, the Washington Conference was 'quite a success for Japan' in that the first line of US defense was stopped at Hawaii and that of Britain at Singapore, 'leaving the vast expanse of the Pacific between the two points' – together with the fate of China – seemingly within Japanese control (Yanaga 1949: 417, 421–7). The Japanese recognized, however, that their country's economy had not yet achieved sufficient growth to allow successful competition on the European continent with the United States (Tiedemann 1984: 6). Japanese of a 'liberal' persuasion gained a special advantage from the conference in that a portion of the country's military expenditures were reallocated to other sectors.

This readjustment had the effect of temporarily lessening the necessity for developing supply capabilities and for the stockpiling of consumer goods. The country could concentrate on becoming a full-fledged industrialized nation (Patrick 1971: 252).

To whatever extent the Japanese appeared to have enhanced their country's status in the international system, these gains tended to be diminished in their own eyes by the US Exclusion Law, passed in 1924, which drastically restricted the immigration of Japanese and other Asians into the United States. Discrimination against Asians in the United States dated back into the nineteenth century, but the passage of this new legislation in the wake of their country's recent successes was viewed by many Japanese as bitter 'proof' of a US attitude of superiority and disdain toward Japan (Borton 1955: 304–5). From this time forward indignation over the refusal of the United States and other Western powers of external 'status equality' to Japan and its people remained a source of resentment among the Japanese populace and their leaders.

JAPANESE IN CHINA DURING THE 'LIBERAL INTERLUDE'

For decades, beginning with the Sino-Japanese War of 1894, Japanese activities and interests had collided with those of Russia in Korea and Manchuria – the fringes of the Chinese empire, so to speak. During World War I and following the issuance of the Twenty-One Demands, however, the Japanese had expanded their activities and interests into China proper, where they collided with the efforts of Chinese nationalists to establish an effective regime.

With an upsurge of nationalism in China after World War I, the Kuomintang, or Nationalist Party, under Sun Yat-sen and his successor, Chiang Kai-shek, had been trying to unify the country (initially with the support of Soviet Russia and a rapidly growing Chinese communist movement), which had disintegrated after the collapse of the Chinese empire (1911–12) into competing local regimes. Among Chinese warlords opposing the Chinese Nationalists was Chang Tso-lin, who, with Japanese encouragement, had declared Manchurian 'independence' while waiting for an opportunity to assert his authority in Peking. From the early 1920s until the end of World War II, expanding Japanese and Chinese activities and interests were continually colliding on the Asian mainland – with the Soviet Union adding to the confusion and seizing, often quite ineptly, whatever advantages seemed to present themselves.

Toward the end of 1926, Chiang Kai-shek undertook a military expedition in order to seize control of Shanghai and eventually Peking. A few months later, in the wake of a financial crisis in Japan (the harbinger of worse events to come), Baron Giichi Tanaka (president of the Seiyukai and an army general) emerged as prime minister. Precipitated by an attempt on the part of the Mitsui and Mitsubishi interests to force a competitor, the Suzuki Company, out of business, the crisis led to the closing of the Bank of Taiwan, a nationwide run on Japanese banks, and a financial panic of unprecedented proportions. As premier, Tanaka presided over a reversal of the relatively liberal domestic and foreign policies that had characterized the 'liberal interlude' in Japan (Reischauer 1964: 151).

As Shanghai fell to Nationalist troops early in 1927 (almost precisely at a time when Chiang Kai-shek was precipitating a break with the USSR and the Chinese communists), Tanaka's advisors – especially leaders of the Seiyukai and Kwantung army (the Japanese garrison in southern Manchuria) – urged an assertive posture to protect Japanese interests. Underscoring a widening deficit in Japan's food supply and raw materials relative to population, Tanaka addressed 'China Specialists' in the Ministry of Foreign Affairs, as well as the Army and Navy, urging positive steps to secure rights and privileges in Manchuria and Mongolia, and to protect Japanese interests in China proper by means of self-defense. Meanwhile, Tanaka dispatched an army brigade to Shantung, and Chiang's expedition was temporarily halted.

Favoring aggressive policies toward communism at home and the USSR and the Chinese Nationalists abroad, Tanaka proceeded on the assumption that a unified China under Chiang Kai-shek and the Kuomintang and recent events in Manchuria (including Soviet activities there) were direct threats to Japan. With the support of his cabinet but without notifying the Diet of his plans, Tanaka dispatched Japanese troops to check the advance of Chinese forces in Shantung (Borton 1955: 312). After a clash in Tsinan, however, Chiang's army bypassed Japanese-occupied Shantung and proceeded toward Peking. Shortly after this confrontation, in June 1928 Chang Tso-lin was assassinated near Mukden, and there were accusations – 'loudly voiced in China and whispered in Japan' – that Japanese officers were behind it. No reliable evidence was available, however, and it was not until after World War II that the story became publicly known; officers of the Kwantung army had killed Chang Tso-lin as part of an abortive effort to seize the city of Mukden – an attempt to accomplish in 1928 what actually occurred three years later (Storry 1960: 175–6).

Japanese interventions not only failed to protect Japan's interests in China but also intensified Chinese nationalism. By the end of 1928, Chiang's forces succeeded in controlling north China, and Chang Hsueh-liang, a warlord in Manchuria succeeding his father (Chang Tso-lin) and armed with strong resentments toward Japan, declared Chinese sovereignty over his territory. The Kuomintang's northern expedition was completed with success. Mean while, Britain, France, and the United States recognized the Kuomintang government in Nanking and agreed on China's tariff autonomy. In Japan, the Tanaka cabinet was forced to recognize the Nanking government.

The assasination of Chang Tso-ling became a political scandal among the leadership in Tokyo. Contrary to the Kwantung army leaders' hope, the government did not authorize them to seize control of Manchuria, and with pressures from opposition parties and the inner court, Tanaka promised to have the incident investigated. The army establishment resisted such an attempt, and even the cabinet was split on the issue. The emperor reproached Tanaka, and his cabinet resigned in July 1929. The president of the Minseito, Osachi Hamaguchi, was then asked to form a cabinet.

INCREASING POLITICAL INSTABILITY

The policies of Premier Hamaguchi were diametrically opposed to those of his predecessor, advocating broader powers for the legislative branch of government, a retrenchment in national expenditures, and a more conciliatory policy toward China (Borton 1955: 313–314). Unfortunately, from a liberal perspective Hamaguchi's appointment coincided with early phases of the Great Depression, and the government's failure to ameliorate conditions – despite, or precisely due to, Minseito promises of retrenchment, deflation, and a return to the gold standard – contributed to the erosion of its political base (Storry 1960: 177).

Although multiplying contacts with the West had brought liberal ideas to Japan, they also made possible the development of a new, modern nationalism that became increasingly militant and ideologically expansionist. By the late 1920s deep divisions had begun to appear in Japan between life and thought in the cities and in the countryside, between the more traditional and more modernized members of the society, between those who had been subject to mass education and indoctrination and the better educated, and between the more conservative and the more liberal sectors of the society (Reischauer 1970: 180).

During the latter half of the 1920s Japan achieved a nearly 100 percent increase in production (and considerable diversity), as well as self-sufficiency in foodstuffs – the latter resulting in large part from extensions in trade, protectionism at home, and the opening of colonial markets. This favorable trend was soon checked, however, by a combination of factors: increased protectionism among Japan's trading partners; the 1929 stock market crash in the United States that triggered a world depression; and, with the introduction of rayon, a general collapse in the silk market. By the end of the decade, as unemployment became a source of discontent, numbers of workers and students moved to the left under Marxist influence, but the predominant trend was rightward.

Although they themselves had become increasingly protectionist since 1922, the Japanese – depending heavily as they did on imports and exports – 'complained bitterly, and with reason,' about the high tariff walls that were being erected against their manufactures in the West. Whenever cheap manufactured goods from Japan appeared to threaten 'even a small segment' of a US industry, for example, 'they were apt to be shut off promptly' (Lockwood 1954: 542–3).

With the onset of the Great Depression, protectionist reciprocations tended to increase in what proved to be a new era in governmental economic policies throughout the world – a widespread shift from the relatively free capitalist enterprise that had characterized the nineteenth century toward government regulation of output, prices, and distribution. The new global trend was away from post-World War I internationalism and in the direction of regionalism and the division of the world into autarkic units.

At about the same time, the raw silk market in the United States and elsewhere – a mainstay of Japanese exports – was increasingly undermined by the competition of rayon, which substituted for natural silk, as well as other textiles. Japan's balance of payments suffered accordingly. During this period the country lost 58.8 percent of its foreign reserves (Patrick 1971: 256), and the Minseito government, for reasons of exchange stability (as well as prestige), decided in 1929 to return to the gold standard – as Western powers had done the year before.

In many respects the effects of the depression on Japan were minor compared to those on other countries, and depressed conditions in the United States, Europe, and elsewhere provided the country with possibilities for renewing some of its gains from international trade. Committed to a belief that Japan's future lay in measures of peaceful economic development based on a multidirectional expansion of foreign trade, the Hamaguchi cabinet had seen economic cooperation and material support from Western political and economic leaders as indispensable for a successful reorganization of the Japanese economy and a reduction of naval expenditures as a means for furthering goodwill and relieving financial pressures.

The success in a reduction of naval expenditure was dependent on the London Naval Conference. Since the Washington Treaty controlled only the battleship, the powers (including Japan) emphasized the buildup of fleets with auxiliary craft. The Geneva Naval Conference was aborted because of the confrontation between the United States and Britain. The Washington Treaty was to terminate in 1931, and the powers were forced to reach a mutually acceptable compromise in order to avoid an arms race.

Japan had built enough new cruisers, destroyers, and submarines to achieve a substantial naval superiority over the United States in the Western Pacific. At the table of the conference, though the Japanese delegation proposed a 10:7 ratio with the United States in cruisers initially, it finally agreed to the same ratio as the Washington Treaty in the larger cruisers to gain a 10:7 ratio in the smaller cruisers and destroyers, and a parity in submarines. This agreement was to be effective for six years, besides which no battleships would be built until 1936. In substantive terms, Japan had only to demolish one battleship, compared with Britain's five and the USA's three, and because the United States agreed not to build any larger cruisers, Japan was to enjoy a 10:7 ratio.

Despite the navy general staff's attack on the compromise and insistence on the original position at the risk of the failure of the conference, the Hamaguchi cabinet had the delegation sign the treaty in April. The premier's troubles over the London Naval Treaty had only begun, however. Sympathizing with expansionists, the Seiyukai, the opposition party, tried not to ratify the treaty, criticizing Hamaguchi for bending under US pressure and for infringing the independence of the high command. The Privy Council was dominated by expansionists, too. A central issue was whether or not an elected prime minister and his cabinet could successfully challenge the militarists, expansionists, ultranationalists, and oligarchs, who in hard times were gaining political influence (Borton 1955: 315). The government was able to overcome military pressures and criticisms from the antagonists in the Diet as well as in the Privy Council; the treaty was ratified.

Map 3   Japan's industrialization between 1868 and 1929

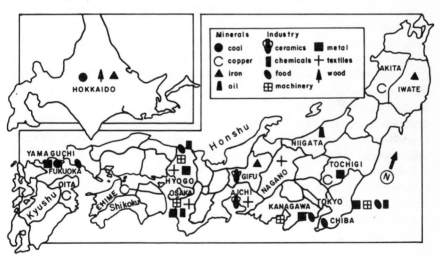

Source: adapted from Barraclough 1978: 218

JAPAN'S 'LIBERAL INTERLUDE' ENDS

Hamaguchi's victory over the oligarchs and the military was short-lived, at best. The Seiyukai did what it could to 'embarrass the Cabinet for having neglected to follow the advice of the military experts' at a time when the world depression and a retrenchment in government expenditures were contributing to economic stagnation and widespread unemployment. Ultranationalists and expansionists in the imperial army and the innumerable secret societies believed that Hamaguchi's conciliation policy toward China and disrespect for the views of the chiefs of staff threatened the base of their political power. In November 1930 the premier was shot by a fanatical patriot belonging to a nationalist party, and he died some months later (Borton 1955: 315–16). The groundwork was now laid for public acceptance of the move into Manchuria by Japan's Kwantung army a year later (Tiedemann 1984: 10).

Rightist groups held Hamaguchi's economic retrenchment policies responsible for the social unrest that seemed to prevail (Yanaga 1949: 497). The impelling disposition of these groups was toward economic and political centralization, government control, accelerated industrialization, and a determined drive for expansion on the Asian mainland (Yanaga 1949: 497, 501, 551). During the spring of 1931, radical elements of the army plotted a coup d'état which was to have been initiated with a mass demonstration planned by Dr Shumei Okawa, a rightist leader of many years' standing. Mobilized troops were to surround the Diet building, cutting off communications with the outside, under the pretext of defending it against a mob of 10,000 rightists and leftists recruited for the purpose. The plot failed to materialize, but toward the end of the following August, Okawa divulged that 'his group of rightists had plans to create an incident in Manchuria sometime around October that would aggravate Sino-Japanese relations and economic conditions' as a first step toward a coup in Tokyo. This plot was preempted, however, through independent actions undertaken by the Kwantung army (Yanaga 1949: 498–9).

Wakatsuki succeeded the fatally wounded Hamaguchi in April 1931. As if economic conditions had not raised problems enough, the Minseito government experienced diplomatic and military problems at home, as mentioned above. Problems abroad were abundant, too. Kuomintang China declared 'a revolutionary diplomacy' to restore its sovereign rights; the management of Manchuria was badly hampered mainly due to the worldwide depression; and the Kwantung army was increasingly out of Tokyo's control. In Japan the rapprochement between the party political system and the self-controlled military, on which the liberal interlude in the 1920s was based, was now severely eroded.

Although Japan had emerged from World War I with a profile that was essentially of the *beta* form (relatively dense population, rapidly advancing technology, and limited access to resources), the silk and other textile industries, in particular, yielded sufficient foreign exchange to pay for imports and provide a context for the country's 'liberal' interlude. By the beginning of the 1930s, however, the collapse of the silk market and the global depression rapidly altered these favorable conditions and prepared the way for almost classical *beta* inclinations and responses.

Chapter 8

Japanese expansion, conflict and escalation

INDUSTRIAL GROWTH AND EXPANDING TRADE

If World War I had provided Japan with its first great opportunity for industrial growth, the abolition of the gold standard system in December 1931 – following the British abandonment of the gold standard in September – provided the country with a second major push. Having reorganized their industries to reduce production costs, the Japanese were positioned to take advantage of cuts in export prices due to depreciation of the yen. The result was the stimulation of export enterprises through increased orders from abroad.

In the meantime, the government had been making large allocations for unemployment relief projects and, following the Manchurian Incident of September 1931, for the manufacture of munitions, weapons, and other military supplies, thus establishing heavy industries operating with little idle capacity. Over succeeding years, Japan's foreign trade climbed steadily, reaching a favorable balance for Japan proper in 1935.

Prior to 1931 the Western industrialized nations had not been seriously concerned with the rise of Japan. Through the years since the end of World War I, however, Japanese industry had been undergoing a marked expansion. During the late 1920s and early 1930s the country achieved considerable diversity and a nearly 100 percent increase in production – as well as self-sufficiency in foodstuffs – which stemmed in large part from extensions in trade, protectionism at home, and the opening of colonial markets. Meanwhile, the Japanese expressed bitterness at the high tariffs against Japan. In the United States, for example, as quickly as cheap manufactures from Japan offered any competitive threat to even a small segment of an American industry, they were blocked. The fact of the matter was, however, that Japan itself had become increasingly protectionist after 1922, and by the 1930s its own industrial tariffs 'invited comparison' with other nations regarded as highly protectionist (Lockwood 1954: 542–3). A steep rise in Japanese duties began in 1932, and in 1934 a Trade Protection Law empowered the government to impose additional duties on imports from countries discriminating against Japanese imports (Schumpeter 1940:

738). The dilemma was that tariff escalations were essentially interactive; an extension or increase of duties in Japan tended to be followed by extensions or increases in Western countries, and vice versa.

Whereas US, British, and other tariffs on Japanese manufactures constrained Western markets for Japanese goods, those duties imposed by the Japanese on consumer goods from the West probably facilitated capital formation in Japan. In 1913 China (including Manchuria, Kwantung, and Hong Kong) and the United States had accounted for 64 percent of Japan's total exports. By 1929 China's importance as a market had decreased, Southeast Asia had begun to figure as a market, British India had become receptive to Japanese goods, and the United States was accounting for approximately 43 percent of Japan's exports. Yet trade, and especially the maintenance of a sufficiently high level of exports in order to pay for imports, was a continuing problem for Japan. As many Japanese saw it, the danger emerging from the depression lay in the flooding of foreign markets with Japanese goods and the growing antagonism in Western countries that this competition tended to generate.

RESISTANCE TO JAPANESE EXPORTS

The constraints that operated on Japan's trade with the West can best be understood against the background of the country's foreign trade relations dating back to 1920. At the beginning of the 1920s Japan's imports and exports per capita were $7.08 and $5.90 as compared with $84.82 and $68.35 for Britain and $70.30 and $105.31 for the United States. By 1930 the numbers were $7.83 and $7.44 for Japan, $80.63 and $50.79 for Britain, and $48.60 and $55.71 for the United States (all in 1906 dollars). Meanwhile, Japan had become increasingly reliant on trade with its colonies. At the close of World War I, Japan's colonial trade amounted to about 12 percent of the country's total, whereas by 1929 the colonies were accounting for nearly a fifth of the total (Allen 1981: 114). See the discussion in Chapters 2 and 5.

The extent to which the increased sales of Japanese goods abroad amounted to a genuine displacement of US and European goods, and the extent to which it was a real expansion of trade, remains open to assessment. In spite of accusations at the time that Japan was a menace to Western economies, Japanese trade by 1934 amounted to only 3.32 percent of the world's total. The depression was changing economic relations both within and between countries, however, and Japan could not escape some of the effects, however indirectly they might come to bear. The era of free trade had ended, and economic nationalism, including protectionism, was spreading almost everywhere. To a large extent, rising Japanese anxieties could be attributed to the interplay between domestic trends in Japan and the effects of the depression in the United States, Britain, and elsewhere.

The collapse of the silk market was a major source of apprehension – especially in the rural areas of Japan. Soon it became evident throughout the country that raw silk could no longer be relied upon to pay for a substantial part of Japanese imports.

In their efforts toward gradual replacement of silk exports with a more diversified export business in cotton, rayon goods, and other manufactures, Japanese merchants looked to markets in less developed areas and particularly in Asia. This shift in market concentration had important political and economic consequences, however – especially with respect to the country's relations with the United States and with China. In the midst of a worldwide depression, with purchasing power universally low, Japan's inexpensive products were well received in many countries. By 1934 several countries of Latin America, where Japanese products had been scarcely heard of a few years before, 'recorded increases in purchases of Japanese goods up to 1200 percent over the previous years,' whereas the United States (and some European countries, including Germany, and South Africa even more) felt the 'surge of incoming Japanese goods on their markets.' Soon the older industrial nations were expressing alarm at the 'seeming flood of Japanese products pouring into many lands' in different parts of the world (*Chugai Shogyo Shimpo* 1936: 4–5). Concurrently, however, higher tariffs in China, boycotts of Japanese goods, and tariff walls erected by British India all contributed to reduce Japan's markets in Asia (*Chugai Shogyo Shimpo* 1936: 3–4).

The balance of Japan's trade and service items combined became so adverse that the country's gold holdings abroad and its favorable balances acquired during World War I were steadily depleted. During the three years following 1930 there were heavy gold shipments from Japan. Toward the end of 1931 the gold embargo was reimposed, but it did not become effective until 1933, when the export of capital and speculation in the yen were prevented by an exchange control law. Thereafter, until 1936, Japanese imports continued to exceed exports, but the export deficit was much reduced, and the credit balance from services was greater than the debit balance.

TRADE WITH THE UNITED STATES: LEVERAGES AND COUNTERLEVERAGES

During the late 1920s and early 1930s the United States became the dominant source of Japan's imports as well as Japan's largest export market. Resulting from increased purchases by Japan of raw cotton, petroleum, iron, and a variety of manufactured goods, the proportion of Japan's total imports accounted for by US goods increased from nearly 30 percent in 1920 to 33.7 percent by 1934. The percentage of exports from Japan to the United States, on the other hand, had declined sharply from over 40 in the pre-depression period to 26 percent by 1933 and down further to 18 in 1934. From a US perspective, the major, but not sole, cause of this decline had been the fall in the price of raw silk (US Tariff Commission 1936: 30). Another important factor, as perceived in the United States, was that during the depression years Japanese imports 'may have caused somewhat more disturbance of the markets' there than might have been expected from the quantities imported. With the collapse of the silk market, Japan had begun exporting to the United States low-priced grades of goods. These were priced lower than any goods of the same type produced in the United States, at a time when demand shifted from higher- to lower-priced goods.

Expanding Japanese inroads into the US market were met by tariff increases on some products, and voluntary quota agreements were reached between certain private manufacturing interests in the two countries such as in cotton goods (including hosiery), velveteens, corduroys, and several other products. Under the Roosevelt administration, the United States, although traditionally a highly protectionist country, was making 'a heroic and not entirely unsuccessful effort to take the lead in freeing the international market from the network of ultra-nationalist trade restrictions' in which it had become entangled during previous years. Yet, partly because of the reaction to Japanese competition and partly as a result of political tensions between the two countries, no reciprocal trade agreement was concluded (Farley 1940: 58–9).

Growing US resistance to imports from Japan may have been attributable less to the low quality of Japanese materials and more to the fact that the cotton textile industry in the United States had 'felt the pinch of Japanese competition,' although many Japanese products that crowded bargain basements and ten-cent stores were indeed inferior (Lockwood 1936: 32). Increasingly, the magnitude and composition of US imports from Japan were determined by the tariff structure including higher levels of duties.[1] It is true that tariff reductions negotiated with other countries in the mid-1930s were extended to Japan on the principle of reciprocal most-favored-nation treatment, but in cases where Japan might benefit substantially from such reductions, the concessions were often 'narrowly limited by precise descriptions' excluding the types imported from that particular country (Lockwood 1936: 34–5).

In spite of these developments, Japan continued to occupy a preponderant place in US trade with the Orient. Of total US imports from East and South Asia (India included) in 1935, Japan supplied 26 percent, and from the total of US exports to that area Japan took as much as 57 percent. With the price of silk remaining low, Japan's share of US imports from Asia had declined since the 1920s, but as a market for US goods – as measured by export values – it had increased until by 1935 it was about four times the size of the Philippines or China, which were the countries of next importance in the area. US export interests were thus bound more closely into the economy of Japan than into any other Asian country, while the dependence of Japan on US markets was even greater (Lockwood 1936: 7).

INTENSIFIED TRADE FRICTIONS

In the course of the Great Depression, more than 40 countries raised tariffs or imposed other restrictions on goods from Japan, which increasingly worsened terms of trade for the Japanese. Coming at a time of industrial expansion and intense feelings of nationalism, such barriers further strengthened the position of military cliques and contributed to a certain paranoia among the populace as a whole. Under these circumstances the country's profile dictated new strategic concerns. With the country's rapidly growing population and dependence on foreign trade for maintaining and improving its standard of living, many Japanese saw their country in a position similar to that of Great Britain in the middle and later decades of the nineteenth century (Allen 1981: 164–5; cf. Choucri and North 1975: 65–85). As a result, the underlying economic problems continued even worsened, but support received by the government from those sectors of the populace who seemed to benefit tended to damp out the warnings of those few who were more prudent.

Japan's cotton exports exceeded those of Britain in 1932, resulting in increased economic tension between Japan and the Commonwealth countries. Commercial relations between Japan and India, Burma, Australia, and Canada were regulated by a series of Anglo-Japanese treaties and conventions concluded during the 1930s (British State Papers, Vol. XXVII, Treaty Series No. 2, 1934, and Vol. XXXI, Treaty Series Nos 50, 1937, 1, 1938, 66, 1938, and 41, 1937). A 1934 convention between Japan and India gave each party the right of 'imposing or modifying from time to time special custom duties on the importation of articles produced and manufactured' in the other 'or higher than those imposed on like articles produced or manufactured in any other foreign country' at such rates as the government might consider necessary to correct the effects of any variation in the exchange value of its own currency with respect to the currency of the other. Subsequent articles of the convention specified the allotments of cotton goods allowed to be exported from Japan to India. A 1937 protocol between India and Japan further tightened these allotments. Similar regulations were agreed upon between Japan and Burma, Australia, and Canada.

Japan in the mid-1930s had 'essentially a single-column tariff' and, with a few exceptions, accorded equal treatment to 'almost 100 percent of its imports.' Penalty rates of up to 100 percent were authorized against countries that discriminated against Japanese shipping or trade. Japan made use of this authority against Canada and Australia in the mid-1930s, with licenses required for the import of wheat, wheat flour, and wool. Except for arrangements with France and Italy, Japan did not pursue an active policy of tariff bargaining. Imports from Japanese colonies were 'for the most part admitted free of duty and other restrictions,' although imports from the Japanese leased territories in Manchuria (Kwantung and the South Manchurian Railway Zone) were 'subject to full Japanese duties.' Formosan camphor was a government monopoly (US Tariff Commission 1937: 6–7).

Overall, by the mid-1930s Japan appeared to be achieving an improved strategic position with respect to basic manufacturers, self-sufficiency in foodstuffs, and access to critical raw materials – all derived in considerable part from its colonial acquisitions and the expansion of its economic interests on the Asia mainland. During the first half of the decade, these trends were strengthened and (apart from exports to Manchuria) achieved a favorable balance of payments. By 1936 Japan, while still importing special steels and steel products, had become a net exporter of steel. Associated with this expansion in production and trade was full employment for industrial workers without reliance on foreign borrowing (Schumpeter 1940: 271–2).

EXPANSIONISM AND COLLIDING INTERESTS ON THE MAINLAND

While Japan's expanding trade activities and interests were generating mixed responses in the West, the country's diplomatic and security undertakings on the Asian mainland were engaging those of China and the USSR – often with much wider repercussions. In fact, not long after the belated withdrawal of Japanese troops from Siberia in the early 1920s, Japanese leaders began to view the rise of Chiang Kai-shek and the Kuomintang – backed at that time by the Soviet Union – as a threat to their own country's expanding economic and strategic interests in Manchuria and elsewhere, including China proper. In this regard, Soviet Russian activities and expanding interests in Manchuria were also perceived as a mounting threat.[2] Throughout the 1920s, moreover, the Chinese Eastern Railway line in Northern Manchuria – with an extensive right of way and resource access on either side of the tracks – had remained under the supervision of a Russian general manager and the protection of Soviet railway guards (Royal Institute of International Affairs 1929: 345).

Japan could exert counterleverages of its own, however. First established as Japanese expeditionary forces facing Russian armies in Manchuria, the Kwantung army, having retained its autonomy despite pressures by the Foreign Ministry seeking to regularize its status and place it under normal channels of control, remained an effective instrument of Japanese penetration. With a total strength of some 10,000 men in the early 1930s, the army was charged with maintaining security in the Liaotung leasehold, to which a division was allocated, and over the South Manchurian Railway system from Port Arthur to Changchun, a sector within which it was allowed to station 15 men per kilometer. 'Manchuria itself, the arena in which the Kwantung army played its role, was . . . Japan's true frontier' – a source of minerals and other raw materials recognized by key groups in Japan as critical to the country's national defense and the front along which the Japanese empire converged on the Soviet Union (Jansen 1984a: 132–3).

Among Japanese officers in Manchuria at this time the government of Chiang Kai-shek was observed with increasing apprehension. Compared with the now-defunct Chinese empire and the succession of feuding warlord regimes, a united Nationalist China could become a serious roadblock to Japanese expansion southward on the continent. Among many Japanese there was a growing disposition to believe that the future welfare of their country depended upon the ability and determination of the regime to strengthen further its military capabilities and to expand national activities and interests on the Asian mainland with greater effectiveness than before and in so doing to reinforce the relatively accommodative leverages of diplomacy with armed force.

Some of these dispositions came to a head on the night of 18 September 1931, when middle-grade officers of the Kwantung army blew up a small section of track, attributed the act to the Chinese, and used the event as a pretext for overrunning the whole province in a series of military actions.

Postwar studies suggest that 'there did not exist what may be termed an "army policy" toward Manchuria and more basically toward China,' but officers of the Kwantung general staff and others in Tokyo, as well as many of their superiors, 'were basically agreed that Manchuria should somehow be placed under Japanese control and treated distinctly from China proper' and that, with increased Japanese military strength vis-à-vis the Soviet Union, Japanese designs on Manchuria 'could be promoted with impunity' without incurring retaliation by the USSR (Iriye 1984: 236–7).

The small explosion on the tracks on the night of 18 September 1931 was a pretext for the Kwantung army to deploy along railways up to Changchun. A few days later Japanese troops in Korea crossed the border. In Tokyo, having been informed of the rumor of the Kwantung army's conspiracy, the Wakatsuki cabinet decided to settle the incident by directing the general staff to order the Kwantung army staffs to create a puppet state rather than to occupy Manchuria directly (Itoh 1976: 36). On 1 March, 1932, in Mukden, the independence of 'Manchukuo' was proclaimed, with Changchun as the capital and Pu-Yi as head of state, the last emperor of the Manchuria-originated Xing (Ch'ing) dynasty of China.

During the five months between the Mukden Incident and the independence of Manchukuo, US attitudes toward Japan worsened. The issue was less Japan's increased influence in Manchuria than its advancement toward China proper. An airborne attack on Chinchou in October and occupation of it in January irritated the US State Department. The Shanghai Incident (directed against a local anti-Japanese movement) in January 1932 angered Secretary of State Stimson. Washington's response to these events – adherence to the Washington Treaty system *vis-à-vis* the integrity of China – became a guideline for US policies toward Sino-Japanese relations (Itoh 1976: 54; Fujimura 1981: 146).

In the meantime the League of Nations, involved in the Manchurian Incident in response to China's appeal, decided to send a mission for an investigation in which the United States, a new member, was asked to participate in the discussion. Japan responded as if to challenge – even irritate – the League. While the mission was in Tokyo, Manchukuo announced its independence, and in September, just before the mission submitted the report to the League, Japan formally recognized its puppet regime as a 'sovereign' State. During the time when the resolution was being drafted, the Kwantung army began to invade in Jehol, the area bordering China proper, which Manchukuo subsequently annexed.

On 24 February the League of Nations adopted the resolution disfavorable to Japan. On 17 March 1933 Japan withdrew from the League (effective in two years); in 1934 it abrogated the Washington Disarmament Treaty; and in 1936 it withdrew from the London Disarmament Conference.

The occupation of Manchuria and the establishment of Manchukuo provided new opportunities for industrial expansion and led also to increases in Japanese military expenditures. As with the United States and the countries of Europe, Japanese military expenditures per capita during this time reflected international trends during the later 1930s. If 1913 is used as a starting point, the general trend (omitting World War I and the immediate postwar years) helps tell the story – see Table 8.1.

Table 8.1 Per capita military expenditures, *1913–37* (1906 US $)

	1913	1921	1924	1930	1936	1937
Japan	1.66	3.24	1.81	2.25	4.33	16.10
Germany	11.30	0.37	1.34[a]	2.17	5.20[b]	n.a.
Britain	9.10	14.31	6.43	7.49	9.67	11.38
USA	9.63	25.12	9.91	11.65	17.62	17.35

[a] 1925 estimate.
[b] This may be a low estimate; all figures should be viewed with caution.

From these figures it becomes clear that the Japanese, while ranking comparatively low in terms of national product per capita, were increasingly willing to invest heavily per capita in order to build their military capabilities.

DISSIDENT COALITIONS AND 'GOVERNMENT BY ASSASSINATION'

The collapse of the silk market had adversely affected both small and large producers, processors, and laborers; and the Great Depression hurt people in many walks of life. In response to these events – along with Western protectionism, US exclusion policies, and Soviet expansionism – increasing numbers of Japanese held the United States, Britain, and/or the Soviet Union responsible for their discontents.

Many Japanese had become disillusioned, restless, apprehensive, and frustrated by the 'liberalism' of the 1920s. Emerging in the country at the same time was a new officer class composed of the sons of rural landowners (and even peasants) as well as army and navy officers – recruited around the age of 16. For its enlisted personnel the army drew heavily from the peasantry also, thus maintaining strong bonds with the peasantry at large. During the 1930s these and associated elements in Japanese society contributed to remarkable coalitions, and coalitions of coalitions, from among the disaffected.

As noted earlier, the active military services – with their unique prerogative of maintaining the war and navy ministries – gave officers and whatever coalitions they might be involved with extraordinary leverage in contests of bureaucratic factions within the regime. In practice, the ranking military could remove a cabinet, commit the regime, through local action, to intervention (as in the Manchurian Incident), prejudice diplomatic negotiations by staging crises (as in China after Japan's invasion of that country), direct propaganda through controlled newspapers, and, if necessary, protect and even covertly sponsor fanatical junior officers in assassinations and other terrorist activities against whoever opposed the government's extreme policies.

Focusing on national economic self-sufficiency, rightist, militarist, and other dissident activities in Japan proper took notable forms after the Manchurian Incident. One cluster of activities gave rise to the National Council of Patriotic Movements, which advocated a merger of proletarian and nationalistic groups and the establishment of close relationships with military activists in a leveraging program to utilize war to bring about the reconstruction of the internal political structure. The establishment of the council was followed during the summer of 1931 by the appearance of the Japan Production Party, which openly identified itself as a fascist organization (Yanaga 1949: 500–1).[3]

The rightward, intensely nationalistic trend contributed to a period of 'terrorism' – violent leverage applied by dissident individuals, groups, or organizations – or what came to be known popularly as 'government by assassination' (Byas 1942: 17–31). A series of such acts occured during 1932, a number of them traceable to the Blood Brotherhood League, organized by an ultranationalist and composed of students and 'the sons of farmers and fishermen' disposed toward direct action (Butow 1961: 54). The group developed a 'hit list' of prominent politicians, financiers, and other influential persons believed to be responsible for domestic corruption, weak diplomacy, and the generally 'deplorable' state of national affairs (Yanaga 1949: 502). The list was kept open for substitutions at the last minute, but those selected for assassination included

> the managing director and the director of the Mitsui Bank, Ltd; the last of the elder statesmen of the Meiji period; the premier, foreign minister and finance minister of the preceding cabinet, as well as the premier of the current cabinet; the speaker of the House of Peers; the Lord Keeper of the Privy Seal; and a privy councillor with a record of long service to the state. (Butow 1961: 54)

In early February, 1932 the former Finance Minister, Junnosuke Inouye, was assassinated, followed a month later by the murder of Baron Takuma Dan of the Mitsui enterprises. On 15 May Tsuyoshi Inukai, the president of the Seiyukai and the premier since December, was killed. His efforts to negotiate with Chiang Kai-shek for a peaceful solution of the Manchurian Incident had angered high-ranking Japanese military officers. Directly or indirectly involved in the Inukai assassination, which was part of an abortive coup d'état, were groups of naval officers, army cadets, and civilian ultranationalists, numbers of whom were subsequently brought to trial. Officials connected with the courts 'received thousands upon thousands of petitions for clemency,' and 'the basic "sincerity" behind the deeds' was 'dinned into the public mind.' Some 40 defendants received sentences, the most severe being hard labor for life, but many were later reduced 'by appeal or amnesty' (Butow 1961: 55–7).

Among the outcomes of the Inukai assassination were an end to party cabinets and the predominance of the army in the Japanese government (Borton 1955: 333). Numerous other assassinations and coup attempts took place over the next few years – including the murder of Finance Minister Korekiyo Takahashi and other cabinet members during the 26 February incident of 1936 by a group of 'misguided young extremist officers' in the 'erroneous belief that they could spare the nation from impending ruin' (Yanaga 1949: 516–17).

Table 8.2 lists 19 incidents between 1930 and 1936 that reflect the mode of 'government by assassination.'

Table 8.2 Major ultranationalist terrorism and coups executed or seized, 1930–6

Month	Year	Incident executed, or plot prevented due to seizure
November	1930	Shot at Premier Hamaguchi
March	1931	Coup plot
October	1931	Coup plot
February	1932	Murder of former Finance Minister Inouye
March	1932	Murder of Baron Dan
May	1932	Coup with murder of Premier Inukai
August	1932	Murder plot against Premier Saito
August	1932	Murder plot against Baron Wakatsuki
November	1932	Murder plot against political leaders
July	1933	Murder plot against the Saito cabinet members and ex-premiers
November	1933	Murder plot against a business leader
November	1933	Murder plot against Baron Wakatsuki and the Justice Minister
June	1934	Bank robbery attempt to fund murder of Premier Saito
June	1934	Murder plot against political and zaibatsu leaders
December	1934	Murder plot against political and zaibatsu leaders
May	1935	Murder plot against General Ugaki
May	1935	Murder plot against Premier Okada
August	1935	Murder of Liet. Gen. Nagata
February	1936	Coup with murder of political leaders

Source: adapted from Itoh 1976:22

EXPANDING ROLE OF GOVERNMENT

With the fall of the Minseito government under Premier Wakatsuki in December 1931, the position of Finance Minister had been taken over by a veteran in the finance field, Korekiyo Takahashi, who had demonstrated his competence in the course of the Russo-Japanese War and again during the financial crisis of 1927. Immediately abandoning the gold standard, Takahashi undertook forthwith a policy of reflation that was calculated to reduce unemployment and stimulate economic recovery without serious risk of cumulative inflation. He also expanded government expenditures, especially for the military buildup, to help the unemployed, and for rural development. In this way, Japan was brought out of the depression 'by methods remarkably close to those espoused by the great British economist, John Maynard Keynes, but not fully expounded until the publication of his *General Theory of Employment, Interest and Money* in 1936, after Takahashi had disappeared from the scene' (Hunsberger, 1964: 18).

The Japanese purpose was not merely to exploit Manchuria – Manchukuo – as it stood, but to 'modernize' the colony, to industrialize it in order to maximize its economic contributions to the empire as a whole. After 1931 government expenditures enabled the home industries to expand their plants so that they were capable of producing a sufficient quantity of durable goods to supply practically the entire domestic market as well as to furnish a sizable surplus for the new Manchurian market. If an investment of some 1.5 billion yen prior to 1931 is taken into account, the Japanese by the end of 1936 had spent in Manchuria 'a total of more than 3.7 billion yen, a sum considerably in excess of the entire budget of the Japanese Empire in any one year' (*Chugai Shogyo Shimpo* 1936: 7).

In budgetary terms, this intent tended to create a certain competition between investments in Manchukuo and the requirements of the imperial military establishment, which in effect had 'spawned' Manchukuo in the first place. It was a tight squeeze. Shaped in large part by demands of the new commitments in Manchuria and demands of the military, but resented by orthodox economists and financiers, the new policy promoted an increase in governmental expenditure, which was financed almost entirely by easy credit terms and borrowing. The outcome was that the proportion of total expenditure on general account attributable to the army and navy increased from 31 percent in 1931–2 to 47 percent in 1936–7. Leaders in Tokyo and Mukden proceeded in both directions – economic promoters developing an ambitious five-year plan for Manchukuo and military officers preparing for an invasion of China proper.

COLONIAL DEVELOPMENT AND ITS LIMITATIONS

During early phases of the twentieth century, Taiwan and Korea – newly acquired – had been valued for their contribution to Japan's agricultural output. For years Taiwan provided sugar and Korea rice, but it was not until the 1930s that any attempt was made to develop industrial resources in either place. But with the Manchurian Incident and the proclamation of Manchukuo as an 'independent' state new horizons opened. As numbers of Japanese industrialists – the 'new zaibatsu' – became interested in possibilities for development in Manchukuo, they began promoting the idea that industrialization could go hand in hand with agricultural advancement there. The expectation was that such a program would help provide *Lebensraum* for Japan's 'surplus' population and at the same time produce sufficient food, raw materials, and manufactured goods to make the home country more self-sufficient. Trade with Manchukuo and the colonies could then be substituted for reliance on foreign markets and imports.

Between 1932 and the invasion of China proper in 1937, the construction of railroads, highways, and hydroelectric projects was a high priority, harbors and navigable rivers were improved, and the country was explored for coal, iron, aluminum, and other minerals (Schumpeter 1940: 376). The Manchukuo government and the South Manchurian Railway Company played active roles in organizing firms for the production of chemical products, synthetic oil, steel products, automobiles, and aircraft. Bonds were floated in Japan and stock subscriptions invited in order to obtain capital for the launching of these and other enterprises. Between 1931 and 1937 the production of iron ore and pig iron more than doubled. Increasing efforts were made toward greater economic self-sufficiency in the Japanese empire as well as in Manchukuo, which were treated as an economic and strategic unit (Schumpeter 1940: 271–3).

Japanese planners tried to link economic development (at home and in the colonies) with measures to relieve the pressures of rapid population growth. A twenty-year plan called for 'pioneers' from the Japanese mainland – 'one million households totalling five million Japanese' – to settle in Manchuria and north China (thus relieving population pressures at home), to increase agricultural output there, industrialize less developed areas, and to 'produce enough raw materials, foodstuffs, and manufactured goods to enable Japan to be more self-sufficient.' In fact, between 1931 and 1945 about a half-million, including about 250,000 farmers, left their villages in Japan proper to develop agriculture and the dairy industry in Manchukuo. 'Even teenagers were recruited, 50,000 of them scattering in the frontier regions' (Iriye 1984: 3–4).

Early in 1937 a five-year plan for agricultural and industrial development was announced in Manchukuo, and it was revised upward the following year. Highest priority was assigned to the production of metals, minerals, electric power, industrial chemicals, dyestuffs, and explosives. With the incursion of Japanese forces into Chinese territory later that year, promotion of intraregional trade with Manchukuo and northern China – the 'yen bloc' – had become an increasingly important concern. Between 1936 and mid-1938 exports to Manchukuo and China 'increased from 25 percent of Japan's total exports to over 40 percent, and imports from these countries from 14 percent to over 22 percent of the total' (Iriye 1984:4).

Despite promotional efforts by the Japanese military, the Japanese government, the Manchukuo regime, and the zaibatsu, colonial successes fell far short of expectations. The limitations were evident not only in Manchukuo but also in the 'old' colonies – Taiwan and Korea. By 1939 Japan proper accounted for over 90 percent of the combined production total of Japan, Korea, and Formosa, with Korea contributing 5.7 percent and Formosa 3.1 percent. The food industry accounted for 67 percent and 22 percent of the Formosan and Korean totals respectively. But Japan was still forced to subsidize whatever industries it wanted to encourage. Benefits to the colonies themselves were even less impressive. The participation of Koreans in their own industrialization had been 'limited, for the most part, to day-labor in Japanese-financed and managed plants'; not a single Korean power plant was under Korean control (Cohen 1949a: 35–6).

In Manchuria the first two years of the Manchukuo five-year plan were completed with reasonably satisfactory results, but severe difficulties were encountered thereafter. Partly as a result of Japan's 1937 invasion of China, production schedules for iron and steel, petroleum, and nonferrous metals were raised substantially, and the period of the plan was extended. Necessary tools, machines, and other equipment which could not be supplied locally or in Japan were sometimes bought in Germany and paid for in soybeans and other Manchurian products – an arrangement that was later disrupted by the outbreak of war in Europe.

At a time when fuel consumption was increasing rapidly in Japan as well as in Manchukuo, advances in coal production were moderate at best. Since oil was in high demand and short supply in Japan, synthetic fuel industries were established in Manchukuo as well as in Korea and Japan, but gasoline obtained in this way had very low octane value and had to be cracked to produce motor fuel. Overall, the expanding Japanese empire relied heavily upon oil imported from the Netherlands, East Indies, Mexico, and primarily the United States, which was also a major source of scrap iron and other strategic materials.

Although there had been considerable change in the direction of Japanese trade during the 1930s, with larger proportions of exports going to Japan's colonies (especially Manchukuo, Kwantung, and regions of northern China as it fell under Japanese control), Japan was still trading with, and to a critical extent dependent on, the United States and other Western nations. In the meantime a perplexing paradox had developed. *Japan had undertaken a program of expansion and colonial development in order to acquire secure access to resources and markets. Since the colonies could not finance their own development and at the same time satisfy Japanese market and resources demands, however, the military required an increasing share of revenues in order to acquire more colonies and thus obtain access to more markets and resources.*

ACCESS TO RESOURCES THROUGH MILITARY INVESTMENT

By the mid-1930s the Manchurian Incident was recalled by many Japanese as an 'easy success' which had enhanced the prestige and influence of the Japanese military. After the apparent failure of free trade policies and the worldwide rise in economic nationalism, the alternative favored by the militarists of developing a self-sufficient empire was seen by more and more Japanese as a viable solution to their nation's problems. The conquest of Manchuria, which had been accomplished at low cost and with practically no expansion of the war industry, had not only served as a measure of new political power but also yielded considerable deposits of minerals as well as other badly needed raw materials. *This experience seemed to demonstrate that high returns could be achieved with a minimum of military investment.*

Although the country's imports continued to exceed exports, the import surplus was substantially reduced because of a boom in exports, and the service credit balance was larger than the debit balance from visible trade. For a five-year period the balance of goods and services combined was favorable by 1,100 million yen or more, an amount that approximately balanced what Japan had invested in Manchuria during the same period, with an excess of Japanese exports to Kwantung and Manchuria contributing to the favorable balance. By 1936, however, imports began to increase more rapidly as a result of a worldwide boom in raw materials, and also because of Japan's own industrial and territorial expansion programs.

The Manchurian takeover had increased the availability of resources and markets, but the costs of colonial administration and development tended to rise commensurately. For the Japanese leadership, further expansion seemed to offer the best solution to this dilemma. Western resistance to this disposition served only to convince many Japanese that wider territorial control was vital to the country's survival.

There were also domestic political consequences. When in June 1936 the newly constituted Hirota cabinet moved to reinvigorate parliamentary government and 'inject new life and spirit' into the regime, the army intervened through the Army Minister, and the premier capitulated with the announcement that ministerial appointments would not be influenced by status or background but awarded to those 'burning with the loyalty to serve the nation.' The swing to the right now became more pronounced, and the zaibatsu about this time 'began to soften its opposition to the army' (Yanaga 1949: 523–4).

The Hirota cabinet paved a way ultimately leading to conflict with the United States through three major policy initiatives. The first one was the revival of the rule to choose army and navy ministers from the active list. While this provision was intended to exclude retired generals who were involved in the rebellion the previous February from coming back and thus to terminate power struggles between army factions, in fact the army was able to thereby strengthen its capacity to take further leadership in national policy making (Itoh 1976: 161–2).

A second initiative, which was partly due to the first one, was the drawing of military and foreign policy plans under the direction of army and naval officers in the general staff. The Japanese government had already decided to withdraw from both Washington and London treaties, and from 1937 on Japan was free to pursue a naval buildup (Nomura 1983: 297–8). The navy prepared an 'outline of national policy,' which provided for a strategy of 'southward offense,' combined with 'northward defense,' in conjunction with a five-year plan of naval expansion. Concurrently the army prepared an 'outline of national defense and national policy' in which a 12-year plan was advanced in order to confront Soviet and other forces in Asia. Based on those documents, the military authorities adopted (a) the third amendment of the Imperial Defense Guideline in which the United States and the Soviet Union were identified as the empire's primary enemies, and China and the United Kingdom as secondary; (b) a National Policy Outline Draft; and (c) a Foreign Policy Guideline Draft in collaboration with the Foreign Ministry. The latter two documents were later combined and eventually approved by the government as the Basis of National Policy in August 1936.

On the Basis of National Policy a closer collaboration was established among the empire, Manchukuo, and the pro-Japanese regime in China, and between a stronger Japanese position in East Asia and Japanese development in the South Seas.

A third initiative expanded public spending to meet military demand. By the year's end (1936) the Finance Ministry, a traditional antagonist of military buildup (for financial reasons) and the last barrier against increasing pressure within the government, had launched an expanding military budget; and during the 1937 fiscal year government expenditures increased by more than 30 percent, with nearly 50 percent of the total being allocated to military spending. On the revenue side, tax increases and further bond-issuing were required. Moreover, the ministry was committed to approve the army's six-year and the navy's five-year buildup plans.

When the policy initiatives were informally reported to the throne, the emperor was informed that his government would work thereafter to acquire a secure position on the Asian mainland, to establish Japan as a 'stabilizing' power in East Asia, to undertake a gradual advance extending the country's influence in the South Seas, and to 'ensure an Asian peace and ultimately the peace and welfare of all mankind.' The government committed itself to the achievement of unity in East Asia by destroying the aggressive policies of other powers, strengthening its army units against Soviet forces in the Far East, and maintaining friendly relations with other nations (Butow 1961: 83).

One result of these pressures was that the political power and influence of military leaders tended more and more to dominate. As the interests of various groups and individuals in the country began to converge, domestic opposition to the military diminished. In pursuit of their own advancement, emerging cadres of bureaucrats in Japan proper, as well as in Manchukuo and other colonial areas, seized opportunities to ally themselves with army and navy officer cliques. Concurrently, the zaibatsu, who had led early opposition to the militarists, were tending to change their attitudes with the growth of governmental allocations for boosting the economy and as they themselves became 'recipients of fat contracts and huge profits, enabling them to carry out their long-awaited opportunity for industrial expansion' (Yanaga 1949: 511). Untangling political from economic motivations is a difficult task indeed.

LEVERAGES AND COUNTERLEVERAGES SURROUNDING JAPAN

Japan's activities on the Asian mainland did not go unnoticed, however. The new and more immediate Japanese threat altered the configuration of alignments throughout much of the Far East. Relations between the Nationalist government in Nanking and the Soviet Union were formalized in December 1932, although communist Russians and Nationalist Chinese continued to view each other with dark suspicion. Meanwhile, Japan's seizure of Manchuria placed the USSR in an awkward position with respect to its control of the Chinese Eastern Railway. In due course, the Soviet government offered to sell the line, and after months of haggling the railway was sold to Manchukuo. The resolution of this controversy did not improve other aspects of Japanese–Soviet relations, however.

In July 1935 the Communist International, now under tight Stalinist control, held its Seventh Congress, which called for a united front against fascism and Nazism in Italy and Germany and approved the initiative by the Chinese communists against Japanese imperialism (Morley 1976: 18–23). On 1 August – in the middle of the Long March – the Chinese Communist Party proposed to its antagonist, the Nationalists, the formation of an anti-Japanese National United Front and issued a proclamation urging 'all classes' to fight against Japan. Chiang Kai-shek viewed the proposal with suspicion and scorn. But in December 1936 Chang Hsueh-liang, then subordinate to Chiang but under communist influence, persuaded him to change the Kuomintang's thrust from anti-communist to anti-Japanese. By the following spring Chiang Kai-shek and Chou En-lai agreed to halt the civil war so as to form such a coalition against Japan.

Contributing to a growing militancy within Japan proper and in the nation's external policies and activities was a fear of Soviet pressures on Manchuria from Siberia to the north and Mongolia to the west. At the other end of the Soviet Union, Nazi Germany was facing the increasing pressure from the east. It was the Nazi foreign department, under the leadership of Joachim Ribbentrop, that approached the Japanese delegation in Berlin in 1935. The Seventh Congress of the Communist International contributed to the collaboration between the two countries. Together with the sense of diplomatic isolation resulting from their withdrawal from the League of Nations, Japan and Germany signed the Anti-Comintern Pact in November 1936, which Italy joined a year later. The pact was carefully drafted so as not to provoke either the Soviet Union or Britain.

Meanwhile, the inability of Britain (and the League of Nations) to halt Italian advances in Abyssinia, the German advance in the Rhineland, and the outbreak of the Spanish civil war suggested that the British Empire was a 'spent force' in the world. Germany and Italy were getting closer, moreover, as their opposition to France and the USSR was consolidated.

The League of Nations appointed an investigating committee – the Lytton Commission – which gathered voluminous data but served only to delay action while Japan proceeded with its conquest. The sole outcomes were that the League demonstrated its inability to act effectively and the Japanese withdrew from the League in apparent high dudgeon; from their perspective the whole affair merely provided further evidence of the Western unwillingness to accord 'status equality' to Japan.

In view of these developments, the militarists and their supporters could maintain that as Japan 'became economically strong and able to compete with the West, the countries of the West used their political power at home and in various colonial areas to prevent her applying this economic strength to her own advantage' (Thompson 1946: 160). Resisting attempts of the West to block the country's development of supply, influence, and other leverage potentials, the militarists and their supporters could claim with some legitimacy – and substantial historical precedent for a country with limited domestic resources – that Japan could not become or maintain itself as a major world power without an empire.

EXPANSION INTO CHINA PROPER

The first substantial move was not long in coming. Just before midnight on 7 July, 1937 some Japanese troops who were on maneuver clashed accidentally with Chinese troops at Marco Polo Bridge (Lukouchiao) near Peking (Reischauer 1970: 204). The incident was 'nothing more than a skirmish started by shots fired by an unknown party in the dark of night . . . Who were the culprits who had fired the shots? . . . the question remains unsolved to this day' (Hata 1983: 248). Unlike the Manchurian Incident six years earlier, this is not believed to have been part of a plot, and it attracted relatively little attention at the time (Yanaga 1949: 572).

With greater self-confidence than it had displayed in 1931, the Chinese government demanded a settlement of differences between the two countries (Reischauer 1970: 204–205), and two weeks later Secretary of State Cordell Hull offered the good offices of the United States in pursuing a settlement of the affair (Yanaga 1949: 572). The Japanese government also demanded a basic settlement, but although few Japanese gave much thought to the possibility of serious resistance by the Chinese, the initial skirmish developed into full-scale fighting by the end of the month. In mid-August, Chinese aircraft dropped bombs on Shanghai while attempting to strike at Japanese warships nearby, and a land battle ensued.

Mounting a major military sweep, Japanese leaders dispatched army units south and west from their bases in North China, and by December the invaders had captured the Chinese capital of Nanking. As the army moved, local regimes responsive to its wishes were established by the military authorities (Usui 1983: 311). Soon the Japanese were in control of all major Chinese ports, the largest cities, most of the railway lines, and nearly all the more productive and highly populated parts of China. Withdrawing to Chungking, where a provisional capital was established, the Chinese Nationalists continued to fight, and the Chinese Communists, who had declared war on Japan (somewhat symbolically) after the Manchurian Incident, launched guerrilla attacks from Yenan in the northwest.

As it became increasingly evident that the war in China was likely to be long and difficult, Japanese leaders tried to develop the country's productive power with increasing vigor. Although Southeast Asia, India, the United States, and other parts of the world continued to provide most of Japan's resources, north China became an important source of supply for the Japanese expeditionary forces (Iriye 1984: 4), but development was a much more difficult problem.

Soon after its initiation, Manchukuo's 1937 five-year plan was extended to include North China. The following year a four-year plan for the mobilization of materials and the expansion of productive capacities was drafted by the Japanese Planning Board, approved by the cabinet, but kept secret from the Diet. Subsequently released information pointed to self-sufficiency within the yen bloc to be achieved by 1942 in coal, iron and steel, zinc, pulp, motor cars, rolling stock, shipping, and the like (Schumpeter 1940: 273–4).

Overall, Japan's expansion programs for the empire tended to place heavy demands on Japanese trade – including trade with the United States – which continued to serve as the lifeline that made the country's other activities possible. The Japanese found that their external economic leverage was limited, however. Because of the nonstrategic composition of the country's exports, the threat of withholding or interrupting trade with other partners was ineffective, whereas these same partners could exert leverage on Japan by refusing to import Japanese products while continuing to profit from exports in response to Japanese demand. *In short, Japan possessed economic leverage only through trade with areas under Japanese control.*

Insofar as Japanese exports to the United States and other industrialized countries were discouraged, the pressures for alternative markets increased – as did the pressure for an expansion of military activities in order to ensure access to such markets.

Under these circumstances, the Japanese government allocated more and more contracts and subsidies to sectors of industry and commerce. According to an index from the *Oriental Economist*, the volume of production – against the base 1931–3 = 100 – jumped from 93.7 in 1930 to 167.3 in 1937 (Farley 1940: 76), and heavy industry showed a tenfold increase from 1930 to 1942 (Borton 1955: 361). This domestic economic growth made possible the further expansion of Japanese activities and interests beyond the home island boundaries that Japan's leaders felt was imperative if access to resources and markets were to be assured – although the economic benefits came at a high price in that almost three fifths of the increase in expenditures prior to 1937 had been allocated for military purposes.

INSTITUTIONAL REFORMS FOR EXPANSION

With his first cabinet (June 1937 to January 1939) Fumimaro Konoye pursued major institutional reforms in the governmental structure and consequently made the nation ready for the war. One of the major reforms was the establishment of the Planning Board. Under the Mobilization Law of 1918, the Japanese government had maintained the Resource Bureau since 1927. Participated in by military officers, the bureau was charged with preparation of a wartime resource mobilization plan and with producing a series of procedures in response to incidents in Manchuria and China. In the meantime the Cabinet Research Bureau, established in the 1930s, was reorganized in May 1937 into the Planning Agency. Supported by military leaders, the Konoye cabinet in October 1937 merged the Planning Agency with the Resource Bureau to create a more powerful Planning Board. Occupying the center of the Japanese mobilization effort, the board was charged with (a) promoting production capacity; (b) regulating demand and supply; (c) adjusting distribution; and (d) achieving and maintaining a balance of payments (Itoh 1976: 202–4).

In order to ensure effective state intervention by the Planning Board, the army demanded new legislation. In fact, even before the merger the Planning Agency had prepared a new law replacing the 1918 mobilization statute. In March 1938 the general National Mobilization Law was passed in the Diet, which provided for a carte blanche delegation of wartime legislative powers to the cabinet, thus enabling the government to legislate by ordinance in a wide range of areas from industrial activities to individual freedoms.

Another notable reform was the establishment on 20 November 1937 of the Imperial Headquarters – a measure previously invoked only in time of war. In order to harmonize military and political strategies, Konoye had actually intended to include the prime minister within the headquarters. The army not only refused Konoye's request, however, but also issued a military ordinance, which did not require the prime minister's approval for enactment, in order to ensure the independence of the military (Fujimura 1981: 181). Thus, established as the Imperial Headquarters, this purely military organization monopolized military operations and exerted a powerful influence on political as well as military policies.

Together the cabinet and the Imperial Headquarters also institutionalized the Liaison Conference as a means of linking military and political policy making, consisting of the prime minister, the Foreign Minister, and four active military officers in the positions of army and navy ministers and army and navy chiefs of general staff. The proceedings of the Liaison Conference could override the Japanese cabinet virtually at will.

The gravest issue for the Japanese government at the time was the pursuit of a settlement with China. In pursuit of this objective, a number of other institutions were established. On 10 June 1938, the cabinet decided on the formation of a five-minister conference, consisting of the premier and the foreign, finance, army, and navy ministers. Originally intended to deal with the policy concerning China, the conference gradually expanded its responsibilities to include other important issues. Despite strong resistance by the Foreign Minister (followed by his resignation), the Asian Development Board was established in order to unify policy implementations in China, and hence the Foreign Ministry's influence on China policy declined institutionally as well. Thus, along with this line of development, foreign policy was subordinated to military policy step by step.

'NEW ORDER' FOR JAPAN'S SECURITY

What tended to emerge after the China Incident of 1937 was a military-civilian oligarchy around which various extremely nationalist, reformist, and dissident military groups could rally. For some time, meanwhile, Japanese military and political leaders had been discussing possibilities for the establishment of what came to be known as the Greater East Asia Co-Prosperity Sphere.

In November 1938 the Japanese government announced a 'New Order in East Asia' to encompass China and Manchukuo, as well as Japan proper. Later, this concept was expanded to include Japanese hegemony over the whole of East Asia now formally called the 'Greater East Asia Co-Prosperity Sphere' (Reischauer 1970: 206–7). At the time of announcement the Konoye cabinet intended to settle hostilities with Nationalist China through the establishment of a pro-Japan, anti-Communist regime. But few Chinese leaders responded affirmatively to the 'new order' proposal, which remained a symbol of Japan's hegemonical aspiration.

As subsequently developed by Japanese leaders the 'co-prosperity sphere' was envisaged as encompassing 'not only Japan proper, its colonies, and all of China north of the Yangtze River, but also the rest of China, Southeast Asia, and ultimately eastern Siberia, India and Australia.' The expectation was that the southern regions would 'supply raw materials and surplus food, while Manchuria and North China provided the materials and basis for a heavy industry complex.' Integrated and defended by Japanese skills, tools, planning, and armed forces, 'the rest of Asia would become a vast market' (Hunsberger 1964: 20). Japan could then achieve self-sufficiency and dominance beyond challenge in the Far East. In addition, there would be commands for military officers, colonial posts for young men, raw materials for industries, and markets for manufactured goods. Two stubborn problems continued to confront the Japanese, however: 'how to exploit resources in areas already secured and how to acquire remaining areas with impunity' (Cohen 1949a: 33).

COLLISION OF THE USA AND JAPAN IN CHINA

As the war progressed, the established 'rights and interests' of the United States, Britain, and other Western powers in China were increasingly threatened. British activities and interests had expanded into China during the late eighteenth century and those of the United States in the first half of the nineteenth. In mid-December 1937 two British gunboats were bombed, and the US gunboat *Panay*, with members of the American Embassy staff aboard, was sunk by Japanese shore batteries (Yanaga 1949: 574; Butow 1961: 123). Five days later the city of Nanking fell to Japanese forces. These and other collisions, together with the indiscriminate bombing of Chinese civilians, aroused public opinion in the United States.

As conflicts between Japanese and US (and British) activities and interests in China worsened, leaders in Japan, Manchukuo, and North China confronted a contradiction, in that Manchuria and North China were never able to supply more than a portion of Japan's needs and demands. As a consequence, the Japanese had to continue reaching outside the yen bloc for cotton, wool, wheat, rubber, nickel, tin, copper, petroleum, and other essentials, which came from India, Southeast Asia, Oceania, Europe, and the United States (Japan's most important trade partner). As the war in China expanded, moreover, and even more as Japanese forces became bogged down, government leaders felt a growing need for an understanding of some kind with the United States and other Western powers.

With respect to certain critical resources, Japanese leaders confronted another serious contradiction. In order to obtain controlled access to Asian resources and markets, they proposed, in effect, to replace Britain, the United States, and other Western powers on the continent and islands to the southeast. To accomplish this, however, Japan had an immediate need for resources to sustain its armed forces – oil (from the Netherlands East Indies), together with scrap iron and aviation gasoline (primarily from the United States). Discussing the problem before an Imperial Conference (in the presence of the emperor), the director of the Planning Board conceded that Japanese steel production would suffer if the USA were to ban the import of scrap metal (as threatened) but he proposed that 'new technologies' could probably be used to produce steel by other methods 'in considerable amounts.' He warned that the banning of copper would be more serious, although 'a considerable amount' had been bought recently from the United States. An oil ban would be most grievous of all (Ike 1967: 6–7).[4]

From time to time the US and British authorities tried to constrain the Japanese by threatening to impose embargoes on shipments of strategic materials to Japan. In June 1938 the US State Department announced the government's opposition to the sale of aircraft and aircraft equipment to countries using such equipment against civilian populations. Extended to the end of 1939, this 'moral embargo' announced in June 1938 was expanded to include technical information pertaining to the production of high-octane gasoline and related materials (Yanaga 1949: 575–6). Years passed before definitive measures were taken, however, and aid to the Chinese Nationalist government remained the primary anti-Japanese leverage exerted.

COLLISIONS WITH THE USSR: A 'HIDDEN' WAR

Meanwhile, the expansion of Japanese power in Manchuria, combined with the more recent invasion of China proper, was rapidly bringing Japanese activities and interests into violent collision with those of the USSR. As indicated earlier, the Manchurian Incident had incited Chinese Communist leaders into a paper declaration of war against Japan, but Chiang Kai-shek had seen the routing of provincial warlord, Communist Red Army, and other domestic anti-Kuomintang forces as the higher priority. The new and more immediate Japanese threat changed all that and soon altered the configuration of alignments throughout much of the Far East. Relations between the Nationalist government in Nanking and the USSR had been formalized in December 1932, but the Soviet Russians and the Nationalist Chinese had continued to view each other with grave suspicion. Now, all of a sudden, Nanking and Moscow found themselves pushed into ever closer relationships by the Japanese threat.[5]

Contributing also to deteriorating relations between the USSR and Japan was a more localized effort to expand Japanese activities and interests in the Manchurian borderlands. Since well before the opening of the twentieth century, Japanese leaders had tended to view tsarist, and subsequently Soviet, expansionism as a major obstacle to their own economic, political, and territorial ambitions. 'At the time of the Russo-Japanese War, Russia constituted the primary hypothetical enemy of the Japanese army,' a Japanese scholar wrote in an analysis of hostilities during the late 1930s. 'The build-up of the latter's organization, equipment and training was based upon a hypothetical war against Russia, with Manchuria the battleground.' In 1933, as a consequence of 'a more favorable position deriving from its occupation of all of Manchuria,' the Japanese army developed new operational plans 'for launching a fierce offensive eastward' against the Soviet Maritime Province, moving northward, and then veering westward. In operation, however, these plans were tempered by new Japanese assessments of Soviet strength (Hata 1976: 132).

Beginning in the mid-1930s, changes in planning and capabilities on both sides led to a rising number of border disputes along the Manchukuo–Soviet–Mongolian borderlands 'from Hulun Buyr to Lake Khanka' (Coox 1976: 115–19) – 155 by the end of 1934, 136 during 1935, 203 in 1936, and by the end of World War II more than 1,600. There was 'uncertainty as to the detailed wording of the various treaties concluded between tsarist Russia and the Xing (Ch'ing) dynasty,' and the Japanese general staff and the Kwantung army 'interpreted boundaries to favor their own interests.' There were also Mongolian and Soviet pressures from the other side. Disregarding ethnic and nationality considerations, Mongolian herdsmen commonly moved back and forth across uncertain boundaries. 'Thus the seeds of dispute could be found in all directions' (Hata 1976: 132–3).

A 12-day skirmish fought in southeast Manchukuo between Japanese and Soviet forces in the summer of 1938 provided a typical example (Reischauer 1970: 206). At issue was the location of the Soviet–Manchukuo border relative to a land . . . of strategic importance overlooking the Tumen-Ula River, the railway, and the roads linking with the Soviet Maritime Province and the city of Vladivostok. Both sides reinforced their border patrols, but as Soviet forces achieved a preponderance of strength in the area, the Japanese government agreed to a cessation of hostilities and restoration of the boundary as the USSR defined it (Butow 1961: 126–7).

Less than a year later a new Soviet–Japanese confrontation occurred, this time along the frontier between Manchukuo and Outer Mongolia – today the Mongolian People's Republic – and on the Amur River between Blagoveschensk and Khaborovsk (Yanaga 1949: 577). As far back as 1933 Outer Mongolia had been referred to by the Army Minister of the time, General Sadao Araki, as an 'ambiguous area' which Japan ought to occupy, and somewhat later Lieutenant General Seishiro Itagaki, chief of staff of the Kwantung Army, identified the extension of Japanese influence and power into the region as one of the army's goals.

From a Soviet perspective, control of Outer Mongolia would place Japanese troops within striking distance of Lake Baikal and the entire Far Eastern sector of the Trans-Siberian Railway (Butow 1961: 128).

By now, Manchukuo's 3,000 miles of frontier abutting the USSR 'were coming alive with barbed wire entanglements, pillboxes, observation posts, armed patrols, reconnaissance planes and gunboats. Incidents occurred incessantly – shootings, kidnappings, highjackings, intrusions.' In late May 1939 what had begun as a border clash rapidly 'assumed major proportions with the employment of aircraft, artillery, and tanks . . . along a front some fifty to sixty kilometers in length and twenty to twenty-five kilometers in depth' (Butow 1961: 128). During the next three months, Japanese, Manchukuo, Mongolian, and Soviet forces fought a 'hidden war' at Nomonhan (near the western boundary between Manchukuo and Mongolia) to which some 56,000 Japanese troops were committed.[6]

The numbers of Soviet and Mongolian troops are difficult to ascertain, but in critical phases of the fighting they were estimated at between two and five times the Japanese strength. Japanese killed and wounded exceeded 17,000; at the postwar Tokyo trials Soviet–Mongolian casualties were reported in excess of 9,000.

MOUNTING TENSIONS

Recognizing the superiority of Soviet air power and mechanized forces on the ground, the authorities in Tokyo assessed the Nomonhan outcome as a defeat for Japan (Hata 1976: 157–8), and the concern of the high command for the country's lack of preparedness led political leaders to consider terminating hostilities in China through diplomatic negotiations – an undertaking likely to require the good offices of the United States and Britain. The Japanese government was consequently 'chagrined' when the US State Department announced in July its intention to abrogate the commercial treaty between the two nations, which came into force in January 1940. Paradoxically, however, instead of 'driving the Japanese to reduce their dependence on America, the announcement made them more determined to placate the United States' (Iriye 198: 48).

Along with the empire's deteriorating relations with Great Britain, the United States, and increasingly the Dutch East Indies, Japan's clashes with the USSR tended to generate a feeling of isolation and to leave the country with few friends aside from the Axis nations with their own shifting coalitions. Political leaders and even competing factions within the army and navy commands developed their own loyalties and policy preferences that made a working consensus at the national level all but impossible to achieve. Among the populace, meanwhile, zealots mounted 'soap-box rallies', distributed pamphlets and handbills, organized protests to the government, and promoted 'inspection trips' to China. Nationalistic societies were formed in rapid succession – many of them by men connected with the assassinations of the first half of the decade. As a consequence, new murders 'were planned' (Butow 1961: 128).

Designed to facilitate access to raw materials and strengthen exports, Japan's expansionist policy generated ever more – and increasingly perverse – side-effects. Because of demands imposed by the China war and the costly administration of occupied territories, Japanese military leaders insisted that governmental controls should be strengthened and integrated into an overall economic plan. Japanese industrialists, on the other hand – the zaibatsu especially – wanted to organize industry into cartels under their own control and independent of the government. As a result of this basic conflict, the national economy was 'partly controlled and partly free.' Wages had been frozen, for example, but 'price controls were more nominal than real,' and although raw materials were officially allocated to essential industries, 'an influential businessman could obtain what he needed if he were willing to pay for it' (Borton 1955: 360).

As regulations multiplied under the National Mobilization Law of 1938, their enforcement became increasingly difficult (Schumpeter 1940: 822). Conditions were exacerbated with the German invasion of Poland in September 1939, which had the effect of accelerating price rises and attempts at tax evasion. In the effort to tighten controls, the National Mobilization Law was invoked to 'freeze prices, freight rates, wages, rents, storage charges, insurance premiums and all other costs and prices at the level prevailing on September 18, 1939' (Schumpeter 1940: 822).

Concurrently, the sudden proclamation of the Nazi–Soviet Pact during the Nomonhan Incident transformed Soviet–Japanese hostilities into a state of uncertainty and confusion. Failing to respond quickly to changing European affairs, the cabinet at the time resigned, leaving the country under an ambiguous leadership.

By the latter half of 1939 – more than two years after the invasion of China – the Japanese army still appeared to be 'bogged down,' with military operations there becoming more and more 'a drain on national resources.' With the outbreak of war in Europe during the late summer of that year, officers of the army general staff and others began to hope that a major struggle among Western powers would draw world attention away from East Asia, provide an opportunity for ending the war in China (Hosoya 1980: 32), and open the possibility of making territorial gains at low cost as Japanese diplomats had been able to do in the course of World War I. With these considerations in mind, members of the army general staff began planning a number of measures for bringing the China war to a close, including 'military operations, plots, and an economic blockade.'

From a lateral pressure perspective, the 'hidden war' between Japan and the USSR during the 1930s amounted to the expanding activities and interests of two states with rapidly growing capabilities colliding *in seriata*. At about this time, a further source of friction was aggravated when the Japanese government accused the USSR of violating the spirit of the Portsmouth treaty with respect to the use of Far Eastern fishing grounds (Yanaga 1949: 576–7). There were moments when a slight tip of the decision making scales might have impelled the Japanese into a full-scale northern invasion of the USSR. What persuaded them to push southward? Many considerations are relevant – struggles between competing factions in the Japanese government, events in Europe, Japan's alliances combined with a sense of acute isolation, the Chinese campaign and its spiraling costs, and perhaps above all an ever more immediate pressure for critical resources.

Chapter 9

Toward the Pearl Harbor decision

DEFINITION AND CONCEPT

On 7 December 1941 (8 December, Tokyo time) top Japanese leaders reached a determination that ranks among the unforgettable decisions of history.

The act of deciding has been defined as a determination arrived at after consideration, but the concept has been dealt with in many different ways. Our approach is simple and pragmatic. A decision is a determination to narrow or close a gap between a perception of fact ('what is') and a perception of value or preference ('what ought to be').

Strictly construed, decisions are made only by individuals. In this connection, many theorists have tended to rely on reification in the treatment of state decisions, that is, by assuming that the determination has been effected by a prime minister, president, dictator, or other powerful leader acting in the name of the state. We find it more useful to interpret state and other collective decisions as an outcome of bargaining among actors. This assumption is that normally such bargaining occurs, even though the leverage potentials between the actors are grossly uneven (Choucri and North 1989: 292–4; North 1990: 12–19, 78–80, 90–102). This approach challenges two widely recognized assumptions.

Conventionally, realist and neorealist theoreticians have tended to proceed from the premise that states are unitary actors that act 'rationally.' A problem with this approach has been that the concepts of unitary actor and rational actions have come to serve as definitionals as well as assumptions, with the consequence that all decisions of all states tend to be viewed through the same narrow lenses. This is not meant as a categorical rejection of unitary and rational actor assumptions. Formal models meeting such criteria can be extremely useful to the extent that they remain analytically falsifiable. Our intention, however, is to replace *de facto* definitions with more readily falsifiable concepts and theoretical propositions.

As commonly postulated among the minimal assumptions of utility theorists, state actors – provided the choices and options of another state are known – possess 'perfect information' with regard to the consequences of their own actions. They can attach precise payoff values to each set of outcomes and calculate 'the payoffs of their rational opponent over all possible outcomes' (Jervis 1971: 125, cited in North 1990: 80). Although the concept of satisfaction may be substituted for assumptions of maximization (Simon 1955: 76–7) – the proposition that the actor is pursuing less than maximum levels of aspiration – several important questions may remain to be answered. Whose aspirations are being pursued? How can levels of aspiration be determined? (Axelrod 1972: 43–4, cited in North 1990: 80).

At this point our relatively simple definition of decision becomes relevant – that is, the determination to close a gap between perceptions of fact and value. The critical word here is *perception*, e.g., perception of 'what is' (or what can be or is likely to be, or both) and perception of 'what ought to be', not only in the long run (*ends*), about which Japanese leaders of the time were in at least vague agreement, but also in the immediate term: the preferred *means* of strategy – 'north' or 'south' – about which for many months they could not reach a consensus. It need scarcely be emphasized that perceptions are extraordinarily subjective.

Whatever the accuracy of Japanese intelligence data bearing on the military and intelligence capacities of the United States (much of it was extremely good), documents of the Liaison and Imperial Conferences, as cited in this chapter, suggest the extent to which the individual Japanese leaders – assessing probable US responses to an attack on Pearl Harbour – were moved by hopes and wishful thinking.

During the autumn of 1941, in particular, Japanese decision makers were hampered by limitations on the information made available to them by the armed forces. 'I was astonished at our lack of the statistical data . . .' Foreign Minister Togo complained retrospectively, 'but even more, I felt the absurdity of our having to base our deliberations on assumptions, since the high command refused to divulge figures on the numbers of our armed forces, or any fact relating to operations.' Even General Teiichi Suzuki, when he was Director of the Planning Board, was unable to obtain critically relevant information about petroleum reserves controlled by the armed forces until a few weeks prior to the strike against Pearl Harbor (Ike 1967: 188).

PRESSURES FOR A DECISION

If Germany's conclusion of the Nazi–Soviet Pact (August 1939) and the outbreak of war in Europe (September 1939) had required the Japanese leadership to rethink foreign relationships, Hitler's invasion of the Low Countries and France the following May and June generated in Tokyo and throughout the empire a new sense of urgency and a feeling that time for coming to a decision was rapidly running out. The Japanese leadership now had to establish priorities, determine who its allies and enemies were, and settle upon a course of action. The fall of the Netherlands and France left the colonial possessions of these two countries unprotected and their oil and other resources up for grabs. Suddenly there was a growing fear in Japan that Germany might impose economic, political, and military control over these regions and thus bring possibilities for the Greater East Asia Co-Prosperity Sphere to a grinding halt (Ike 1967: 3). Japan must move quickly, an army memorandum warned. 'Never in our history has there been a time like the present.' Japan must grasp the opportunity that had presented itself (Tsunoda 1980: 247–8).

As Japanese leaders had recognized for a long time, however, a 'southward advance' would surely invite intervention by the United States and Britain, neither of which could tolerate the alienation of these vital regions. Any movement of Japanese forces into southern Indochina, Singapore, and the Netherlands East Indies would expose their left flank to naval and air strikes from the east. These circumstances and the attendant dilemma immediately brought the cabinet of Admiral Yonai under attack as a 'status quo government friendly toward the United States and Britain' (Butow 1961: 139). On 22 July 1940 it was replaced by a second Konoye cabinet in which pivotal posts were occupied by the so-called Manchurian group, including as Army Minister Hideki Tojo (perceived until recently as advocating a tough policy toward the USSR), Foreign Minister Yosuke Matsuoka (former president of the South Manchurian Railway), and president of the Planning Board Naoki Hoshino (a key figure in the formation of the Manchurian industrial structure).

Konoye's domestic goal – 'perfection of national defense on the basis of total defense structure' and on an early 'termination of the China War' – required a planned economy including 'the control of production, distribution and consumption' as the primary means of achieving 'self-sufficiency in food, rationalization of trade policies, expansion of chemical and machine industries, promotion of science, increase of population, improvement of national health, and the equalization of sacrifices and services to be rendered by the people to the state' (Yanaga 1949: 540–1).

BARGAINING AND LEVERAGING IN BERLIN

Matsuoka, meanwhile, pursued negotiations in Berlin toward a tripartite alliance with Germany and Italy. Fascist tendencies had been growing in Japan throughout the 1930s, and events – particularly in China and along Soviet–Manchukuo borders – had been viewed with alarm by right-wing groups and the army general staff. Initially, on the other hand, the navy had opposed a tripartite agreement on the ground that such a commitment might lead to serious confrontations with the United States and/or the USSR. Even after the Anti-Comintern Pact was signed, Navy Minister Yonai (February 1937 to August 1939), Vice-Minister

Yamamoto (December 1936 to August 1939), and others in the Navy Ministry contended that *Japan could not win a war against Britain and the United States – especially in view of US naval and air capabilities*. Further confusion was injected into these discussions by the sudden conclusion in August 1939 of the Nazi–Soviet treaty – 'at a time when Japanese and Soviet troops were locked in a desperate battle at Nomonhan . . . and relations between the two countries were at their lowest ebb' (Hosoya 1980: 17).

Events continued to push many Japanese in the direction of closer relations with the Axis powers, however. Just as there was a disagreeable feeling among some leaders that Germany 'had betrayed them by violating the spirit of the Anti-Comintern Pact,' they were 'also apprehensive that the Soviets, feeling secure on the west because of the Nazi pact, might either embark on military adventures in the Far East or increase pressure on Japan from the north to make the settlement of the Sino-Japanese war more difficult' (Hosoya 1980: 17). These possibilities seemed to require a formal understanding with the Axis powers. As for the Navy Ministry, views there began to change as plans were formulated for a possible advance into Southeast Asia and the South Seas. Consequently, authorized by decisions reached at an Imperial Conference including the emperor, cabinet ministers, and top army and navy officers a week earlier, Japan on 27 September, 1940 concluded a tripartite alliance with Germany and Italy (text and accompanying letters in Morley 1976: 298–304).

The Tripartite Alliance, the Nazi–Soviet Pact, Japanese apprehensions about a possible Soviet attack, and the costly slowdown of Japanese forces in China combined to direct Japanese attention toward the possibility of a rapprochement with the USSR. The Chinese Nationalist regime, having withdrawn under Japanese attack to Chungking, had been receiving economic assistance from the outside by the way of three main routes – through Burma in the southwest, through French Indochina, and through the northwest from the USSR. With the outbreak of war in Europe, it seemed possible to cut the Burma and Indochina routes by applying diplomatic pressure on Britain and France and the northwestern route through a political rapprochement with the Soviet Union – this last requiring a remarkable turnaround made easier by the Nazi–Soviet Pact (Hosoya 1980: 32–3).

The idea of overtures to the Soviet Union was not new. As far back as 31 December, 1931 Soviet Foreign Commissar Maxim Litvinov had proposed conclusion of a Japanese–Soviet nonaggression treaty, and the following year the USSR offered to sell Japan its share of the Chinese Eastern Railway in Manchuria. The general disposition had been against any such rapprochement, but now, in the early years of World War II, new exigencies seemed to provide a rationale. As early as the opening weeks of 1940 two diametrically opposed viewpoints were being expressed in governmental circles. A pro-Anglo-American group urged that Japan should exert major efforts to obtain a diplomatic settlement with Great Britain and the United States, whereas an opposing group argued that Japan should strengthen its ties to Germany and Italy and, with German help, improve diplomatic relations with the USSR. The latter faction, including officers of the Japanese general staff concerned with settling the Sino-Japanese War, tended to be motivated more by the dynamics of international power politics as contrasted with those of deep ideological commitments (Hosoya 1980: 14–15, 17, 23–6). Such conflicts and confusions may help to explain the nagging uncertainty among Japanese leaders over whether to strike 'north' or 'south' in the latter months of 1941.

Matsuoka appeared to have persuaded himself that the Tripartite Pact 'would intimidate the Soviet Union into joining the "four-power entente," or at least into signing a nonaggression pact with Japan, and that the "four-power entente" would in turn serve to pressure the United States into abandoning its hard-line policy toward Japan.' He shared with the Germans a naive assumption that 'Soviet cooperation in the elimination of spheres of influence of the four powers could be assured' by an offer of territories like Iran, Afghanistan, or India, over which they had no control. At the same time, he insisted that the Soviet Union abandon much more vital interests such as the Balkans and Finland, or northern Sakhalin and the Maritime Province which Japan hoped to control in order to complete its 'East Asia Co-Prosperity Sphere' (Berton 1980: 8–9).

In fact, the idea of a four-power entente had been put forward in Japan before the conclusion of the Nazi–Soviet nonaggression pact at a time when Japanese generally were perceiving the USSR as 'the principal object of the tripartite cooperation among Japan, Germany and Italy.' Immediately after conclusion of the pact, notably, it was a segment of the Japanese right wing that activated a movement 'calling for a nonaggression treaty with the Soviet Union as an important step toward the realization of a four-power entente.' This perspective was supported by the German Embassy in Tokyo, and thus 'the movement began to gather strength' – leading to the conclusion on 13 April 1941 of a treaty of neutrality between Japan and the USSR. Over succeeding months and years, despite changing circumstances and uncertainty and agonizing on the part of Japanese leaders, this treaty survived until 5 April 1945, when, in accordance with provisions that had been written into it, the USSR gave notice that the pact would not be extended when it expired the following year. 'Four months later, on August 9, the Soviet Union launched its attack on the Kwantung Army' (Hosoya 1980: 24, 78–85, 114).

As it turned out, Germany's spectacularly successful invasions of Norway, the Netherlands, Belgium, and France six months after the conclusion of the Nazi–Soviet treaty and the Tripartite Pact reassured Japanese leaders with respect to the Reich's capabilities and intentions and at the same time aroused pressing concerns about German plans for the disposition of French

Indochina and the Netherlands East Indies. There was a growing fear that Hitler might seize control of these territories, which Japan had hoped to bring into the co-prosperity sphere, before Japanese forces could be set in motion. This anxiety, coupled with Germany's clear demonstration of power on the European continent, had the effect of strengthening the leverage of right-wing nationalist groups in Japan (Borton 1955: 359; Ike 1967: 3–4).

UNEASY AXIS COALITION

As early as 1936 the Japanese navy had begun planning for an advance into Southeast Asia and the South Seas, but in view of Japan's expanding commitments on land, the project was not easy to justify. During the German invasions of Denmark and Norway, however, section chiefs within the navy general staff concluded that the time had come to occupy the Dutch East Indies. Germany's western advance into the Low Countries and France accelerated matters, and the French surrender to Germany on 17 June 1940 seemed to provide Japan with a favorable opening. By July the Japanese army was developing a plan for an early invasion of the Dutch East Indies. Seemingly at the last moment, however, the navy vetoed this undertaking in favor of an early invasion of French Indochina, but no decision was reached in support of that alternative, either. The navy view was that any plan for military operations in the south would mean war with both Britain and the United States. Chief of the navy general staff intelligence division Takuzumi Oka asserted that, whereas preparations for military operations against Britain and the Netherlands had been completed, the important task now was 'preparation for war against the United States' (Tsunoda 1980: 290–1).

Meanwhile, German–Japanese discussions continued. After informal conferences with the German ambassador and other German diplomats in Tokyo, Matsuoka undertook extensive negotiations in Moscow first (following Ribbentrop's advice) and later in Berlin. Molotov showed little interest in Matsuoka's grand perspectives for dividing up remote parts of the British empire, however, and the Moscow talks degenerated into a near-squabble over spheres of interest. In Berlin neither Hitler nor Ribbentrop revealed to Matsuoko their plans – already in progress – for an attack on the USSR, although Ribbentrop observed that, if Stalin were to threaten Germany, Hitler would crush the Soviet Union. Precisely what conclusions Matsuoka drew remains unclear, but his signature of the neutrality pact with the USSR of 13 April 1941 may have been precautionary. Although the Nazis were taken by surprise and angered, Ribbentrop made it clear that, if the Soviets should compel Germany to strike, the common cause would best be served if Japan, undiverted, were to attack British-held Singapore. Ribbentrop told Matsuoka that the conquest of Britain was only a matter of time and assured him that 'if Japan got into conflict with the United States, Germany on her part would take the necessary steps at once' (Yanaga 1949: 591–2).

To confuse matters further, even as Hitler and Ribbentrop were hinting at a reversal of tripartite policies toward the USSR, ongoing attempts by private intermediaries to initiate negotiations between Japan and the USA led to a US proposal. In retrospect, it seems evident that these negotiations had no prospect of success in that those in the Japanese regime who favored the proposal were not in control of the government at that time. Perceiving these efforts as an attempt to detach Japan from the Axis, Matsuoka saw the negotiations as a threat to his personal position. After resorting first to tactics of delay, he tried to prejudice whatever negotiations might take place by conveying to Secretary of State Cordell Hull the unshakable confidence of the Axis powers in a complete victory and their firm belief that, although the entry of the United States into the war might prolong the hostilities, the outcome could not be altered. In a subsequent message he proposed a Japan–USA nonaggression pact. In Washington, meanwhile, Ambassador Nomura opened negotiations with the United States that dragged on for months as drafts and counterdrafts were exchanged.

At the same time that Japanese leaders were 'politely but persistently' refusing German pleas for strong action in Southeast Asia (including an attack on Singapore), Japanese diplomats in Washington were trying to convince US officials that the Axis powers were not a threat to US interests in Asia (Iriye 1984: 13). As for the Americans, quite apart from their feelings about Germany or Italy, there was a 'rational' tendency in Washington to consider it unlikely that Japan would challenge the United States 'to a war that would be tantamount to national suicide' (Iriye 1984: 21); and from Tokyo, Ambassador Grew articulated a US desire for 'an early return to mutually good and helpful relations with Japan' – especially in view of the current condition of world affairs (US Department of State 1940: 341–2). Matsuoka, Konoye, and other civilian leaders in Japan thought, for their part, that peace in the Pacific could be maintained if only the United States would pledge not to interfere with Japan's building of a new Asian order (Iriye 1984: 13).

JAPAN'S POLICY AND DECISION MECHANISMS

Central to Japanese policy and planning during these years were two decision-making bodies: the Liaison Conferences and the Imperial Conferences. Whenever a major policy decision was reached by a Liaison Conference of leading civilian and military policy makers, it had to be ratified at an Imperial Conference, which was likely to include 'the members of the Liaison Conference plus the President of the Privy Council,' meeting 'in the presence of the Emperor, who sat in front of a gold screen "mounted on a dais at the superior end of the chamber," while the "others would sit down at two long, brocade-covered tables and were at right angles to the Emperor's throne-like sanctuary."' Imperial Conferences were opened by the prime minister, who made a formal statement setting forth the object of the meeting.

> The ostensible purpose of these proceedings was to inform the Emperor – who would normally sit quietly and not utter a single word-about the situation, so that after the Conference he could give his 'sanction,' thereby making the decision legal . . . binding on all . . . and very difficult to change at a later date.

In fact, the emperor 'never made personal decisions but always followed advice given him by his ministers and military leaders' (Ike 1967: xvi–xvii).

Foreign policy decision making in Japan at this time was essentially a group function – a process closely approximating the group bargaining and decision model developed by Cyert and March (1963: 26–38). The goal of leading figures within the Liaison and Imperial conferences was to obtain decisions by inducing coalitions in support of preferred options. Members discussed, debated, and 'bargained' among themselves, but some – notably the army and navy ministers – tended to possess more leverage than others. Increasingly during the 1930s the army and navy general staffs functioned as 'standing' subcoalitions within the conferences, but these two subcoalitions were often subdivided into 'sub-subcoalitions' with respect to particular issues. This perspective on Japanese decision making leading up to the Pearl Harbor decision is quite different from the stereotype of 'the Japanese nation and particularly the Japanese military in this period as a highly disciplined, monolithic force, responding as one to the emperor's command' (Scalapino 1980: 121) – or of Tojo as an Hitlerian dictator leading Japan into the attack on Pearl Harbor.

A central – but never resolved – issue confronting the imperial leadership was whether the gains of expansion and conquest were 'commensurate with the political risks and financial outlays which were the overhead of this pattern of overseas development' (Lockwood 1968: 537). *Associated with each territorial acquisition, in short, were new costs of development and defence which seemed to outstrip the yield of colonial resource availabilities and markets and thus to generate demands for the further extension of their military activities.* Retrospectively, the persistence of the Japanese in pursuing their expansionist goals may appear arational (or irrational), but once aboard the imperial express, it was not easy to step down. At the time, moreover, Japanese leaders persuaded themselves, on balance, that the dangers of failing to control access to resources and markets outweighed the risks of further expansion.

An immediate problem was what to do about the United States and

Britain. The time was ripe for moving into Southeast Asia, and it was crucial to sever Japan's resource dependency on those two nations. The probabilities were high that a military advance into that region would trigger a war with both countries. With the concluding of the Nazi–Soviet Pact, however, and as Japan had moved closer to Germany, the Amur Valley and the frontier between Manchuria and Mongolia–Japan's 'rear' during a southern advance – had been relatively peaceful. The pressing problem was that if Japan were to cut off its relations with the United States, the navy's petroleum would last no more than a year, and current supplies of nickel, molybdenum, tungsten, copper, zinc, mercury, mica, asbestos, aluminum, cobalt, and rubber were sufficient for no more than a year and a half. 'Such a situation would finish us,' ship procurement headquarters chief Toyoda declared. Navy Minister Yoshida added the warning that, in case of hostilities, Japan – because of oil and related shortages – could not fight a war against the United States for more than a year, whereas the United States could probably plan for a protracted war. And once a decision for war had been taken, navy chief of staff Prince Fushimi confided to the emperor, Japan would require at least eight months of preparation. 'The later war comes, the better,' he asserted (Tsunoda 1980: 257).

US LEVERAGES: RESOURCE EMBARGOES

In response to German victories in Europe, the United States launched 'an Act to Expedite the Strengthening of the National Defense' in July 1940. In combination with the abolition of the Treaty on Commerce and Navigation with Japan in January, this act served to legalize 'moral embargoes' against Japan (Feis 1950: 72–3). Having obtained an agreement with the Vichy French authorities, Japan in September 1940 dispatched a troop contingent from China on a limited advance into northern Indochina – a move that helped to trigger a series of US sanctions that became increasingly severe over succeeding months. One after another, scrap iron, iron ore, pig iron, ferro alloy, certain finished and unfinished steel products, copper, bronze, zinc, nickel, brass, caustic potash, and other materials were added to a rapidly expanding embargo list (Nagaoka 1980: 147–8, 212).

Still uncertain about what course to take, Japanese leaders decided that a full-scale southern advance should not be executed unless the United States undertook a program that endangered imperial defenses in the Far East (Tsunoda 1980: 291). What were referred to as 'close relations' with Thailand, French Indochina, and the Dutch East Indies were to be obtained by diplomatic means, but if 'the empire's self-existence' were threatened by embargoes imposed by other powers, the empire would exercise military force (text in Morley 1980: 303). Not until the following April was a unified army–navy draft of an 'outline of Policy toward the South' finally agreed upon.

Meanwhile, a series of intermittent exchanges took place, directly and indirectly, between Japan and the United States. During the autumn of 1940 an informal US effort had been made to avoid a collision between the two countries when two Maryknoll priests arrived in Japan with letters of introduction from financial leaders in the United States addressed to a former official of the Japanese Ministry of Finance who was associated with a semiofficial bank in Tokyo. One of the priests turned over a memorandum he had written 'from the point of view of a Japanese,' which proposed a 'Far Eastern Monroe Doctrine' for Japan and the calling of a high-level Japanese–American conference to be held in Tokyo or Honolulu. Returning to the United States, the two priests prepared a second memorandum, differing somewhat from the earlier one, which was presented to President Roosevelt. Secretary of State Cordell Hull urged caution, but the priests were encouraged to maintain their contacts in Japan (Ike 1967: xx–xxi).

Further overtures were made to the United States by the Japanese government – but always on Japanese terms – and the year 1941 'opened with ominous shadows over the Far East and the Pacific.' Asserting before the Diet that the Netherlands East Indies lay within the Greater East Asia Co-Prosperity Sphere, Foreign Minister Matsuoka insisted that Japan had no course open to it other than to secure 'economic self-sufficiency' in this way. Such claims, in addition to Japan's established policies of expansion and military conflict, did not go unnoticed in Washington (Ike 1967).

Addressing the United States Congress early in the new year, President Roosevelt warned that the country's security had never been so seriously threatened and that the democratic way of life was under persistent attack through arms as well as propaganda (Yanaga 1949: 589). Later in the month Ambassador Grew reported from Tokyo that, in anticipation of possible hostilities with the United States, Japanese military forces were believed to be planning a surprise attack on Pearl Harbor (Jones and Myers 1941: III 260–7). All but blind to the consequences of their own policies, however, Japanese leaders found it difficult, if not beyond their capabilities, to interpret US protests and sanctions as anything but aggressive warmongering. Later, speaking before the budget committee of the Diet, Matsuoka asserted that 'ultimately diplomacy is force, and it goes without saying that diplomacy not backed by strength can accomplish nothing' (Yanaga 1949: 589–90) – a claim scarcely unique to the Japanese, it might be added.

On 12 May 1941 Japan proposed normal trade relations between itself and the United States, each country supplying the other with needed commodities. The further suggestion was made that the United States 'cooperate in the production and procurement for Japan of natural resources such as oil, rubber, tin and nickel in the southwestern Pacific' (Borton 1955: 366). Secretary of State Hull recalled Ambassador Nomura's statement of a few days earlier 'to the effect that it would be an incalculable loss to the two countries as well as to civilization should the United States and Japan become engaged in war.' From the perspective of a postwar Japanese writer, this was 'clearly an American bid for Japan's cooperation' (Yanaga 1949: 593).

Early in June the Netherlands refused – not for the first time – 'to comply with Japan's demands for oil, rubber and tin from the Netherlands East Indies' (Borton 1955: 357). Shortly thereafter the United States indicated that it would not assist Japan in acquiring these strategic materials; and on 27 May, President Roosevelt proclaimed 'an unlimited national emergency' (Yanaga 1949: 593). In the meantime, Foreign Minister Matsuoka had summoned the ambassadors of Britain and the Netherlands to assert Japan's need for continued access to Southeast Asian rubber and tin (Ike 1967: 43–44).

PRESSURES OF ALIGNMENT

In February 1941, Ribbentrop had invited Japanese Ambassador Hiroshi Oshima to his country estate at Fuschl for a discussion of future German–Japanese relations. Then, early in March, Hitler issued a basic order regarding collaboration with Japan, and later that month Japanese Foreign Minister Matsuoka visited Berlin and had a series of conversations with Hitler and Ribbentrop. Hitler wanted the Japanese to enter the war as soon as possible, but against Britain, not the Soviet Union. Matsuoka was assured that the war in Europe was virtually over, and Britain would soon be forced to concede defeat.

> An attack by Japan on Singapore would not only have a decisive effect in convincing Britain that there was no further point in continuing the war, it would also provide the key to the realization of Japanese ambitions in Eastern Asia at a time when circumstances formed a unique combination in her favor. (Bullock 1959: 577)

In early June 1941, Ambassador Oshima received an invitation to visit Berchtesgaden, where Hitler and Ribbentrop issued statements about their attitude toward the USSR which could be 'construed as advance notice to the Japanese government of the German intention to attack.' Hitler asserted that one should never make concessions to Soviet Russia. 'I am a person who will always draw the sword first if I am convinced of my opponent's hostility,' he declared. Ribbentrop noted that the possibility of war had 'greatly increased' and promised that if Japan were 'encountering difficulties in preparing for a southern advance, Germany would welcome Japanese cooperation against the Soviet Union.' Neither Hitler nor Ribbentrop indicated that the decision to attack the USSR was final (Hosoya 1980: 91).

The ambassador's report to the Japanese Foreign Ministry had 'created a suddenly tense situation within the government and the military' – giving rise to bitter arguments over the military actions that the country should take (Hosoya 1980: 90–4). As a consequence, Matsuoka, who had negotiated the nonaggression pact with the USSR while urging closer ties with Germany at the same time, soon found himself in an untenable position. Hoping to extricate himself, he urged the emperor to approve 'entering the war on Hitler's side' while 'advancing southward in the Pacific' (Borton 1955: 57). When Matsuoka's failure to warn the Japanese government led to his fall in July, Hitler thereby 'lost his best ally in the Tokyo Cabinet' as the Japanese 'quickly made up their minds to follow their own plans and keep the Germans in ignorance' (Bullock 1959: 579).

NORTH OR SOUTH? BALANCE OF COSTS AND BENEFITS

Japan now faced again the old dilemma. An attack on British and Dutch territories in the Pacific promised substantial disutilities, but Japanese leaders were persuaded, on the other hand, that submission to US pressure for disengagement in China was out of the question (Russett 1967: 98) – a consideration which seemed to leave their country with no alternative to a southward expansion. The raw materials vitally needed in Japan could be obtained only by seizing Thailand, Malaya, and the Netherlands East Indies, but the likelihood of an Anglo-US intervention in such an eventuality appeared stronger than ever.

The failure of Japan's top leadership to reach a decision was aggravated by the inability of military and naval commands to agree on a strategy. In early June 1941 three different policies were being advocated within the armed services. The army's military affairs section urged decisive military advance to the south, whereas the operations division of the general staff proposed a 'green persimmon' policy ('shake the persimmons down while green'), whereby the Japanese would work in concert with the Germans, who were known to be planning an invasion of the USSR. This proposal was opposed, in turn, by the military section of the Army Ministry and the war guidance office of the general staff, which supported a 'ripe persimmon' policy of strengthening military power in Manchuria, advancing into Indochina, and 'waiting for the fruit to ripen' (Hosoya 1980: 92–3). Thereafter, altered circumstances (some resulting from Japanese activities, others set in motion elsewhere), a change in the navy position, and shifts in the pattern of leverages within the Liaison and Imperial Conferences pushed the country into the situation that seemed to make a Pearl Harbor strike inescapable. 'When the Pacific War broke out,' however, 'Japan still faced the problem of disunity between its services' (Hata 1980: 208).

In Washington, on 21 June, Secretary Hull gave Ambassador Nomura a detailed oral statement of the US attitude – together with a draft proposal for the improvement of relations between the two countries. At dawn the following day German armies invaded Soviet territory. Presenting himself at the imperial palace with news of this latest turn of events, Matsuoka proposed to the emperor that 'Japan should cooperate with Germany and attack the Soviet Union,' temporarily refraining from action in the south. He warned, however, that ultimately Japan would 'have to fight simultaneously the Soviet Union, the United States and Britain.' The Emperor was 'alarmed,' but hoped that war could be avoided (Hosoya 1980: 94).

The ambiguities, frustrations, dilemmas and conflicts plaguing Japanese decision making surfaced again. At daily Liaison Conferences held the ensuing week, there were heated discussions over basic policy. Should Japan strike northward against the USSR? Or south as planned? 'Until the end of last year,' Matsuoka recalled,

> we thought of moving south and then north. We thought that by moving south, China would be taken care of, but it didn't work out. If we advance in the north and get, say, to Irkutsk, or even only half the distance, it would have an effect on Chiang Kai-shek, and I think an overall peace might ensue.

Tojo asked if Matsuoka thought it advisable to move north even though it meant 'giving up the struggle in China.' Matsuoka did think it advisable – although he conceded at a Liaison Conference a few days later that, if the high command persisted in its determination to strike south, he would acquiesce. 'I have forecast events several years in advance,' he said, 'and never missed the mark. I predict that touching the south will be a very serious move.'

On 2 July at last the Imperial Conference was convened, and a policy outline was adopted. In essence, it was southward offensive: a southward advance with the anticipation of hostilities against Anglo-American intervention and preparedness for attack on the Soviet Union contingent on the war in eastern Europe.

Previously Matsuoka had advocated a southern advance, but now he was switching to the north. 'A great man can change his mind,' he insisted. If Japan dealt with the USSR 'promptly,' he thought, the United States would probably not enter the war. (During the Tokyo war crimes trial after World War II, 'Matsuoka tried to defend himself by claiming that he had advocated an attack on the north knowing that the military would oppose it, a tactic that would help delay the Japanese attack in the south') (Berton 1980: 7; Hosoya 1980: 97–8).

Generally, an attack on the Soviet Union was favored by middle-level army officers and especially by young staff officers of the Kwantung army. In addition, Army Minister Tojo, who had advocated an aggressive policy toward the USSR all along, advocated a general staff proposal for Kwantung army maneuvers involving the mobilization of up to 850,000 men and a flotilla of ships loaded with troops, weapons, and supplies sailing toward Korean and Manchurian ports. The plan for these maneuvers had been drawn up under the supervision of operations division chief Shin'ichi Tanaka, who urged the intentional creation of a '"favourable opportunity" for an attack on the Soviet Union' while it was under attack by Germany. 'Even in Japan proper a general defense headquarters was established on July 12 and consideration given to instituting a system of air defense. . . . Japan was clearly on the brink of war with the Soviet Union' (Hosoya 1980: 97–9, 102–4).

How, then, in view of these developments – and with the German invasion of the USSR well underway – did Japanese leaders decide to move south and risk the almost certain triggering of a war against the United States instead? For one thing, the military affairs bureau of the Army Ministry opposed a northern attack in favor of an attack in the south, and the army general staff concluded that Japan should attack the USSR only if the total Soviet war potential in the Far East were reduced by one half as the result of troop transfers to the western front, which, as observed by the Japanese chief of staff and by the head of the Russia (fifth) section of the general staff, were not taking place on anything approaching such a scale. On the contrary, Soviet troops along the main front with Japan were reported as being strengthened.[1] And although German forces were progressing 'favorably,' their advance was thought by Japanese intelligence officers to be 'slowing down.' The probability of bringing the current German operation to a successful conclusion was viewed as 'diminishing' (Hosoya 1980: 102–3, 105–6).

Another part of the answer seems to have been associated with the army's desire to block Chinese access to supplies reaching them from the British by way of Burma and from French Indochina as steps toward closing down the war in China. An even more fundamental concern, however, was almost certainly the rising Japanese demand for the resources needed if the country's military and naval operations were to proceed successfully in either direction. 'Moss-covered tundras, vast barren deserts – of what use are they?' demanded vice-chief of the navy general staff Yoshimasa Nakahara as he persuasively advanced within the Navy General Staff his conviction 'that Japan's destiny lay to the south' (Tsunoda 1980: 241–2). Increasingly, 'the chain of events that seemed inevitable to many Japanese leaders was: occupation of French Indochina, leading to a more rigid American embargo, leading to a Japanese attack upon the Dutch East Indies, leading to war with the Allies, including the United States' (Scalapino 1980: 118–19). Yet even now the die had yet to be cast decisively.

The German invasion of the Soviet Union meant the collapse of

Matsuoka's ambition to form a four-power entente as a leverage to solve both the mounting friction with the United States and his country's unproductive struggles in China. In mid-July, Konoye resigned and was reappointed as the premier so as to replace Matsuoka by Admiral Toyoda, bearing in his mind that the expulsion of Matsuoka and the appointment of a navy representative as Foreign Minister would convince the US government of his serious commitment to negotiation (Nomura 1983: 216). What Japan did during the following weeks failed to reflect such an intention of Konoye, however, and tension between the two countries continued to increase until 7 December.

SOUTHERN ADVANCE AND CRITICAL EMBARGOES

Based on the imperial decision, Japan had decided to prepare, if necessary, for war with the United States and Britain (Ike 1967: 77–90; Nagaoka 1980: 236). On 21 July, the French government at Vichy, having allowed the Japanese garrisoning of air bases in northern Indochina the previous September (1940), yielded to Axis pressure by granting Japan 'the right to maintain troops and establish air and naval bases in southern Indo-China' (Yanaga 1949: 595; Butow 1961: 192, 122). When Japanese convoys left Hainan Island for Indochina on 25 July, the United States immediately froze Japanese assets in the country and established the Far East Command, headed by MacArthur in Manila.

On 1 August, Roosevelt imposed a complete embargo on the export of US oil, scrap iron, and other war-relevant materials upon which Japanese military and naval establishments had become critically dependent. In this connection, the advance into southern Indochina had been intended as leverage against the Netherlands East Indies, which had so far refused to sell petroleum to the Japanese. Under these circumstances, the embargo came as a grievous blow. Hostilities with the United States and Great Britain had been accepted as a likely eventuality, but the possibility of a US oil embargo had not been taken into serious account (Nomura 1983: 255). Yet with or without Dutch or US oil, the occupation of southern Indochina by Japanese forces looked more and more like a 'point of no return' (Iriye 1984: 63).

The freezing of Japanese assets by the United States and the cessation of US shipments of key materials left the Japanese economy 'in severe straits' and the country's war-making power 'directly threatened' (Russett 1972: 46). There was a disturbing realization, moreover, that whereas a northern war against the USSR was now 'virtually impossible' and a southern expedition 'virtually inevitable,' the United States was 'hardly likely to stand by while Japan helped itself to Borneo, Malaya, and the Dutch East Indies' (Kennedy 1987: 343).

As the summer of 1941 progressed, Japanese leaders told each other again and again that war would be risky – especially a long war – but each further delay in its initiation would only place them at an even greater disadvantage. The longer war was put off, army chief of staff Sugimoto asserted, the more unfavorable the armament ratio (between the United States and Japan) would be (Ike 1967: 234).

Prime Minister Konoye concluded that the empire must 'quickly prepare to meet any situation' that might occur and at the same time 'try to prevent the disaster of war by resorting to all possible diplomatic measures' (Ike 1967: 138). If by the early part of October there was still no prospect of the country's demands being met; the decision was that 'we shall immediately decide to open hostilities against the United States, Great Britain, and the Netherlands' (Butow 1961: 250). On 6 September the Imperial Conference was convened, and despite the emperor's tacit objection, the decision was made to prepare for war against the United States and the United Kingdom. But the debate continued.

THE OIL SQUEEZE

Time may have been running out for Japan, but the leadership continued for the better part of six months, nevertheless, to debate and waver. Because of its shortages of oil and other critical strategic materials, the empire was getting weaker, president of the Planning Board Suzuki told the fiftieth Liaison Conference on 3 September. 'By contrast,' he asserted, 'the enemy is getting stronger. With passage of time we will get increasingly weaker, and we won't be able to survive' (Ike 1967: 130–1).

Suzuki's assertion was not an overestimate. As determined retrospectively, Japan's national income for 1941 (1906 dollars) was $5.8 billion as compared with $184.3 billion for the United States and $16.0 billion for Britain. In per capita terms, the figures were $80.89 for Japan, $1,381.77 for the United States, and $331.85 for Britain. Japan's military expenditures for the year were $3.15 billion as compared with $11.13 billion for the United States and $744 million for Britain (1940). Military expenditures per capita for the three countries were $44.3, $83.6, and $15.6 (1940) respectively.

By the autumn of 1941 'Japanese leaders, rightly or wrongly, had come to believe that they were being pushed into a corner by the United States and her allies' (Ike 1967: xxiv). The problem concerned material resources. The country, 'traditionally dependent' on trade with Britain and the United States, was heavily reliant on foreign sources for supplying many of its vital resources. Since the China Incident, special efforts had been made to 'develop resources' in the areas Japan controlled and to increase production in these areas. But the country's dependence on the United States, Britain, and the Netherlands still remained. With the war between Germany and the Soviet Union, however, it was now vital to put an end to this reliance. It was a cornerstone of US policy for the defense of extensive American activities and interests in China – the fruits of its own commercial, cultural, and other expansions – that no country should obtain political control of China and that Chinese markets should remain open to all nations. Thus, ever since the Japanese invasion of China in 1937 and the extension of US aid to Chiang Kai-shek's Nationalist government, the two countries had been on a collision course. 'The United States demands that there be no discrimination in trade in the entire Pacific region including China,' Tojo would complain some weeks later, 'whereas Japan cannot agree to the demand unconditionally because of a problem of obtaining resources in China.' He added, however, that Japan would accept the US nondiscrimination policy if the same principle were observed worldwide.

Reference materials for discussion prepared after consultations between the government and the high command warned that, unless the United States changed its policy, the Japanese empire would be placed in a 'desperate situation,' where it must resort to war 'to defend itself and assure its preservation' (Ike 1967: 152).

Japanese leaders thought that they could bring the war in China to an end by offering generous concessions; they could withdraw Japanese troops from North China as the United States was demanding; and they could then 'settle back to profit economically from the new war in Europe', as they had done 'with such splendid results' during World War I. From a strictly utilitarian perspective this policy had much to be said for it. As perceived by some of the top leadership, however, withdrawal from China could mean severe loss of face and an open admission 'that the militarists' program of prosperity through conquest had failed.' The only satisfactory solution, from this viewpoint, was to 'break the economic blockade by war on the Western democracies' (Reischauer 1964: 192).

Increasingly, top figures in the Tokyo leadership saw an overriding, if subjective, 'utility' in their current course of action. If necessary, the country could impose trade relationships on Korea, Taiwan, Manchuria, and North China, but commerce with Britain and the United States was a two-way concern, and by the autumn of 1941 such possibilities had been foreclosed. In addition, just beyond the empire's perimeter there existed ample supplies of badly needed resources (Borton 1955: 364). But Foreign Minister Matsuoka had seen the United States and Britain 'encircling' and 'surrounding' the country, and Japanese leaders had warned again and again that the empire's 'existence' was at stake (Ike 1967: 12, 66, 101, 129, 135, 138, 148, 152, 212, 237, 282). The intensified perception of increasing threat from the outside, the oil squeeze, and a sense of time running out now forced Japanese leaders to see the range of available alternatives narrowing sharply (cf. Hermann 1969: 21–36).

The Japanese assessments of their own capabilities, relative to those of other major powers, remained confused and ambivalent. Seemingly, almost with each passing day, the 'time factor,' from a military point of view, was becoming ever more compelling. In a sense, the crucial problem confronting Japan at this time could be reduced to one simple factor – the oil squeeze. In 1940, 60 percent of Japan's supply had come from the United States, 'but since the freezing of Japanese funds in July 1941, no oil had been imported from America. Efforts had been made all along to build up stockpiles; but at best the supply of oil would last only eighteen months' (Borton 1955: 364; Ike 1967: 188). Each day of added delay meant an added expenditure of 12,000 tons of oil (Butow 1961: 243; Ike 1967: 186). The navy alone was consuming 400 tons of oil an hour.

The danger was great, however, that the United States would mobilize while oil and other vital resources became increasingly difficult for Japan to obtain. According to Admiral Nagano, the ratio of the Japanese fleet to that of the United States was 7.5 to 10, but only 60 percent of the US fleet was available in the Pacific, the rest being in the Atlantic. There was consequently a strong motivation for Japan to act quickly. As time went on US naval and air forces would 'improve remarkably,' and defensively Japan's three main adversaries – Britain, the United States, and the Netherlands – would grow stronger. By the autumn of 1942 'the increasing military preparedness of the United States Navy' would surpass the naval power of the Japanese empire, 'and we will finally be forced to surrender to the United States and Great Britain without a fight' (Ike 1967: 33, 154).

War Minister Tojo admitted to 'some uneasiness about a protracted war,' but how could Japan 'let the United States continue to do as she pleases'? Tojo is reported to have told Konoye that 'at some point during a man's lifetime he might find it necessary to jump with his eyes closed from the veranda of the Kiyomizu-dera' temple – the minister's way of asserting that 'he and others in the army believed that there were occasions when success or failure depended on the risks that one was prepared to take and that, for Japan, such an occasion had now arrived' (Butow 1961: 267).

BARGAINING AND LEVERAGING IN PURSUIT OF A DECISION

By mid-October, having reached an impasse in negotiations with the United States – partly because of the stubborn resistance of War Minister Tojo and partly because of obstructionist activities of pro-Axists and other extremists – Konoye resigned from the premiership, and two days later the Tojo cabinet was installed with a 'clean slate' mandate to undertake 'a thoroughgoing study of the situation' *without being bound by the Imperial Conference decision of 6 September* (Butow 1961: 301–2). If oil scarcity were a demon, then it appeared to be a demon which, paradoxically, only the 'demon war' seemed capable of exorcising. The problem of how to ensure resource access was becoming a near obsession. If war began in November, naval aircraft gasoline – including whatever might be obtained from the Netherlands East Indies – would last no more than 30 months, and with passage of time the supreme command's strategic position 'would deteriorate' (Ike 1967: 7, 138, 192, 202).

Tojo plunged immediately into what he subsequently referred to as 'the gravest crisis ever encountered in the history of Japan.' Filling the post of chief cabinet secretary was one of the new prime minister's early concerns; Tojo selected Hoshino, whom he had known in Manchuria sometime back and with whom he had served in Konoye's second cabinet. Serving as spokesmen for the supreme command, army and navy chiefs of staff 'requested' a prompt national review and a quick conclusion – with Admiral Nagano, reemphasizing that the navy alone was consuming 400 tons of oil per hour, underscoring the need for a speedy solution to the impasse (Butow 1961: 302, 314).

Almost daily Liaison Conferences were held throughout the remainder of October. During the Liaison Conferences of 24 and 25 October the 'northern question' was raised again. Question three on the agenda was: 'If we begin hostilities in the south this autumn, what situation will we face in the north?' The Foreign Ministry, the army, and the navy were largely in agreement on this issue. With the USSR fighting for survival against German troops in the west, there would be no aggressive action in the north during early phases of the war, but the United States might use Soviet bases, or, enticed by the United States and Britain, the Soviet Union 'might engage in machinations.' If the war should be prolonged, Japanese–Soviet hostilities could not be 'ruled out' (Ike 1967: 189).

By 30 October this much had been concluded; in the negotiations with the USA 'there was absolutely no prospect of Japan's being able to attain her current "minimum" demands.' If anything further were to be expected from the Washington negotiations, new proposals would have to be submitted. A war against the United States, Britain, and the Netherlands would enhance Chinese Nationalist resistance against Japan, but a southern thrust by the Japanese into Southeast Asia 'would subsequently result in a weakening of Nationalist morale and increased defections' to a Japanese puppet government that had been established in Nanking. There was no way to escape the oil–time dilemma (Butow 1961: 318–19).

Increasingly, the imperial leadership perceived the country's stakes rising, its most fundamental interests threatened, the range of alternatives narrowing, and the time available for effective action decreasing – all tendencies that tend to characterize crisis situations (Hermann 1969: 21–36).

The dilemma created by the unavoidable consumption of limited supplies of oil and the time required for naval operations continued to hover over the conference table 'like a demon.' Japanese leaders, old and new, 'never once asked themselves *why*' they confronted such a difficult choice. 'They did not look at the record or otherwise seek in past policies an explanation for present difficulties. . . . When agreement was fairly unanimous, it was easier to join the group than to cause trouble by insisting on further analysis.' If any member of the decision making group had 'attempted to probe deeply, he would very likely have been told not to quibble – not to raise frivolous objections. He might even have been thought a coward' (Butow 1961: 215).

DECISION – NOW OR NEVER

The sixty-sixth Liaison Conference of 1 November adopted a proposal that the deadline for negotiations was 1 December – with the proviso that diplomacy would continue in pursuit of one of two plans (Proposal A, the more complex and favorable to Japan, or Proposal B), and if one or the other were successful, war would be called off (Ike 1967: 200, 203). At this long session, which lasted from 9:00 a.m. on the 1st until 1:30 a.m. on the 2nd, Japanese leaders, civilian as well as military, were 'so imbued with the idea that war was preferable to any compromise' that they closed their eyes to the danger of the policy that was unfolding (Butow 1961: 320).

Finance Minister Kaya: 'Well, then, when can we go to war and win?'

Navy chief of staff Nagano: 'Now! The time for war will not come later' (Ike 1967: 202).

Japanese leaders 'did not deny that war was a gamble; they simply treated it as a gamble that had to be faced.' Japan might be defeated, but if the chance were not taken, the country might be defeated anyway. War was thus viewed as 'a now-or-never proposition' (Butow 1961: 320). There was no other realistic alternative.

Planning Board director Suzuki spoke up:

Kaya feels uneasy because we are short of materials. . . . But there is no reason to worry. In 1943 the materials situation will be much better if we go to war. We have just been told that with the passage of time the Supreme Command's strategic position will deteriorate. So we can conclude that it would be better to go to war now. (Ike 1967: 202)

Ultimate victory could not be regarded as certain, but if Japan were to hesitate, another opportunity would never present itself (Butow 1961: 320).

The second Imperial Conference in two months was called for 5 November to approve a war plan which only fueled further debate. This time a decision was reached to make war on both the United States and Great Britain and to invite the European Axis partners to join in the struggle. The issue whether or not to fight the Soviet Union was more difficult to resolve (Borton 1955: 369). 'While it is stated that our plans are to occupy the greater part of the South Pacific in about 100 days,' president of the Privy Council Hara noted,

> it is usual for predictions to turn out wrong. Although at the time of the Russo-Japanese War the capture of Port Arthur was expected to be accomplished in the summer . . . it was actually achieved on January 1 the following year. The same is true of German plans in the war between Germany and the Soviet Union. Although I believe that our Supreme Command's plan is most realistic, would you transfer some troops in the South to the North in case the war is prolonged . . . ? (Ike 1967: 234)

Under circumstances as they were unfolding, Japan's relations with the USSR remained a 'touchy' issue. On 6 November a protest was lodged with the Soviet Union over the sinking of the *Kehi Maru* by Soviet mines, and the USSR was disturbed, in turn, by renewal of the Anti-Comintern Pact a day before the Liaison Conference of 27 November. In Tokyo the decision was made to 'keep in mind the possibilities of arranging a peace between Germany and the Soviet Union . . . bringing the Soviet Union into the Axis camp . . . improving Japanese–Soviet relations . . . and encouraging the Soviets to push into Iran and India' (Ike 1967: 254–6).

At the Liaison Conference of 15 November, a document entitled 'Draft Proposal for Hastening the End of the War against the United States, Great Britain, the Netherlands, and Chiang' was presented. This amounted to a general 'war-guidance scheme' (Butow 1961: 328). Engaging in a 'quick war,' the empire would 'lure the main fleet of the United States' near Japan, destroy it, and demolish British bases in East Asia and the Southwest Pacific as well. In the meantime, Germany and Italy would be encouraged to carry out operations in the Near East, North Africa, and Suez; connections between Australia, India, and Britain would be broken and Britain blockaded and invaded (Ike 1967: 248–9). As long as Germany remained undefeated, 'the United States, it was felt, would not dare to concentrate much of her military might in the Pacific' (Reischauer 1970: 209–10). Prime Minister Tojo assured the conference that the 'first stage of the war' would not be difficult, but there was 'some uneasiness' about a protracted war.

On 17 November special Japanese envoy Saburo Kurusu arrived in Washington and was introduced to President Roosevelt (Feis 1950: 307). In discussions with Secretary of State Hull the following day, Ambassador Nomura put forward a proposal – without authorization from Tokyo (Ike 1967: 249) and as if it were his own – that, in order to avert immediate trouble, at least, the United States and Japan might reach a partial agreement restoring the situation between the two governments to what it had been prior to July when Japan had moved into southern Indochina, and the United States and Great Britain had imposed their embargo. According to this proposal, neither the United States nor Japan would make an armed advance into Southeast Asia and the South Pacific except for that part of Indochina where Japanese troops were already stationed. Upon restoration of peace between Japan and China, Japanese troops would be removed from Indochina. The United States and Japan would cooperate in the acquisition of resources and goods each needed from the Netherlands East Indies. The two governments would restore their commercial relations to those prevailing prior to the US freezing of Japanese assets, and the United States would supply Japan with 'a required quantity of oil.' The United States would also refrain from measures and actions prejudicial to the 'restoration of general peace between Japan and China' (Feis 1950: 307; cf. Proposal B, Ike 1967: 210).

On 17 November, Tojo, addressing an extraordinary session of the Diet, served notice that third powers 'were expected not to obstruct the conclusion of the China Incident' – an assertion amounting to a demand that the United States 'step aside to permit Japan to land the knock-out blow' (Butow 1961: 330–1). Three days later, Japanese negotiators presented Hull with the basic proposal: the two governments would agree that neither would undertake an armed advance into South Asia and the Western Pacific, except for Indochina, but would cooperate to assure the acquisition of materials that both needed from the Netherlands East Indies. Commercial relations between the United States and Japan would be mutually restored to the level that had existed before the freezing of assets, and the United States would agree to supply Japan with 'a required quantity of oil' (Ike 1967: 207–67). Hull's response, handed to Ambassador Kurusu on 26 November, made clear that it was up to the Japanese, who had adopted a program of force, to take the initiative by abandoning it. The Japanese leadership chose to interpret this response as an ultimatum, which it clearly was not (Yanaga 1949: 601). On the following day, 27 November, a unanimous agreement was reached 'that the decision for war should be confirmed at an Imperial Conference scheduled for December 1' (Butow 1961: 335–9).

DECISION CONFIRMED

The agenda for the Imperial Conference that would sanction war was agreed upon at the seventy-fourth Liaison Conference on 29 November. The question of what to do about the United States during the interval prior to the firing of the first shot remained unsettled, however. Discussions had to be continued as long as possible. Foreign Minister Shigenori Togo asked if there were enough time left to carry on diplomacy. 'We do have enough time,' navy chief of staff Nagano replied. Togo wanted to know when the fighting would start. 'Tell me what the zero hour is,' Togo demanded. 'Otherwise I can't carry on diplomacy.' Nagano complied. 'Well, then, I will tell you. The zero hour is –' he lowered his voice, 'December 8 [Tokyo time]' (Ike 1967: 260–2).

Arrangements were made for the emperor to consult with senior statesmen – specifically, the ex-premiers – who gathered at the palace on the morning of the 29th. Since Tojo refused to answer questions dealing with operational matters, 'the senior statesmen learned nothing at all about the projected naval strike against Pearl Harbor or about any other phase of Japan's war plans,' but the Prime Minister did explain why war with the United States and Great Britain 'could not be avoided.' After lunch the emperor, who had not been present during the morning session, 'spent an hour in the imperial study listening to the views of the ex-premiers.' First to speak, Baron Wakatsuki 'testified to his faith in the "spiritual strength" of the Japanese people but expressed concern over Japan's ability to fight a protracted war from the point of view of material.' Admiral Yonai urged that great care should be taken against 'going for broke in a single throw,' and Mr Hirota, 'the only former premier with practical diplomatic experience,' thought that 'the true intentions of parties engaged in diplomatic negotiations . . . only became clear after two or three crises had occurred.' He wondered, therefore, what purpose could be served 'by going to war immediately' (Butow 1961: 345–7).

When the Imperial Conference of 1 December convened, the Japanese task force 'whose mission was to attack Pearl Harbor had set sail, under sealed orders, from Hitokappu Bay in the remote Kuriles. . . . The issue of war or peace had been debated at length, and now it was time to formalize the decision.' In an opening statement, Prime Minister Tojo emphasized that the United States, Great Britain, the Netherlands, and China had 'increased their economic and military pressure against' Japan, and that the leadership had now reached a point where the situation could no longer be allowed to continue. 'Under the circumstances,' he asserted, 'our Empire has no alternative but to begin war against the United States, Great Britain and the Netherlands in order to resolve the present crisis and assure survival.' Foreign Minister Togo summarized his interpretation of Japanese–American negotiations, and questions were raised and comments offered by other participants in the conference. In response to doubts raised by president of the Privy Council Hara about the maintenance of domestic 'solidarity' during a long war, Prime Minister Tojo concluded with the assertion that the regime was 'prepared for a long war' but would do everything possible 'to bring the war to an early conclusion.' In the event of a long war, the leadership would do its utmost 'to keep the people tranquil, and particularly to maintain the social order, prevent social disorganization, and block foreign conspiracies' (Ike 1967: 271–2).

The Liaison Conference of 4 December approved a long note prepared by the Foreign Ministry and accusing the United States, Britain, and others of pursuing a dominant role in East Asia, destroying Japan's position there, and rendering further negotiations useless. Because of decoding delays in Washington, Japan's ambassador handed the note to Secretary of State Hull about an hour after the attack on Pearl Harbor.

Chapter 10

Modeling Japan's lateral pressure to World War II

This chapter looks at the interwar period from a quantitative perspective. The purpose of the inquiry is to identify recurrent patterns and processes that characterize the decades between World War I and World War II. Utilizing the same basic analytical structure and model presented in Chapter 6, we now ask, what can now be said about the underlying trends, the overall dynamics, the processes obscured by day-to-day stresses, tensions, and pressures for decision?

We would expect the transition from a developing (*epsilon*) state to an industrializing (*beta*) power to entail different patterns of external behaviour. Earlier we have discussed the pre-1914 phases of Japanese development in order to draw similarities and contrasts between Japan, on the one hand, and Britain, Germany, and tsarist Russia, on the other. The fact remains, however, that examining the pre-World War I and interwar periods separately may run the risk of obscuring feedback relationships and other statistically significant relationships that operate over long periods of time, persisting throughout the entire span of years between the Meiji Restoration and Pearl Harbor.

Although Japan's growing population and advancing technology consti-tuted a strong and continuing source of lateral pressure in the pre-World War I period, the influence of population 'drops out' when the interwar period is analyzed separately, without reference to the earlier, back-ground conditions. By contrast, however, the strong positive linkages and interconnection between imports and exports, significant after World War I, remain significant throughout; the greater the imports of raw materials (to a resource-poor Japan), the greater were the production possibilities of manufacture and exports of finished goods, the larger was the volume of goods produced for export, and the greater was the need (or demand) for raw materials. The apparent decline in the direct impact of imports of raw materials, however, so strong during the preceding period, reveals that other factors were becoming increas-ingly important throughout the interwar years. What we begin to see statistically is the new and significant influence – the crystallization

– of factors whose effects had been nonsignificant during the earlier period.

PIECES OF THE GROWTH AND EXPANSION PROCESS

Analysis of the quantitative materials shows a notable pattern; the linkages that appear strong over the span of 65 years can be described in terms of three dominant feedback processes which unfolded over time. These feedback relationships are generated – and set in motion – by domestic pressures.

First is the strong *positive feedback structure relating the imports of raw materials to the export of finished goods and generating ever greater demand for the import of raw materials*. Exports of finished goods earned foreign exchange that enabled the acquisition of raw materials; and raw materials were then transformed into finished goods to pay for more imports of raw materials. This relationship manifests a strong positive feedback loop: more imports, more exports, more imports, and so forth. If access to raw materials or markets were blocked from one source, another source of access had to be found. 'Exports make it possible to expand import capacity' (Minami 1986 253). This self-sustaining dynamic process was strong, positive, and statistically significant.

Second is a *dynamic feedback structure relating navy expenditures, colonial area, and imports from the colonies*.[1] Navy expenditures contributed to the expansion of colonial holdings, but sheer size of the colonies did not have the same expansionary effects on imports from the colonies (as the sign is negative). When considered in conjunction with the effect of imports from the colonies upon navy expenditures, on balance this negative link – constraining somewhat the spiraling conflict dynamics – contributes to a strong, positive, and statistically significant feedback loop. This dynamic process contributed to the militarism of the interwar period and to the enhanced budgetary allocation to the army and the navy.

These two dominant feedback relationships provide an empirical basis for the proposition that Japan was propelled into a conflict situation, with few countervailing influences. In the decades following 1914, the positive import – export loop generated a moderately stronger impact on navy expenditures. This effect was not statistically significant before 1914. It took shape during subsequent decades but receded in importance over the 65-year period in the sense of being overshadowed by other factors.[2] As long as trade 'worked,' the pressure for military investments was constrained (and did not grow). When trade relationships 'operated' effectively, they limited the tendencies toward armed conflict. As long as lateral pressure was manifested successfully in trade, military investments did not expand, and probabilities of armed conflict with the major powers were lessened. To the extent that trade dampened the spiral toward violent conflict, it served almost as a surrogate for military activities. Successful exports facilitated unimpeded imports, which contributed in turn to further exports. As this relationship persisted, there was no statistical evidence of links to military expenditures or to expansion in noncommercial modes. Trade, in such circumstances, emerged as the dominant mode of lateral pressure, and the imports–exports linkage continued as a self-propelled, but self-contained, process.[3]

Third is the consequent *feedback linkage relating military expenditures, colonial area, and imports from the colonies.* During the 1915–41 period national income (roughly connoting technological advancement, productivity, and the attendant higher demands for raw materials) and colonial area (indicating expansion due to lateral pressure and resultant acquisition of new resource bases) were significant in influencing colonial imports. The greater the military expenditures, moreover, the larger were the colonial areas and the greater the volume of imports from the colonies (and, with efforts at industrializing the colonies, especially Manchukuo, the greater was the demand for even more resources). In conjunction with the dynamic and strong positive feedback structures, this piece represents a weaker structure; however, although not statistically significant, it appears to hold the pieces of the process together.

CHARACTERISTICS OF A *BETA* POWER

During the interwar period two distinct dynamic relationships characterized as feedback loops crystallized: trade linkages and military linkages relating to colonial expansion and imports from the colonies. Domestic economic factors – notably national income (an indicator for technological advancement) – generated new demands and pressures leading to imports from the colonies (and thus the 'need' for territorial expansion). The export of finished goods became indispensable, in turn, as a source of foreign exchange to pay for imports – especially from noncolonial sources. Closely related to this nexus were increases in expenditures for sustaining the army and navy forces required if colonies were to be acquired and maintained. Figure 10.1 shows the results for the *beta* profile of Japan during the interwar period.

While the process of colonial expansion was strong throughout the 65 years leading up to Pearl Harbor, Japan extended its colonial holdings almost unimpeded after World War I. Over 70 percent of the variance in colonial expansion is explained during the interwar years as the 'lurching' process described in Chapter 5 tended to 'smooth out' with continued expansion. For the later years military expenditures were also significant, which responded in part to perceived threats and contributed to territorial acquisition. For the entire period from the Meiji Restoration to war in 1941, military expenditures and raw materials imports, roughly representing force capabilities and demands that could not be satisfied domestically (together with other variables), explain 69 percent of the variance in colonial territory.

Directly or indirectly, other variables affected the two feedback loops. Population size, through rising demands, contributed to imports of raw materials and national income variables, and the industrial labor force shaped the export of finished goods, especially in earlier years. Merchant marine as an indicator of a specialized capability was also significant. All these variables provided strong, persistent, and regular influences on Japan's overall characteristics; they were not periodic or erratic in their effects.[4] See Figure 10.2.

Both government revenue and imports from the colonies become significant factors in Japan's *beta* profile. Together with colonial area, imports from the colonies shaped governmental expenditures directly – colonial area remaining a significant factor pushing for greater government expenditures for colonial administration throughout the entire period. Between 1915 and 1941 the explanatory power of the equation increases substantially to account for over 90 percent of the variance.

The linkage between imports of raw materials and exports of finished goods was tight. Whereas prior to 1915 Japan's essential imports were used primarily for meeting domestic consumption needs, after 1915 the country's imports of raw materials were used increasingly as initial inputs for producing goods to be exported by Japan. And exports led directly

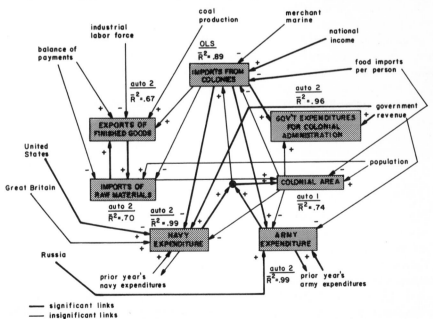

Figure 10.1 Robust linkages, 1915–41

to growth. This strong, significant feedback loop was a dominant feature of Japan in its *beta* profile phase during the 1915–41 period. Sixty-seven percent of the variance in exports of finished goods for 1915–41 is explained by these factors. Between the two world wars exports of finished goods are a significant determinant of raw materials imports. And for the entire period, over 80 percent of the variance in imports of raw materials is explained by population, exports of finished goods, and the previous year's balance of payments.

MILITARY EXPENDITURES AND EXTERNAL EXPANSION

From the Meiji Restoration until 1941, Japan – emulating Britain, France, Germany, and other countries of the West – relied increasingly on military (and naval) leverages and the acquisition of colonies as a means of assuring and protecting access to raw materials and markets. It is therefore not surprising to find that army and navy expenditures influenced imports from the colonies, which in turn necessitated greater army (beginning in the earlier period) and navy (increasingly in the later period) expenditures. For the span of the entire period until 1941, over 90 percent of the variance in army expenditures is accounted for by the variables in the equation.

Japan's army expenditures – in response to Russian/Soviet expenditures, past army expenditures, government revenue, colonial area, and percentage of total imports obtained from the colonies – continued to grow. During the interwar years imports from colonies, past army expenditures, and Russian/Soviet military expenditures were significant positive predictors of Japanese army expenditures. Imports from the colonies overshadowed the earlier significance of government revenue and became a dramatic push factor strongly influencing levels of army expenditures.[5]

During this period government revenue provides a significant basis for the expansion of military expenditures. The higher the financial resources available to the government, the larger were the allocations to the military. This relationship provides further evidence of strong, self-propelling dynamics for expansion.

Naval expenditures

Trends in Japan's navy expenditures deserve special attention for the span of the entire period between 1878 and 1941. It is clear that Japan's allocations to the navy can best be explained by government revenue, past naval expenditures, and US naval expenditures – all pushing Japanese navy expenditures upward. Dampening, or countervailing, influences were provided by raw materials imports and by colonial area. During the interwar period US naval expenditures became particularly salient, as did the level of raw materials imports, imports from colonies, and government revenues, as well as the bureaucratic factors (previous year's allocations).

US navy expenditures constituted the single most powerful influence on Japan's naval expenditures (other than Japan's own commitments to its navy in previous years) during the 1915–41 period. The impacts of the United States as a perceived adversary during the interwar period are thus significant. Conversely, raw materials imports, colonial area, and imports from the colonies all exerted a negative dampening influence on naval expenditures, reflecting Japan's success in obtaining resources from its colonies. This factor is important to the extent that it indicates a 'downward escalator' operating at the time. On this basis we infer that navy expenditures also take shape as a *consequence* of imports from the colonies and not as a cause.[6]

External expansion and military competition

From the late nineteenth century the expanding activities and interests of Japan – including colonial acquisitions – increasingly intersected with the expanding activities and interests of other countries, notably Russia/the USSR, Great Britain, and the United States. Insofar as the Japanese associated threats to raw material and market access with particular adversaries, Russia/USSR emerged in the long run as the major determinant of Japanese army expenditures, whereas the United States increasingly after World War I became the major threat influencing Japan's navy expenditures. During the early decades of the entire period, in these terms, tsarist Russia was the main adversary, but during the late 1920s and the 1930s the USA as an adversary became increasingly salient, although the USSR remained a prime land target. In sum, Russian *army* expenditures and US *navy* expenditures each significantly affected Japanese army and navy expenditures (based on the significance of the 'adversary' variable).

Army and navy expenditures generated the usual upward spirals inherent in arms race dynamics, fueled further by perceptions of the United States and Russia/USSR as the arch-enemies. Compared with the relatively quiescent nineteenth century (Japan not being seriously threatened by China in 1894–5), and with allowances for the Russo-Japanese War and the relative quiet of the 'liberal interlude,' the interwar period was characterized by increasing reliance on negative leverages and concomitant increases in military expenditures.

Notable during pre-World War I decades was the impact of Japan's government revenues on army allocations (reflecting Japan's concern for its Russian adversary which, during the 1930s, led to articulation of the 'northern strategy'). In advance of Pearl Harbor, however, government revenue shifted to exert a significant impact on navy expenditures, an indicator of the development of Japan's competing 'southern strategy.'

During the decades prior to World War II it was US navy expenditures that provided the impetus for greater allocations by Japan to its own navy expenditures, whereas, by contrast, British expenditures were not a significant influence. (See Figure 10.2 for a comparison of strong results during three periods: prior to World War I, during the interwar period, and throughout the entire period from the Meiji Restoration to World War II.)

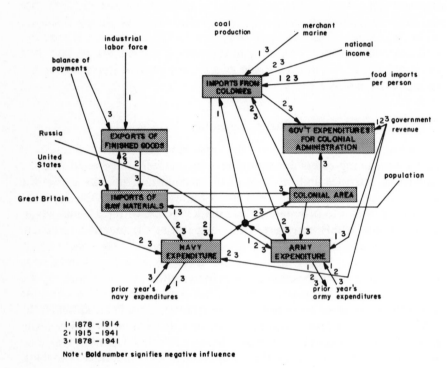

Figure 10.2   All links, 1878–1941

Chapter 11

Comparing lateral pressure processes
World War I and World War II

In Japan the overall development process seems to support the proposition that population growth and rapid modernization and industrialization contributed to substantial increases in armament capability, investment in the military and colonial expansion, and varying degrees of intermittent warfare. From the perspective of quantitative analysis, the system of simultaneous equations represents the processes in question – exports, imports, military expenditures, colonial expansion – accounting for the historical record successfully. Although many questions remain unanswered, and despite complex interactions among the endogenous variables in the interwar period, overall the country's external expansion was clearly shaped by the growing weight of domestic factors. Japanese leaders used the country's expanding military capabilities as leverage for territorial occupation, the establishment of spheres of influence, and ensured access to the raw materials and markets of mainland Asia.

Theoretically, in the system of simultaneous equations depicting the case of Japan, there may be several causal paths between an exogenous variable and an endogenous variable, and the interactive feedback loops may be expected to complicate the individual relationships. In order to assess the total influence of a particular variable (such as army expenditure) on another (such as imports from colonies), the various ways in which the relationship takes place must be taken into consideration.[1]

In order to improve our understanding of growth and expansion, we have examined both *direct* and *indirect* factors that have influenced Japan's activities during the earlier phase (the *epsilon* years) and the later phase (the *beta* years). Population thus had a direct impact on colonial acquisitions as well as an indirect impact on imports from the colonies (because of its direct effect on colonial acquisitions, which in turn influence imports from the colonies). Similarly the colonial area had a direct impact on imports from the colonies (positive) as well as an indirect effect on navy expenditures (through its effects on increasing

Table 11.1 Direct and indirect impact matrix based on path coefficients, 1878–1914

IMPACT OF	ON Exports of finished goods	Imports of raw materials	Army expend- itures	Navy expend- itures	Colonial area	Imports from colonies	Government expenditures (overseas)
Exports of finished goods	1.10	0.51	0.11	0.15	0.45	−0.19	0.07
Imports of raw materials	0.50	1.25	0.27	0.36	1.09	−0.46	0.16
Army expenditures	0.02	0.04	0.80	−0.03	0.16	−0.31	−0.02
Navy expenditures	0.02	0.04	−0.20	0.97	0.16	−0.31	−0.02
Colonial area	0.03	0.05	0.33	0.19	1.13	−0.42	0.17
Imports from colonies	−0.05	−0.08	0.71	0.18	0.09	0.66	0.13
Government expend- itures (overseas)	0.00	0.00	0.00	0.00	0.00	0.00	1.00
Industrial labor force	0.45	0.19	0.04	0.06	0.17	−0.07	0.02
Coal production	0.29	0.12	0.03	0.04	0.11	−0.05	0.02
Balance of payment (t–1)	0.00	0.05	0.01	0.02	0.05	−0.02	0.01
Home population	0.43	1.08	0.26	0.33	1.02	−0.42	0.15
Russian military expenditures	0.01	0.02	0.38	−0.02	0.08	−0.15	−0.01
US military expenditures	−0.01	−0.02	0.09	−0.42	−0.07	0.13	−0.01
UK military expenditures	0	0	0	0	0	0	0
Food imports per capita	0.00	0.00	−0.14	−0.05	−0.17	−0.03	−0.04
Merchant marine tonnage	−0.07	−0.11	0.95	0.24	0.12	0.89	0.18
National income	−0.01	−0.01	0.07	0.02	0.01	0.07	0.01
Government revenue	−0.05	−0.08	−1.57	−0.04	−0.36	0.69	0.56
Army expenditures (t–1)	0.03	0.04	0.87	−0.04	0.17	−0.34	−0.02
Navy expenditures (t–1)	0.02	0.03	−0.15	0.75	0.12	−0.24	−0.01

imports from the colonies). (These results should be seen in the context of the evidence presented in the Appendices as well.)

The direct and indirect effects among variables measuring growth, expansion, and military allocations are shown in Tables 11.1 and 11.2.[2] Prior to World War I, for example, the impact of trade on colonial expansion was

Table 11.2 Direct and indirect impact matrix based on path coefficients, 1915–1941

IMPACT OF	ON Exports of finished goods	Imports of raw materials	Army expend- itures	Navy expend- itures	Colonial area	Imports from colonies	Government expenditures (overseas)
Exports of finished goods	1.69	1.12	−0.02	−0.12	0.12	−0.06	−0.02
Imports of raw materials	1.06	1.72	−0.04	−0.18	0.19	−0.10	−0.03
Army expenditures	0.05	0.12	0.91	0.07	0.51	−0.24	−0.07
Navy expenditures	0.05	0.12	−0.09	1.00	0.51	−0.24	−0.07
Colonial area	0.10	0.23	−0.17	0.00	0.95	−0.47	−0.14
imports from colonies	−0.22	−0.50	0.16	−0.07	−0.04	1.02	0.38
Government expend- itures (overseas)	0.00	0.00	0.00	0.00	0.00	0.00	1.00
Industrial labor force	−0.30	−0.02	0.00	0.02	−0.02	0.01	0.00
Coal production	0.64	0.43	−0.01	−0.05	0.05	−0.02	−0.01
Balance of payment ($t-1$)	0.12	0.03	0.00	−0.00	0.00	−0.00	0.00
Home population	0.50	0.84	−0.08	−0.08	0.43	−0.21	−0.06
USSR military expenditures	0.03	0.07	0.55	0.00	0.31	−0.15	−0.05
US military expenditures	0.01	0.01	−0.01	0.12	0.06	−0.03	−0.01
UK military expenditures	0.01	0.01	−0.00	0.06	0.03	−0.01	0.00
Food imports per capita	0.06	0.13	−0.03	0.02	−0.08	−0.27	−0.10
Merchant marine tonnage	0.00	0.01	0.00	0.00	0.00	−0.02	−0.01
National income	−0.31	−0.72	0.23	−0.10	−0.06	1.47	0.54
Government revenue	0.03	0.07	−0.27	0.81	0.30	−0.14	0.58
Army expenditures ($t-1$)	0.08	0.07	0.52	0.00	0.30	−0.14	−0.04
Navy expenditures ($t-1$)	0.14	0.02	−0.02	0.20	0.10	−0.85	−0.01

pronounced, whereas during the interwar period the influence of military allocations on colonial dynamics was more prominent. In both periods, interdependence between the trade variables was high. The display of coefficients in these tables shows, as we have presented earlier, the linkage between the three sets of dynamic feedback processes and shows that these processes operated in the pre-World War I period and in the interwar period.

First is imports–exports, linking imports of raw materials and exports of finished goods.

Second is military–expansion, relating navy expenditures, colonial area, and imports from the colonies.

And third is military–colonial imports, which links military expenditures (that is, the combined army and navy expenditures) and imports from the colonies.

During the 1915–41 period, when Japan's transition to a *beta* profile was accomplished, the military and colonial relationships were highly interdependent, but trade did not have much influence on these other factors. It was during the latter part of this period, of course, that Japan was involved in its vicious cycle of military engagements with and invasions of Manchuria and China proper. These three sets of relationships are shown for the two different periods in Figures 11.1 and 11.2 respectively. In Figures 11.3 and 11.4, only the strong coefficients are presented. For both the earlier period, when Japan was developing from a traditional society to an industrializing state, and the later period (1915–1941), when Japan became fully industrialized and expansionist, several exogenous variables have particularly strong influences on the model as a whole and on its individual endogenous variables. These exogenous variables, which seem to drive, or shape, the Japan model, are population, national income, merchant marine, and (lagged) army and navy expenditures.[3]

Among the factors that were found to be strongly influential during *both* phases of Japanese development, both periods, were the production of coal and government revenue – the first showing the continued efforts to extract or squeeze out valuable resources, and the other underscoring the government's own financial resources available for the pursuit of its objectives. In the earlier years, Japan's domestic population and merchant marine tonnage were the two most influential variables driving the system, whereas in the later period national income, government revenue, and domestic population were the more influential exogenous factors.

Population (before World War I) and national income (before World War II) have direct and/or indirect impacts on all modes of lateral pressure, that is, trade, military, and colonial expansion. During the earlier period colonial area acquisitions were driven by imports of raw materials, and imports from the colonies, in turn, led to army expenditures. But during the interwar years, *only* the military variables directly affected colonial area. Japan's competition with the Soviet Union was an important factor in the Japanese army buildup and expansion into Manchuria and China proper. And Russian influence on army expenditures in both periods and on colonial area in the later period are especially apparent.

SOURCES OF LATERAL PRESSURE: THE MASTER VARIABLES

The analysis highlights how domestic growth is 'causally' related to – and results in – Japanese external expansion and how expansion had multiple and identifiable roots, channels, and relative impacts. Clearly, no single variable can be thought of as the source of all the external pressures. We are still confronted, however, by the need to isolate the root elements, and there are some observable patterns. Below are the *direct* coefficients. They are not those presented in Table 11.1 and 11.2.

Population

Japan's population had a significant impact upon imports of raw materials and upon colonial expansion. For the earlier and later periods, the coefficients measuring the direct impact of population on raw material imports were 0.86 and 0.44 respectively. Pressures from population creating demand for raw materials were greater prior to World War I than during the interwar period. The coefficients for the impact of population on colonial area for the same two periods were 0.07 and 0.36 respectively, the impact being greater throughout the interwar period when Japan's population grew by 28 million as opposed to 18 million during the earlier period.

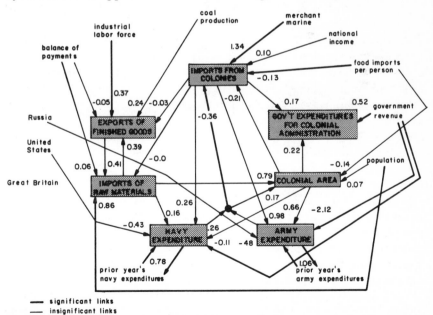

Figure 11.1 Normalized beta coefficients, 1878–1914

Raw materials in general appear to have been a major Japanese concern during the first period, whereas *particular* raw materials, especially oil, became more important during the 1930s and 1940s – in large part because of increasing military demand.

Population was influential in a different way at different points in time. Throughout the earlier period, population influenced the imports of raw materials more than the acquisition of colonial area. Subsequently, during the interwar period, the impact of population on expanding colonial area increased and was more influential than in the earlier period. Nonetheless, the influence of population on imports of raw materials persisted throughout.[4]

Technology and national income

While leaving much to be desired as an indicator of technological development, national income generally connotes the degree of economic performance and development. The relevant coefficients show that the only remarkable impact of national income is on imports from the colonies during the interwar period. The impact of national income is positive, that is, the higher the increase, the greater are the resulting effects on the system as a whole. The negative, or dampening, effects of national income during this period are on finished goods exports, on imports of raw materials, and, to a lesser degree, on colonial area. In isolation, therefore, these results

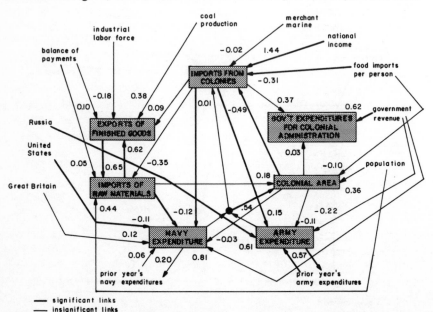

Figure 11.2   Normalized beta coefficients, 1915–41

indicate that the direct impact of internal growth (represented by national income) was immediately influential in the growth of expenditures on the army, on colonial area, and on imports from the colonies.

As income grew, however, its direct impacts on exports and imports, on army expenditures, and on colonial acquisitions led to a dampening effect. By the same token, as income slowed down, the effects on these factors were positive – pushing for greater imports and exports, higher navy expenditures, and more colonial acquisitions. The total impacts of national income on the endogenous variables in the model are as follows:

	Before 1914	Before 1941
Exports of finished goods	−0.01	−0.31
Imports of raw materials	−0.01	−0.72
Army expenditures	0.07	0.23
Navy expenditures	0.02	0.10
Colonial area	0.01	0.06
Imports from colonies	0.07	1.47
Government expenditures for overseas colonies	0.01	0.54

These patterns show, again, that the greater the domestic productivity, the more extensive was Japan's dependence on its colonies as suppliers of

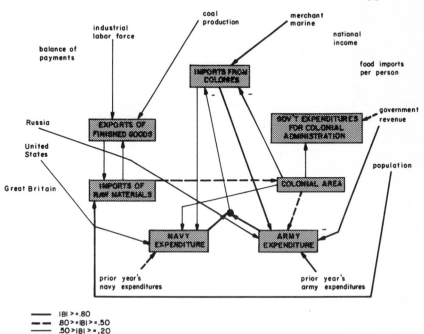

Figure 11.3 Robust linkages, 1878–1914

resources and raw materials, and the greater were the expenditures for colonial administration.[5]

RESOURCES AND TRADE

Imports of raw materials

Imports of raw materials from the colonies have been very important for Japan as a measure of the country's serious domestic resource constraints. Raw materials inputs have *direct* impacts on three variables – exports of finished goods, navy expenditures, and colonial area. We see evidence of the structure of lateral pressure in Japan; resource constraints lead to imports of raw materials, leading in turn to exports of finished goods, which then require further imports of raw materials. Imports of raw material, therefore, create pressures for increasing navy expenditures, which then contribute to colonial acquisitions. Such additions to territory significantly influence expenditures for colonial administration.

The roots of this process are to be found in the domestic population and the industrial labor force. Both variables are exogenous to the system as a whole, but shape it significantly by influencing the direction and magnitude of outcomes and effects on other variables indicating expansion and competition.

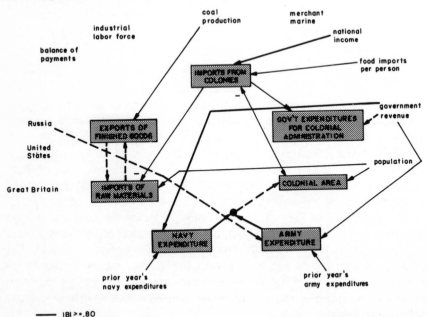

Figure 11.4   Robust linkages, 1915–41

The coefficients indicating the *direct* impact of raw materials imports on each of these three other endogenous variables are as follows:[6]

	Before 1914	Before 1941
Export of finished goods	0.39	0.62
Navy expenditures	0.16	−0.11
Colonial area	0.79	0.18

When the interdependence of the endogenous variables is taken into account, the *indirect* influence of raw materials imports becomes more clearly observable, and takes into account the various 'paths' through other intervening variables as well. (For example, there is no direct effect of imports of raw materials on government expenditures for colonial administration; however, there is an impact through the intervening variable of colonial area – see Figure 11.4 for illustration.) The total influence is summarized through the following coefficient values:

	Before 1914	Before 1941
Export of finished goods	0.50	1.06
Navy expenditures	0.36	−0.18
Colonial area	1.09	0.19

The *indirect* impact of raw materials imports on the other endogenous variables in the model is as follows:

	Before 1914	Before 1941
Army expenditures	0.27	−0.04
Imports from the colonies	−1.46	−0.10
Government expenditures for colonial administration	0.16	−0.03

We infer, therefore, that the demand for resources, met through importing from the colonies, influenced colonial expansion during the earlier period and was highly interactive with exports of finished goods throughout the entire period leading to 1941. Other links were not as strong except for the moderate impact of these processes on military buildup. In the later period (between 1915 and 1941), the strength of the feedback loop linking imports of raw materials to exports of finished goods is pronounced. This linkage represents the rationale for Japanese foreign activities and foreign policy. Again, exports were essential for growth, and raw materials were essential for producing finished goods for export. The greater the amount of exported goods, the greater was the demand for raw materials. Because Japan had no significant amounts of raw materials domestically, imports were a necessary solution. The statistics strongly reflect this Japanese reality.

Exports of finished goods

Since Japan relied upon the export of finished goods to pay for the import of raw materials required by its industries, we would expect the analysis to show the effect of the export of finished goods – as a function of industrial product – on other variables in the model. The *direct* impacts of finished goods exports are as follows:

	Before 1914	Before 1941
Imports of raw materials	0.51	1.12
Army expenditures	0.11	−0.02
Navy expenditures	0.15	−0.12
Colonial area	0.45	0.12
Imports from colonies	−0.19	−0.06
Government expenditures for overseas colonies	0.07	−0.02

The negative coefficients can be interpreted as dampening (or tension-reducing) effects; during the earlier period the exports of finished goods influenced all the other variables noted here, pushing the system toward military allocation, colonial expansion, imports, and expenditures on the colonies. During the later years we see some dampening effects in that exports of finished goods did not contribute to greater military expenditures, but rather to lower allocations. This means that the impact from finished goods exports was negative (though weak), and not that the level of military expenditures was lower. This is the source of the dampening effects we see in the model; by the second period there were some 'brakes' in the system, or 'downward escalators,' but they were not strong enough to control the spiraling system and underlying pressures toward conflict.

An example of the increased pressures pushing the system toward conflict can be seen in the comparison of the influence of exports of finished goods on raw materials imports during the earlier and during the later periods. The interwar years witnessed twice as much impact of finished goods exports on actual demand for raw materials imports as the prewar years, and the influence was strong and positive.

PATHS TO WAR

Japan responded to many pressures – real as well as perceptual. From an actual or statistical point of view, the country was characterized by a variety of pressures pushing for expansion of activities and interests beyond home frontiers and for larger allocations of resources required by the military and the colonial administrations in order to ensure territorial control. Treated as an exogenous variable, population generated strong demands for raw materials imports in the earlier period and, by influencing territorial expansion, later as well. Subsequently, during the interwar period, the important demographic factor was the size of the industrial labor force (a variable that had significant positive impact on the exports of finished goods). Technology, as indicated by national income, also exerted both direct and indirect influences on external expansion – generating more allocations for the military, more demands for territory, and more demands for imports from the colonies. But technology also had dampening effects, notably on exports of finished goods, imports of raw materials, and to a lesser degree on colonial area (especially during the interwar period).

The period before World War I saw lateral pressure expressed in terms of both industrial growth and territorial expansion. In the formative years of the Meiji Restoration, this expansion – as generated by population growth leading to raw materials imports and technological advances indicated by exports of finished goods – directly influenced military buildup and colonial expansion. During the interwar period, when expansion was even greater, the already positive import–export feedback relationship strengthened over time.

Insofar as trade was inadequate, military leverages (indicated by army expenditures) led to colonial acquisitions (including controlled access to resources), which led, in turn, to higher navy allocations (leverage for the defense of colonies and sea routes). Identified as primary adversaries were those countries that the Japanese perceived as blocking (or threatening to block) their safe access to resources and/or markets – whether through normal trade or as a consequence of colonial expansion. The dynamics of Japanese growth, development, and expansion were such that a strong endogenous and self-propelling element – a kind of governmental inertia – was built into the system in that the strongest impact on military expenditures (dating from the earlier period) was exerted by Japan's own government revenues (that is, the strong influence on each year's allocation of the previous year's allocation).

The trade–security links were clearly in evidence. One of the most distinctive features throughout the overall period under scrutiny was the feedback relationship between exports of finished goods and imports of raw materials – the latter being constrained by the former. Continued success in exporting manufactured goods was an important factor diverting expanding Japanese activities and interests *somewhat away* from military action – a trend that became stronger during the interwar period. Thus, in conjunction with the self-propelling element (bureaucratic inertias 'built into' military allocations), the shorter-term positive feedback import–export loop served as a partial 'downward' escalator. Meanwhile, a second impulse constraining army (and navy) spending to a degree resulted from the country's *successful* colonial expansion – a tendency countervailing military competition with other powers to some extent – although the drift toward war continued.

These patterns suggest the following processes relating territorial expansion to international conflict and war. A growing population (combined with an advancing technology) generated increasing demands. Since these demands could not be satisfied by domestic resources, the Japanese found themselves caught in a *tight positive feedback loop*; the acquisition of more imports (raw materials) required the export of more finished goods (to pay for imports). Effective trade (at least sufficient exports to pay for imports), which was a critical variable in this situation, became the prime manifestation of lateral pressure (the expansion of activities and interests beyond home frontiers).

Chapter 12

Simulating growth and expansion
Paths to war

In this chapter we explore the reliability of the model and the results in representing the actual historical processes. How can we ascertain whether or not our conclusions are correct? Conducting a dynamic simulation of the modeled processes described in the previous chapters, and then exploring the counterfactual – what would have happened if . . . ? – provides a related and especially important dimension of analysis.[1] Simulation of historical processes can be a powerful method for exploring what may have transpired as various interactions and dynamic feedback processes evolve over time.

SIMULATING GROWTH AND EXPANSION

In a dynamic simulation all the dependent (endogenous) variables are simulated simultaneously. A forecast of colonial area, for example, would use the historical or known values for all the exogenous variables in the colonial area equation along with the coefficient estimates from the equation – as well as simultaneously simulated endogenous variables such as military expenditures.[2]

To simulate a dynamic system is usually much more difficult than to forecast a single equation. Errors may accumulate across equations when jointly dependent (that is, endogenous) variables are simulated, causing iteration values to oscillate and even diverge. In this chapter, simulation techniques and quantitative data are used in order to see how accurately the model could predict known observations of Japan's colonial area, imports of raw materials, exports of finished goods, army and navy expenditures, and allocations for governing the colonies. The simulation is then exercised by raising questions of an 'if . . . then . . .' nature – systematically inserting changes in the model and observing the outcomes. The findings reveal in some part the fit of the theory and data and the extent to which Japan's growth and expansion from the years immediately following the Meiji Restoration to war in 1941 have been successfully represented.

Effective simulation depends on the success of the analyst in obtaining coefficient estimates that are robust and valid. These parameter estimates (the coefficients) are then combined with historical or known data for the exogenous variables at the starting date so that the initial values of the endogenous variables can be predicted. Thereafter, the procedure continues through the use of *simulated* values for all endogenous variables.[3] Because a simulation involves all equations and estimates of the jointly dependent variables without recourse to their historical or known values, it is self-contained, allowing for a fairly controlled method of varying parameters and observing the implications of the system as a whole.[4] Simulation requires four types of information: the structure of the model itself, historical or known values for the initial endogenous values for the variables, data for the exogenous variables, and constant files (coefficients and parameters that have been estimated earlier).[5]

The model for the Japan case is composed of a set of simultaneous equations presented in Chapter 6 and analyzed in Chapters 5 and 6 (for the period before World War I) and 10 and 11 (before World War II).[6] In the course of estimating the parameters of the model it became clear that there were indeed significant differences between the earlier (pre-World War I) and later (interwar) years; we therefore incorporated these differences in the structure of the simulation. Simulation for the period 1878–1941 was done with two sets of coefficients, one generated by the 1878–1914 period and one derived from estimates from the 1915–41 period. These are the coefficients described in presenting the results of the estimations for before World War I and during the interwar years. The results of the simulation for the seven *jointly dependent* variables, the endogenous variables, in the system of simultaneous equations, reveal how the system can be reproduced by the explanatory variables.

The simulations turned out to be strikingly close to the historical record, but in some cases the simulation 'overshoots' actual data, indicating that the dynamics of the model push the endogenous variable to a greater degree than is warranted when compared with the actual data – the 'reality' that serves as our reference point. In other situations, the simulation 'undershoots,' signaling that the estimated coefficients are weaker than would be required to represent reality more accurately, or that some important explanatory variable has been omitted at the estimation stage earlier. Although our discussion of the simulation presented below proceeds equation by equation, the results are based on the *complete system simulation.*

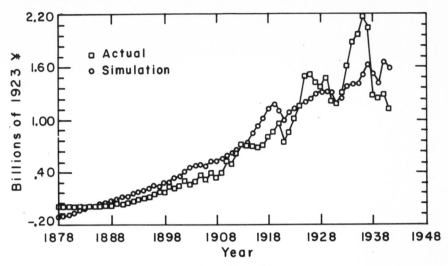

Figure 12.1   Simulation: imports of raw materials

IMPORTS OF RAW MATERIALS

Over time there is a notable shift in the simulation of Japan's imports of raw materials. During earlier decades the simulation overshoots its empirical referent, thus indicating that the model 'generates' more lateral pressure than would be necessary to reproduce reality. This was a period when the key coefficients were statistically significant – particularly the effect of home population. After World War I there is a systematic underestimation in simulating imports of raw materials; the model does not generate as much lateral pressure as historical reality produced at that time – see Figure 12.1. The empirical (actual) observations for imports of raw materials in this post-World War I period are consistently higher than the simulation. Although the major peaks are not fully reproduced, the slight trough, or decline, in imports during the early 1920s is well simulated. The subsequent growth of raw materials imports is also captured rather successfully. The growth in actual imports of raw materials from 1920 to 1935 is generally in excess of the simulated trend, followed by a dramatic drop in imports from then until 1941. This pattern reflects the increasing reliance of the Japanese empire upon oil from the Netherlands East Indies, Mexico, and the United States, which was also a major source of scrap iron and other strategic materials, whereas the sharp decline in the imports of raw materials in the mid-1930s is a dramatic illustration of the trade constraints imposed on Japan at the time. The imports simulated show a smoother line than the historical trend, and a higher end-point by 1940–1. The simulated trend can be interpreted in terms of the imports of raw materials that had been generated by domestic demands and export capabilities.

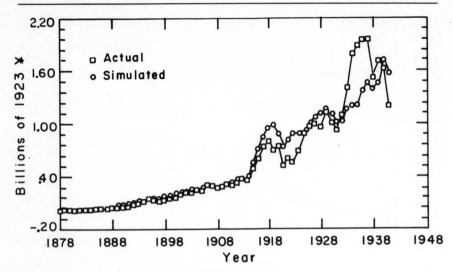

Figure 12.2 Simulation: exports of finished goods

In sum, then, the model somewhat overestimates raw materials imports until the end of World War I, and then seriously underestimates them; the actual pressures for imports were much greater than the model was able to reproduce.

EXPORTS OF FINISHED GOODS

Prior to 1914 the simulation of exports of finished goods is nearly perfect. This means that the explanatory variables – exogenous variables (population, coal production, industrial labor force, balance of payments) and endogenous variables (imports from the colonies and imports of raw materials) – fully explain the exports of finished goods. But there is some divergence in the post World War I period; until the mid-1930s the simulation overshoots reality, but subsequently there is a notable undershooting. Our explanation for exports of finished goods is somewhat incomplete for the years immediately preceding war in 1941, and some significant factors are not included in the model – see Figure 12.2.

The simulation underestimated the domestic sources of lateral pressure in the trade mode from about 1925 onward. The actual (historical) push for exports was stronger by far than that reproduced and explained by the model. During the late 1920s and early 1930s the United States was one of Japan's largest markets. Since the historical trend of exports was much greater than the simulated trend for those years, we can discern once again the heavy reliance of Japan on exports of foreign trade above and beyond what we have been able to explain statistically. Note, however, the precision of the simulated reproduction for the period 1878–1914, or thereabouts. For those years, the statistical analysis and simulations are consistent with the historical record.

Between 1920 and 1930 the simulation shows a decline in Japan's exports relative to previous years (and certainly relative to the succeeding decade). In 1927 a Foreign Office spokesman had declared that Japan must expand its industrialization efforts so that increases in the number of people would generate more trade rather than provide cause for war. Here, at least, we find evidence – if not an adequate explanation – of the problem. The simulated trade – being larger than the actual trade for these years – might be viewed as that which *could have taken place* had there been fewer external constraints.

Recall that, whereas trade grew between 1925 (or thereabouts) and 1938, a sharp decline in imports and exports took place from then until the attack on Pearl Harbor. During this entire period there was full employment for industrial workers without reliance on foreign borrowing. Yet despite such economic growth and territorial expansion – or, in part, because of it – resource constraints appeared to worsen and external threats to multiply. In retrospect, Japanese efforts at industrialization and development in Korea and Manchuria, as well as on the home islands, together with the expanding requirements of military operations in China proper, appear to have increased Japanese demands for resources in the late 1930s. These efforts contributed at the same time to external resistance to territorial expansion (including large-scale collisions with Soviet-led forces along the Mongolian–Manchurian border) and new constraints on resource access.

NAVY AND ARMY EXPENDITURES

The military simulations are particularly striking. The sharp upward spiral in the mid-1930s is well reproduced by navy expenditures as well as by army expenditures. The spurt of increased allocations during the Russo-Japanese War of 1904–5, on the other hand, is somewhat overemphasized in the simulation, and the simulated values exaggerate the historical record for the World War I period. This pattern suggests that the underlying processes would have generated the lumpy military expenditures during the warring years if they had not been inhibited by some factor not included in the analysis. Whereas Japan was not a very active participant in World War I, the economic and military capabilities necessary for propelling military expansionism were in effect present – see Figures 12.3 and 12.4.

Both the simulated and the actual military expenditures (army and navy) show an exponential rise from 1928 or so through the attack on Pearl Harbor. The model replicates actual data almost to perfection. This trend reflects the course of events from the occupation of Manchuria, the establishment of Manchukuo, the invasion of China proper, the attendant

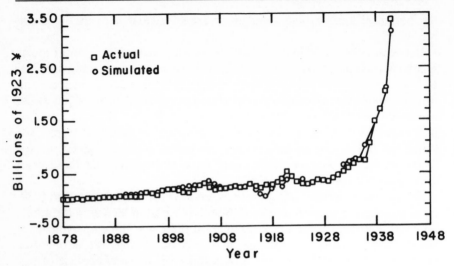

Figure 12.3   Simulation: navy expenditures

extension of Japanese military activities and territorial holdings, and the expansion of Japanese industrial capacity in order to supply both the home market and the new colonies. The system of simultaneous equations and the replication also reflects how economic, political, and military variables *interacted* to create the vicious cycle of growth, development, rising demand, resource insufficiency, territorial expansion, external resistance, and further growth, development, rising demand, resource insufficiency, expansion, resistance, and so on.

In view of the increasing political influence of militarist factions during this decade and a growing demand for more armaments, an economic policy of deflation was out of reach, and the consequent reflation contributed to expanding government expenditures which further fuelled the escalation of armaments. Between 1931–2 and 1936–7 the percentage of the general account allocated to army and navy expenditures increased from 31 percent to 47 percent. The Japanese leadership was also reacting to the expansion of Soviet activities and interests in East Asia (the statistical analysis identifying the USSR as a major influence on Japan's army allocations and the United States as an influence on the empire's navy allocations). Thus, confronting threats from the 'north,' a growing dependence on oil and other materials from the 'south,' and a consequent fear that the United States might intervene from the 'east,' Japanese leaders found it difficult to choose from strategic options that appeared hopelessly contradictory.

There were also serious economic problems. Sharp declines of imports and exports for several years prior to Pearl Harbor demonstrated the accumulated effects of economic problems throughout the decade of the 1930s (including those resulting from loans undertaken to meet up to one third of government expenditures following the Manchurian Incident).

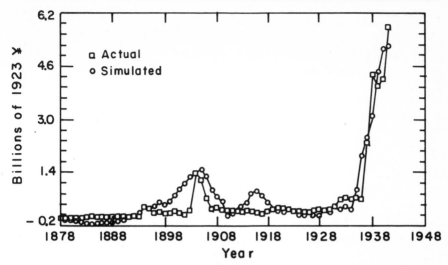

Figure 12.4   Simulation: army expenditures

The import simulations below also replicate the downturn of exports at the end of the decade. What we will see, then, are the combined interactive effects of the import–export relationships that had a strong positive feedback relationship, which together with army and navy expansion contributed to a strong upward spiral and an escalation of adversarial conflict.

COLONIAL EXPANSION

Japan's colonial expansion increased in stepwise fashion, making it difficult to model specific acquisitions. Nonetheless, the simulated values track the overall record of expansion persuasively – see Figure 12.5.

The occupation of Manchuria presents a sharp, quantitative turning point and the beginning of what became a large-scale expansionist activity – an exponential 'step function' within a long-term trend set during the nineteenth century and leading to rising demands for raw materials from the 'south,' and proposals for a Greater East Asia Co-Prosperity Sphere, which, to the extent that it was pursued, seemed to require a shift from a northern to a southern strategy, and, for flank protection, a preemptive strike to the east.[7]

IMPORTS FROM THE COLONIES

Imports from colonial holdings were crucial for Japan. The simulation roughly undershoots the actual values for the entire decade between 1895 and 1905, by 1908 tracking the historical record almost perfectly until Japan's entry into World War II. The Russo-Japanese War may

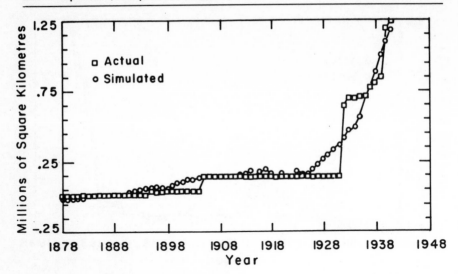

Figure 12.5   Simulation: colonial area

account for the underestimate, at least in part. Overall, the simulation is very robust – see Figure 12.6.

GOVERNMENT EXPENDITURES FOR
COLONIAL ADMINISTRATION

Budgetary allocation for management of the colonies is well simulated. The minor underestimations during the World War I years and around 1932–3 are noted as the latter years coincide with the Japanese expansion into China proper which, apparently, is not fully 'budgeted for' in the simulation. The costs of expansion rose as the Japanese government tried

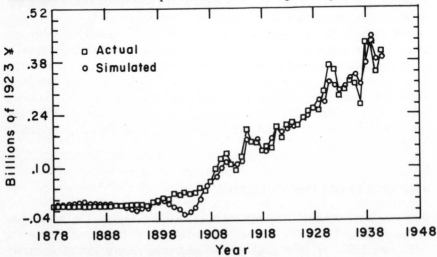

Figure 12.6   Simulation: imports from the colonies

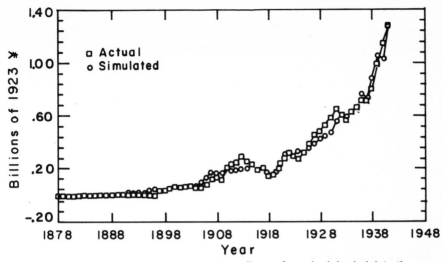

Figure 12.7 Simulation: government expenditures for colonial administration

to establish effective government over colonial areas – especially Manchuria
– and to push economic development. New capital investments were
required, and government expenditures for the colonies were accelerated
– see Figure 12.7.

WHAT WOULD HAVE HAPPENED IF . . . ?

To the extent that the simulated model accurately represents and replicates
the reality of the Japanese case, what would happen if Japan's empirical parameters had been different? As a form of policy experiments
counterfactual analysis is especially useful to help assess quantitatively
the degree of intervention in the system that would be necessary to alter the
outcomes as shown by the historical record (that is, by reducing government
expenditures, for example, or changing allocations to the military).

Military expenditures

Figures 12.8, 12.9, 12.10, and 12.11 provide a series of counterfactual
inquiries focusing on determinants of Japan's army expenditures. In
these exercises, four explanatory variables are individually changed (by
10 percent) and the impacts on army expenditures observed. Covering
the entire 63-year span between 1878 and 1941, the analysis examines the
impact on army expenditures of (a) the previous year's army expenditures;
(b) government revenue; (c) imports from the colonies; and (d) perception
of the potential enemy.[8]
    The impact of the previous year's army expenditures on the current
year's army expenditures reaffirms the bureaucratic inertia in the budgetary

process. We find that the effect in the prior year's expenditures on army expenditures of the 1920s and 1930s is minimal, whereas prior to 1914 a 10 percent increase in the spending of a prior year would have increased army expenditures considerably. We thus find that, after about 1918, a 10 percent increase or decrease in the previous year's spending would have made no difference to subsequent trends. The tendencies were set, and the new upward spiral would not have been changed by such an intervention – see Figure 12.8.

The effect of manipulating government revenue appears to approximate the effect of bureaucratic inertia with respect to army expenditures through time. In the pre-World War I period, the effect of a 10 percent increase or decrease is great. However, by the 1930s, when an expansionist military policy had already been set in motion, changes in government revenue did not have much impact on the direction of expenditures in that it appeared to reinforce (rather than change) the trends of history. By the 1930s, then, alternatives on this variable had little effect on other variables in the system. Once government expenditures had influenced army expenditures – and the effects were set – a 10 percent change in government revenue, one way or the other, had no impact on the path of any allocations after 1935 and up to 1941. As Figure 12.9 shows, only during the 1910–15 period (or thereabouts) did changes in government revenue have an impact on the level of allocations for the army.

Conceivably, increasing imports from Japan's colonies could have influenced army expenditures insofar as heightened commitments to colonial defense were indicated. Yet changes in colonial imports appear to have had little effect on army expenditures, particularly during the later period, whereas the effect was greater during the first two decades of the century. Again, this may signify that colonial imports were a stronger determinant of army expenditures during the earlier decade when a basic pattern of military expansionism was being set in response to bureaucratic inertia and other factors – see Figure 12.10.

USA and USSR

What about perception of the 'enemy'? What would have happened if Russia/USSR had not been seen by the Japanese as a major competitor or serious threat? Throughout the whole period, if we assume that there was no perceived threat from Russia/USSR (and the adversary threat is eliminated), simulated army expenditures tend to decline relative to the actual expenditures. More important is the simulation result that if *no* country had been identified as a threat to Japan, there would have been *no* army buildup in the 1930s – see Figure 12.11.

We turn next to the potential effects of outside threat on Japanese naval spending, particularly with respect to the United States. First,

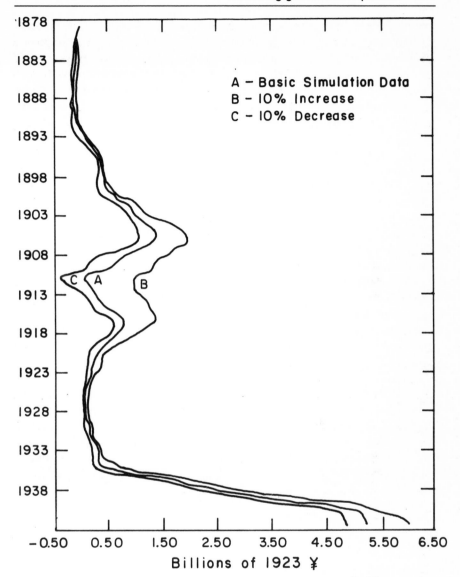

Figure 12.8 Impact of army expenditures (*t*–1) on army expenditures

would removal of the USA as a perceived threat significantly reduce Japanese navy spending? And second, would increases *or* decreases in US naval expenditures have changed the levels and dynamics of Japanese naval spending? In other words, would trends in Japan's navy expenditures have changed substantially in the absence of a US threat?

We looked at the *removal* of the United States as a threat by setting Japanese perception of the United States as a threat to zero – see Figure 12.12. The results showed, beginning with the year 1907, consistently *lower* navy expenditures than those estimated when the United States

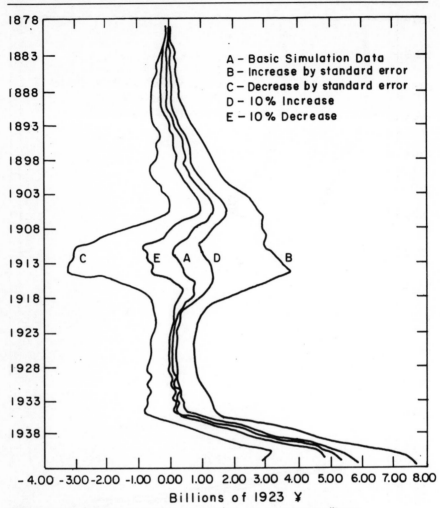

Figure 12.9   Impact of government revenue on army expenditures

was considered a threat. But this reduction in expenditures was minor, and the same general patterns were obtained. More importantly, the dramatic rise in Japan's expenditure from roughly 1925 through 1940 remained. Further, there was relatively little sensitivity to US navy allocations with respect to their possible influence on levels of Japanese naval expenditures. Even a 20 percent increase or decrease on the US side would appear to have had no discernible impact on Japan's expenditures for its navy. This result supports the view that Japanese naval spending was not predominantly an arms race in response to US navy spending, and that neither increased nor decreased US spending would have had significant impacts on the Japanese naval buildup – see Figures 12.13a and 12.13b.[9]

Combining these results with those of the previous chapter, we now conclude that while the impacts of the US threat on Japan's navy expenditures

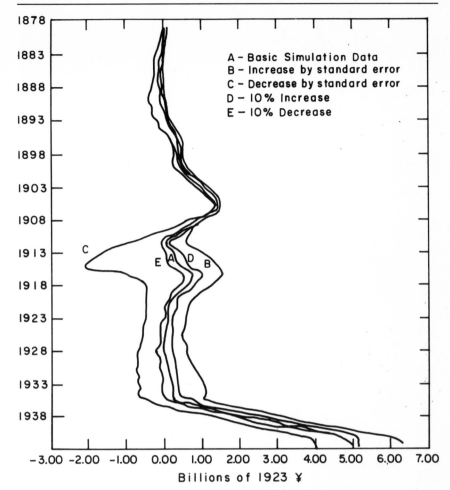

Figure 12.10 Impact of colonial imports on army expenditures

were present (confirmed by the significance of the estimated coefficient for
US navy expenditures on Japan's expenditures for the navy), nonetheless,
had there been *no* US threat perceived by Japan, the path of Japan's own
navy expenditures would not have changed substantially until war in 1941.
Indeed, the overall path to conflict may not have changed at all.

Northern or southern strategy?

The simulation results confirm that Japan was indeed very sensitive to
the Russian/Soviet military buildup; without it, a de-escalation of Japan's
military expenditures might have been feasible. This possibility appears at
two points in time. First, following the Russo-Japanese War, had Russia no
longer been perceived as an 'enemy' (and its army expenditures thus dis-
counted), Japan's own allocations might have been reduced accordingly. As

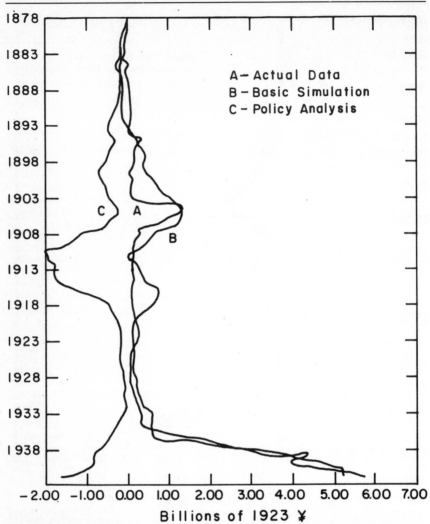

Figure 12.11 Impact of enemy on army expenditures: Russia/USSR as a potential enemy

indicated in Figure 12.11, however, the decline in expenditures was short-lived – with Japan's allocations increasing after 1914 as a consequence of World War I rather than as a response to a perceived Russian threat (although Japan, following the Bolshevik Revolution, participated in the Siberian expedition and was notably slow in the withdrawal of its troops).

The second point was from 1933 onward when, had there been no Soviet threat, Japanese army allocations would have declined (as reflected in Figure 12.11) – an indirect confirmation of the northern strategy at this time. Overall, however, the Japanese were responsive not only to Russian army expenditures, but also to their perceptions of shifts in Russian foreign policy and military strategy with implications for the Far East. Among the irritant factors were Russian antagonism to the Washington Conference; subsequent Soviet–Japanese frictions during the mid-1920s (which can be interpreted as setting the stage for a new operational plan, developed by the Japanese army in 1933, for launching an offensive from Manchuria against the USSR); and border disputes followed by the 'forgotten war' along Manchukuo's borders with Mongolia and the USSR. This succession of events had led to the nagging choice between a northern strategy against the USSR and a southern strategy (motivated in large part by a continuing but increasingly more pressing need for access to oil and other resources). The latter required preemptive action to neutralize the US fleet if the eastern flank of Japan's advance were to be protected.

To highlight the dilemmas of strategy: removal of Japanese perceptions of Russia/USSR as a threat greatly altered army expenditures: No buildup occurred during the 1930s when the role of the USSR as threat was set at zero. By contrast, perception of the United States as an adversary was statistically significant in framing Japan's navy trajectory. Yet statistically we determined that this response was rather marginal, in that even the removal of the United States as a threat entirely had little impact on the overall thrust of Japanese naval expenditures. We conclude, therefore, that the overall path of Japan's prewar navy buildup would have remained, with or without, a perceived US threat. Japan's navy buildup had dynamics of its own. (Note the impact of merchant marine tonnage and colonial area.) The United States was a significant factor in influencing the Japanese navy expenditures, but the United States had no appreciable impact once the trend path was set.

COMPARING JAPAN AND THE EUROPEAN POWERS

At this point we compare briefly the simulations of Japan and those of the European powers as presented in *Nations in Conflict*. The comparisons are imperfect in that the European cases cover the period 1870 to 1914, while the Japan simulations span the decades following the Meiji Restoration to Pearl Harbor. Since the Japan case encompasses those years for which we do have comparable results for the six major powers of Europe, however (but the models are not identical), this comparison can shed light on the underlying processes, though not on the specifics. The following discussion addresses 'what would have happened if . . . ?'

Simulating colonial area

In the British case, all trends in colonial acquisitions were well simulated. Occasional outlying points were not captured (notably sharp gains in Africa in 1890), but the overall trend was replicated well. The simulation for

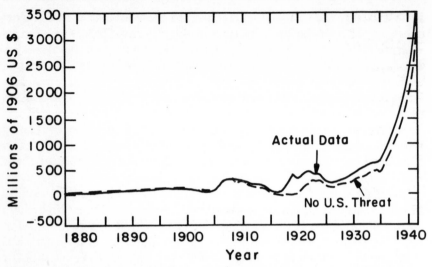

Figure 12.12 Removing the US threat: simulated values of Japanese naval expenditures with actual data and with US threat removed

Germany was less successful for the earlier period (1884–1914), beginning after Germany's initial acquisition of territory. This simulation correctly generated a positive trend of approximately the right slope, but major discontinuities in German colonial area were not reproduced. Like Germany and Britain, Japan acquired colonies in a stepwise manner that was difficult to replicate. The specific timing and size of the increments of colonial area acquired were not well explained by the model, but the general trend, timing, and increments were effectively simulated.

Simulating military expenditures

British military expenditures were simulated successfully, despite the inability to fully capture upsurges in military expenditures attributable to conflicts in colonial areas. Simulation values for the 1870s (representing the Ashanti Wars) and the turn of the century (Boer War) were below historical levels. Some aspects of British military expenditures were missed entirely; by contrast, however, German military spending was accurately simulated throughout. For Japan both navy and army expenditures were well simulated. The navy simulation tracks actual expenditures, including the spiraling processes, almost perfectly. The army simulation was somewhat less successful, undershooting the expenditures coinciding with the Russo-Japanese War and overshooting the World War I period. It seems probable, however, that Russian expenditures prior to World War I – which feature prominently in the simulation of Japan's expenditures – reflect responses to the European conflicts rather than to the Japanese threat. The relevant issue here, however, is the nature of Japan's own responses (rather than the Russian motives).

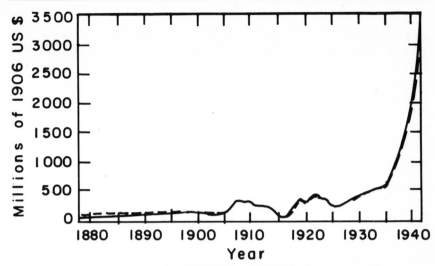

Figure 12.13a Reducing the US threat: simulation of Japanese naval expenditure with actual US naval spending and with US naval spending reduced by 20 percent

REWRITING HISTORY: COUNTERFACTUAL INQUIRY

As a form of policy experiment, counterfactual analysis involves changing the values of variables (or of their coefficients) from their empirical or estimated values and then simulating the model using the altered values. In *Nations in Conflict*, the values of coefficients were changed experimentally, whereas the policy analysis in the Japan study involved changing the actual values of the variables and leaving the coefficients intact.[10] In the World

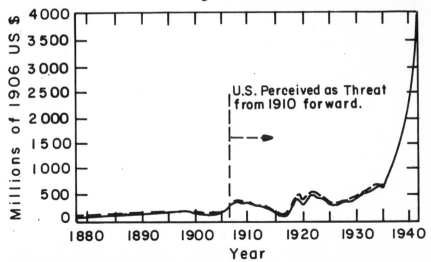

Figure 12.13b Increasing the US threat: simulation of Japanese naval expenditure with US actual naval spending and with US naval spending increased by 20 percent

War I study, policy experiments were done only for Britain, since the predictive power of the British model had been particularly successful. The coefficients endogenous to the system were altered, and only one coefficient was changed at a time. We found that changes in the coefficient value for intensity of intersections, as these affect violence behavior, resulted in a decline in colonial area, military expenditures, and alliances (although increases had a greater impact on violence behavior than decreases did). These findings indicate a high degree of interdependence among the equations of the system such that increasing the intensity of the intersections coefficient affected one set of relationships or feedback loops, whereas decreasing the coefficient affected another.

The most striking result concerns the impacts of the previous years' military expenditures. We found – for Britain, at least – that military expenditures, while probably contributing to escalation and war in the long run, had inertial or 'runaway' effects along the way, whereas decreases in the same bureaucratic momentum yielded relatively small payoffs.[11] For Japan, the values of four variables – army spending, level of government revenues, level of imports, and Japanese perceptions of Russia/USSR – were altered experimentally (upward and downward), and the effects of these alterations were simulated from the Meiji Restoration to war in 1941. As indicated earlier, when army spending $(t-1)$ was increased prior to 1914, the 10 percent increase in each previous year's military spending yielded a major increase in subsequent spending, suggesting therefore that trends in military spending are set in motion early (rather than later) in a given phase of expansion. Changes in the level of government revenues yielded results similar to that of previous spending. Prior to World War I, any changes in government revenues had a considerable impact on military spending and colonial area, reflecting the sensitivity of military allocations to budgetary levels. Alterations in the level of imports from colonies had relatively little effect on simulation outcomes, and whatever impact did appear was greater in the first part of the twentieth century.

In comparative terms it seems clear that the overall impact of bureaucratic momentum was more influential in the case of Britain than in the case of Japan. While increasing the coefficient of past years' military expenditures in the British case led to a massive increase in the simulated level of military spending, analogous increases in the level of the military expenditures $(t-1)$ in the Japanese case had less impact overall and very little impact on the simulated levels of spending for later decades. Other factors influencing military (specifically army) spending in the Japan model – colonial area, imports from the colonies, and particularly the Russian/ Soviet threat – seem to be stronger. These made the simulation results fairly robust against changes in the level of previous military spending.

We conclude, therefore, that for the interwar period, when Japan consolidated its profile as a *beta* power, the sources and manifestations of lateral pressure were strongly interconnected. The entire system – the state, its master variables, its capabilities, and its behavior patterns – seemed to be propelled along the path to conflict. On quantitative grounds, as a consequence, we can infer that Japan remained considerably less responsive than Great Britain to changes in military expenditures. Further, in part, as a result of this relative rigidity, the feedback processes contributing to de-escalation rather than escalation of competition and conflict were not in statistical evidence. The policy deliberations leading to the decision for war, which we have described in an earlier chapter as particularly ineffective in the wake of mounting pressures, can now be thought of as almost irrelevant, given the robust pressures at work.

Part IV

Postwar Japan

Reconstruction, growth, expansion

Chapter 13

Lateral pressure after World War II

JAPAN AT WAR

After the Pearl Harbor decision, Japanese troops expanded rapidly into Southeast Asia, the Aleutian chain, the Philippines, New Guinea, and other Western possessions in the Pacific. The course of events thereafter effected a succession of changes in the global configuration of power and the position of Japan in the international system. Yet the country's resource dependencies, import and export patterns and requirements remained remarkably consistent.

During the postwar decades Japanese growth was in many respects spectacular, and the country soon became a strong participant in the global economy, but the external expansion of its activities and interests was manifested in new ways, and the leverages applied to other countries tended to be expressed within a mode that contrasted sharply with prewar patterns. To a considerable extent, Japan's position after the war was shaped not only by wartime events, but also by the geographical positioning of troops at the close of hostilities.

The course of wartime events in China, as well as military activities in the Pacific, had a great deal to do with the policies that were applied to Japan by the United States and other Allied countries during the postwar decades. Established in remote border areas of China's Kiangsi Province a few weeks after the Manchurian Incident of 18 September 1931, the Chinese Soviet (or Juikin) Republic declared war – on paper, at least – against Japan. Although in principle Chiang Kai-shek's Nationalist forces were also operating in opposition to the Japanese, Chiang appeared to be engaged in 'extermination campaigns' against the Communist Red Army as a first priority. Subsequently, the Chinese Communists undertook their Long March across China to Yenan Province in the northwest. After Japan's 7 July 1937 invasion of China proper, the advance of Japanese armies across northern China was rapid, and by the end of that year nearly all the chief cities and their connecting communication lines were in Japanese hands. As the struggle wore on, the 'united front' of Nationalists

Map 4   Japan's expansion abroad, 1928–45

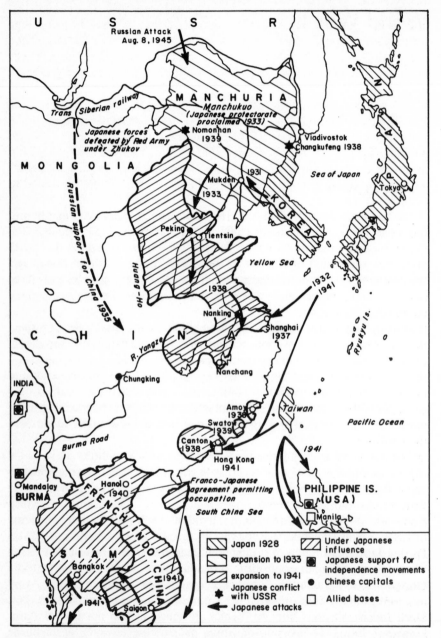

Source: adapted from Barraclough 1978: 268

and Communists came to look more and more like an armed truce, if not a continuation of the civil war. Mao Tse-tung's guerrilla forces launched attacks upon Japanese garrison troops and puppet (Chinese) forces along north–south supply routes as they fell under Japanese control. Then negotiations were initiated between the Yenan border region government of the communists and Chiang's Nationalist government which led to an uneasy alliance in September 1937. Remarkably, during this period, the USSR was sending military supplies by truck caravans across Sinkiang Province to the Nationalists, but not to the Communists. As an aspect of the Nationalist – Communist truce, the Communist eighth route army was paid a regular subsidy by the nationalists, who remained wary, nevertheless; and in practical military and political terms, Mao Tse-tung and his colleagues treated the Japanese conflict as a national crisis which could be turned to Communist advantage.

The Japanese attack on Pearl Harbor galvanized the whole situation, but the reforming and expanding of US naval and army forces in the Eastern Pacific took time, and the war in Europe was awarded the overriding priority. It was only with successful US amphibious landings in the Solomons, the Marshall and the Gilbert islands, and in the Aleutian chain that the tide unmistakably began to change. From this time forward it became increasingly evident to many Asians – the Nationalist and Communist leaderships in China, for example – that the US forces were beginning to win. But it was not until the summer of 1943, with the Japanese defeat on Saipan and the launching of Nagoya- and Tokyo-bound bombers from that island and adjacent Tinian, that Senator Mike Mansfield reported that the Kuomintang and the Communists, apparently sensing a sharp turning point in the war, appeared 'more interested in preserving their respective parties . . . than in carrying out the war against Japan' in order to enhance their respective positions, because both felt that the United States would 'guarantee victory' (US Department of State 1949: 61).

For Japan, war in China and the Pacific was resource-consuming. In particular, battles with the United States proved Japan's high vulnerability with respect to the availability of natural resources. Japan expected the US troops eventually to lose their morale. But this did not happen. The scale of US war mobilization exceeded that of Japan by far – several times over. During wartime, for instance, Japan built only 15 aircraft carriers, while the United States built as many as 102; Japan made some 65,000 airplanes, the United States, 197,000; Japan built commercial vessels to a total of 3.3 million tons, and the United States, 52 million tons (Masamura 1988: 15–16). Since Japanese troops lost control of both the skies and the seas, the prolonged war exhausted Japan's industries and its population. Direct airborne attack on factories destroyed production capacities. The damage to convoy capability resulted in the shortage of raw materials for military supplies. The supply of petroleum was so insufficient as to restrain operations.

CONFIGURATIONS OF POWER

According to US military intelligence, it seemed evident that the defeat of Japan would create a new configuration of power, with the USSR threatening to regain the dominance tsarist Russia had lost in 1905 and to become the sole military land power in Asia. 'Deprived of her empire in China, and with her cities and industries smashed to pieces,' Japan would be 'back where she started at the dawn of her modern era, a group of relatively worthless islands, populated by fishermen, primitive farmers, and innocuous warriors.' The clock would be turned back 'some eighty years to the time when the rivalry between Russia and the Western democracies in China began.' How could the military and political vacuums in the Far East be filled after the defeat of Japan? Intelligence officers saw the answer depending to a considerable extent on the future moves of Soviet Russia. There was a persuasive logic behind Western hopes that the USSR might join in the war against Japan, but if that should occur, the course of events would depend upon the ability of the Western Allies to prevent a division – like the one already beginning to take place in Europe – between a US – British sphere and a Soviet zone of operations in China and other parts of the Far East (*US War Department* 1945: 2309). The full implication of these dynamics did not become clear, however, until the outbreak of the Korean War in 1950.

As events turned out, the defeat of Japan 'ended a balance of power that had previously restrained Soviet pressures in China and the Pacific' and enabled the USSR to consolidate its strategic position in the Soviet Far East and in China 'north of the wall' – although the Soviet Union later withdrew its troops from Manchuria – and also in northern Korea, Sakhalin, and the Kuriles. There was apprehension at the National Security Council level of the US government that, if Japan were absorbed into the Stalinist bloc, 'the Soviet Asian base could become a source of strength capable of shifting the balance of world power to the disadvantage of the United States.' If Pakistan and India subsequently fell to communism, the United States and its allies might find themselves 'denied any foothold' on the Asian mainland. The industrial plant of Japan would be 'the richest strategic prize in the Far East for the USSR.' The Soviets, however, could not 'quickly build up a powerful self-sufficient war-making complex in Asia without access to and control over Japan' (US Department of Defense 1971: 239, 255–8, 412).

Accordingly, the strategic value of the Far East to the United States and its Western allies was articulated by the US leadership in terms of three fundamental considerations. First, a denial of Soviet control over Asia could block the acquisition by the USSR of power advantages 'which might in time add significantly to the Russian war making potential.' Second, insofar as indigenous forces of Asia opposed Soviet expansion, they would assist the United States in containing Soviet advances in the region and possibly reduce the drain on the US economy. Beyond this, the 'indigenous forces of Asia, including manpower reserves, would also be a valuable asset if available for the support of the United States in the event of war.' And third, Asia was perceived by the US leadership as 'a source of raw materials, principally tin and natural rubber,' which were 'of strategic importance to the United States' – but indispensable to Japan, whose access to the basic resources of Asia must be assured if that country were to reestablish itself economically, politically, and industrially and prove resistant to Soviet encroachments. Japan could maintain an adequate standard of living on a self-supporting basis only if it were able 'to secure a greater proportion of its needed food and raw material (principally cotton) imports from the Asiatic area, in which its markets lie,' rather than from the United States, in which its export market was small. Until the outbreak of the Korean War, however, US efforts on the Asian mainland were largely confined to support for Chiang Kai-shek's Nationalist government in China and for French forces stationed in Indochina (US Department of Defense 1971: 255–6, 412).

SURRENDER AND OCCUPATION

On 6 August 1945 the first atomic bomb ever used in warfare was dropped on Hiroshima. As reported to the Japanese army general staff the next day, the whole city had been 'destroyed instantly.' On the following day the USSR declared war on Japan, effective 9 August. On the same day a second bomb was dropped on Nagasaki.[1] With the reservation that the status of the emperor should remain unchanged, on 10 August the Japanese government accepted the Potsdam Declaration, an appeal issued on 26 July by Truman, Churchill, and Stalin, which required the revival and strengthening of democratic tendencies among the people, the occupation of Japan 'until Allied objectives had been achieved' and 'a peacefully inclined and responsible government' had been established, and surrender on unconditional terms (Borton 1955: 390–2). The emperor announced the surrender on 15 August.

The formal surrender – which took place on 2 September aboard the United States battleship *Missouri*, and in the presence of General MacArthur, who, as Supreme Commander of the Allied Powers (SCAP), would be in charge of the occupation – marked an abrupt collapse of Japanese activities and interests from the Asian mainland and far reaches of the Pacific back onto the home islands, at a time when US and Soviet activities and interests were expanding and colliding. Defeat deprived the former empire of nearly half of its land area and was estimated to have cost the economy 'more than nine-tenths of its merchant marine, one-fourth of its housing, and one-fifth of its industrial plant, machinery, equipment, and other durables.' A quarter of the country's national wealth is believed to have 'vanished' between 1941 and 1945 (Denison and Chung 1976: 10).

During the next two years, Japan experienced 'the full force of a social and cultural revolution' inspired by General Headquarters, (SCAP) – General MacArthur, in short (Storry 1960: 239–45). The Treaty of Peace with Japan, signed on 8 September 1951, brought the occupation to an end. From 'start to finish a US operation,' the occupation stripped Japan of its imperial holdings including Manchuria, Korea, Taiwan, the Pescadores, and mandated islands in the Pacific. Acting under provisions of the Yalta Agreement of February 1945, moreover, the USSR took possession of the Kurile Islands and southern Sakhalin; and for the time being the Ryukyu Islands (Okinawa) and the Bonin Islands were taken under US administration.

The next task was the destruction of the country's armed forces and war potential. Chapter II, inserted into the 1947 constitution by General MacArthur himself, renounced war 'as a sovereign right of the nation and the threat or use of force as a means of settling international disputes' (Tiedemann 1955: 82–6). Later, especially with US involvement in the Korean War, the Japanese were subject to continuing pressure from the US government to increase their armed forces and assume greater responsibility for their own defense. The military equipment and troop strength of Japan's Self-Defense Corps, established in accordance with the Mutual Security Assistance Pact of 1954 with about 150,000 men (Tiedemann 1955: 93), were steadily increased. Yet by the early 1980s the country's military expenditures still amounted to less than one percent of GNP (as compared with 5 percent in the USA, and 10.7 percent in the Soviet Union).

Meanwhile, preoccupied with immediate problems of demilitarization and security, SCAP officials soon found themselves confronted with an economy in a state of collapse. In sum, the wartime destruction of the country's production had been 'nearly complete.' A total of 119 major cities had been destroyed, foreign trade had been suspended, and agricultural production 'drastically reduced' as a result of fertilzer shortage and other agricultural inputs during the early postwar period. Inflation was rampant, and food was in seriously short supply (Okita 1975: 2–3). As chief occupying power, the USA played a major role in rebuilding the country's economy. Massive aid was made available, and factories were supplied with badly needed materials. At the same time, Japan began to benefit from events in the rest of the Far East. The rise of the People's Republic of China and the Korean War turned Japan into 'an essential base for the deployment of American power,' with the result that US special procurement expenditure substituted for aid, which ceased in 1951. With the constraints that had been placed on Japan's military establishment, defense expenditures were reduced to one or one and a half percent of national income, and the burden of colonial administrative costs no longer existed (Allen 1967: 3–4).

RECONSTRUCTION

Early in the occupation, the Japanese government was instructed to draft a land reform program that would liquidate 'those pernicious ills which have long blighted the agrarian structure' wherein three quarters of all Japanese farmers were 'partially or totally tenants and paying rentals amounting to half or more of their annual crops.' Ten months later, in October 1946 a Land Reform Law was enacted, and by the end of the year 'tenants were able to begin buying land from the government' (Yanaga 1949: 638) – on their way toward becoming proprietors (Allen 1967: 13–14). Stimulated by the reform, farmers began adopting better methods of production and improving their living standards. Fertilizer was used on a larger scale, and by the late 1950s tractors, cultivators, and other agricultural machinery were being introduced at an increasing rate (Okita 1975: 30–1). With capital substituting more and more for labor (Allen 1965: 94–6), Japanese agriculture was growing at the rate of 4.2 percent per year by the mid-1950s (Maddison 1969: 50).

Despite these vigorous measures, Japanese reconstruction was slow at first. 'Generals are not economists,' wrote Jerome Cohen, and even after four years – spent 'tearing down Japan' as effectively as possible – 'there were too many related problems of security and demilitarization to allow any great concentration of time and effort to be devoted to methods of rebuilding' the country (Cohen 1949b: 418). By 1948, however, it was already becoming evident that 'in the future the main consideration before SCAP would be to rebuild Japan as an ally of the United States against Communism' (Storry 1960: 243). A target for the achievement of Japan's 1930–4 standard of living was framed for 1952. This disposition to press for renewed Japanese development was strengthened by the Communist victory in the Chinese Revolution, the Berlin blockade, the outbreak of war in Korea, and the conclusion that 'a strong, robustly anti-Communist Japan must become a prime American aim' (Storry 1960: 243). By 1951 the advance of Japanese industrial growth compared favorably 'with what was achieved in the most productive European countries' (Allen 1965: 104, 108).

Initially, these and other policies were imposed on Japan by the occupation, but over succeeding years the country's remarkable growth and economic development were attributable to Japanese initiative and effective administration (Allen 1967: 4–5). Even during the war, several groups in the country had begun to work secretly on postwar problems, and during the summer of 1946 an informal advisory group for Prime Minister Shigeru Yoshida was organized, and a letter addressed to General MacArthur urged a program for increasing the production of basic commodities – especially coal and steel – and requested the importation of heavy oil in order to facilitate steel production. A priority production program was soon established by the Japanese government. With the Korean War and 'fast-growing demand from abroad,' the economy began to recover from the postwar depression and to boost its foreign currency earnings abroad. 'Thereafter, the independence of the Japanese economy through normal export trade was made a major goal in Japan's economic policy' (Okita 1975: 3–5).

Underlying problems of Japanese economic reconstruction were the persistent constraints of 'too many people on too little land' together with adverse trade balances. In 1945, 72 million people populated war-devastated Japan proper. During less than two years, more than 5 million soldiers and civilians returned home and thus worsened economic (and food) conditions. By 1947 Far Eastern countries were sending 'only about one percent of their exports to Japan' and receiving 'only about three percent of their imports from Japan,' as contrasted with Japanese receipt of 20 percent of these countries' total exports in 1936 and Japanese provision of 30 percent of their imports. 'Obviously, because of the low level of output, Japan had not been shipping enough goods abroad to pay for her necessary imports' – with the result that continuing US expenditures were necessary 'to prevent "disease and unrest"' (Cohen 1949b: 494–5).

With the 'loss of traditional markets and sources of supply due to political and economic chaos in China, Manchuria, Korea, Burma, etc., and in view of persisting anti-Japanese sentiments in Australia, the Philippines, etc.,' it was extremely difficult to lessen this dependence. Although the rate of industrial production had been rising prior to the Korean War and was strengthened during hostilities, there were other, less encouraging indications. The population growth rate was 'distressingly high'; the rice crop in 1954 was 'the worst . . . in years', and with the cessation of the Korean War, the temporary excess of Japanese foreign receipts – provided by US and Allied procurements, the money spent by US and other troops in Japan, and the dollar costs of maintaining these forces – was soon wiped out, and the old problems returned (Cohen 1949b: 494–5). But the country's subsequent economic growth was described by Shigeru Yoshida as 'a "dream" to those who had experienced the immediate postwar collapse' (Olsen 1978: 84).

RETURN TO INTERNATIONAL COMMUNITY

The Treaty of Peace with Japan was signed on 8 September 1951 in San Francisco. The completion of the occupation in April 1952 made Japan independent, but Japan's mutual security treaty with the United States left it dependent on the US global strategy. In fact, Japan became one of the closest and most reliable allies of the United States in the

Asia-Pacific region. With numerous US bases and facilities on hand, the islands of Japan remained a vital pivot in the United States' containment of communist forces in Asia. By the same token, the Japanese government had to accept delayed normalization of its diplomatic relationship with the Soviet Union and the People's Republic of China in spite of strong public opposition. In retaliation the Soviet Union blocked Japan's entry to the United Nations.

The restoration of independence brought the occupation's political purge to an end, and many conservative politicians became active, criticizing the Yoshida cabinet. The role in government of Japan's conservative factions became fluid; merger and separation of conservative parties continued until they consolidated to create the Liberal Democratic Party in November 1955. Meanwhile, denouncing Yoshida's dependence upon the United States, Ichiro Hatoyama became prime minister (December 1954 to December 1956) to launch an 'independent national diplomacy.' He decided to initiate negotiations with Moscow designed to normalize bilateral relations. The two countries established diplomatic ties on 12 December 1956, but the territorial issue of the northern islands was not settled. On the same day the United Nations Security Council voted to admit Japan to the organization.

Another step to be undertaken in the course of rejoining the international community was for Japan to normalize relations with its Asian neighbors, those which had been the target of Japanese aggression less than a decade earlier. The San Francisco peace treaty obligated Japan to make war reparations, but the terms were relatively favorable in that they did not impose an unbearable burden. Some countries, like the Philippines, expressed strong anti-Japanese sentiments, and the Japanese government tried hard to pay as few reparations as possible. It took more than a decade to settle all the reparation questions; Japan was to make payments totaling US $1 billion between 1956 and 1976 (Yamakage 1985: 136–141). In addition, Japan agreed to pay 'semi-reparations' and provide yen loans in concessional terms to other Asian nations.

Despite the reluctance to make reparations and related payments, Japan took advantage of the forced payments in several respects. First of all, reparations were to be paid mainly in the form of capital goods and services, so that Japan was able to save scarce foreign exchange. Second, the Japanese government regarded war reparation as part of a broader economic cooperation package; and in fact, these payments were later counted as the grant-in-aid of Japan's official development assistance. Third, the making of reparations was intended not to compete with Japanese exports. (The government suggested that reparations and exports were complementary strategies designed to promote Japanese interest in Southeast Asia.) Fourth, Japanese engineering and trading companies were involved in reparations from the earliest days, thus paving the way for Japanese economic expansion in the region. In sum, war reparations for Japan resulted in the establishment of the foundation for the expansion of commercial activities some years later.

Furthermore, it was clear that Japan needed to join the postwar international economic regime in order to promote foreign trade. The US government was very supportive of Japan's endeavors, but other Allies were not. In August 1952, a few months after independence, Japan was admitted to the International Monetary Fund (IMF) and the International Bank of Reconstruction and Development (IBRD). But the admission process was not smooth. There was a difference in opinion among Allied nations concerning Japan's share. The United States (and Japan, of course) preferred a larger share, while Britain and others insisted on a smaller share. Japan wanted the same share as West Germany (US $330,000), which was to be admitted at the same time as Japan. The IMF's compromised offer was $250,000, which Japan accepted after some months of hesitation (Akaneya 1985: 111–12). But four decades passed before Japan was awarded a share equal to that of West Germany – in 1990.

Japan's entry into the General Agreement for Tariffs and Trade (GATT) was even more troublesome. The question of Japan in GATT created controversy among Allied nations even before Japan gained independence. Representing the opposition, the British government pointed to Japan's unfair trade practices before the war and argued that the country's future export potentials would threaten the Commonwealth nations. The United States government, on the other hand, wanted not only a reduction in Japan's dependence on American aid but also more trade with Western countries – lest the Japanese tilt toward the potentially extensive market of Communist China (Akaneya 1985: 121–4). For Japan, formal trade agreements with GATT members constituted a substantive precondition for participation in the new multilateral trade regime. But it was not until September 1955 that Japan was formally admitted to GATT.

POLICY MIX FOR RAPID INDUSTRIALIZATION

Economic reconstruction took place at a rapid pace throughout the early 1950s in concurrence with a boom in special military procurement generated by the Korean War. By the end of the 1950s basic economic statistics indicated that reconstruction was over and that the Japanese economy had embarked on a surge of economic expansion.

Containing a large population demilitarized and demobilized in rural areas, Japan's prosperity depended as ever on rapid industrialization and secured imports of industrial raw materials. But the World War II defeat had pushed the Japanese economy back to the level of the 1920s. External conditions – and probably domestic dispositions as well – barred Japan from following its 1930s path. The modes of expansion and territorial conquests of the 1920s and 1930s were out of the question. Both war destruction and democratization during the occupation required a new approach to rapid industrialization and commercial expansion.

There were four obstacles to rapid industrialization, however: scarcity of electricity, shortage of steel, damaged capacity for merchant shipping, and scarcity of coal (Nakamura 1983: 215). The government introduced several policies to overcome those obstacles and facilitate reindustrialization. As early as September 1949, however, the Yoshida cabinet adopted an industrial 'rationalization' plan that included, among other measures, the government's role in designing the future industrial structure and the establishment of guidelines for individual industries. The 'rationalization' was implemented under the strong leadership of a government whose policy instruments were extensive.

One of the most fundamental policy instruments was the provision of low-interest loans for the public sector. A government institution created by the Yoshida cabinet in 1947 to pursue the priority production methods, the Postwar Reconstruction Finance Bank, was replaced by the Japan Development Bank (JDB), established in 1951 to promote the modernization and rationalization of key industries. The particular targets for support were the electric power industry and merchant shipping (loans to merchant shipping companies eventually went to the shipbuilding industry). Japan also utilized IBRD loans to build electric power plants, shipbuilding facilities, and large-scale industrial plants of various kinds. Starting in 1953, there were 21 contracts (in the total of US $300 million) during the 1950s, and all but two were borrowed by the JDB to finance private companies.

A second policy instrument was the provision of financial support for the private sector, including tax incentives and subsidies. The Special Tax Measures Act (1951) and the Enterprises Rationalization Promotion Act (1952) provided companies in key industries with accelerated depreciation programs, tax-deductive reserve programs, subsidies for research and development, and so on. Also, infrastructure reconstruction was undertaken largely by governmental direct funding in order to promote planned industrial development in various locations. As a consequence, individual enterprises were able to pursue an extensive strategy of capital accumulation.

The set of foreign trade regulations also provided effective policy instruments. Under the Foreign Exchange and Foreign Trade Act (1947), the government was able to control imports. It allocated scarce foreign reserve to key industries to accelerate their development and consequently protected the manufacturing industries by not allowing imports of competitive products, such as automobiles. Import tariffs were imposed strategically. On the one hand, relatively high import duties levied on manufactured goods protected the new industries; on the other, low tariffs on industrial raw materials helped Japanese industries gain international competitiveness. The policy on foreign investment was also targeted strategically. The Japanese government discouraged foreign investment in Japan, but it promoted massive technology imports by Japanese firms.

In sum, by introducing various types of economic leverage, the government prepared a very favorable domestic environment for private enterprises in the early 1950s and maintained it throughout the rest of the decade. Together those policies have recently been labeled an 'industrial policy' or a 'targeting industrial policy' to reflect an integrated approach to industrialization and economic policy. The assessment of such policies differs from one scholar to another. (See, for example, Johnson 1982; Komiya 1984.) A former Economic Planning Agency economist, Kosai (1988), warns that a simplistic view of Japan's success story might be misleading:

> The popular notion in the 1970s that there was a so-called Japan Incorporated, a close alliance between government and business, with the government directly guiding the activities of private firms, rested largely on impressions of how the Japanese economy operated during this period [of the 1950s]. But it would be a mistake to regard Japan as a 'planned economy' or the government as an 'economic general staff' even in this period. Government and business did share information with each other and make their views known to each other, but the final investment decisions were in the hands of the business firms. (Kosai 1988: 517–18)

ECONOMIC DEVELOPMENT AND INDUSTRIAL STRUCTURE

In 1956 the Economic White Paper of Japan declared that it was no longer in the postwar era; growth through recovery was over. Half a year earlier the Hatoyama cabinet had announced the five-year plan for economic self-reliance, the first of its type. The plan set two goals: first, to establish a self-reliant economy with a balance of payments equilibrium without resorting to special procurement or foreign aid; and second, to achieve full employment in order to absorb expansion of the labor force. The annual growth rate was targeted at 5 percent. During fiscal years 1956–60 the average annual rate of growth achieved in fact was 9.1 percent. Until the oil crisis shook the Japanese economy, all succeeding midterm economic plans always underestimated the rate of economic growth. Japan's economic expansion to unprecedented scale began.

Industrial structural change took place in profound ways. Heavy industries replaced light industries as the leading mode of economic development. New industries began to flourish. In particular, the petrochemical industry started to rise very rapidly. The transfer of technology from abroad and the long-term strategy of the Ministry of International Trade and Industry (MITI) (which adopted a petrochemical industry development policy in 1955) helped the rise (Nakamura 1983: 228). The electric appliances industry took a comparable turn.

At the core of such a structural change, the pattern of energy use began to change as well, shifting from coal to petroleum – hence from domestic to imported resources. The logic for the shift seemed compelling. First of all, while the demand for electricity was increasing, sites suitable for hydroelectric power plants were becoming less and less available. Huge oil reserves were found in the Middle East, and the price of petroleum continued to decrease. (Increasing demand for petroleum not only in Japan but throughout the world helped the Japanese shipbuilding industry to become the major supplier of gigantic oil tankers.) The Japanese coal industry could not rationalize itself so as to gain price competitiveness against imported petroleum. Moreover, leading industries called for the cheapest possible energy in order to export their products competitively. With continued economic growth and expanded exports, Japan's balance of payment improved sufficiently to enable the allocation of foreign currency directly for petroleum imports. Finally, petroleum became not merely an energy resource but more importantly the key raw material necessary for the country's fast-developing petrochemical industry. Japan's vulnerable dependence on foreign petroleum was embedded in the core of its industrial structure during these decades of the postwar period.

Economists Kazushi Ohkawa and Henry Rosovsky explained Japanese growth in terms of a 'long swing' in the Japanese economy – 'especially in terms of rates of growth'; a spurt in nonagricultural private investment; the 'extensive and gradual quickening' of most indicators 'within the long swing framework' of the previous 70 years; and a differential structure with respect to 'growing labor productivity and wage gaps between the modern and traditional sectors of the Japanese economy.' This analysis rested upon assumptions of

a gap between technology actually applied in Japan and the increasing capability of borrowing and absorbing more advanced methods based on well-functioning sociopolitical infrastructure; a flow of autonomous investment based on borrowed technology providing the major driving force in the country's economy; a two-sector growth model including 'modern' and 'traditional' elements; and the strengthening and further development of forces already in operation before the war.

The technology gap took form as a dualistic structure of industry and labor market developed. There were marked differentials in productivity (reflecting scarcity of capital and different capital intensities in modern and traditional sectors) and new wage rates (resulting from such labor market institutions as permanent employment and seniority payments). Wages in the modern sector were high in spite of a labor surplus (Ohkawa and Rosovsky 1973: 39–40).

In accounting for the 4.6 percentage point spread between Japanese growth (8.8 percent a year between 1953 and 1971) and that of the other ten countries then examined (4.2 percent for eight European countries plus the United States and Canada) Denison and Chung found greater contributions of capital, accounting for 1.2 percentage points; a greater contribution from the application of new knowledge and skills to production, accounting for 1.0 points; 'an above-average contribution from changes in employment, hours of work and the distribution by age and sex of total hours work,' accounting for 0.9 points; and 'greater than average contributions from the allocation of resources away from agriculture and from nonagricultural self-employment,' accounting for 0.3 points. All of the sources enumerated to growth in the other countries in the periods analyzed, with the sole exception that Italy (1950–62), are 'estimated to have gained more from the reallocation of resources away from agriculture and non-farm self-employment' (Denison and Chung 1976: 46–47).

Economist Minami (1986) explained the postwar economic expansion 'partly' as an extension of the prewar trends; acceleration in investments and productivity rates due to 'factors peculiar' to this period; and modernization of equipment and declines in military expenditures. Minami singled out the impact of technological change in other countries on Japan and Japan's own export expansion (Minami 1986: 419).

OUTWARD EXPANSION: NEW STYLE

Throughout the early postwar period, exports were recognized as 'a vital necessity for the survival of the Japanese economy,' even though the country was cut off from overseas trade. Because of a 'pessimistic outlook' that many people entertained at first, 'views were expressed that Japan must live mainly on indigenous resources.' It became evident, however, that, without 'the advantages of the international division of labor,' the country would be condemned to 'economic inefficiency and low living standards' (Okita 1975: 48). In this respect, Japan's requirements remained unchanged: 'The need to export was reinforced by Japan's limited raw material endowment and dependence on foreign suppliers for modern equipment, which kept the propensity to import high and therefore required a large volume of exports to finance the growth of imports.' In the postwar situation, the rebuilding and modernization of the country 'required not only a high capital formation ratio, but also a large expansion of exports' (Ohkawa and Rosovsky 1973: 41).

The end of World War II found Japan's foreign trade 'in ruins and the foundations on which it might be rebuilt apparently insecure.' During the latter phases of violence many 'large industrial establishments had been destroyed by air attacks; raw materials were very scarce; and formerly efficient trading organizations had been broken up.' Foreign trade remained directly under SCAP control at first, but 'foreign trade was entrusted to a number of trade corporations between early 1947 and the end of 1949,' when 'a single exchange rate was introduced,' and 'the Ministry of International Trade and Industry (MITI) was set up in place of the emergency organization for trade control.' From 1950 onward, many of the former trading concerns 'began to re-establish themselves, and exchange and mercantile business to resume its former character' (Allen 1967: 35).

The first stimulus to Japanese exports was provided by the Korean War, and even after this opportunity was spent, the demand for certain Japanese products was sustained, for a time, by other external factors. Japan was already benefiting from its special relationship with the United States, which continued after the end of the occupation. And in the mid-1950s a global investment boom generated demands for capital goods which the United States and other Western producers could not fully satisfy. Dollars acquired during this period through procurement expenditures, resulting from the presence of US troops in Japan and South Korea, enabled the financing of a high proportion of Japanese imports. By the time the boom had come to an end, Japan had successfully reduced production costs and was highly competitive over a considerable range of products (Allen 1967: 38). From this point forward, Japan's new outward expansion – its postwar manifestation of lateral pressure – took shape as a steady proliferation around the world of the country's commercial, financial, and industrial activities, interests, and influence.

Chapter 14

Economic growth and vulnerability

Surrendering unconditionally to the United States in August 1945, Japan lost its colonial holdings, and its land area was reduced to the size it had been 80 years earlier, when the country was opened to the West. Many characteristics of the Japanese past were eradicated, and the country confronted the need for a major transformation.

As pointed out by Organski and Kugler from an investigation of what has been termed the 'phoenix factor,' after a war the losers often 'begin and maintain a steadily accelerating recovery rate and overtake the winners' thereafter as 'levels of power return to points one would have anticipated had no war occurred' (Organski and Kugler 1980: 130–46). 'Japan performed best' after World War II, then Germany, then Italy (Organski and Kugler 1980: 210–13). Our analysis supports that conclusion. Overall, postwar Japan did more than overtake the winners technologically and economically; Japanese society also transformed itself in social and political terms, developing new organizational forms for production and taking a lead in the substitution of commercial and diplomatic for military influence and leverages in the global environment.

By the late 1950s the Japanese economy was growing rapidly. The average annual rate of GNP growth in real terms during 1956–60 was as high as 8.5 per cent. This was already startling, but the performance in the 1960s turned even higher. The rate stood at 10.0 per cent during 1961–5 and at 11.6 per cent in 1966–70. But Japan's economic activities still depended on the import of natural resources, technology, and capital goods. Exports, however, began to take off at even high rates. Since 1965 Japan's exports have tended to exceed imports, thus generating a continued surplus in balance of trade. Throughout this period both the style and the standard of living changed drastically. The process was complicated, shaped by mutually reinforcing interactions among industrialization, urbanization, increase in employed labor forces, increase in wages, and the expansion of consumer durables. Kosai summarizes this process as follows:

In response to industrial development, people changed both their jobs and their residences. From 1955 to 1970 the number of employees increased 15.22 million, from 18.77 to 33.39 million; the cities' population increased from 50 to 75 million, and their percentage of the total population increased from 56.3 to 72.1 percent. (Kosai 1988: 514)

Between 1955 and 1970 wages increased 2.12 times in real terms (Masamura 1988: 252). The manufacture of consumer durables was upgraded in both quality and attractiveness, from black-and-white television sets, washing machines, and refrigerators in the early 1960s to color television sets, air conditioners, and passenger cars in the late 1960s.

During this period Japanese enterprises, particularly the large-scale ones, established many characteristics that were quite distinct from those in the prewar Japan or Western companies. These companies came to be known for their distinctly Japanese style of business practices and management. For instance, the relationship among enterprises was effectively transformed: zaibatsu, financial cliques which controlled prewar Japan's economy and which were ordered to dissolve by the occupation authorities, were replaced by keiretsu, affiliate enterprise groups whose members mutually hold stocks and conduct more or less exclusive transactions with one another. Managerial positions, within individual enterprises including the chief executive officer, were located on the promotion ladder in ways calculated to further the development of so-called career employees (arrangements characterized by lifetime employment, the seniority rule of wages and promotions, membership of company unions, and so on). Those characteristics may be summarized in terms of what was called 'peoplism,' which amounted to enterprises of the employee, for the employee, and by the employee (Itami 1988). By the same token, company strategy tended to focus on larger market share rather than higher-yielding share and on long-term growth rather than short-term profit.

Rapid urbanization affected rural areas and agriculture in various ways. Industries in urban areas attracted labor, so that rural communities declined in population, and household composition changed as well. The farming population declined from 14.9 million in 1955 to 9.3 million in 1970. Nevertheless, agricultural outputs increased throughout these decades of rapid economic growth primarily due to the mechanization of already highly labor-intensive farming and the introduction of new crops and chemical fertilizers, insecticides, and pesticides. In the background, however, there were strong political factors that shaped these developments. Both the agricultural sector and the industrial sector received various forms of government assistance. On balance, agriculture benefited more, especially with respect to rice, the staple food in Japan, which was under strict government control both during and after World War II. In 1960 incentives for rice farming were provided by the continuous increase of government-controlled rice prices to reflect the increase in wages. Furthermore, the Agriculture Cooperative Union Law (1947, revised in 1954) and the Agricultural Fundamental Law (1961) deeply influenced Japanese agriculture and village life during this era of rapid economic growth. As a consequence, living conditions in rural areas improved, and farmers' incomes rose at a more rapid pace than those of urban dwellers.

POLITICS OF ECONOMIC GROWTH

On the political scene the Liberal Democratic Party (LDP), as a result of the merger of two conservative parties in 1955, assumed strong leadership under Nobusuke Kishi and led the nation to a series of political controversies toward the end of the 1950s. Domestically the Kishi cabinet (1957–60) began to take the offensive against left-wing forces such as trade unions and teachers' unions while at the same time attempting to strengthen the power of police officers. Externally Kishi pursued a policy of 'self-reliant national diplomacy.' (For instance, he attempted to strengthen the defense forces.) Kishi's highest priority was to rectify Japan's submissive relations with the United States due to the occupation. Following his visit to Washington, in June 1957, the issue was refocused toward the revision of the mutual security treaty in favor of Japan. In the course of these developments, political tensions increased both within and outside the Diet. Although revision of the security treaty was successful, the attendant political turmoil forced Kishi to resign.

Over time the LDP adopted less controversial postures. Throughout the 1960s the consecutive leaderships of the LDP-controlled government assured continuous growth of the economy and the improvement of living conditions. Hayato Ikeda, a bureaucrat formerly with the Ministry of Finance, succeeded Kishi and launched an 'income doubling plan.' In reality it was less of a plan than an assessment of prospect, the basis of which was a conservative estimate of the annual growth rate (7 per cent) during the following ten years. This figure was lower than the actual performance of the previous five years. Nevertheless, the plan had some utility; its announcement provided an image of the future, and a target for the Japanese people. In contrast to prevailing views in the late 1950s, they gained self-esteem and enhanced their confidence in economic performance and capacity for hard work. The LDP was in essence an alliance of less conservative factions, however, and the struggle for power within the party produced a challenger, Eisaku Sato, who criticized Ikeda's growth policy. But once he had taken power, his government (1964–72) let the Japanese economy expand based upon the gains of its own dynamic momentum.

Although the LDP maintained rural constituencies as its stronghold, it was funded largely by business interests. From an LDP perspective the government pursued a so-called dual-track policy – an economic policy in favor of industrial business at the relative expense of agriculture, and an income distribution policy in favor of farmers at the expense of the urban population. On the one hand, the government was supportive of rapid industrial development and enforced various interventions in order to make Japanese industries competitive internationally. On the other, the government effectively utilized redistribution mechanisms in favor of the rural population, such as rice price control, and revenue transfers from the central government to local governments for rural areas, or more specifically, for farmers. By contrast, living conditions in urban areas worsened due to overcrowding, insufficient social infrastructure, expanded pollution, and so on. In major cities like Tokyo and Osaka, LDP-supported governors were defeated by the contenders. Although it did not lose much in the Diet, the LDP continuously declined in its percentage of votes throughout the 1960s. As a consequence by the early 1970s the LDP had transformed itself into a broader (catch-all) party in order to maintain a majority power base.

Economic growth changed the political attitudes, voting behavior, and self-image of Japanese citizens, and consequently it affected the ruling LDP, as well as the other parties. In 1955, the year that two conservative parties merged in the LDP, the divided Japan Socialist Party (JSP) was united, and the Japanese people expected to see the beginning of a bi-party system. In the 1958 elections to the House of Representatives, the LDP and the JSP gained 287 and 166 seats respectively. As it turned out, the bi-party system failed to establish itself, and the JSP continued to lose support during the 1960s. The Democratic Socialists (the right faction of the JSP) formed a new party; and a Buddhist sect created the Clean Government Party to win support from more or less alienated people. While the LDP maintained dominant power, the opposition forces were in disarray. More importantly, an increasing number of Japanese citizens expressed no party preferences and chose to abstain in each election. (For a more detailed, but still concise, summary of the developments in Japanese politics during the era of rapid growth, see Fukui 1988: 207–13.)

'TRADING STATE' STRATEGY

When the Japanese government decided, in the 1950s, to develop a substantial petrochemical industry and to depend primarily on petroleum for its energy supply, the nation's increasing dependence on foreign trade became incorporated into the dynamics of economic growth. But this did not mean that Japan became a 'trading state' at the same time. Despite the country's entry into the Bretton Woods system and GATT, its external transactions were still heavily controlled by the government. It was not until the 1960s that the government liberalized various regulations and restrictions in order to transform Japan into a trading state closely linked with, and dependent upon, the world economy.

With respect to exports, the Japanese government adopted promotional measures early in the postwar decades in order to earn foreign currency for imports of vital goods. In 1950 the Japan Export Bank was created, which was transformed into the Japan Export–Import Bank the following year. In 1954 the Overseas Trade Promotion Organization was formed, which, in 1958, became the Japan External Trade Organization (better known as JETRO, whose literal translation of the official Japanese name is Japan External Trade Promotion Organization). A rapid increase in textile exports caused trade frictions with the United States and European countries in the late 1950s, and the government found it necessary to impose voluntary restraint on cotton textile exports vis-à-vis the United States, the first of the kind in postwar US–Japan relations.

The international environment was not favorable to Japanese exports. Even though Japan was admitted to GATT in 1955, 14 important trade partners, including Britain, Australia, and France, applied Article 35 of the agreement to Japan. This meant that Japan was excluded from most-favored-nation (MFN) treatment by those countries. The Japanese government had to negotiate with each of its counterparts bilaterally. While accepting the safeguard clause, the sensitive goods issue, the voluntary export restraint, and/or the promotion of imports, the government went through painstaking efforts to conclude treaties of commerce and navigation with one country after another. In this process of complex negotiations MITI decided not to apply Japan's trade liberalization program to ten countries that still discriminated against Japan. It took nearly a decade for the Japanese to repeal Article 35.

Import restrictions had been introduced as early as 1931 and were kept in force for nearly three decades. As exports rose, however, the Japanese government was increasingly pressured to lift these restrictive controls, which had often been used as a pretext for those countries that did not provide Japan with most-favored-nation (MFN) treatment. In 1959 MITI began to prepare import liberalization and in June 1960 the government adopted the Basic Outline for the Liberalization of Foreign Trade and Foreign Exchange, whose main objective was to increase the rate of liberalization from 40 per cent (as of April 1960) to 80 per cent within three years. In February 1963, in response to GATT's request, Japan became an Article 11 country of GATT, which meant that the government could not restrict trade for balance of payments adjustment. In fact, the trade liberalization plan was accelerated to reach well over 80 percent by the end of April 1963. By 1967 the rate had gone up to 97 per cent. Import restrictions remained on automobiles, special steel, petrochemicals, and electronic products, however, due to MITI's policies.

The country's manufacturing enterprises competed with one another to introduce foreign technology, to modernize plant facilities, and to export as much as possible. MITI, not being confident in the strength of Japanese industries (especially those sections that were in charge of manufacturing industries), was intent on supporting the steel, automobile, and petrochemical industries in particular. Although MITI drafted the International Competitiveness Enhancement Bill in 1963, it was never passed in the Diet.[1] Gaining momentum, the business community rapidly expanded. It was reluctant to accept government intervention. Moreover, business leaders preferred an environment that allowed enterprises to behave freely. Tax incentives, soft loans, and constrained applications of the antitrust law were all welcomed. Failing to introduce more direct policy instruments, MITI postponed the trade liberalization of those products that were considered important to the ministry's industrial strategy.

Throughout the 1960s the Ministry of Finance relaxed the extensive foreign exchange restrictions step by step. In February 1963 the IMF altered the status of Japan from an Article 14 to an Article 8 country. This meant that Japan was not to allow restrictions on foreign exchange with respect to current transactions. The Japanese government accepted the decision. And Japan became a full-fledged member of the IMF in April 1964.

Earlier, in 1962, Prime Minister Ikeda had visited Europe to pave the way for Japan to join the Organization for Economic Cooperation and Development (OECD), a consultative institution founded the previous year based on the Organization of European Economic Cooperation with new members such as the United States and Canada. The OECD had become a club of advanced countries, and the Japanese wanted to join. The organization admitted Japan in July 1963, and full membership was conveyed in April 1964. The cost for Japan to buy entry into the advanced societies' club was to liberalize capital movements. In June 1967 the government adopted the 'Fundamental Plan for Capital Liberalization' and took stepwise measures to liberalize both foreign investment in Japan and overseas investment by Japanese enterprises. While the Ministry of Finance and the business establishment were in favor of rapid liberalization, MITI insisted on more protective treatment of industries. By the end of the 1960s the government formally converged on a position of rapid liberalization.

The liberalization of trade, foreign exchange, and capital unleashed the growth potential of the Japanese economy. It not only accelerated modernization investments but also brought about mergers and an amalgamation of big enterprises in order to prepare for competition with foreign capital in Japanese as well as foreign markets. Together these various liberalization measures made the Japanese economy not only more closely integrated with the world economy, but also more competitive internationally. Japan's prosperity began to emerge from its own industries' outward expansion as the country became a 'trading state.' By the end of the 1960s Japan's

GNP ranked third on a global basis, behind only the United States and the Soviet Union. But the Japanese market was not sufficiently open to foreign industries despite the government's concerted strategy of liberalization.

Between 1963 and 1964 many important developments took place with respect to Japan's external economic relations. As a result, the country acquired the status of an advanced industrial society. In 1964 the Olympic games were held in Tokyo, and the bullet train system, which was constructed with a World Bank loan, began operation. The Japanese people began to sense the political implications of their rapid rate of economic growth through visible changes in Japan's status in international society.

FOREIGN POLICY INITIATIVES

If tense in Europe, the cold war in Asia had been hazardous and violent. US–Soviet confrontations had created four divided states in the postwar international system: one in Europe and three in Asia. While Germany was divided by allied forces according to occupation policies, each of the three Asian states was divided by bitter hostilities among its people – China's civil war, the Korean War, and the Vietnam War. As an ally of the United States, Japan's position was clear. The government could not pursue an Asia policy independent of the United States. The problems were inescapable. First of all, Japan's posture, always a domestic political issue, evoked harsh criticism from opposition parties and the intellectuals. For additional reasons, but primarily because of prewar colonial history, Japan's relationship with Korea was further complicated. It took more than 14 years and some 1,500 formal meetings for Japan to normalize diplomatic relations with South Korea. Even after the normalization in 1965, bilateral relations remained unsettled.

Beneath the surface, however, the Japanese government allowed informal and unofficial relations to develop with the Communist side of each divided state. With respect to Communist China the government adopted the principle of separating economics from politics, implying that private enterprises could enhance commercial relations with the mainland insofar as they observed the restrictions of the Coordinating Committee for Export Control to Communist Areas (COCOM). North Vietnam provided the Japanese steel industry with high-quality coking coal, one of the vital materials to produce iron. As for North Korea, the Japanese Socialist Party (JSP) played an important role in keeping contacts open. Even some LDP members of the Diet were involved in the maintenance of Japanese ties with those Communist countries.

Coinciding with an upward swing of the Japanese economy and with an enhanced international status for Japan, the government began to pursue a more 'visible' foreign policy, especially in Asia. The first major initiative was taken in the formation of the Asian Development Bank (ADB). The Japanese government not only offered the largest contribution but also invited the ADB to establish its headquarters in Tokyo. Although Japan was asked to contribute the same (and the largest) amount (20 percent of the total share) as the United States, at a ministerial meeting in November 1965, Manila was chosen for the location of the headquarters despite Japan's optimistic expectation.[2] The ADB was established in 1966, and Japan learned once more that its initiatives were not yet welcomed without reservation.

Shocked by such an embarrassing failure, the Japanese government was quick to respond by seeking to improve Asian sentiments toward Japan (Yamakage 1985: 145–47; 1990: 152–3). In April 1966, barely half a year after the setback of the ADB, the government convened the Ministerial Conference on Economic Development in Southeast Asia (MCEDSEA). The conference agreed to reconvene once a year thereafter, hosted by a different participating government on each occasion. Although Tokyo invited all Southeast Asian countries except North Vietnam, Burma refused to attend because of its strict neutrality, and Cambodia and Indonesia sent only observers because of their nonalignment policy.[3] Asian states interpreted Tokyo's scheme as reflecting a broader US strategy, irrespective of the real intentions of the Japanese government. In fact, the government tried to elicit its Southeast Asian counterparts' support for Japan in exchange for Japan's official development assistance (ODA). But Tokyo was always careful to obtain US approval of Japan's initiatives. Washington welcomed Japan's 'burden sharing'. In defense of noncommunist Asia Japan would exercise its economic power to support development in Asian countries while the United States would concentrate more on military-strategic commitments.

Another manifestation of the policy of 'burden sharing' with the United States was participation in the Asia–Pacific Council (ASPAC) (Yamakage 1985: 154). Proposed by South Korea, the organization consisted of allies of the United States such as Australia, New Zealand (ANZUS), the Philippines, Thailand (SEATO), Taiwan, South Korea, and Japan (through a bilateral agreement), as well as South Vietnam and Malaysia. Although the United States was not a member, the international political implications of the establishment of the ASPAC were obvious. However, the Japanese government continued to oppose an explicit reference to a military or political objective. Instead, offering ODA, Japan sought to emphasize economic and social cooperation for development so as to dilute the most stark political implications.

Increasingly the Japanese government played an active role – and sometimes seized the initiative – in regional organization (the ADB, the MCEDSEA, and the ASPAC). While the major source of leverage was Japan's economic power, the objective that the government pursued was not entirely self-interested economic expansion in favor of Japanese industries. The government, especially the Ministry of Foreign Affairs, wanted to reflect Japan's growing position in the world economy onto its foreign policy posture. Tokyo was fully sensitive to the implications of the cold war in Asia, on the one hand, but it sought ways to contribute to the changing international society in the context of North–South problems, on the other. In this way economic cooperation in a wider sense could go along with Japan's economic interests. And the government could exercise more political influence, domestically and internationally.

THE US FACTOR

At the meeting of Prime Minister Ikeda with President Kennedy in 1961, the 'equal partnership' between the two nations had been emphasized. Although few believed at the time that their relationship was in any sense equal, the decade from the early 1960s to the early 1970s can be characterized as one in which the process of equalization took place. But the two governments had different views of equalization. The US government kept trying to persuade the Japanese to become an equal ally, defined as having a more 'open' economy and playing a more active role in the Western strategic alliance. For Japan, on the other hand, policy toward the United States was dominated by efforts to alter the submissive relationship since the unconditional surrender. In this sense the revision of the mutual security treaty in 1960 had been a success. But clearly, Japan continued to depend on the United States in both the security and economy realms; American power looked omnipotent to the Japanese. The LDP leadership never intended to jeopardize close relations between the two countries, only to maneuver within these constraints. However, during the eight years of Sato's leadership (1964–1972), the longest cabinet in the country's modern history, the Japanese experienced new strains.

Because the two nations saw their bilateral relations from different perspectives, the issues each side was concerned with during the decade of equalization were paradoxically both uniquely mismatched and closely intertwined. The key issues of contention were as follows.

First was liberalization of foreign economic relations. The US government was increasingly critical of the slow liberalization process, not only of import restrictions but also of foreign investment in Japan; the Japanese side agreed to accelerate the process at the end of the 1960s. Second were trade frictions over Japan's textile exports. While the conflict over Japan's cotton exports was finally settled when the long-term agreement was signed in 1962, the US government requested voluntary restraint of wool and synthetic fiber in 1969, which lasted for two years, and a wider managed trade of textiles was initiated. Third was disagreement over the status of the mutual security treaty after 1970. According to the treaty as revised in 1960, each side was to be able to terminate it, with prior notice, after 1970. The concern of governments with the stability of the alliance, on the one hand, and with the possibility of another spasm of political turmoil in Japan, on the other, resulted in an agreement of nonaction as late as 1969. And fourth was conflict over Okinawa (the Ryukyu Islands) and the Bonin Islands. Premier Sato decided to negotiate with the US government on the return of territories under US control to Japanese sovereignty in 1967. The Bonin Islands were returned in 1968; but Okinawa's key position in US global strategy in general, and for operations in Vietnam in particular, made the negotiations difficult.

Each of these issues was important to both countries and difficult to settle.[4] The Japanese government placed the highest priority on the fourth issue (the Okinawa question) and made compromises on the economic issues (first and second items above) as much as necessary. A final agreement was reached in 1971, and Okinawa was returned the following year.

It is fair to say that the Japanese government was fully aware of its position within the US alliance system and pursued foreign policy in accordance with such a perception. Nevertheless, Japan's relations with the United States were not conflict-free. The US factor in Japan's international relations could not be denied; but this did not mean that Japan's foreign policy was always subordinate to US strategic objectives nor that it could only be explained by reference to American pressure. Especially with respect to its Asia policy, Japan sought to increase its own power.

ADJUSTING TO 'NIXON SHOCKS'

While Tokyo was busy negotiating with Washington on bilateral issues, US foreign policy was on the verge of a change so drastic such that the international environment that Japan had taken for granted suddenly disappeared. Since the late 1960s the US economy had shown unhealthy signs, including a high deficit and a decline in gold reserves (from 59 percent of the global total in 1955 to 27 percent in 1970). As a consequence, the United States suddenly abandoned the role of guardian of the Bretton Woods system.

By this time a new threat to US–Japan relations was beginning to emerge as the Nixon administration and the Beijing regime undertook the reduction of tensions between the two governments. 'Feelers' date back to the late 1960s, but as late as October 1970 Sato and Nixon, meeting in Washington, had agreed on close consultation with respect to the China question. On 1 July President Nixon's visit to China was announced. It therefore came as a 'shock' to Japanese leaders to discover during the summer of 1971 that the US government, without consulting with Japan, had taken the lead in its rapprochement with the People's Republic.

A month later, with an embattled US economy, Nixon announced emergency economic measures, including a 10 percent import surcharge and depreciation of the dollar. Even today the Japanese people still remember the two Nixon 'shokku' that shook Japan during the summer of 1971.

It would be a mistake to underestimate the psychological and political effects of these events.

In both strategic and economic terms, this fundamental shift of US foreign policy made it necessary for Japan to adapt to a new international system, but the change was too unexpected and too sudden. The Japanese government found it difficult to adjust immediately to either the Asia policy or its own economic policy. Although fully realizing that reorientation of the country's foreign policy was necessary, especially toward China, governmental authorities could not agree as to when, how, or precisely what it was that had to be changed. Lengthy discussions and deliberations among them led to a decision to abandon support for the Kuomintang government in the United Nations. It was also clear that Japan could no longer maintain the level of 360 yen per dollar, the fixed rate since 1949. But the country's financial and monetary authorities failed to appreciate the Japanese yen promptly or to close its foreign exchange market in support of that move. Worried about the impact of appreciation, the Japanese government tried to maintain the yen as cheap as possible and therefore proceeded to relax its financial policy to help the country's industries.

The two 'Nixon shocks' unleashed extensive criticism of the Sato cabinet. Sato tried to tone down the external influences upon Japan, but feeling that the prime minister had been in the premiership too long, the Japanese public looked forward to a new leadership suitable for new policies. Soon thereafter Okinawa reverted to Japan's sovereignty, Eisaku Sato's major foreign policy success, but in June of 1972 he announced his resignation. In the following month Kakuei Tanaka became prime minister, defeating Takeo Fukuda in the LDP presidential race.

The Tanaka cabinet (1972–4) was quick to normalize diplomatic relations with mainland China. The government in Beijing, which consistently refused negotiations with the Sato government, welcomed the change in Japanese premiership. As early as September 1972 Japan and China agreed to establish diplomatic ties, and Japan immediately terminated its official relationship with Taipei. Although Japanese business was quick to expand transactions with China, economic relations between Japan and Taiwan could not be neglected. Japan applied to Taiwan the principle of separating politics from economics, the same principle which had been applied to China for years.

After the decline of the Bretton Woods system, the international economic situation remained unstable. The Smithsonian Agreement – devaluing the dollar by raising the official price of gold from $35 to $38 per ounce – established the first major departure from the original fund agreement and effectively introduced a new regime.[5] The new regime did not last long. In fact, the response of the Tanaka cabinet was not different from that of its predecessor. The Japanese government attempted to appreciate the value of the yen as little as possible and emphasized further liberalization of the Japanese economy. A rapid increase in the country's foreign reserve, on the one hand, and in the US trade deficit, on the other, induced Japan to appreciate the yen significantly – by 26 percent from 360 yen to the dollar before the Nixon shock to 265 yen in early 1973.

STRAIN IN THE 1970s

As it turned out later, the era of rapid economic growth had in fact been over by the early 1970s, and since then the growth of Japan's GNP has never reached a 10 percent annual rate level. At the time, however, there was a widespread expectation that the Japanese economy would continue to grow rapidly. The Tanaka cabinet adopted an ambitious plan of economic expansion, which was often called 'the Reform of the Japanese Archipelago,' named after Tanaka's book written a few years before he became prime minister. Governmental expenditures expanded, and the financial authorities assumed a loose hold over monetary policy. As a consequence, the price level rose. 'The freedom of action that the government had acquired with the end of balance-of-payment constraints was misused, thereby incurring inflation and bringing to an end the period of high growth' (Kosai 1988: 537).

Economic conditions abroad were also in trouble. Inflation was becoming a worldwide trend, and in February 1973 foreign exchange markets were attacked by yet another sudden devaluation of the dollar. A shaky world economy affected the Japanese economy.

Before the really dramatic increase in oil prices had achieved its full impact, however, the Japanese economy had already shown signs of difficulty. The oil crisis of October 1973 and the subsequent rises in oil prices were a major blow for Japan. At the close of the year, after 'five consecutive years of larger balance-of-payments surpluses, Japan recorded a deficit of $10 billion. . . . This sharp turnaround reflect[ed] greatly reduced trade surpluses and large outflows of long-term capital' (Frank and Hirono 1974: 5).

The oil shock triggered panic as consumers tried to buy and stock not only petrochemical products but also various commodities for daily use. The government abruptly shifted to a tight monetary policy and called for extensive energy-saving measures. In 1974 Japan experienced 'stagflation,' with inflation at about 30 percent according to the wholesale price index and some 20 percent on the consumer price index, and with – 1.4 percent growth of GNP. Negative growth in the economy was experienced for the first time since Japan had begun its postwar recovery.

In the midst of this economic turmoil, Prime Minister Tanaka's popularity sharply declined as the opposition parties blamed him for mismanagement of economic policy. Even within the ruling LDP harsh criticism erupted, and the party leaders entered into a struggle for power. In July 1974 three cabinet ministers criticized the prime minister and resigned. In October, Tanaka's political fund-raising techniques were made public, disclosed, and criticized in a monthly magazine. Tanaka was forced to announce his resignation in November; and a year and a half later, with a few other LDP politicians and company managers, he was arrested with the allegation of the 'Lockheed scandal.' Takeo Miki, the leader of a small faction, was chosen to succeed Tanaka as a compromise measure following the harsh confrontation between Takeo Fukuda and Masayoshi Ohira, leaders of larger factions. The Miki cabinet (1974–6) was bound to fail due to weak leadership. Fukuda took office in December 1976.

The Japanese economy was heavily affected by these external influences. Industrial production declined by nearly 20 percent from the end of 1973 to the beginning of 1975. Enterprises tried to rationalize both production facilities and tighten labor force uses. Trade unions were by and large cooperative with managers to help their companies to survive, even though the wage increase rate declined significantly after the oil crisis. The Miki cabinet, concluding that Japan was in an era of 'low growth,' adopted a tight monetary policy. Inflation calmed down, but domestic demand was frozen. It was not until the end of 1976 that industrial production recovered to the level of early 1973. In retrospect it was during 1978 – when economic performance exceeded the peak attained before the oil crisis – that Japanese industries sought large-scale outward expansion.

VULNERABLE ECONOMIC POWER

Japan's economic expansion generated not only significant trade friction with the industrial nations, notably the USA, but also a marked rise in anti-Japanese sentiments in Southeast Asia. As stated in the previous chapter, Japan's economic return to Asia had been made possible by war reparations. Throughout the 1960s trade with Japan occupied an increasingly larger share of total trade for the Southeast Asian nations. By the same token Japanese investment in the region became increasingly visible year after year. By the early 1970s opposition forces, or contenders within the economic and political establishments, in countries like Indonesia and Thailand made use of anti-Japanese sentiments to fuel antigovernment movements. When Prime Minister Tanaka visited Southeast Asia in

January 1974, he was welcomed by anti-Japanese demonstrations in Bangkok and by riots in Jakarta.

At a conference organized in the mid-1970s by the Institute of Southeast Asian Studies in Singapore, academic and governmental representatives from Japan and from the Southeast Asian countries discussed the status and implications of Japanese activities and interest in the region. Japan's postwar economic growth was generally characterized as dramatic and the expansion of Japanese trade and investment as even more phenomenal. There was less consensus with regard to the implications of these activities and interests for Southeast Asia. Even severe critics conceded that Japan did not extend its trade by force. The expansionism was economic and was not achieved by 'gunboat diplomacy,' but it did involve collaboration with local groups. Impressive statistics of the rapid expansion of foreign investment and of the economy as a whole were not being matched by 'developments in host countries' (Sandhu and Tang 1974).

Most of the responses, however, although less favorable than the assessments of the Japanese present at the conference, were far more judicious. While taking cognizance of Japanese aid programs in the region, the positive aspects of Japanese trade and investment, and the relatively low priority assigned by the Japanese to their military establishment, other delegates were critical, nevertheless, of Japan's relationship with their respective countries, the negative impact of Japanese commercial activities on local cultures, the bargaining and leverage power of Japanese multinationals, and so forth. The Japanese were taken to task also for allowing themselves to support traditional ruling elites in Southeast Asia. All of these attitudes could undoubtedly be interpreted as indicators of Japan's new status as a commercial, financial, and industrial power.

The oil crisis of 1973 made the Japanese realize the vulnerability of their economic prosperity – what Keohane and Nye (1977) call 'vulnerability interdependence' – with respect to energy, the nation's vital resource. The government adopted an 'energy security' policy and ventured into 'resource diplomacy.' The potential Arab threat in the form of an oil embargo was so effective as to succeed in changing Japan's policy toward Israel and its position on the Palestinian question.[6] For Japan it was of vital national interest to guarantee a secured supply of energy. But the Japanese government was reluctant to support Kissinger's initiatives at the time and shifted its Middle East policy about a month after Japan had been informed that it would be subject to oil supply cuts.

In order to establish friendly relations with Arab oil-producing countries, the government employed an instrument of Japan's economic power – in this case overseas development assistance. Egypt ranked fifth as recipient of Japan's ODA (5.9 percent of bilateral assistance), and Iraq, ninth (3.5 percent); but during the next few years these and other Middle East countries (Egypt most notably) occupied increasingly significant shares of Japan's total foreign assistance. The support of Egypt's economic reconstruction by Japan was designed in part to repair deteriorating relations with the United States during the oil crisis itself. At the same time Japan tried to project an image of independence in foreign policy toward the Middle East by appearing not to be tied automatically to US assessments or policy preferences. But this was not an image that was sustained by reality. In fact, Japan continued to reflect American policy priorities in this area.

In essence Japan remained hostage to its dependence on imported raw materials. Fully aware of its overall dependence on natural resources from abroad, the Japanese government extended its ODA policy as a means of securing supplies of resources other than crude oil. The 'develop and import' scheme was given top priority in financing ODA projects designed to enhance natural resource exploitation. Among these were Indonesia's aluminum refinery, Peru's copper mining, Nigeria's uranium mining, and so on (Inada 1985: 295). Japan also began to emphasize the diversification of resource suppliers as well as the stockpiling of strategic resources. These policies, in addition to energy-saving measures, facilitated adjustments to continuing resource-related vulnerabilities.

In April 1975 the Conference on International Economic Cooperation was convened – followed in November of the same year by the first economic summit, which was, like the conference, convened in France. The Japanese government was involved in both of these organized efforts to induce stabilization of the world economy. But neither Japan's own vulnerability nor the problem of the management of its own economy reduced the country's growing and internationally recognized influence in the world economy. Although not entirely as equal as one might infer, the trilateralism of the United States, the European Community, and Japan began to be seen as a reality. It was already becoming obvious that, in the determination to overcome their major economic difficulties, the Japanese would in effect influence the course not only of their own future but also of the world economy as a whole.

Chapter 15

A new model of lateral pressure in postwar Japan

THE TRANSFORMATION OF JAPAN

The previous chapter has shown that Japan's economic recovery after the war was rapid, especially during the 1960s, when technology and GNP advanced at phenomenal rates. Japanese economic growth and development since World War II, in fact, are often referred to as a 'miracle.' At the same time, however, some of the country's characteristic features have persisted. There have been no major discoveries of energy or other domestic natural resources, for example, and resource constraints similar to those of the nineteenth century continue to present a problem – for the economy, for the leadership, and for the public. With respect to its economic activities, Japan remained almost wholly dependent on foreign trade for raw materials and for the foreign exchange to pay for them.

Deprived of its imperial possessions through defeat in war, Japan has enjoyed the advantage of not being burdened by decolonization or anticolonization struggles as were Britain, France and the Netherlands. Virtually all the Japanese who had settled in Manchukuo and overseas colonies returned home after the war, and for the most part the country has been spared the minority and post-imperial problems confronting other former empires.

Unlike their US and Soviet counterparts, Japanese military and naval units returned after the war to stay, and Japan itself was largely spared the cost of the cold war arms race. The constitution restricted Japanese forces to defensive capabilities and purposes. Japanese material and human resources were set free to rebuild the country and invest in its reconstituted economy, to innovate and expand its productive capacities. The Japanese government has sustained its reluctance to play other than limited and peaceful roles in the international system or to claim major responsibility for activities therein. It was in large part under pressure from the United States and from world events, Japan began in later stages of the cold war to assume a greater – though still limited – role in the military complex of the Western Alliance.

Japan placed primary emphasis on participation in international commerce and other economic activities. The country's first foreign trade ties following the war were with East and Southeast Asian countries, whose early demands for reparations were gradually transformed into a basis for substantial trade and investment. During the occupation, and thereafter, trade with the United States – which, in spite of the many conflicts, had become a major prewar trading partner – increased rapidly.

POSTWAR MANIFESTATION OF LATERAL PRESSURE

Japan's traditional sources of lateral pressure – population density, resource constraints, and technological advancement – were now even more acute than they had been previously. But, in contrast to pre-Pearl Harbor decades, the country's expanding activities and interests were predominately technological, economic, financial, and cultural rather than military. Foreign trade and investment activities replaced colonial expansion and military activity as a dominant mode of lateral pressure. Yet in some respects the country's resource problem had worsened. Raw materials that remained limited in supply were in some cases also being depleted, thus adding to the country's external dependence. Whereas in 1930, for example, Japan had met 50 percent of its energy demands with domestic coal, by the 1970s domestic coal supplies were meeting less than 10 percent of the country's needs, and imported oil was relied upon for 70 percent of Japanese demand. Despite greater frugality in oil consumption resulting from higher world prices, Japan's fundamental reliance on foreign sources was not, and could not be, reduced. Such dependency extended to resources other than energy, moreover, including metal ores and vital foodstuffs. Characterized by severe resource scarcities, in short, Japan's profile on this dimension remained in fundamental ways unchanged by the catastrophe of war, the occupation, and subsequent reconstruction. The constraints were essentially the same: high population density and dependence on external resources, combined with continued demands for technological advancement. New ways had to be devised, however, for successful adaptation to an industrial and postindustrial age of competing powers. Central to this adaptation were drastic changes in the mode, style, and characteristic features of Japan's foreign (as well as domestic) policy and behavior.

The postwar economic growth of Japan was made possible initially by imports of technology and advanced 'know-how' – knowledge and skills – primarily from the United States. In combination with domestic technological innovations, such imports made the country by the 1970s the third economic power in the world (after the United States and West Germany). Critical in this rapid development was Japan's technology policy. From wholesale importation in the immediate postwar years, the country gradually progressed to imitation, then to adaptation, and finally, by the 1960s, to new levels of innovation. By the 1980s, these were posing serious threats to the once unquestioned technological supremacy of the United States and West Germany (Gilpin 1987).

Before examining – and modeling – Japan's post-World War II growth, development, and expansion within the lateral pressure framework, we need to touch upon some of the extensive work, highly relevant to this perspective, that has been accomplished in recent years by both Japanese and Western scholars. Especially noteworthy for our purposes are studies concerned with competing growth paradigms, Japan's transformation from 'borrower' to investor and global economic challenger, and the leverage exerted by direct foreign investment as a manifestation of lateral pressure.

APPROACHES TO JAPANESE ECONOMIC GROWTH

Economic analyses anchored in the neoclassical growth paradigm have been widely used as a basis for explaining the type and nature of Japanese economic output. By definition, the economic paradigm de-emphasizes the role of government and minimizes the role of the state in exploring Japan's postwar performance. Yasusuke Murakami (1987) and others extended this notion to the 'Japan Inc.' model (Kaplan 1972), arguing for the weakness of government intervention and a balance between regulation and free competition. This paradigm tends to discount sociological and/or anthropological explanations in favor of training, productivity, investments, and related factors. Emphasis is placed on labor and on 'sophisticated managerial, organizational, scientific, and engineering skills capable of rapidly absorbing and adapting the best foreign technology' (Patrick and Rosovsky 1976: 12).

Focusing on the relationship between political power (politics and state) and economic power (economics and market) in seeking explanations for Japanese growth and development since World War II, a number of scholars in the West as well as in Japan have followed somewhat different paths. Alexander Gershenkron (1962), for example, pursued the historical perspective of 'late development' in shaping centralized, authoritarian regimes pushing for growth rather than equity. In his study of Japanese bureaucracy, on the other hand, Chalmers Johnson (1982) proposed a more formalized view of the 'developmental state' characterized in part by an elitist economic bureaucracy with a strong leadership in supportive relationships with entrepreneurs. In part, at least, this political-economy approach reflects a statist perspective founded on the 'strong state' concept (as defined by Krasner 1978) wherein Japan is viewed as more 'statist' than 'corporatist' (Katzenstein 1988).

Within this perspective students of Japanese politics generally have focused on the interaction and coalition building among major actors – including the Liberal Democratic Party (LDP), the Ministry of International Trade and Industry (MITI), and the Ministry of Finance (MOF). MITI and MOF exercised influence over the private sector through the unique practice of *amakudari* (literally 'descent from heaven'). This practice involved placing former government officials in corporate positions. Proceeding from this strong statist disposition, the institutional approach has been applied to a wide range of specific issue areas, such as the semiconductor industry (Okimoto 1984).

Elaborating on statist views, Yamamura (1986) argued further that rapid economic and technological growth throughout the 1970s was due to 'protection and nurture.' MITI encouraged the 'investment race' for high-technology growth in the private sector. Extending the market-oriented and the statist models, Okimoto proposed the concept of a 'network' of relationships between public and private spheres in the formation of economic policy. Signaling an 'intermediate zone' between the state and private enterprise, Okimoto stressed the social and sociological nature of the support systems enabling institutions like MITI to exert influence (Okimoto 1986: 41). And Samuels (1987) raised important questions about prevailing views of the state for business and for managing the country's resource strategy. In this connection he argued for the 'reciprocal content' between the state and business and emphasized bargaining among economic and political actors for jurisdiction over markets. Friedman (1988) suggested that Japan's economic development can be explained best by the activities of small firms and enterprises of a modest scale, not by the actions of the state and those of big business.

In contrast to neoclassical and political-economy perspectives, Michio Morishima (1982) has focused on social customs, norms, and common practices, such as the Confucian heritage. Others, like Ezra F. Vogel (1979), have stressed the efficiency and effectiveness of Japanese institutions based on group loyalty and collective consciousness; and still others, notably Hadley (1970), have focused on consensus formation and maintenance.

Explanations of why and how nations invest abroad have developed largely in a US setting, and the attendant theories owe their origin to the American experience. Macro-level explanations of foreign direct investment (FDI) – a powerful 'leverage force' in Japan's post-World War II lateral pressure – have been made in terms of oligopolistic market structures and market imperfections as the major determinants (Kindleberger 1969: 13–14; Hymer 1976). Micro-level explanations have centered primarily on firm behavior with a 'product cycle theory' as a dominant hypothesis (Vernon 1966). The emergence of Japanese foreign direct investments during the postwar years generated new explanations and new theories for the phenomenon. For example, Kojima (1973a) proposed that foreign direct investments achieve efficiency in allocating resources through international divisions of labor – although more recently Minami (1986) has argued for recognizing Japan's role in such divisions, summing the problem succinctly: 'Technological innovation has played a decisive role in the modern economic growth of Japan and will continue to be important in the future.' But the added caveat that 'technology borrowing from abroad may become increasingly difficult' interjected a note of concern for Japan's continued access to foreign knowledge and skills (Minami 1986: 426).

The change in status from 'borrower' to 'innovator' still required access to technological advances elsewhere. Between 1983 and 1986 Japan spent 2.8 percent of its GNP on research and development; only 22 percent came from government sources (Lederman 1987: 1125–8) – despite the acknowledged shift to creation and innovation.[1] Compared to other industrial societies, Japan attained a leadership with respect to patents. A 'citation ratio' ranks Japan first (1.34) in patents, followed by the United States (1.06), the United Kingdom (0.94), France (0.80), and West Germany (0.79) (*New York Times*, 7 March 1988, citing the National Science Foundation).

Comparing the Japanese experience in foreign direct investments with that of the United States, Kojima (1973a) postulated that Japanese FDI are more export-oriented, more resource-oriented, and more labor-intensive, while US foreign direct investments are more oriented toward domestic markets. He concluded that Japanese direct investments abroad were situation based, varied among countries or regions depending upon patterns of comparative advantage and changes over time. Ozawa also argued that foreign direct investments were an inevitable outcome of growth-oriented industrial policies. Recognition of fundamental space and resource constraints, he thought, was leading to a realignment of industrial policies and structures to pollution-free, technology-intensive industries and to promoting foreign direct investment as a means of relocating industry externally (Ozawa 1979: 88). In short, Ozawa and others have argued that Japan's investments overseas in labor-intensive industries evolved as a new mode of economic expansion, and access to low-wage labor in Asia thus enabled Japanese firms to maintain their international competitiveness. Implicit in this logic, of course, is the necessity of continued access to productive assets abroad.

Technology exports and technology 'transfer' appear as correlates of Japan's foreign investments. The distinction between US and Japanese modes of technology transfer closely parallel explanations of differences in patterns of direct foreign investment. US technology transfers are shaped by the operations of the multinational corporations and favour within-firm transfers. By contrast, Japanese technology exports were considered by some Japanese scholars to be more 'orderly' and congruent with the characteristics of the host economy and the direct foreign investment undertaken (Kojima 1977a: 1–2). Interpretation and theories aside, the fact remains that Japan's foreign direct investments and technology exports expanded dramatically during the postwar period, emerging as a distinctive feature of the *gamma* profile and the lateral pressure that it generated.

MODELING POSTWAR JAPAN

In setting out to represent the Japan case for the postwar period within the conceptual framework put forward in Chapter 1, we found that the components of the prewar model were not appropriate for the 1948–76 period when the country not only had a new profile but also faced conditions that were significantly new. Overall, the new Japan was characterized (as before) by (a) growth and development, (b) resource demands, and (c) expansion internationally. In the contemporary instance, however, the expansion has been economic and peaceful (though not without conflict) rather than territorial and violent. The sources of difference are traceable to the country's new profile, moreover, as well as to changes in its relationships with the international and global environments.

Military competition and colonial expansion, so central to the *beta* profile of Japan until Pearl Harbor, were no longer part of the new reality. Tables 15.1 and 15.2 highlight the features of the new framework and its theoretical basis, indicating the components of the model, description and rationale, measures used, and specific equations representing growth, development, and economic expansion.

Table 15.1 The Japan model: post-World War II

Component of the model	Description and rationale	Measure
Growth and economic capability	National economic capability resulting from the interactive effects of population growth, technological developments, economic productivity, and domestic resource exploitation	Gross national product
Resource demand	Demands for resources resulting from the interactive effects of population growth, technological development, economic productivity, and domestic resource exploitation	Nonfuel imports Energy imports
Expansion in economic mode	Expansion of economic activity outside national boundaries in search of external economic control for resource acquisition and establishment of markets	Total exports Japanese foreign direct investment

Table 15.2 The Japan model: postwar growth and expansion

Gross national = $\alpha_1 + \beta_{11}$ (industrial labor force as percentage of total labor
product   force) + β_{12} (foreign direct investment in Japan) + β_{13} (Japan's
                   foreign direct investment) + β_{14} (exports of technology) + β_{15}
                   (imports of nonfuel commodities) + μ_1

Nonfuel imports= $\alpha_2 + \beta_{21}$ (population) + β_{22} (wheat consumption) + β_{23} (capital
                   stock) + β_{24} (copper consumption) + β_{25} (merchant marine
                   tonnage) + β_{26} (total exports) + μ_2

Energy imports= $\alpha_3 + \beta_{31}$ (domestic energy supply) + β_{32} (population) + β_{33}
                   (gross national product) + μ_3

Total exports = $\alpha_4 + \beta_{41}$ (merchant marine tonnage) + β_{42} (exports of
                   technology) + β_{43} (gross national product) + β_{44} (energy
                   imports) + β_{45} (Japan's foreign direct investment) + μ_4

Foreign direct = $\alpha_5 + \beta_{51}$ (exports of technology) + investment β_{52} (gross
                   national product) + μ_5

Deflator: wholesale price index (1870–1970). Sources of the Japanese price
   indices include the Asahi Shimbun Index (1868–1900), the Bank of Japan Index
   (1901–65), and the International Monetary Fund Index (1966–76). Differences
   among base years were standardized.
      Instrumental variables were used to estimate the following independent
   variables: Japan's foreign direct investment (13, 45) imports of nonfuel
   commodities (15), total exports (26), gross national product (33, 43, 52),
   and energy imports (44). Figures in parentheses refer to the coefficients in
   the model equations.
      Instrumental variables (IV) were selected from among a wide range of
   instruments checking also for multicolinearity and autocorrelation among IVs.
Instrument List: steel production, pig iron production, copper consumption,
   national income, gross domestic capital formation, total imports, imports of
   raw materials, merchant marine tonnage, foreign direct investment in Japan,
   exports of technology, and the index of productive capacity (capital stock).

In the postwar model, economic growth, so central also to the prewar
model, is measured by change in GNP. Among the explanatory variables
are labor indicators, investment variables, and a critical import–export
relationship so salient in earlier decades. Resource demand is measured
by changes in energy imports and by changes in nonfuel imports. They
in turn are shaped by population, resources, and technology. Economic
expansion is measured by changes in total exports and in Japanese foreign
direct investment. The prominence of technological factors is taken into
account by the exports of Japanese technology as a determinant of Japan's
own overseas investments.

By far the most compelling change in modeling the postwar period is the
sheer scale and momentum of growth and change. Since all the economic

variables were shooting upwards so rapidly, it is technically impossible to untangle their interconnections.

The extent of post-World War II Japanese growth has thus dictated the use of *change* in the variables at hand, rather than the absolute values employed in the prewar analyses.

System of simultaneous equations

The system of simultaneous equations put forth in Table 15.2 is composed of five equations with five jointly dependent variables. As in the analysis for the earlier periods, this joint dependence among the key variables depicts the simultaneities and interconnections that make it difficult to pull the pieces apart in any meaningful way.

The first equation in the model measures Japan's growth and economic capability, a major indication of potentials for lateral pressure and outward expansion. The dependent variable in the first equation in the modern model – the variable to be explained – is Japan's *gross national product*. Population is indicated in the equation by the industrial labor forces (as a percentage of the total labor force). Resource demand is represented by nonfuel commodity imports, and technology is indicated by three variables: Japan's foreign direct investment abroad, foreign direct investment in Japan, and the country's technology exports.

Technology has played two major roles in Japan's postwar development; foreign investments in Japan represent that country's demand for foreign technology (inflow) and the attendant penetration of Japanese markets by foreign firms. The other side of the coin is Japan's own foreign direct investment, an indication of the country's growth and technological capability, manifesting itself in external investments (outflow). The country's exports of technology demonstrate this expanded technological base and the source of lateral pressure as manifested in commercial and technological modes.

Nonfuel imports are based on demographic factors – population and food consumption. The industrial factors (the index of productive capacity and copper consumption) and trade factors reflect the country's transport capabilities for imports (merchant marine tonnage) and its export capacity (total exports). Merchant marine tonnage is a particularly important capability enabling the transport of traded goods, whereas the export variable reflects the country's capacity for producing goods and distributing them 'outward'. These resource demands and constraints are specified in the second and third equations, depicting energy imports and nonfuel imports.

The second equation represents one component of resources. *Energy imports*, the second component, is determined by population and GNP, the two conventional determinants of energy use anywhere. Resource constraints are reflected in domestic energy supplies, which directly affect energy demand and hence energy imports.

Since Japan's postwar lateral pressure has been manifested in economic rather than military (or territorial) expansion, the fourth and fifth equations focus on two specific forms of activities, total exports and foreign direct investment. *Total exports* are shaped by technology (measured by Japan's ability to earn income from sales of technology), economic growth (measured by GNP), energy demand (energy imports), and foreign direct investment. This last linkage – between foreign direct investments and total exports – is an area of considerable controversy wherein analysts still debate both the theoretical and the empirical bases upon which such a relationship can be posited, let alone demonstrated. Nonetheless, we believe the relationship of foreign direct investment of Japan to its export performance is an important feature of the new postwar Japan.

Foreign direct investment is shaped in this model by Japan's growth, economic capability, and exports of technology. (In many ways, foreign direct investment can be seen as functionally equivalent to colonial expansion in the prewar model.)

In schematic terms the relations among the five jointly dependent variables in the model are represented in Figure 15.1. The distinctive features of this model are the interdependence among economic growth, energy imports, foreign direct investments, exports, and nonfuel imports. These relations can be summarized in two major positive feedback loops. First is the linkage relating economic growth to demand for energy imports, which in turn affects the growth of the economy – thus generating more demand for energy. (In a simplified fashion this loop depicts the resource

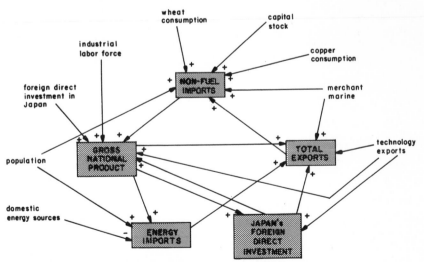

Figure 15.1 Japan postwar model: overview of the sytem, 1946–76

dilemma for Japan.) Second is the interactive relation between economic growth and expansion in economic activity of Japan's own direct foreign investment. An expansion of direct foreign investment, and similarly any disruption in foreign investments, will constrain growth. The model in Figure 15.1 represents our broad hypotheses about the postwar Japan case. The test is whether this model is supported by the evidence at hand.

Database and estimation procedures

The data employed to estimate the parameters of the model for postwar Japan are composed of annual observations of a series of variables over the entire 30-year span based on government, Bank of Japan, and international sources.[2]

The strong interconnections (severe multicolinearity) among the variables, due to Japan's phenomenal growth in economic activity, trade, investments, and almost every indicator of economic and technological performance, was in itself an indication of the postwar processes. Everything grew at the same time. The excessive colinearity further underscores added indication of Japan's post-World War II phenomenal growth.[3] As for earlier periods, the final estimation of the model utilized a two-stage least squares estimation technique.[4]

THE RESULTS

Growth and development

Among the most significant determinants of growth and development in postwar Japan were (statistically) technology exports, nonfuel imports, and Japan's foreign direct investment. Of these, Japan's own foreign investments abroad and exports of technology were particularly significant influences contributing to changes in the country's GNP. This finding does not reduce the importance of investments of multinational firms in Japan. However, on statistical grounds alone we can state with confidence that the country's own technological variables were considerably more influential in shaping changes in its economic activities than were the particular factors labeled foreign investments in Japan. Overall 66 percent of the variance in changes in the country's GNP is accounted for by these combinations of factors.

Unequivocally, the important conclusion here is that Japan's technological advancement, together with its foreign economic activity, contributed most to increases in its economic activity.[5]

Resource demand and constraints

The resource demand issue was explained with less success. Only 33 percent of the variance in nonfuel imports is accounted for, primarily by copper consumption, merchant marine tonnage, and total exports – all contributing to such imports.[6] The most significant positive impact on changes in nonfuel imports is the changes in total exports. This result reflects, once again, the import–export dynamic so prevalent in the pre-World War II period. The positive feedback trade loop linking imports and exports remains apparent, reinforcing the essentiality of trade for growth – even survival.

The links are obviously complex. The greater the exports were, the higher was the demand for nonfuel imports. And when this result is combined with the first equation (recall that nonfuel imports have significant effects on the country's GNP), the central role of external trade is further underscored. In the equation explaining changes in exports we will show that domestic economic activity, GNP, in turn has an impact on Japan's exports.

Changes in the imports of energy are explained a little more successfully than nonfuel imports (and influence). Forty-seven percent of the variance is accounted for. The country's GNP is the more influential explanatory factor (the other is change in the domestic supply of energy), underscoring again the importance of access to energy and energy use for the country's economic activity.[7]

Economic expansion

Japan's economic expansion is modeled in two equations, one specifying the determinants of total exports, and the other representing the growth in Japan's direct foreign investments abroad. Both exports and investments are central features of Japan's transformation and crucial for the country's economic performance. Over the postwar period, Japan accumulated a large surplus in balance of trade (and in its overall balance of payments). The competition that Japanese companies have given to the United States and Western Europe is already legendary. (Expansion of competition in the banking sphere has now become a significant feature of this legend.) Japanese investment overseas continues to expand in search of new markets and new opportunities – a clear indication of lateral pressure in an economic rather than a military mode.

The model generates a good fit, or explanation, for changes in Japan's total exports during the postwar period, accounting for 65 percent of the variance. Two influences on exports are particularly significant – energy imports and merchant marine tonnage. If a brief interlude around the oil crisis of 1973 is allowed for, energy imports can be seen as pushing forth the almost continuous growth of exports throughout the postwar decades.

Since exports of technology, which became important later in the 1950s decade, did not exert a positive impact on exports (the influence is significant but in the wrong direction, which may imply lagged relationships), our hypothesis is not confirmed. Also puzzling is the fact that changes in GNP and foreign direct investments exert a negative impact on changes in the volume of exports, whereas, consistent with the thesis of upwardly spiraling sources of lateral pressure. We had expected a positive relationship. However, since changes in GNP and changes in exports are similar in trend prior to the 1970s, and both take nose dives prior to the events of 1973, one possible interpretation is that changes in exports preceded or anticipated changes in GNP. It may also be that changes in GNP affect changes in exports – with a lag.

The explanation of the results with respect to foreign investment is of a different nature. Since Japan did not begin its overseas direct investments until the mid-decade of the 1960s, and the growth was not noteworthy until the end of the decade, what appears as a strong, significant, and negative influence may perhaps be a statistical artifact. The negative change in imports following the oil price increases of 1973 was also experienced by foreign direct investments, but on a much smaller scale.

THE FEEDBACK PROCESSES

The five equations, although discussed separately, are in fact highly interdependent, as the coefficients were estimated within a system of simultaneous equations. Figure 15.2 shows the interactions of the five jointly dependent variables and the basic results (beta coefficients and relative impacts). The linkages among the endogenous variables themselves are all significant. For example, there is a strong, mutually reinforcing, and positive relationship between changes in economic activity (GNP) and Japan's direct investment abroad. This interdependence truly characterizes the case of Japan – domestic growth generates demand for imports of raw materials and energy resources as well as direct foreign investment, all leading to further growth. There are also some revealing effects of the 'master variables' – population, technology, and resources.

The *population* factor in the model is represented by two variables, changes in population size and changes in the industrial labor force. Population size has had a dampening (negative) impact on changes in energy imports and on changes in nonfuel imports. The country's family planning program, seeking to bring the population factor under control, appears to be effective in the sense that population changes have not 'pushed up' energy demand; *in fact, the population variable is not statistically significant in this model.*[8] The impact of the industrial labor force (the second population variable) on economic performance is positive, but not statistically significant.

The *resources* variables in this model truly depicts the constraints on Japan's own resource base and the inevitable effects; the lower the domestic energy resources, the higher were the energy imports. Consumption of copper also led to greater nonfuel imports. Domestic food consumption contributed to nonfuel imports as well, reflecting critical population demands.

The *technology* variable is the most elusive. Technology plays a multifaceted role in the 'real' world and in our representation of this reality in the post-World War II model. New knowledge and skills introduced into Japan during early postwar years were brought in largely through foreign direct investment. The well-known profile of Japanese technological change – proceeding through imitation to innovation to maintaining a competitive edge – began with observation of foreign enterprises established in the country. These investments had a significant positive influence on Japan's economic performance. By contrast, however, when the relative impact of GNP is compared with the impact of Japan's direct investment abroad, we find that Japan's own external investments had the greater impact on changes in the country's gross national product.[9]

DYNAMIC FEEDBACK

Together four feedback loops dominate this system and show the distinctive features of Japan in the post-World War II period:

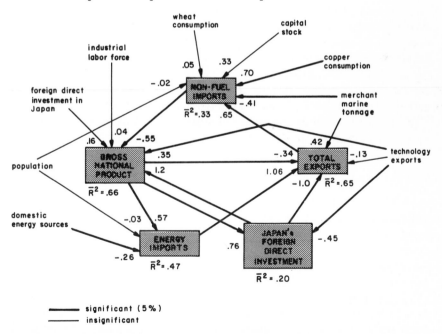

Figure 15.2   Basic results: Japan postwar model

First is a positive feedback loop connecting the change in GNP with the change in foreign direct investment and representing the relationship between domestic economic growth and capability and external financial and commercial expansion. The greater the domestic growth, the stronger its foreign investment performance is, and, in turn, the greater is the economic growth.

Second is also a positive loop, connecting the change in GNP, the change in total exports, and the change in nonfuel imports, representing Japan's production cycle with respect to its imported and exported goods and their contribution to economic activity. This feedback relationship shows the vulnerability of Japan to its export sector.

Third is the negative feedback connecting changes in GNP to changes in energy imports, changes in total exports, and changes in nonfuel imports. This loop – which involves the same variables as the second one, except for the role of energy imports – shows that energy dependence has a negative effect on economic growth.

Fourth is the positive feedback connecting changes in GNP, changes in foreign direct investment, changes in total exports, and changes in nonfuel imports. This feedback loop shows the importance of foreign investments in reducing the constraints of energy dependence at home – see Figure 15.3.

Three of these four feedback relationships are positive or self-reinforcing, and one is negative. The negative loop provides restraints on the country's domestic growth and external economic expansion. Access to energy is the constraining factor as the costs of imports become an economic burden. Japan became a major importer in the late nineteenth century, with no prospects for self-sufficiency. All the other feedback loops in the postwar model – which relate level of changes in GNP (the major indicator of economic activity) to exports, to imports, and to direct foreign investments – are positive. They propel the growth spiral and expansion upward and 'outward,' reflecting the push from internal sources.[10]

Relative impacts of major variables

As with our analysis of pre-World War II Japan (1876–1941), the beta or path coefficients serve as indicators of the relative impacts in the model, indicating the influences of certain variables upon others.[11] (The beta coefficients for the 1946–76 model and relative impacts of each variable are shown in Figure 15.2 above. The strong interdependence among the endogenous variables is immediately apparent.

The strongest beta value (1.21) represents the effect of Japan's direct foreign investment on GNP. Another high coefficient is the impact of GNP on Japan's direct foreign investments. Both effects connect GNP with the change in direct foreign investment.[12]

Changes in merchant marine tonnage directly and significantly affect trade; and changes in technology have a strong positive impact on GNP, pushing economic performance upward, but exert a somewhat weaker impact on Japan's direct foreign investments. The strongest impact of all the exogenous variables, changes in copper production,[13] signifies the effect of increased consumption of minerals, a result of industrialization, and an attendant increased demand for imports.

Overall, as one would expect, economic growth and technological advancement in postwar Japan are far more significant than population. The receding role of population in Japan's lateral pressure is itself an outcome of economic growth. The postwar family planning programs in Japan can be credited with the transformation of the demographic parameters, although resource access remains a critical concern for future growth and development – and the effects of aging of the population were not yet fully apparent.

The initial feedback loops in the model, representing the systematic relationships in postwar Japan, account for many of the changes in the variance of the jointly dependent variables representing processes of economic growth, resource constraints, demand for foreign markets, and economic expansion internationally.

COMPARING JAPAN BEFORE WORLD WAR II AND AFTER

The postwar Japan model differs from the prewar case in several respects.

First, the nature of the population variable has changed. Whereas population was a significant determinant of lateral pressure in the prewar

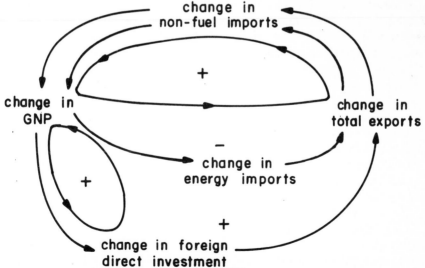

Figure 15.3   Feedback loops in the postwar Japan model

model, it is significantly less so in the postwar case. This is not to suggest that population as a master variable was irrelevant after the war but that, specifically, changes in population size and in the industrial labor force have had little noteworthy effect. (And the impacts of an aging population have not yet become evident.)

Second, since a full military option was not available in the postwar period, the role of economic modes of lateral pressure was structural; the salience and significance of these economic factors are remarkable.

Third, there are strong elements of continuity over time with respect to the role and relationship of imports and exports in the overall growth and expansion process.

In postwar Japan – still characterized by high technology, high (but controlled) population, and limited domestic resources – lateral pressure cannot be attributable to population but rather to technological capability and resource constraints, both factors generating demand for external sources. (Again the population is relatively negligible and not significant.) We would not expect to find empirical results – and the four feedback loops – in a country with high population, low technology, and high resources; nor in countries with low population, low technology, and high resources; nor in countries with high population, low technology, and low resources.[14]

CONCLUSION

The postwar Japan model demonstrates that the dynamics of expansion in Japan's economy are based on *positive, mutually reinforcing interactions between economic capability and performance, imports of energy and other resources, and foreign economic expansion.* Statistically, a close interactive relationship between GNP and Japan's direct foreign investment (a manifestation of lateral pressure in an economic mode) is apparent. Statistically, also, the country's economic performance is strongly tied to its trade sector (its exports and imports).

The continued predicament for Japan is its dependence upon these linkages and its vulnerability to interruptions if any of these linkages are threatened. At the beginning of 1986, beyond the scope of our quantitative analysis, Japanese companies accounted for 6.8 percent of the world's total foreign direct investment; this was close to the German (8.1 percent) or Dutch (8.6 percent), but far behind British (18.1 percent) or US (36.1 percent) multinational companies (*The Economist*, 5 December 1987: 15).

The prominence of technological advances and technological exports further characterizes Japan's contemporary situation. Enhanced competitiveness and technological dominance are the country's distinctive characteristics today. We can expect, therefore, greater reliance on, and use of, economic leverages in interactions with other countries.

The analysis in this chapter provides further confirmation of changes in the influence of the 'master variables' in shaping the dramatic expansion of Japan after World War II and generating lateral pressure in several behavioral modes. It is a system that is spiraling upward, in economic and political rather than military terms. On statistical grounds, at least, there are overwhelming indications of trends in growth and explosive processes. In statistical parlance, Japan's international economic activities appear to be overdetermined – too many factors pushing for external economic expansion in too many ways. The implications of these trends are compelling; Japan is 'pushing outward' on various economic fronts, and will continue to do so. How will other states accommodate this strong pressure? How will the international system as a whole adjust to a new dominant power, where economic expansion has been strongly demonstrated?

This emphasis on lateral pressure should not obscure the fact that each statistic, each figure, represents the outcome of discrete individual decisions (Choucri and North 1972). The outcomes are those processes we have modeled, and they provide the arena for public policy, the realm of choice for decision makers, and the substance of diplomatic discourse and contention. They become elements of 'high politics' when fundamental national interests and concerns are evoked.

Chapter 16

Simulating Japan's post-World War II expansion

Earlier chapters have reported on the use of simulation to test the plausibility of the model and its behavior as applied to the pre-World War I and the interwar periods of growth and expansion and to explore the impacts of a variety of (hypothesized) alternative conditions or policy interventions. This chapter employs the same techniques to test the system of post-World War II equations. The intent was to model *changes* in the endogenous variables – not their absolute values – and accordingly, also, to simulate the changes. Thus, since the variables are essentially 'detrended,' the first difference transformation does not carry the serial correlation that often serves to generate better-fitting simulation when compared to the actual (or historical) record. To generate good 'fits' for *changes* in the variables of interest requires by necessity especially strong and robust estimation of the coefficients.[1]

The chapter closes with some brief comparisons between the post-World War II simulations and those of the pre-World War I and inter-war periods.

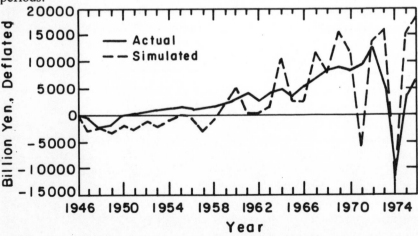

Figure 16.1 Actual and simulated changes in gross national product, 1946–76

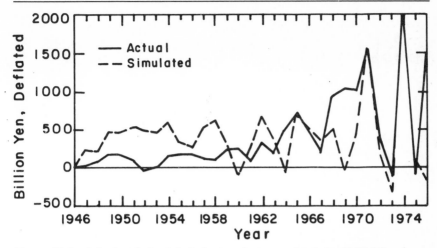

Figure 16.2 Actual and simulated changes in energy imports, 1946–76

SIMULATING CHANGES IN THE DYNAMICS OF LATERAL PRESSURE

In the post-World War II period, Japan's lateral pressure was manifested primarily in terms of economic expansion – initially because the country had been disarmed following its defeat, partly because the new constitution forbade engagement in war, partly as a widespread response to the nuclear bombing of Hiroshima and Nagasaki, and partly because the United States had raised its defense umbrella over the island nation. The military option was thus essentially absent in the post-war Japan case, and trade, investment, and associated activities have constituted the primary mode for lateral pressure.

The country's national output – a fundamental element of lateral pressure – was underestimated by the specifications in the postwar model. The empirical ('real') indicators of lateral pressure were higher than the estimated values, indicating greater pressure in actuality than we were able to explain successfully.

The simulation of *changes in GNP* shows greater fluctuations than occur in actual changes in GNP, but the two series are appreciably close – see Figure 16.1. During the first decade of the postwar period, the historical GNP record shows changes at levels higher than those simulated.[2] For example, the volume and change in Japanese economic activity during the immediate postwar period exceeded those. From this we infer that some important components or elements of the early decade are not well understood. From 1960 on the 'fits' of simulation and the historical record improve appreciably, taking more accurately into account the spectacular growth of subsequent decades.

The simulation of *change in imports of energy* shows the same upward trend in the 1950s and 1960s, as does the historical record – see Figure 16.2.

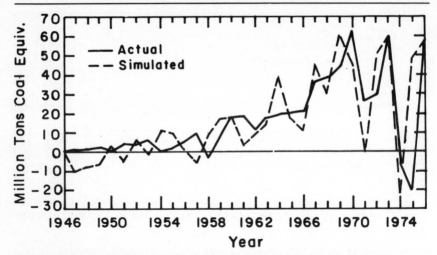

Figure 16.3 Actual and simulated changes in nonfuel imports, 1946–76

The simulation follows the trend well. In the 1970s the gap between the actual values and the simulated values is greater than in the earlier years, which means in part that our explanation of the factors that generate nonfuel imports is less successful for those later years than for the earlier ones.[3]

The simulated change in *nonfuel imports* shows fluctuations less sharp than revealed by the historical record, but the discrepancy between the two traces of these imports is small – see Figure 16.3. This is clearly an effective simulation.

The simulation of *changes in total exports* reproduces a record that is higher than the actual changes in total exports for the period 1947–59 – see Figure 16.4. In the 1970s the simulation remained close to historical values despite the enormous fluctuations at that time.

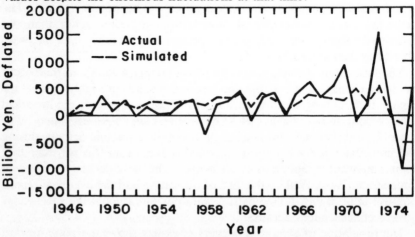

Figure 16.4 Actual and simulated changes in total exports, 1946–76

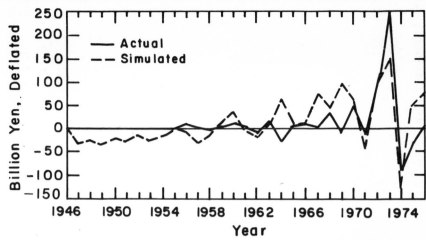

Figure 16.5   Actual and simulated changes in foreign direct investment,
1946–76

The simulation of *change in foreign direct investment* is lower than the
actual change in the 1950s and higher than the actual change in foreign direct
investment in the 1960s – see Figure 16.5. So while we remain essentially on
track, we may be off in terms of timing. This discrepancy is due to the fact
that in reality Japanese export performance and growth in foreign direct
investment did not take place on a substantial scale until well into the 1960s.

Such efforts at pinpointing where the fit is good and where the replication
efforts are not successful constitute a form of validation that goes beyond
the initial assessment of goodness of fit for conventional statistical or
econometric estimates, based on significance of the individual variables,
or variance in the dependent variables accounted for by the independent
variables. Simulating absolute levels of any variable is easier than capturing
their fluctuations in changes. The analysis of the 1946–76 period yields
further support to our model of Japan's lateral pressure. (Summary
statistics for the simulations are in Appendix IV.)

We have shown, for example, that during prewar periods Japan's military
expenditures were influenced by the size of Japanese colonial holdings.
We also indicated how perceptions of the adversary affected the level of
Japanese army and naval expenditures. In the postwar period, when the
military option (as a mode of lateral pressure) was no longer available,
it was appropriate to determine how changing trade and investments –
both manifestations of lateral pressure in economic modes – contributed to
changes in economic performance. The simulation was intended to indicate
how successfully we could replicate the historical record with the model and
to reveal at what points the changes were not well simulated.

For technical reasons, a simple question remained unanswered: could
we simulate accurately the levels and trends in the key variables on the
basis of the changes? The problem can be summarized as follows. In

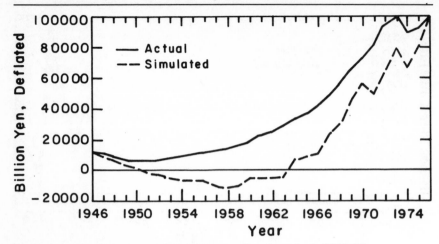

Figure 16.6   Actual and simulated gross national product, 1946–76.

the post-Japan model, growth in all the national attribute dimensions contributed to lateral pressure – for historical reasons largely in economic modes. Thus, in statistical terms, everything was related to everything else, and untangling individual causal inferences was not feasible. So we resorted to an indirect way of answering the question.

COMPARING SIMULATION WITH THE HISTORICAL RECORD

To explore the robustness of the results further, we compared the simulated levels of each variable with its actual levels. Because high multicolinearity precluded estimation of the coefficients and since such estimation is a prerequisite to simulation, we transformed the simulated changes (first differences) back into their respective absolute levels. These simulated,

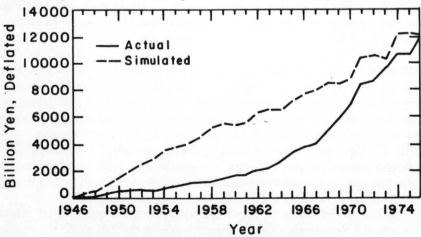

Figure 16.7   Actual and simulated nonfuel imports, 1946–76

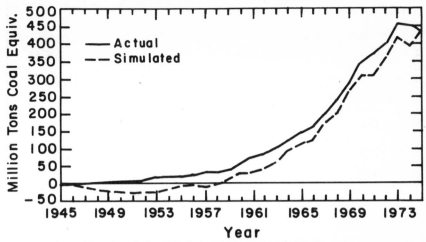

Figure 16.8 Actual and simulated energy imports, 1946–76

transformed level variables were then compared with the actual, historical observations to yield degrees of fit. In this way we could compare *levels* of historical reality directly with *levels* of simulated reality:

First, the *simulated gross national product* is consistently lower than the actual GNP for the entire period. The model does not generate as much economic activity (and hence lateral pressure) as is reflected in the actual data – see Figure 16.6. The two tracks diverged in the early 1950s and did not re-achieve close coupling at any point within the entire period (signaling some elements excluded in our modeling of Japan's economic growth). The oil shock of 1973–4 had notable effects on the Japanese economy, however, and at that point the simulation began to catch up with the actual GNP levels. When economic growth was curtailed (due to oil price increases), output declined, and the simulated output represented the process fairly accurately. Either there is a component missing, however, or some of the

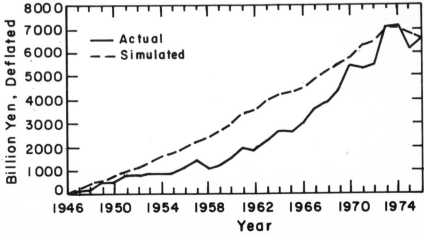

Figure 16.9 Actual and simulated total exports, 1946–76

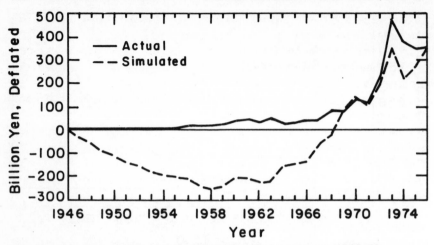

Figure 16.10 Actual and simulated direct foreign investment, 1946–76

coefficients are underestimated. Overall the results suggest that we have not been able to capture the full impact of increased knowledge and skills, innovations, or enhanced efficiencies.[4]

Second, the *simulated nonfuel imports* were consistently higher than actual imports.[5] Although the trends are in the same direction (an important consideration), the simulation overshoots the historical path until the early 1970s – see Figure 16.7. Again it appears that we do not capture successfully the domestic sources of resource demand in a period of sustained prosperity, whereas the model creates excessive nonfuel imports. But when the economy contracts in the early 1970s, the fit is better, and the model becomes more consistent with known reality.

Third, in contrast with our first two results, the *simulation of energy imports* is extremely successful, being only slightly – though consistently – lower than the actual energy imports for the entire period – see Figure 16.8. In effect, therefore, Japan had imported somewhat more energy than was simulated by the model.

Fourth, the *simulation of total exports* is much higher than the actual total exports – see Figure 16.9. In the 1950s and 1960s the historical divergence is especially great, whereas in the 1970s the simulation fares better. With respect to sheer volume, the simulated model generates more goods and services for export than Japan exported historically. Again the trends between simulated and actual exports are closer in the early 1970s.

Fifth, we find that the actual levels of *direct foreign investments* are considerably higher than those simulated by the postwar model.[6] On conceptual grounds we cannot properly explain the levels of changes in Japanese investments abroad before the late 1960s, although we do quite well subsequently. (The two significant explanatory variables in the equation are exports of technology, an exogenous variable, and the GNP, an endogenous variable.) More direct foreign investment was in fact taking place than we could account for – see Figure 16.10.

To summarize the post-World War II model, three patterns emerge in our comparison of the simulated historical variables: overestimation (nonfuel imports and total exports), underestimation (GNP and direct foreign investment), and close approximation (energy imports). The model overstates Japan's trade activities and underrepresents its economic output. The model also suggests that Japan must expand foreign trade activity to maintain its GNP performance, even at levels lower than the actual GNP. This illustrates again the dependence on trade. Continued access to goods and services from the external environment is essential, as is the sustained export of goods and services.

The model is particularly reliable in representing Japan's economic activity and foreign economic expansion when the country encounters external constraints unfavorable for domestic economic conditions. The simulation is on balance closer to reality in the 1970s than in the earlier post-World War II period. In the 1970s international economic conditions were much more constrained than they had been earlier, as Japan's economic growth adjusted to the 1973 oil shock.

We interpret the overestimates of simulated exports (when compared with the actual levels of exports) as indicating that the postwar Japan model does not sufficiently represent the constraints on Japanese exports.[7] These constraints, we believe, were external to Japan and part of the international environment, including commercial relations among industrial powers. We interpret the simulated export levels to represent the exports that *would have taken place* (based on domestic production capacity and bases for lateral pressure) had there been fewer (or no) constraints from the international environment. The simulated trend in exports thus indicates the potential for manifestation of lateral pressure in an unconstrained environment.

RECONSTRUCTING REALITY

The quantitative analysis was accomplished in three parts: (a) estimation of the model; (b) simulation of the system – a means of checking and evaluating results; and (c) experimenting with counterfactuals ('what if' evaluations of historical options that were available but were not acted upon). Because our results showed that the coefficients estimated for the period before World War I (1878–1914) differed from those of the 1915–41 period, indicating in effect a system break, we were able to obtain quantitative confirmation of shifts or changes in the Japan model. But when the simulations of these two periods are compared with the post-World War II simulation, the results indicate a much more radical system break.

These two sets of coefficients – drawn from two different historical periods – provided new inputs into the simulation. In this regard it is both methodologically and historically appropriate to stress that the simulations were based solely on the estimated coefficients of the system of simultaneous equations without resort to the historical record (or known data) at any point in the simulation aside from the initial starting point.[8]

In simulations of the earlier pre-World War I and interwar periods, the trend toward expansion (lateral pressure) was manifested by territorial (colonial) acquisition, which was 'explained' in large part by imports of raw materials driven, in turn, by population growth. The 'system break' during the interwar period, however, was indicated primarily by a shift from lateral pressure generated by resource demand to a pattern of military investment in response to a perceived Soviet threat – including collisions between Japanese and Soviet/Mongolian troops along the Manchurian (Manchukuo) border in the late 1930s and US opposition (including violent 'incidents') to Japanese expansion (especially in China proper).

Imports of raw materials 'overshoot' during the earlier, pre-World War I years, indicating more simulated pressure than was historically the case; but later and throughout the interwar period, raw material imports are notably underestimated – more was there than we could account for; as noted, the actual pressures for imports were greater than the model was able to reproduce. The same is generally the case for exports of finished goods; between 1920 and 1930 the simulation reveals a decline in exports relative to previous years (and to succeeding decades); and drawing on historical analysis, we inferred that the simulated trade for this decade represented what could have taken place had there been fewer external constraints.

The navy and army expenditures were well simulated, although the simulated value exaggerated the allocations during the Russo-Japanese War, and also the World War I years. Our interpretation was that the economic and military conditions for the lumpy expenditures were in place.

The strength of bureaucratic inertia was such that variations in previous years' military allocations did not matter substantially during the earlier decades, but subsequently bureaucratic inertia had set in to a point where a certain rigidity was in place. The same is generally the case with respect to government revenues; there, too, inertia was established. And variations in imports from the colonies overall had no substantial impacts on simulation of any expenditures. We concluded, again, that the basic patterns pushing for militarism had been established, and the system could not readily accommodate to 'downward escalators.'

In general, the simulations turned out to be 'strikingly close to reality' (cf. p. 201). The most difficult variable to simulate was colonial expansion – largely because of the stepwise acquisitions. Because this form of expansion was embedded in an integrated system, however, the simulation was remarkably accurate. Japanese trends leading to Pearl Harbor were closely replicated, and our hypothetical treatment of internal pressures, bureaucratic affects, and the dynamics of competition was further confirmed. Except for the years around World War I and 1932–3, the simulation of government expenditures for colonial administration was generally successful. The latter instance suggests that administrative and management expenditures sustaining Japanese expansion may not have been adequately 'budgeted for.'

When subjected to counterfactual analysis, the simulations produced some valuable correctives. If we look now at various pieces of the model – each endogenous variable (replicated through system-wide simulation) – we observe, as in earlier chapters, some instructive patterns. There are periods of 'over-' and 'undershooting' as well as nearly exact convergences with reality. Recall the earlier discussion in Chapter 12

In the case of the navy, when the United States was 'removed' as a potential adversary, the pattern of Japan's navy expenditures was not affected. It made no difference. Neither additional increases nor decreases of US navy allocations would seem to have exerted much impact. The United States was an important factor in shaping navy expenditures, but once these were set, the actual path of Japanese navy expenditures assumed its own course.

With respect to army allocations, on the other hand, 'removing' Soviet Russia as an adversary did have an impact on Japanese army allocations; without Russia, Japan would have spent less on the army. By contrast, removal of the United States as an adversary had no appreciable impact on Japanese navy expenditure despite the fact that Japan was statistically sensitive to US allocations. The Japanese navy path had been set, and there was little the United States could do to influence or change its path.

If *no* country had been perceived by Japan as an adversary, would there have been military competition? The exercise suggests that if there had been *no* country identified as a threat, there would have been *a* military buildup in the 1930s.

Applied to post-World War II Japan, the counterfactual analysis used for earlier periods produced no significant changes in the simulated variables. Compared to earlier periods, the postwar decades were less politically volatile, more economically stable, robust, and expansive. Consequently, with political and economic functions more tightly integrated with other domestic and external activities, Japanese society as a whole was better able to withstand interventions and stresses (both 'real' and the methodologically induced counterfactual) than had been the case in the two earlier periods under scrutiny.

Part V

Conclusion

Emergence of a global power

Chapter 17

Adaptation to a new international environment

The first full phase of Japan's postwar economic 'miracle' was shaped by the immediate postwar recovery and rapid growth of the 1950s and 1960s, making the country an economic power of consequence. This phase ended with the oil crisis of 1973. Paradoxically, the second phase occurred during – and was even made possible by – the global recession in the latter half of the 1970s, when the world economy was subject to multiple strains; and Japan, possibly the most vulnerable of the industrial economies, appeared to present itself as 'a fragile blossom.'

Responding quickly to the oil price hike in 1973–4, Japanese industries, apparently sensitive to theories of the market economy, accelerated their own structural change with consequences beyond textbook expectations. Not only did they reduce their demand for petroleum in response to higher prices, but more importantly, they took extensive energy-saving measures in order to reduce energy input per product unit as much as feasible. In retrospect Japan appears to have been least affected among industrial economies by the second oil crisis in 1979. In any case, new technological innovations took place one after another in various fields, and were disseminated at a rapid pace. A major contribution to Japan's successes was the microelectronics revolution, leading to the widely touted 'miracle.'

Leadership during this transformation of the Japanese economy shifted from industries depending on cheap imported raw materials and energy to those seeking higher value-added. Automobiles, fine chemicals, electronic equipment, and numerical-control machine tools began to characterize Japanese manufacturing industries. Second, and closely related, was the fact that 'made-in-Japan' products were characteristically more energy efficient in both production and use, relatively inexpensive, and of high quality. As a result, Japanese products gained international competitiveness and a high profit margin. Despite the yen's appreciation against the dollar following the oil crisis (from 300 yen per dollar in 1976 to 240 yen in 1983), the volume of Japanese exports remained high.

Having successfully overcome the most serious economic crisis since defeat in World War II, Japan now turned its attention to the outside world. During the premiership of Takeo Fukuda (December 1976 to December 1978), the Japanese leadership set up two basic foreign policy strategies that were to define the nation's future contribution to the international community. The first was an active Asia policy. Since the early 1970s Japan had been seeking new policy guidelines toward this area. Combined with the US–China rapprochement, and increased resentment against Japanese activities in Asia, the victory of Communist forces in Indochina was forcing Japan to redirect its policy vis-à-vis the Asian mainland. Prime Minister Fukuda decided it was necessary to conclude a peace treaty with the People's Republic of China. While Prime Minister Tanaka had visited Beijing in 1972 to establish diplomatic relations with China, further enhancement of bilateral relations faced a range of obstacles. Finally, in August 1978 a peace treaty between the two countries was signed, and Japan began to play the role of major patron for China's modernization.

Japan's second basic foreign policy strategy centered on economic assistance under its official development assistance (ODA) program. In 1977 the Japanese completed their war reparation program – dating from 1956 – which the government regarded as an ODA grant-in-aid arrangement – and now the time was considered ripe for establishing a new framework within which long-term ODA commitments could be implemented. During the same year Japanese exports began to generate a huge foreign exchange surplus, and the government was asked to increase the amount and to improve the quality of ODA, whereupon Fukuda assumed leadership in arguing for a doubling of the ODA. In May the government announced plans to double foreign assistance within five years (see below). In the next year it revised the plan again, reducing the doubling period to three years. Since then the Japanese government has periodically revised mid-term doubling targets for foreign assistance and has achieved the goal each time.

Throughout this process Japan insisted that the development program remain the focus of its foreign policy approach toward Asia. During a tour in August 1977, Fukuda established a new economic involvement with Southeast Asian countries where he made Japan's new Southeast Asia policy public. As a result, through expanding ODA programs, Japan increased its commitments to the development of the Association of Southeast Asian Nations (ASEAN) countries and at the same time espoused a formal commitment to 'peaceful coexistence' in the ASEAN region. Overall, China has received the largest share of ODA disbursements.

Among Fukuda's main objectives were to sustain the phoenix-like recovery of the Japanese economy, to expand Japan's active role in the international system (especially among Asian countries), and to validate rising expectations abroad regarding his country's participation in the management of the world economy. His initiatives were also directed toward the furtherance of Japan's relations with the United States. Viewed retrospectively, the influence of the United States on Japanese foreign policies of the late 1970s becomes apparent. During a meeting with Fukuda in March 1977, President Carter had endorsed Japan's further contribution to Asian development and stability and encouraged Fukuda to define and expedite his country's active role in the international system.

Two months later, at the Conference on International Economic Cooperation, Fukuda announced a program for doubling Japan's external assistance. A meeting between Ambassador Strauss and Minister Ushiba in January 1978 – where Japan's ODA was on the agenda – was followed by an announcement at the Carter–Fukuda meeting in May of the ODA plan for doubling in a shorter period (Inada 1985: 298–302). At that meeting Carter was said to have persuaded Fukuda to sign the peace treaty with China on the ground that a closer Sino-Japanese relationship was consistent with the US decision to normalize diplomatic relations with China (Tanaka 1985: 250). Japan's active diplomacy in the late 1970s may appear to have initiated an independent foreign policy; in reality, however, Japan continued to pursue a policy of close coordination with the United States.

THE JAPAN PROBLEM OF THE LATE 1970s

The problem with Japan appears to, a large extent, as the result of Japan's successes during earlier decades – but notably during the late 1970s. During the early 1980s an acute imbalance in US–Japan economic relations began to emerge, due partly to Japan's tight financial policy to reduce the public deficit successfully and partly to US macroeconomic policy, which led to twin deficits. Japanese products penetrated into the American market while the US dollar was allowed to accumulate in Japanese accounts – and was then redirected to the American market in the form of direct and indirect investments. Thus the US dollar circulated between Japanese and American accounts. This mechanism worked on a larger scale each year throughout the early 1980s, resulting in an increased imbalance in balance of trade accounts. The expansion of Japanese activities and interests in the United States became even more visible through 'made-in-Japan' products and 'owned-by-Japanese' assets.

The flow of Japanese manufactured goods into the American market was – and still is – widely believed to be a serious threat to the viability of US manufacturing industries. Postwar economic friction between the Japanese and the US governments was, of course, not new. Difficulties concerning Japanese textile exports dated back to the late 1950s. Managed textile trade started in the early 1960s and has lasted until today. Commercial conflict and the settlement of disputes in the form of managed trade on a particular commodity became a recurrent pattern between the two countries. Over time a significant portion of bilateral trade covering a wide range of commodities from steel to semiconductors has been managed under the free trade system.

What was now referred to in the United States as the 'Japan problem' appears to have been intended by the Japanese as a program in response to domestic economic pressures that included a strengthening of the country's economic and financial capabilities and a mode of sustained economic expansion. The problem was perceived as new because the external expansion of Japanese economic activities and interests had not been a prominent feature of Japan's earlier postwar foreign policy, and also because the country's emerging *gamma* profile had not given rise to a characteristically *gamma* military establishment.

In the modern era of interdependence, Japan's new expansionism has taken a form very different from the country's pre-World War II pattern of imperialism. Nevertheless, the penetration of Japanese products into foreign markets and the investment of Japanese capital abroad – in land, factories, bonds, and so forth – have commonly been referred to in the United States and elsewhere as an 'invasion.' Confronted with failure in its attempts to control this new expansionism, the United States has tried to find the 'solution' by exploring ways of influencing the Japanese state and society. Specifically, US officials presented 'Japan Inc.' as developmental capitalism. They cited MITI's industrial targeting policies, *gyosei-shido* (administrative guidance), premodern business practices, 'unworkable' antitrust legislation, and so forth, as evidence that the Japanese government had not acted in good faith. US officials argued that domestically Japanese business had failed to maintain a free market environment, and as a consequence, existing social and economic mechanisms at home allowed Japan as a nation to behave aggressively abroad.

Increasingly during the 1980s, US–Japan economic friction gradually shifted from commodity-by-commodity negotiations to an emphasis on major sector-by-sector issues and then to engulf overall social relations. In the course of an intensifying friction, the 'Japan problem' attracted public attention in both countries. The basic argument of those critical of Japan emphasized different aspects of the problem but centered on the consideration that, with its own constitutional and unique code of action, Japan is a deviant state that cannot easily adhere to the consensus in an international community whose members share with one another some more or less common international norms. Underlying such an assessment lie misgivings and fears about Japan's seemingly endless economic expansion.

American tendencies toward defining the solution to the 'Japan problem' in terms of altering the internal structure of the country's economy and society can be seen as an implicit recognition that only changes in domestic factors may lead to changes in external behavior. A connection between today's growth and expansion in Japan and the occupation period comes to mind. But there are other crucial considerations. It seems obvious that lateral pressure in Japan has increased markedly since the Japanese responded to the oil crisis of the 1970s and overcame attendant economic hardships. And the greater the country's lateral pressure, the greater has been its economic expansion worldwide. During the post-oil-crisis years, the Japanese have vastly extended their reach, expanding economic activities to meet the nation's domestically induced pressures. At the same time, however, Japan has remained a very limited market for foreigners, essentially protecting itself against the economic expansion of others. Scarcely a day goes by without complaints from the United States that Japan relies on 'unfair' practices in order to protect its own closed markets.

CHANGES IN EXTERNAL POLICY

Unlike its pre-World War II territorial expansion, the postwar Japanese government has not attempted to extend either military or overt political power outside Japan proper. Instead, the nation's security and prosperity have depended upon international arrangements, such as the US nuclear umbrella and the IMF–GATT regime. Under these conditions Japan's domestic pressures were successfully channeled into acceptable modes of lateral pressure, manifested by transnational activities in the economic arena.

Japan's contribution to the support of the GATT economic regime and the US-dominated security regime upon which the country depends has remained relatively small. Nevertheless, a significant increase in financial commitments to 'defense' can be observed since the late 1970s. First, Japan modernized its defense capabilities, not only to counter a direct medium-sized attack on the territory for a short period of time – which had been a long-standing objective – but also to integrate Japanese forces with US strategy and to maintain surveillance over its territory. Second, the government also agreed to cover a part of the local expense of maintaining US troops in Japan. Third, in terms of the international economy, especially in finance, the Japanese government began to play an active role in facilitating the recirculation of Japan's huge trade surplus worldwide.

While Japan's increased participation in GATT and other global regimes was welcomed, its expansive tendencies were not. Both at home and abroad demands were raised that Japan engage in domestic structural reforms aimed at shaping a more mature and less aggressive economy. Under three prime ministers during the 1980s – Zenko Suzuki, Yasuhiro Nakasone, and Noboru Takeshita – the Japanese government committed itself and the society at large to extensive reforms. State-owned businesses were privatized one after another; budgetary controls resulted in a significant decline in the overall deficit; and tax reform was introduced despite strong opposition.

Many reforms, proposed as supports for a liberal system, were not unrelated to Thatcher's program or to Reagan's. As in Britain or the United States, such proposals were widely supported, especially by the business establishment. A Japanese business community that had acquired international competitiveness and strength under governmental protection for decades no longer wanted governmental intervention and called for liberalization and a reduction in the role of government. The deregulation of intertwined governmental controls meant also the 'internationalization' of the Japanese economy. On a much larger scale than the past, a formerly well-protected economy and society were increasingly exposed to foreign elements, ranging from primary agricultural products to manufactured goods. In ways reminiscent of Perry's ships of the mid-nineteenth century, external forces were again pushing for an 'opening' of Japan. The principle of reciprocity long pressed for by the US government now helped 'reopen' Japanese society.

The opening process turned out to be slower than expected, however. Domestic political inertia and bureaucratic resistance were strong, and the leadership was too fragile to surmount these obstacles. When the Japanese leadership faces contradictory alternatives, it typically tends to postpone making a decision until international and/or domestic circumstances leave only one option perceived as feasible. Under such circumstances Japanese leaders then find themselves forced to adopt a previously unacceptable alternative because no other options are available. (Recall earlier discussion of the Pearl Harbor decision.) Conversely, when options are thought to have widened, Japanese leaders have tended to allow patently foreign pressures (*gaiatsu*) against the country to increase and then, in these circumstances, to wait for domestic opposition forces, including those within the ruling party, to abandon their resistance. Currently it seems probable that Japanese society will become increasingly more 'open' (and responsive to changing circumstances) – however slowly.

In trying to explain such attempts at national reform in terms of a lateral pressure frame of reference, our expectation is that the expansion of Japan's activities and interests may well be redirected partly (even absorbed) domestically and hence less overtly expansive externally; that lateral pressure may be relaxed in the course of its own dynamics; and that Japan may be reciprocally able to absorb the lateral pressure of other states directed toward it to a larger extent than ever possible in the past. Conversely, however, it is theoretically possible that deregulation may allow private corporations to act more freely. Freer economic activities might thereby exacerbate existing misgivings and fears about Japan's expansion.

TECHNOLOGICAL ADVANCES AND LATERAL PRESSURE

Despite dramatic changes in profile (from *epsilon* to *beta* to *gamma*), some persisting features of Japan remain salient. As projected to 2100 (actually a very long shot) the population of the country continues to be large relative to domestic territory and other resources (see Kito 1983 for projections to 2100). Since World War II the level and rate of change of Japanese technology have advanced spectacularly, and there are strong indications that this trend will continue for the foreseeable future. Increases in demands by the population for food and other basic resources and industrial demands for raw materials are unprecedented in Japanese experience, and, despite efforts to restrain and redirect some of the potentially debilitating aspects of economic growth, this tendency is likely to continue for a long time to come.

So far technological advancement has both reduced and increased Japan's lateral pressure. The constraints have been shaped by the need for the acquisition of energy resources and raw materials, but simultaneously there have been powerful economic pressures for expansion abroad designed to open new markets and enhance the prosperity of the Japanese economy.

At the time of writing, Japan's remarkable technological performance emerges as a successful combination of two factors: technological 'push' policies such as the organization of national research projects and sustained expenditures in research and development, and other technology-promoting measures such as research subsidies, favorable tax schedules, and administrative guidance for expanding the nation's technological capabilities, termed 'demand-pull' policies (Okimoto 1986).

In the final analysis, technological capability remains the essential element of Japan's national profile amenable to policy intervention. While technological advances are not entirely within Japan's control, of course, nonetheless, relative to resource constraints or population characteristics, the technology factor can be influenced directly by government and private-sector corporate policies (Shishido 1983: 259).

As one might expect, the dominant modes of Japan's postwar lateral pressures have been economic and financial. Over succeeding decades the country produced goods of increasingly high quality with a technological 'edge' and various instruments of protectionism. Although theories of Japanese competitiveness differ in their central explanations, but all converge on the extraordinary rates of technological change and investment overseas. The postwar model of lateral pressure sought to capture this change while retaining elements of continuity of the profile.

By 1988 Japan's economy was two-thirds the size of that of the United States. The two countries together accounted for one-third of the global output. The United States had become Japan's largest export market, and trade surpluses with the United States – on the order of $50 billion – were (and are) a sore point in the relationship. Charges of protectionism were raised in response to US business attempts to penetrate the Japanese market. In recent years the Tokyo stock market has expanded its influence. As of October 1987 the higher yen and rise in Japanese stock prices made the Tokyo market the world's largest exchange in dollar value, capitalized at $2.677 trillion, compared to the New York Stock Exchange at $2.254 trillion (*New York Times*, 7 December 1987).[1] Figure 17.1 gives a snapshot of the world in terms of equity investment according to national scale.

Put succinctly, Japan's diplomatic and economic difficulties crystallized by the end of the 1980s around a simple reality: the great economic success since World War II could not be sustained in the same form and in the same manner. The export-led growth strategy was under siege, and Japan was pressured by industrial powers to show 'restraint' and admonished to expand domestic demand. Minami (1986: 428) stated what became the official stance of the industrial powers toward Japan: 'it is important that Japan practice self-restraint with exports and increase industrial imports.' Anticipating the range of pressures confronting Japan by the end of the decade, we note here that Japan could no longer expect that its own economic performance would dictate the rate and pace of growth. A new transition was in the offing, and the terms of change were yet to emerge clearly. For Japan 'self-restraint' called for a new strategy of growth and expansion, new international policies, and new images of the future.

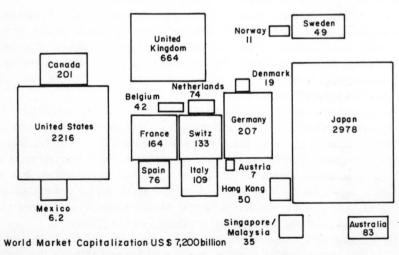

Figure 17.1   Equity investor's map of the world in 1987 (US $ billion).
Source: Salvatore 1990: 247

Whatever the future trajectory of Japanese growth might be, the international implications are varied and profound. In 1988 Prime Minister Takeashita proclaimed 'three pillars' as a foundation for a policy of international cooperation on the part of Japan: (a) active participation in cooperation for peace; (b) further economic cooperation for development; and (c) promotion of cultural exchange. Like past statements on foreign policy guidelines, Takeashita's message neither proposed substantial changes nor suggested major departures from the country's previous low posture in foreign policy. Nevertheless, Japan's involvement in the international political arena has been increasing.[2]

Technological advancement is almost certain to remain the basis for Japanese strategy in an international environment where competition for access to knowledge and skills will continue to grow. Japan's current profile – characterized by *high but stabilizing population, rapidly advancing technology* and *resource access through successful trade and external investments* – derives primarily from its technological development and capacity for exchanging goods for resources. To the extent that such a profile can be successfully sustained, internal as well as external developments need to become increasingly and reciprocally supportive. Other major traders in the international system – and the rules and regimes of global exchanges – are likely to become increasingly sensitive to the market and resource needs of countries approximating the Japanese profile. And Japanese leaders need to continue adapting to the requirements of other nations (including the resource-rich) and the international system as a whole. The challenge for Japan, its allies, and its trading partners rests on these unusual and intensely interactive imperatives.

Against this background Chapter 18 provides speculations about the Japanese future. How will, or can, the international environment accommodate to the requisites and demands of a growing Japan and its expanding interests, leverage potentials, and capacity for active presence internationally and in penetrating the economies of even the major powers? How successfully can the Japanese accommodate to a rapidly changing international (and increasingly global) system?

Chapter 18

Retrospection and thoughts for the future

In the Prologue we noted how some writers before and after the attack on Pearl Harbor had attributed Japan's expansionist policies and actions to 'overpopulation,' the search for raw materials and markets, the expansion of profits, and other economic factors, whereas others had 'debunked' these ideas – in part, seemingly, as a reaction to Marxist-Leninist 'materialism.' Among the 'debunkers' the tendency had been to explain Japanese expansionism, territorial conquests, and colonialism by any one or two of a wide range of factors, from 'nationalistic sentiment and pride' or identification of themselves as a 'chosen' (and hence privileged) people to out-and-out power politics – the pursuit of dominance for its own sake, or to Japanese 'fascism.' For years these fundamental differences in perspective have remained unresolved, but recently a number of scholars have called for a reopening of the issue and, in view of Japan's spectacular successes since World War II, a reexamination of the 'pathological' as well as the 'healthy' aspects of Japanese economic growth and modernization strategies.

Part of the problem has emerged from a conventional tendency of long standing to look for one, two, or at most a very few 'causes' of expansion and war to the exclusion of all others. If, by contrast, a 'multicausal' approach is undertaken, it becomes feasible to identify complex networks of interactive factors – some direct, some indirect, and one (or a very few) with demonstrably more influence than others. We have treated a number of these variables as elements in a network of factors contributing in many different combinations to the growth, development, and actions of states in general and Japan in particular. Our selection of such factors is informed by historical sources and wide arrays of data with which we are familiar, but our list is not exclusive. Other variables for which appropriate data are available can always be added.

At the generative center of this 'causal' network, the three 'master' variables – the people, their technology (overall knowledge and skills), and their access to resources – provide the intensely interactive matrix from which all human capabilities and activities can be derived. Countries differ, however, according to their structures or profiles, that is, the ratios of their respective levels and rates of change along these same three dimensions. In this chapter we provide an overview of how the profile and behavior patterns of one country – Japan – were twice transformed in the course of slightly more than 100 years.

A CENTURY OF JAPANESE GROWTH AND DEVELOPMENT

Beginning in the 1870s as an *epsilon* country (large and growing population, 'underdeveloped' technology, and relatively limited access to resources), Japan – under Meiji leadership – initiated a 'development' program which drew heavily upon Western knowledge and skills (economic, industrial, and military), which effectively transformed the country in the course of a century. Critically important consequences of this growth and development were the expansion of Japanese activities and interests (commercial, diplomatic, military, *et al.*) beyond national borders, and the intersection – and not infrequently the 'collision' – of these activities and interests (lateral pressures) with the expanding activities and interests of other countries. The action–reaction elements in the military equations reflect these relationships.

The generation and consequences of this Japanese growth and expansion are traced in some detail throughout the book and do not require detailed discussion here, but a number of observations may be worth underscoring.

The uneven growth and development of the three master variables *within and between states* (a) contributed to a vast diversity in their respective sizes, capabilities, demands, and other characteristics; (b) led to competitions among them for resource access, market advantage, and power (as relative *capability*, relative *outreach*, and relative *influence*); (c) virtually assured that consequential relationships would generate – *and be shaped by* – widely varying cognitions, motivations, and affects (positive and negative) that are known to infuse human interactions in environments of such intensities and import; and (d) in line with the security paradox discussed in Chapter 1, disposed Japan, through its leaders, to undertake measures *in protection of its own well-being* that were interpreted by other states as *threatening their well-being*.

Pre-World War I

Relevant also is the fact that in the 1870s, during initial phases of the country's 'modern' growth and development, Japan's *epsilon* profile approximated that of numbers of 'developing' nations today. This suggests the strong possibility that at least some contemporary states with *epsilon* profiles may already be well on their way toward *gamma* profiles (stabilized population, advanced technology, strong and favorable import – export ratios). Insofar as these possibilities exist, the question arises as to which countries are most likely to achieve *gamma* status and what some of the consequences are likely to imply for themselves and for the international system as a whole.

Outstanding features in the early development of Japan included the preeminent role of its domestic population (*combined with an advancing technology*) in exerting claims for imports of raw materials; the development of specialized capabilities (not excluding the navy and merchant marine), and allocations for investment in the military as important determinants of imports from the colonies; the role of government revenues and their availability for spending on colonial administration; and the strong inertia effects involved in army and navy expenditures.

During the pre-World War I period strong interplays between domestic and external activities (including military expenditures and arms competitions) contributed to a major collision with the forces of expanding Russian activities (the Russo-Japanese War).

The trade–security link is one of the most distinctive features of the Japan case (a strong positive feedback relation between exports of finished goods and imports of raw materials). We interpreted the results as showing that, in the long run, *continued success in exporting manufactured goods* was important in diverting Japan's lateral pressure away from the military form or mode. This positive loop appeared to serve as a 'downward' escalator. A second 'downward' impulse on navy and army spending came from successful colonial expansion, countervailing to some extent military competition with other powers.

Interwar period

During the interwar period Japan, like the powers in pre-World War I Europe, shared a tendency for bureaucratic processes to affect the levels of military spending. In the historical chapters surrounding this analysis we identified the internal bargaining and leveraging and the factions that gradually won out. The sensitivity of the Japanese leadership to British moves and to US calculations fueled the bargaining and shaped the politics of the interwar period in relations with the United States.

Two distinct dynamic relationships (or feedback loops) were especially evident prior to World War II – the trade linkages (imports and exports, mutually contingent and mutually reinforcing) and the military–colonial expansion linkages (connecting military allocations to colonial acquisitions, in turn leading to more imports from the colonies). By necessity statistical analysis renders simplification of complex dynamics, but the evidence continued to show that population, through rising demands, 'drove' the system by contributing to imports from the colonies, and the specialized capability of the merchant marine facilitated these acquisitions. The government revenue provided the financial basis for expansion. It is not surprising to find that army and navy allocations contributed to greater imports from the colonies and, closing the feedback loop, in turn led to more expenditures on the military.

But it would not be accurate to conclude simply that the dynamics of growth and expansion generated sustained pressures for increased military expenditures, which in turn contributed to competition among the powers. The realities are more complicated in that there were indeed some countervailing influences. We identified the salutary role of raw materials imports and territorial acquisitions. In other words, unimpeded access to external resources and unimpeded lateral pressure (in this case, in the territorial expansion mode) provided dampening effects. The important empirical finding, therefore, pertains to the relative strength of these factors. Over time the positive feedback loops pushing toward conflict were stronger.

What can be said about locating the sources of lateral pressure? Where did it all come from? Individually and in combination, the master variables were close to the source. Population, as an exogenous variable, had different influences at different times: in the earlier period by pushing for more imports of raw materials, and later by statistically influencing external territorial expansion.

We have accepted national income as a rough indicator of technological capability and growth – less than satisfactory, but the best at hand. Throughout the period under scrutiny, accelerating knowledge and skills contributed directly and indirectly to Japan's external expansion. Yet there were also dampening factors; unidirectional linkage and growth were not unconstrained. There were periods of swing when national income 'pushed' additional allocations for the military, and intensified territorial expansion and imports from the colonies; and other times when the effects of national income were constraining. During the interwar period, for example, trends in national income had a 'dampening' effect on finished goods exports, on imports of raw materials, and to a lesser degree on colonial area. By the same token, as income 'slowed,' the effects on these other factors were positive – pushing upward. The overall effects, over the long run, are well reflected in the raw data themselves, the 'upward' and 'outward' thrusts in lateral pressure.

We have addressed the linkages of commerce and security on both sides of Japan's trade loop: imports of raw materials and exports of finished goods. The strong positive feedback relationship throughout the entire pre-World War II period is clearly apparent. In effect, we confirm again what several Japanese economic historians have stressed: the greater were the exports of finished goods, the greater was the demand for raw materials. Our analysis also revealed the statistical and quantitative links between this trade loop (which we referred to earlier as a trade trap) and other manifestations of external expansion.

Japan responded to many pressures – 'actual as well as perceived.' In the narrative historical chapters we examined modes of pressures and perceptions of threat. From an 'actual' or statistical point of view, we identified some of the pressures for greater military allocations and outward expansion. Since the import–export feedback relation remained strong throughout, we interpret this result as indicating ways in which lateral pressure took shape. During the interwar period we found that the short-positive feedback loop linking imports to exports became stronger, and at the same time a self-propelling element, a kind of bureaucratic inertia, was 'built into' the military allocations, pushed by government revenues and by the previous year's military allocations. The trade loop and the expenditures inertia factor can thus be thought of as an 'actual' (as distinct from 'perceived') element of the interwar Japan case. The colonial linkages also became stronger during the interwar period, serving as a set of 'actual' factors as well.

To a large extent the transformation of Japan's profile over time reveals the strong role of government policy and interventions. It becomes evident that a state's profile can change, and be transformed, both as a result of government intervention and public policy and as an outcome of bargaining and leveraging among private and public entities, groups, or individuals. The transformation of Japan – from an *epsilon* to a *beta* to a *gamma* state – reflects government intervention, choices, politics, and bargaining: all elements of volunteerism. And for Japan, as for other states, the essence and definition of national security changed as the national profile changed, and as new demands were formulated and articulated, and old ones reinterpreted or dropped entirely.

THE PEARL HARBOR DECISION

Relevant in addition to Japan's (changing) profile, the interactive network of variables contributing to the country's generation of lateral pressure, collision with tsarist Russia in 1904, and the decision to attack Pearl Harbor, were a wide range of cognitive and affective phenomena. Conceptually and theoretically, these variables – the perceptions, expectations, evaluations, preferences, emotions, and feelings of individual leaders and rank-and-file subjects of Japan – are important in accounting for Japanese behavior throughout the pre-World War II period. For reasons we shall touch upon further along, however, such phenomena are difficult to analyze rigorously within the quantitatively defined framework – although the time series data provide a valuable context for achieving a better understanding of governmental decisions, policies, and actions.

It is evident that Japanese decision-making did not fit neatly into a unitary or rational actor framework. The decision to seize control over Manchuria, for example, was made by high-ranking military officers on the scene and presented to the Tokyo regime as a virtual *fait accompli*. And the years of 'government by assassination' were characterized by scattered pockets of private and interest-group violence, often planned and carried out by lower-ranking military officers. It was only later, as Japanese armies penetrated deeper into China proper, that most of these violent elements were absorbed by the regime in the form of a military–civilian oligarchy.

Just as earlier Japanese cabinets had been unable to comprehend why the United States opposed their expansion into China, the oligarchy found it difficult to understand why the United States opposed their plans for expanding into Southeast Asia. Hence they resented all the more the US embargo on scrap iron, oil, and other resources – needed for their conquest of China – that the United States (however illogically) had previously allowed Japan to import.

Throughout the autumn of 1941 Japan's top leaders felt severe pressures to do *something*, but they found it difficult to agree on an option that did not appear profitless or with great risk. The problem was how to obtain critically needed resources for winning the war in China and at the same time to obtain reliable long-term access to the further resources (and markets) that the economy required.

In this regard the historical narrative reveals the extent to which Japanese leaders were aware of – and sought to emulate – the expansionist solutions relied upon by great powers of the past, and the measures employed by them in order to maintain and protect territories so gained. After all, it was the expansion (and defensive dispositions) of British, US, and – most immediately in the late 1930s – Soviet activities and interests in East Asia that Japanese expansionism was directly colliding with.

A strong coalition within the leadership favored a *northern expedition* against the USSR.

If the time-series data highlight the Japanese demand (even, under the circumstances, objective *need*) for resources, foreign exchange, and markets, the historical narrative underscores the policy dilemma that immobilized the oligarchical leadership during much of the 1940–1 period of uncertainty and in analytical terms defied rational actor assumptions. Proponents of a *southern expedition* emphasized the Japanese navy's immediate need for oil to fuel its warships and pointed to the extensive resources and markets of South and Southeast Asia that appeared available for the taking. Since there were no critical resources to appropriate on the road to Irkutsk, a Japanese conquest of Southeast Asia provided the only feasible solution – immediate access to the oil required for winning the war in China and establishment of a Greater East Asia Co-Prosperity Sphere, controlling raw materials and markets from the Dutch Indies to Burma and even to a 'liberated' India.

The 'catch' associated with a *southern* expedition was the near-certainty that such an expedition would bring a potentially invincible United States into the war. Relying more on hope than on rational calculation, however, proponents successfully argued that – with a preemptive strike against the US Pacific fleet, rapid Japanese successes 'in the south,' Axis victories in Europe, the surrender of Britain to the Germans, and 'a great change in American public opinion' – the war 'might end' (Ike 1967: 208–49).

So much for the 'driving power' of Japan's resource-and-market-access predicament. The Pearl Harbor decision amounted to a Hobson's choice – the only possible escape from what the oligarchy came to perceive as an otherwise inescapable dilemma.

This is not to imply, however, that a more rational option did not – in *principle*, at least – exist. On the contrary, the post-World War II analysis demonstrates Japan's newly developed capacity for economic – and 'peaceful' – alternatives to territorial expansion and colonization as means for expanding national accesses to raw materials and markets. In *reality*, however, such an alternative, to be available, would have required in 1940–1 a deeper and broader understanding of the country's resource-and-trade predicament and a wholly different course of action dating from the early 1920s.

JAPAN'S POSTWAR GROWTH AND EXPANSION

Analyses of postwar Japan reveal a new model, a new structure, and a new system of simultaneous equations – new data, new estimations, and new results. The transformation of the society, reconstruction, and recovery were all synthesized in this model. Alterations in population, technology, and resource ratios, for example, combined with restrictions imposed by the new constitution on the country's military establishment, transformed Japan's profile from *beta* to *gamma* (roughly comparable to the postwar profiles of Britain, Germany, and France).

Notable among these changes was the reduction of Japan's population growth rate – rendering the country's density relatively stable and reducing its demographic contribution to lateral pressure. Meanwhile, the rapid advancement and increased sophistication of Japanese knowledge and skills became more and more influential – along with continuing domestic resource constraints – in shaping and strengthening the expansion of the country's activities and interests worldwide. Demands were increasingly generated by technological requirements and expectations for higher standards of living. At the same time, as mandated by the new constitution, military requirements were under constraint, and the costs of colonial expansion disappeared – both replaced in effect by an intense concentration on economic modes of expansion, which led to the persisting importance of import–export linkages. Meanwhile, technological exports resulting from greater sophistication in knowledge and skills became leading factors in Japanese trade, and all these factors combined led in turn to a powerful new thrust in the country's foreign direct investment.

In setting out to represent the Japanese postwar model succinctly, we stressed three kinds of 'macro-processes': growth and attendant leverages; resource demands and constraints; and expansion in economic modes of international activity. The same methods of estimation, simulation, and analysis were undertaken, and the same basic line of inquiry pursued; however, an important change in data was necessary, namely, the use of first differences rather than absolute levels. The use of first differences was required initially because of excessively high collinearity, but it was needed subsequently because the transformation and rates of growth during the postwar period were so rapid that *change* had to be embedded in the model itself. And in the postwar case, *growth* dominated all patterns of change. Rapid growth dominated Japan's patterns of change throughout most of the post-World War II period.

As the major indicator of growth, GNP was well accounted for by Japan's direct foreign investments abroad, by exports of technology, and to a lesser extent by nonfuel imports. While investments into Japan were important, their influence was dwarfed by Japan's technological change. Imports into Japan, disaggregated according to energy and nonfuel imports, reaffirmed the linkage to exports so prominent in earlier decades. Again a positive loop prevailed: the more were the exports, the greater were the imports.

Four feedback relationships between economic performance and international economic exchanges also dominated the postwar decades. Three of these loops were positive, indicating mutually self-reinforcing growth and expansion, and one was negative, reflecting constraints on growth. The positive loops connected (a) GNP with foreign direct investment: the greater domestic growth, the stronger external economic performance, the greater the domestic growth; (b) GNP with exports and nonfuel imports, linking domestic output to trade activity and revealing the vulnerability of Japan to fluctuations in its trade; and (c) GNP, foreign direct investment, exports, and nonfuel imports, showing the importance of foreign investment activities in reducing the constraints on energy dependence. The constraining or negative loop connected GNP, energy imports, exports, and nonfuel imports. The distinctive feature of this loop is linkage to energy imports, which served as the major factor constraining growth.

The successes and failures of the simulation help to underscore some of the highly relevant characteristics of Japan's 'reality.' While reproducing 'real-world' trends with considerable fidelity, the simulation underestimated the strength of some indicators and overestimated others. Overall, we underestimated Japan's economic growth (the simulated GNP undershooting the actual for notable periods) – along with the true role and importance of knowledge and skills. Other elements pushing for growth and expansion which we failed to capture included more direct measures of productivity, organizational and institutional capabilities, and 'softer' measures for economic performance, such as motivation. We also understated the momentum and scale of Japan's investment outreach;[1] more was taking place than we could account for and effectively estimate, especially in the sphere of expanding activities and interests.[2]

In general, we overestimated fuel imports. The 'fit' was relatively poor during years of prosperity but improved when the economy contracted in the early 1970s. The simulation of total exports also overshot the actual record – the model generating more goods and services for export than was actually the case (although again, with economic contraction in the early 1970s, the 'fits' were better).

JAPAN TRANSFORMED

In this study we have demonstrated the transformation of Japan from a developing society to a major power and an economic giant reliant on the international environment for its economic requirements for survival. Beyond the changing conditions indicated above, however, there remain some persisting features of the Japan case.

Remarkably, in the global environment of the 1980s, characterized by superpower confrontations, crises, the arms race, North–South conflicts, and terrorism, Japan has continued to 'dedicate itself not to duplicate the tragedy of war' but to making 'relentless efforts to become a peace-loving nation' and contribute to the 'establishment of permanent peace.' Nonetheless, increasingly since the occupation, Japanese leaders have been subject to countervailing pressures, both domestic and external, for preserving 'the inalienable right of self-defense' as a prerequisite for survival 'as an independent sovereign state' (Japan Institute of International Affairs 1982–3: 46).

Dating from the late 1960s, Japan's annual spending on defense had been widely advertised as only 0.9 percent of its GDP. Actually, it was nearly 1.6 percent within the NATO definition, which includes such items as military pensions. In these terms West Germany in the early 1960s was spending 4.3 percent of its GDP on defense if West Berlin is included, France 4.1 percent, Britain 5.3 percent, the United States 6.6 percent, and the USSR anything between 12 and 17 percent.[3]

Though small, Japan's defense industry was growing twice as fast as the rest of its manufactures. Remarkably, the country after the war acquired *latent* capabilities sufficient to manufacture nuclear weapons as early as 1959 (Meyer 1984: 41). By the 1970s, moreover, additional pressures were pushing Japan toward a gradual, incremental defense buildup and more joint undertakings and exercises with US forces (McNelly 1986). Some of these pressures had originated with Japanese leaders, some from large corporations in search of defense contracts, and some from the United States with the hope that the Japanese would accept a larger share of responsibility for defenses in the western Pacific. By the fiscal year starting March 1988, unofficial observers estimated that Japan would be spending 1.5 percent of its GNP on the military, about $40 billion – making it the world's third highest military spender after the United States and the Soviet Union (*The Economist*, 23 January 1988: 28).

Historically (in line with the security paradox), the distinction between defense and regional or global influence and dominance has often been thin and difficult to ascertain. Records of the past provide few precedents for economic dominance in the absence of commensurate military power. The two have tended to develop interactively. That Japan has remained under the United States' strategic umbrella is well understood and taken into account. Less clear are the eventual outcomes of bargaining and leveraging as today's dominant military power attempts – or is pressured – to share the burden, and cost, of security commensurate with Japan's emergence as an economic power. Indeed, Japan is 'moving into new and uncharted terrain' (Katzenstein 1988: 304).

If (in view of the post-World War II insistence by the United States on Japan's renunciation of force) US cold war pressures on the country to rearm appear somewhat incongruous, a further touch of irony was provided by US expressions of indignation at the Japanese refusal to commit troops during the Middle Eastern war of 1991, in which access to oil was a prominent issue.

The Japanese face a dilemma of their own, however. As a global economic power, the country is dependent on the stability of the world economy; but at the same time, Japanese actions invariably affect the global community, contributing to an interdependence that is likely to increase in future decades. This interdependence, in turn, has enhanced Japanese feelings of vulnerability and a sense of being hostage to external forces.

It is within this rapidly changing context that Japan's future needs to be assessed. Comparing Japan with the United States, the Soviet Union, China, and European states over a relatively long period has yielded at least a rough indication of the positioning and ranking of these nations today and how their relative capabilities may evolve during the more immediate future.

TENTATIVE FUTURES

What guidelines do we have for envisaging Japan's future role in the world? Are current trends likely to continue into the twenty-first century?

In Japan, as in Western Europe, the post-World War II era – characterized by reconstruction and the availability (during the 1950s and 1960s) of cheap capital for growth – may well be over. What is likely to follow it?

One way to answer this question is to extrapolate the growth, development, policies, and actions of Japan and other major powers from recent decades into the future.

Experimentally, in an effort to sense the early future prospects of Japan relative to those of the United States, the Soviet Union, China, and major European states, we anchored a rough indication of the positioning and ranking of these nations in 1970 indicators and made projections of their respective levels, average changes, and consequent rankings beyond the empirical base of 1985 through the years to 2010. The presumption implicit in this exercise made no allowance for 'breaks' or discontinuities in national growth and development patterns that could alter the structure of the system or the capabilities of its individual components. Accomplished in a straightforward way, with all of the qualifications that such a method conventionally implies, the projections created a challenging future for the next three decades.

Soon after the exercise was completed, however, the events of 1989 and 1990 – notably the remarkable and universally unexpected changes in the USSR, the unraveling of the Soviet client states in Eastern Europe, and the reunification of Germany – served as sharp reminders of the many indeterminacies in human affairs and greatly reduced the credibility of our 'futuristic' graphs, which at best might merit filing for future reference and comparison with some future reality. Conceivably, however, the projections may contribute to a crude 'if this, then probably that' approach to the future of Japan and other leading countries of the world.

Japan's current profile (characterized by *high but stabilizing population, rapidly advancing technology*, and *resource access through trade and external investment*) derives primarily from its technological development and capacity for exchanging goods for resources.

Relative to the demographics of other powers, Japan's share of the global population may be expected to decline somewhat. The most notable demographic change will be the aging of the Japanese population – the number of those over 65 doubling between 1983 and 2000.[4]

Explanations of Japan's competitiveness differ in detail, but all converge on the extraordinary rates of technological change and overseas investment. Currently there are strong indications that this course of development will continue into the next century. Characterized by 'demand-pull' dynamics, this trend derives in large part from a combination of sustained expenditures in research and development, government-sponsored research projects, research subsidies, favorable tax schedules, and administrative guidance in the expansion of the nation's technological capabilities (Okimoto 1986).

Despite current efforts to restrain and redirect some of the potentially debilitating aspects of economic growth, the combined demands of the population for food and other basic resources, and industrial demands for raw materials are likely to continue increasing. The country may be expected to maintain its reliance on high-quality products, competitive pricing, and various instruments of protection to retain favorable balances between exports and imports.

Expressed primarily in economic and financial terms, Japanese lateral pressures – expansionism – have penetrated throughout most of the world. As Japan's largest export market, the United States has provided the Japanese with trade surpluses in the order of $50 billion – a sore issue leading to charges and countercharges of protectionism aimed against efforts of US business to penetrate Japanese markets. Whatever means are undertaken to alleviate these tensions, the competition is likely to continue for the foreseeable future.

The MITI forecast of Japan's energy prospects to the year 2010 provided some indication of official views in Japan (Sogo Enerugi Chosakai 1990). Taking into account various assumptions, such as the scenario on the global energy prospects up to 2005 issued by the secretariat of the International Energy Agency (IEA), the extensive applications of energy-saving measures, and related factors, the Ministry projected total energy demand in 2010 to the equivalence of 666 million kl. of crude oil, or an increase by 38 percent from the level of 1988. In these terms dependence on petroleum would decrease between 1988 and 2010 from 57 to 46 percent, while the use of nuclear energy would grow from 9 to 17 percent in the same period (see Table 18.1). Nonetheless, it is clear that unless major technological advances relax the need for energy, Japan will become increasingly sensitive to domestic energy constraints. The 1990 crisis in

Table 18.1 Long-term prospects of energy supply: composition of primary sources of energy (in percent)

Fiscal year	1988 (actual)	2000	2010
Petroleum and LPG	57.3	51.6	46.0
Coal	18.1	17.4	15.5
Natural gas	9.6	10.9	12.0
Nuclear	9.0	13.2	16.7
Hydraulic	4.6	3.7	3.7
Geothermal	0.1	0.3	0.9
Others	1.3	2.9	5.2
Total (%)	100.0	100.0	100.0
Crude oil equivalent (million kl)	482	597	666

Source: Sogo Enerugi Chosakai 1990

the Persian Gulf is illustrative. Japan continues to be vulnerable to foreign protectionism of any type. Will the Gulf crisis provide the opportunity for an expanded role for Japan? Will Japan attempt to secure its prosperity by trying to control foreign markets and/or foreign suppliers?

If the future is assessed in terms of security interdependence – economic, political, strategic, and environmental – a number of variables become critically relevant not only for Japan but for countries worldwide. Most, if not all, of the pertinent issues can be approached through the three master variables – population, technology, resources – and the combinations and permutations resulting from their interactivities.

TOWARD 2010

In the past Japan's population growth, size, and density were critical issues contributing to the country's economic, political, and strategic *insecurity*. (As construed today, environmental insecurity was not current in most people's thinking in those days.) In the future Japan – having accomplished a demographic transition (in large part through technological advancement) – is likely to experience slower population growth than many other countries (with the probable exception of the European Community).[5]

With respect to size of GNP, our projections suggested a pairing of Japan and the former USSR in an economic race until 2000, when the former would surge ahead and overtake the latter within the following decade.[6] Now (following major changes in the USSR and Eastern Europe) the bets are off – although Japan could take third place after the United States and the EC. On a per capita basis Japan could be a strong candidate for first place somewhere along the line.[7]

The country's overall exports seem likely to continue growing, making the country the world's second-largest exporter in total value (and as a percentage of GDP) by 2000. (In export of manufactured goods, the Japanese already rank first – in total value, as a percentage of GDP, and on a per capita basis.)

If these observations are placed in a slightly different context, Japan's position in the world can be viewed in 'world-share' terms, that is, as percentages of global aggregates for key indicators. For example, Japan (in 2010), with only 2 percent of the world population (2010), could account for 15 percent of world trade, 15 percent of world GDP, and 17 percent of world exports (and first place in exports per capita). But according to our projections (admittedly tentative), Japan's imports could remain at about 8 percent of world imports by 2010.

If trade is accepted as an indicator of lateral pressure, Japan in 2000 may rank third (after the EC and the United States) in volume (and as a percentage of GDP) but first on a per capita basis.

As projected, Japan's military expenditures remain low as a percentage of GNP (at 1.5 percent in 1988) but high (third largest) in absolute terms. While recognizing that the projection of military commitments is a singularly hazardous exercise, while writing we find no basis for fundamental changes in rates of increase in Japan's military allocations.

IMPLICATIONS FOR THE FUTURE

What we have presented so far has been an extrapolation of the growth, development, policies, and actions from the recent past into an uncertain future – essentially a 'no surprise' projection. What could trigger a 'surprise' future for Japan?

To the extent that with such a profile a country like Japan can maintain itself effectively, its domestic and external activities need to remain (or become) reciprocally supportive. Before and after the turn of the century, other major powers in the international system are likely to undergo comparable growth and development, and to become increasingly sensitive to the resources and market needs of countries approximating the Japanese profile; and the European Community may well become increasingly competitive. As a consequence, the Japanese may be expected to sustain or possibly to accelerate their country's technological advancement within the international environment, where competition for access to knowledge and skills – as well as resources – is likely to intensify.

Putting these trends together (and with allowance for indeterminacies), we expect a continuation of the trade mode of lateral pressure among major powers and the persistence of strong export performance. Beyond this, however, in the context of a stylized five-power world (with the European Community's statistics adjusted accordingly), the strength of Japan and its lateral pressures may well continue its salience. But in a 'surprise' alternative future, three potentially critical changes could transform the country from the world's leading creditor power to a net importer of capital: significant reductions in Japan's large trade surplus; declines in current high personal-savings rates; and increases in government welfare expenditures required by an aging population. Major world conflicts, or other massive economic or other global disruption, could trigger even more dramatic change in Japan (as well as in the rest of the world). A conjunction of these tendencies might result in mutually reinforcing pressures, potentially transforming Japan's basic *gamma* profile.

If we assume that Japan can avoid or resolve problems of this order, the country will almost certainly find itself, along with other nations of the world, confronting unprecedented challenges of global consequence. These include gross differentials between the economies and living standards of the industrialized countries and those of many developing nations of the world, for example; environmental issues that are rapidly becoming global; and the challenge of peacekeeping in an era of increasingly accurate and massively destructive weapons. In each of these three spheres of concern Japan is singularly qualified for a leadership role.

Having evolved from a developing *epsilon* to a tumultuous *beta* and thence to a prosperous and innovatively industrialized *gamma* nation, Japan has accomplished a demographic and democratic transition along the way. In a world that is changing much faster now than in the past, Japan can serve as a model to many Third World countries today in the pursuit of economic, political, strategic, and environmental security.

In this connection, only determined skeptics would fail to recognize Japan's post-World War II progress in economic and political spheres, but many might call attention to the convenience of the US strategic umbrella that went a long way toward making the country's 'peace-prone' policies more feasible than is usual among major powers. Yet Japan's cautious approach to management of its armed force has served a worthy purpose in the international arena and deserves emulation. Emerging from a background of territorial expansion (lateral pressures of violence), wars of conquest, and the reduction of neighboring countries to colonial submission, the Japanese have succeeded in the achievement of major power status through *economic* lateral pressures and without resort to warfare or threat of violence in the conduct of their diplomacy.

Although, like other countries of the world, Japan still has a long way to go in meeting the environmental challenge, the country has made noteworthy progress in developing energy-efficient fuels and technologies, and enhancing the quality of life for its people.

As the twenty-first century approaches, however, there are historical lessons to be taken seriously not only by Japan but possibly even more by other nations of the world.

FORCES OF GLOBALIZATION AND MULTI-NATION STATES

From today's perspective, Japanese leaders undertook their emulation of Western territorial expansion (lateral pressure) and colonization just as the age of the great empires was approaching its denouement. Some of the world's imperiums collapsed virtually under their own weight. Others were dismantled in part, at least, because of the wars which they had instigated (or had at least participated in). Still others, finding the costs of empire untenable, divested themselves more or less 'voluntarily.' The record of these events is worth sober consideration. But first we need to enlarge upon – and qualify – our use of the 'empire' concept.

Almost from their emergence the so-called *nation* states of Europe transformed themselves during and after the sixteen century into *multi*-nation states, in that by conquest or other means they expanded into distant regions of the earth and 'colonized' vulnerable tribes, nations, or even other – presumably weaker – multinational states or empires. By the early twentieth century it was commonplace that many empires practised 'democracy' at home and authoritarianism (if not tyranny) abroad. Among these empires were those which late-nineteenth-century Japan chose – late in the traditional imperial game – to emulate.[8]

Early in the new century (1911), however, the age-old Chinese empire collapsed, followed by the tsarist Russian, Austro-Hungarian, upstart German, and aging Ottoman Turkish imperiums during or in the immediate aftermath of World War I. Then during the interwar period Mussolini's Italy and Hitler's Germany built new-style empires, only to go down in defeat – along with imperial Japan – as an outcome of World War II.

Within the decades immediately following, the overseas empires established by vastly expanded 'nation' states of Western Europe – Britian, France, Belgium, the Netherlands, and what remained of the Spanish and Portuguese imperiums – were dissolved more or less 'peacefully' (often as a result of prolonged agitation and/or revolutionary activities on the part of nationalistic, if not *patriotic*, nationals within the colonies).

At the time of writing the Soviet Russian 'empire' has lost its East European satellite states. While struggling to hold the multinational USSR together (by threat of force), it has further unravelled through the entire imperium.

Many of today's Third World nations are fragments of these great empires of the past. Many of them, inhabited by populations of differing nationalities and/or religions, are held together in part by boundaries imposed generations ago by the imperiums of which they were unwilling constituents. Many of them – like the empires of which they were once a part – are multinational (or at least multiethnic). Numbers of these countries – Lebanon, Iraq, Iran, Turkey, Sri Lanka, Yugoslavia, and the Philippines, to name a few – are in danger of further fracturing. Several developed or 'more developed developing' states confront similar problems: Britain in Northern Ireland, China with respect to Tibet and other ethnic areas, Canada vis-à-vis Quebec. And so it goes – how far remains unclear.

The Gulf war of 1990–1 occurred precisely in a region of the world characterized for centuries by the expansionist processes referred to above.

In the meantime, a global countervailing force can be identified – the growing realization by many nations that a process of 'globalization' is taking place. Powered in part by exponentially advancing knowledge and skills, extensive population growth has been enveloping the planet for millennia and exerting increasingly powerful anthropogenic impacts on global ecologies. In recent times supersonic transportation, 'instant' communications, and the wide diffusion of advanced technologies are bringing the farthest reaches of the world closer together. The globalization of trade and finance is making countries throughout the world increasingly interdependent. Confronted now with the aftermath of the Gulf war, we need to remind ourselves that whoever controls access to and consumption of oil – a contributing factor in this conflict (as *raison de guerre*, as an element in 'collateral' damage, and as a weapon of destruction) – remains a major source of local, regional, international, and global environmental degradation.

In this connection, it is worth recalling that razing of the environment as a wartime strategy dates at least as far back as Sennacherib (699 BC), who leveled the city of Babylon and flooded the ruins with waters of the Atakhatu Canal.

Within this century weapons exploded over Hiroshima and Nagasaki (and development of successive generations of other instruments of war with massively destructive potentials) completed the 'globalization' of warfare. Beyond this, however, during the twentieth century the 'normal,' everyday activities of all of us have exacted unprecedented environmental costs on both social and natural environments.

JAPAN AND THE PURSUIT OF GLOBAL SECURITY

The globalization of warfare and degradation of the planetary environment raise critical issues about the globalization of economic, political, strategic, and environmental security on local, regional, international, and planetary levels. In this regard it is necessary to recall the extent to which large (even world) wars – including Japanese events leading to the attack on Pearl Harbor – often begin locally and escalate to regional and even global levels. In modern wars the escalation of weaponry (from conventional to massively destructive) is frequently threatened when at least one party to a conflict, facing possible defeat, considers a nuclear 'solution.'

In pursuit of security (economic, political, strategic, and increasingly environmental), a number of European countries are already engaged in the development of specialized suprastate security communities – loose 'regional' regimes operating somewhere between conventional state 'governments' and the potentialities for a global regime. Possibilities for developing *security regimes* of one scope or another are being discussed, however informally, in the Middle East, East Asia, and other parts of the world.

Events in the Middle East demonstrated the extent to which global distributions of weapons of mass destruction, lateral pressures, boundary disputes, and competition for resources could raise a local conflict to the global level almost overnight. Many observers welcomed the initiative (and strength) of the United States and its coalition to work through the United Nations in resolving this particular conflict. But the course of the Gulf war raised questions pertaining, on the one hand, to the initiative of the United States (a high lateral pressure state and the world's surviving superpower) to assume a leading role in the command and prosecution of the war – and hence a major share of responsibility for its intended and unintended consequences – and, on the other hand, the reluctance of Japan (however understandable) to commit combat forces to a 'peacekeeping' mission under United Nations auspices.

Japan's role in the Iraqi war was notable in two respects. First, a strategic resource – oil – was a critical issue (as it had been for Japan in 1940–1); and second, the Japanese government, while contributing funds and other support to the UN-sponsored coalition against Saddam Hussein's Iraq, refused – citing Japan's constitution – to dispatch combat forces in support of the intervention. There was also a strong feeling among many Japanese that whereas they had increased their own energy efficiency substantially and had reduced their oil imports, the United States had made little or no progress in either direction.

Would the Japanese have been more willing to contribute troops if the action against Iraq as a United Nations operation in support of regional security and less an intervention of the United States, its European allies and its Middle Eastern clients against an overly ambitious Third World dictatorship? In this context Japan's reluctance (as well as the US initiative and failure to foresee its unintended consequences) may have reflected the persistent disinclination of the community of nations to commit itself seriously and effectively to the globalization and institutionalization of the peacekeeping role.

Competition for resources (and other sources of conflict), violent lateral pressures, splintering tendencies, and the violation of boundaries are not likely to disappear for a long time – if ever. In the meantime, as the earth becomes more crowded, the technology (including weaponry) more advanced, the demands on resources more pressing, and the weapons 'smarter,' more lethal, and more globalized, the issues of international management, international security, international law, and global peacekeeping become increasingly critical. Japan may be expected to exert a powerful influence in this complex environment.

Chapter 19

Epilogue
A critical assessment

With the publication of *Nations in Conflict* nearly two decades ago, we reported on a first effort to frame the elements of lateral pressure in econometric terms, estimating and simulating the parameters of simultaneous equations. Studies of the European states prior to World War I and of the Scandinavian countries over the span of a century (1870–1970) have provided clues to the differences between propensities for war and 'peace systems.' Our concern since then has been less with specific events, such as the outbreak and conduct of war, than with general trends and processes.

The analysis in *Nations in Conflict* focused on the sources of lateral pressure and then on the impacts of expansion on military competition, alignments, and arms races and violent interactions. The lateral pressure framework accommodates (and allows the connection of) such processes of change as growth, decline, decision (conditioned by cognitions and affects), bargaining, leveraging, coalition formation, competition, adversarial identification, and conflict (violent and nonviolent). The dependence of all social undertakings on the intense interaction between economic and political processes can be made explicit. Similarly, warmaking and peacemaking can be accommodated within the framework and their processes systematically linked.

The choice of estimating and simulating a system of *simultaneous* equations represented an effort to apply economic methods to international relations. The decision to estimate and simulate is driven by the belief that an appropriate representation of a relationship posited by the theory of lateral pressure was an essential and necessary first step in validation. The simultaneous *estimation* procedure allows – and forces – the analyst to specify the *components* of the system (that is, the particular modules or 'pieces' of the model) that are supported by the attendant dependent and independent variables and then to pull the components together into an identifiable *system*. In this system the same variable can serve as an independent variable in one component and as a dependent variable in another. (Military expenditures, for example, can explain alliance formation as an independent variable and, *at the same time*, be influenced by alliances and other variables as well.) This interdependence and, in many instances, the feedback relations constitute a more appropriate and realistic way of representing aspects of lateral pressure theory than does the emphasizing of correlations alone, or using single equation formulations with one dependent variable and several independent variables and no references to, or connections with, other components of the reality at hand.

MEASUREMENT ISSUES: EMPIRICAL INQUIRY

The equations themselves are signals of reality; they are not the reality itself. The Japan study represents a more sophisticated version of this procedure. The challenge in submitting lateral pressure theory to the empirical test lies in the fact that the theory stresses the dynamic relationship between national attributes (profiles) and international activities. Because the theory seeks to articulate the strong interdependence, critical feedback relationships, and time-dependent processes, the methodological and analytical techniques appropriate for such contingencies must be utilized.

In its verbal statements moreover, the theory stresses the nonlinearities in interstate interactions, and the complexities associated with realities that are at once equifinal and multifinal realities – characterized, that is, by many paths to the same outcomes and multiple outcomes deriving from similar sources. These complexities of the real world are difficult to capture.

From the start our procedure has been to move from a general statement of theory to formal representation for empirical inquiry *prior to quantitative analysis*. This involves specifying the *components* of the model (because the theory addresses complex relationships, both internal and external), the description or rationale for *decomposing* the system as we have done (that is, providing the theoretical justification for the specification of the system of *simultaneous* equations), and then moving to *measures* or *indicators* for depicting the dependent variable in this particular component – with the full expectation that this variable may be (and, in fact, often is) specified also as an independent variable in another equation. This point is important to stress, because critics who focus *only on a single equation* ignore the underlying reality that the equation in question is embedded in a more complex set of relationships and that this arbitrary decomposition constitutes a serious error.[1] Therefore, inferring the theory only from a reading of one equation could be tantamount to misplaced empiricism. The equations and the estimated coefficients represent and depict a 'partial' theory about reality.

The second phase in our research agenda focused explicitly on simulation and forecasting. The purpose was to model the highly interactive features of the lateral pressure process by first stressing the major feedback loops, forecasting over the data base, and then forecasting beyond the existing record (see Choucri and Bousfield 1978). The US case over the period 1930–70 served to illustrate the essential interactions between the demand and capability components of lateral pressure, 'pushing' the system in its expansionary path. In the course of this work we learned the essential differences and contributions of each mode of modeling, simulation, and forecasting by experimenting with system dynamics as a methodology in contrast to econometrics estimation and simulation.

Since national attributes change over time, it is not surprising that most of the important theoretical and empirical developments in our research involved *transformations of national profiles* generally with consequential implications for patterns of international activities. In fact, we had selected Japan as our focus precisely because of what was already widely known about changes in Japan's profile. Yet when we began the Japan study we did not foresee the extent of the useful insights that such changes over time would provide. For our purposes, in short, the Japan case is particularly instructive in that it demonstrates how *changes* in national profile affect the forms and *modes of lateral pressure* and vice versa.

From this study we have enriched our theoretical understanding of shifts in modes of lateral pressure and explored what would (or could) happen if Japan had adopted different policies or had been confronted by different adversaries. However, we have yet to model rigorously the connections between short-term events, such as a provocative act, and their underlying long-term causal structure relating national profiles to international activities.

The next step, simulation, also involves serious challenges. Because errors can readily accumulate, simulating a system of simultaneous equations is not an easy task; it entails simulation without reference or resort to empirical or historical data. The *only* empirical observation is the first data point of each variable in the system of equations. *All* of the other observations are estimated simultaneously, and *all* are simulated accordingly.

Once estimation and simulation are successfully completed (that is, with very small errors), the third step is to 'exercise' the simulated system and to experiment with 'what if' questions. (For example, what would be the effects on a country's military expenditures if it were not confronted by hostile alliances, or if the alliances were becoming increasingly strong or increasingly hostile?)

The power of simulation – if properly undertaken – lies in helping clarify contingencies: what would have happened if . . . ? In this book we have explored a variety of contingencies; all point to the inescapable conclusion that interactions shape networks of conflict and that no single state can be held responsible for a given conflagration. The interactions – actions and reactions – shape hostilities; World War II in the Pacific, especially, was not merely the product of Japan's unilateral policies or Japanese actions alone but must be viewed as endemic to the fabric of interstate relations at the time.

DECISIONS IN TIME SERIES ANALYSIS: A SPECIAL PROBLEM

In Chapter 1 we defined decisions in terms of efforts to narrow or close gaps between an actor's perceptions of 'what is' and 'what ought to be.' We also stated our assumption that such perceptions (and actions generated by them) are driven and shaped, in part, by motivating human affects (or emotions) and cognitions. For methodological reasons, however, we did not incorporate these phenomena into the formal analysis. The reason for this exclusion was at once simple and complex. The growth, development, and expansion data were collected and aggregated at annual intervals over the span of a century – a continuous time series which in practical terms we could not duplicate for affective and cognitive data by any content analysis methodology available to us. This does not mean that the integration and analysis of such data would not be desirable – or at some time in the future even feasible. In principal, at least, the challenge is 'out there' for someone to meet.

Meanwhile, we assume that the materials used – the population, production, allocation, trade, and other time series data analyzed (as well as the narrative analysis of the Pearl Harbor decision) – are bona fide historical 'tracks' left by the Japanese people and their leaders as a consequence of what they perceived, felt, and decided from within their country's changing profile – itself an outcome of interactions among the Japanese themselves as well as with the world outside.

A RECORD OF SELF-EVALUATION

Entitled 'A Critical Assessment,' the next-to-last chapter in *Nations in Conflict* provided a self-evaluation of the research that the book had reported upon. In it we conceded that objections could be raised 'with respect to our choice of variables and their measures and even the sources from which the data were drawn.' Today after more than sixteen years of additional experience, we confront many of the same problems with data, but it is clearer now what the nature of the problems is. In a sense we, like many others working in comparable fields, are captives of those who gather data for national and international sources and of the problems that *they* confront. At this writing the results of the 1990 US census, and reservations about its flaws, are becoming available; and reading the relevant reports, one can only guess at the problems that a vastly poorer or more densely populated country must face when counting its people (or calculating its GNP, its military expenditures, or its energy consumption per capita).

Embedded in the larger model, the colonial expansion equation before World War II illustrates many of the problems associated with theory development, model specification, and quantitative measurement. Despite our ability to account for a large proportion of the variance in colonial area, we are not particularly satisfied with our specification of the theory. Much of the variance is accounted for by the constant term, that is, by preexisting dynamics – not explicitly specified – incorporated in the model. Further, the resulting statistics only imperfectly reflect what transpired at the time. Always, with any statistics, the results must be interpreted with care.

There is another, in some respects more pernicious problem, however, namely, how to match conceptual *variables* with appropriate *indicators*. Colonial area produces only a crude measurement of national expansion, for example, and GNP as an indicator of technology is admittedly vulnerable to criticism. Currently, as a direct consequence of our analysis of more than a century of Japanese growth and expansion, we are leaning toward energy efficiency and energy consumption as better indicators of technology. It is worth noting, however, that GNP and national consumption of energy tend to correlate relatively well. In any case, like the data quality issue, this is only one of several difficult problems that remain largely unresolved.

Given the analytical tools and modes of analysis that are currently available, the extended lateral pressure framework remains too inclusive, extensive, and loosely joined to qualify or be tested as a general theory – although 'quasi' or 'partial' theories are testable within the definable boundaries it provides.

The major strength of the lateral pressure framework, in our view, lies in the capacity it provides for linking in intensely dynamic – and at the same time testable – modes the processes of (uneven) growth, development, and behavioral outcomes among states (demographic, technological, economic, military, and so forth) that have been treated separately in conventional studies rather than interactively, and usually dismissed as poor 'causal' agents (in conflict and war, for example).

Once brought together and 'allowed' to interact, however, each variable process begins to claim its 'causal' share – direct, or more commonly indirect – in territorial and other forms of expansion, competition, conflict, and, not infrequently, war.

Development of the country profiles has provided a useful (though still unrefined) tool for comparing nations in terms of their respective levels and rates of change in population, technology, and resource access. An initial motivation for defining the country profiles was to clarify and informally demonstrate the differences between an *epsilon* country ('high' population density, 'low' technology, 'limited' resource access) and an *alpha* ('medium to low' population density, 'advanced and advancing' technology, 'extensive' resource base) or a *beta* country like pre-World War II Japan ('high' population, 'advanced and advancing' technology, but 'limited' resource base). It was only toward the end of the empirical analysis that we recognized the value of comparing profile transformations (changes in 'master variable' ratios) as a means of exposing and comparing the dynamics of national growth, expansion, and behavioral consequences across countries and *through time*. Currently, we are tightening the profile concept for testing of lateral pressure theory.

In all cases that we have examined so far, the prevailing level of technology has exerted a powerful discriminating influence on population and resource access – the other two master variables.

Procedures of this kind will provide a focus for future research into the structural transformations that occur when a developing country like South Korea, for example, approaches (or achieves) industrial status. Similarly, a comparison of countries with similar *profiles* ('master' variable ratios) but significant different *sizes* (territorial and/or population and/or technological and economic) – South Korea and China, perhaps – should allow us to ascertain which variances of outcome are explained by structural ratios and which by structural 'size' combinations.

Comparable comparisons can be made of industrialized countries (growth and development trends in a United Germany and Japan, for example, or Germany and Luxembourg).

In this and other respects several of the hypothesized relationships in Chapter 1 lacked the precision that we would have preferred. The system of simultaneous equations we developed has successfully decomposed the more falsifiable and measurable aspects of the conceptual framework and submitted them to empirical test. The result was a first-order (and rough) approximation of the linkage between domestic growth, development, and international behavior, but we are not entirely satisfied with either the model specification or the theoretical guidelines. If we had known at the beginning what we have learned since, we could have done better.

In passing, it is worth noting that we often regret having labeled the country profiles – *alpha*, *beta*, *gamma*, and so on – for the reason that such designations, however convenient, convey a notion of rigid, in fact arbitrary, boundaries which can be theoretically and empirically misleading.

As with all quantitative (and other) methods in the social sciences, the procedures we have employed are constrained, again and again, by data requirements, and the data bases are never as robust as we would wish. Thus, the trade-offs among empirical fit, parsimony, and falsifiability are especially difficult to make with any degree of satisfaction. We need to learn better ways of correcting for the inadequacies of the data which are available to us.

There are other self-criticisms – theoretical and analytical limitations, if you will – that gnaw at us (in the middle of the night, all too frequently). We need to examine and reexamine our analytical 'output' – 'eyeballing it,' 'immersing ourselves in it,' searching for patterns, incongruities, discrepancies between hypothesized and actual results (residuals, for example). Then, drawing upon what we have missed previously, we need to improve on the specification of national profiles (and their transformations, completed or in progress) and their relationships with forms of lateral pressure (economic, military, other), competition, conflict spirals (and recesses), and the like. We also need to improve the system of simultaneous equations described in earlier chapters. Initially we had a tendency to aggregate key relationships which in some instances may need to be disaggregated. We need also to improve upon our indicators (and, as far as we can, the quality of available historical data upon which we are continually drawing).

It is well known that issues of methodology commonly involve difficult trade-offs. Costs and benefits are attached to almost every major choice made in the development and testing of theory. Clearly, it would have been desirable to be able to specify and correct the errors in the analysis so far, and thus be able to present a complete, consistent, and fully tested theory. But the lesser job that we *did* accomplish took the better part of a decade and a half of slow and often discouraging trial and error investigation – with the major returns occurring only in the last year or so. On a long journey one needs to put up at least a rough milestone now and then or risk losing one's sense of movement and direction.

Despite limitations imposed by the use of regression analysis, extensions in estimating parameters of a system of simultaneous equations, and then simulating the system, we are generally satisfied with the methodology we used in this phase of our work. In order to capture the dynamic changes over time more fully, however, the regression algorithm is not entirely adequate. As for the counterfactuals – the exploration of what could have happened under alternative conditions – the results have been suggestive but fundamentally incomplete in that two crucial processes have not been adequately represented: (a) processes and politics of other nations, and (b) contextual and environmental implications of interstate relations.

In the next phases of our research we expect that the methodologies, as in the past, will move along with theory, the quality of data available, and the complexity of the tasks that confront us.

A RETROSPECTIVE

Since the publication of *Nations in Conflict*, earlier phases of our research program have been reviewed by a number of scholars in international relations and related fields and disciplines. Many of the critiques have been extremely helpful as we have worked toward further refinement and testing of the lateral pressure framework and the fundamental assumptions and propositions that constitute the overall theory. We are especially grateful for suggestions that have helped us to improve theoretical specification and the generation of more elegant theoretical structure.

Several other criticisms seem to have fallen into two general categories. First among them are those that we consider essentially trivial or nonilluminating, such as disagreements over a particular coefficient or indicator (especially when no better alternative is identified) or debates over functional form. Similarly, being profoundly aware of the usual data problems, we feel no need to be reminded of them unless some new or better source is brought to our attention. Somewhat the same sort of thing can be said about choice of indicators; we are delighted to have specific and viable alternatives brought to our attention (although we often cannot change over until the 'next project'). There is always room for improvement, which is what we want, but it will be more helpful to us when the criteria for recommending a specific substitute are made explicit.

A second set of critiques derives from attempts to replicate our analyses but which in our judgment do not in reality replicate them. Among these are 'replications' that treat the 'master' and 'derivative' variables separately, rather than interactively, without attention to the interconnections, dynamic linkages, feedback relations, and simultaneities of influences that connect internal and external actors. It seems only reasonable to us that any fair replication must either use a methodology appropriate to the theoretical directives or indicate step for step in what respect(s) the original methods are challenged and the substitute methods more appropriate. In this respect the use of bivariate linear equations to test and/or replicate lateral pressure theory and our analyses thereof is singularly inappropriate.

Another recurrent misunderstanding of the theory and the empirical analysis associated with it has been attributable to critics who have simplified the underlying premises and erroneously assumed a direct link between national population, treated 'causally,' and international conflict – a 'Lebensraum' effect. In fact, from the publication of *Nations in Conflict* (and in journal articles before and after), we have underscored (and in research reports demonstrated) the intense *interaction* of the three 'master variables' – population, technology (knowledge and skills), and resource access – as the ultimate (but not the sole) source of uneven growth, development, competition, conflict, and war.

Beyond this, we have been nonplussed by charges of 'determinism,' which in view of our predilection for propositions including words like 'greater,' 'lesser,' 'higher,' 'lower,' 'more,' 'less,' 'likely,' and 'probable' seems more than a little incongruous. Middle East events during the winter and early spring of 1991 have reinforced our inclination (growing out of our study of events leading into World War I and strengthened by the course of Japanese policies and actions before and after World War II) toward reliance on such concepts of *uncertainty*, '*noninevitabilities*' (especially in wars, which are continually being characterized as 'inevitable' by those who wage them), *a-rationality*, *disequilibrium* (which we have also been criticized for), and *unintended* consequences. We frequently remind ourselves of Karl Popper's distinction between 'clock-like' assumptions about reality and the indeterminate, equifinal, multifinal 'cloud-like' improbabilities in human affairs. At the same time, however, we are fully persuaded that decision and policy making can be illuminated by systematic studies of the behavior of 'clouds.'

FUTURE RESEARCH

The next phases of our research, while addressing these and related issues that remain outstanding, are 'nested within' and 'linked into' the global system and its natural and social environments and processes. By this we mean that all states of the world, their structures, growth, development, and behavior patterns are examined as 'shares' or percentages of global totals. Or, from a more general perspective, the First, Second, and Third Images of our research in the past (including their 'natural' as well as 'social' environments) are 'nested within' and 'linked into' the global environment and its natural and social environments and processes – the Fourth Image.

With respect to the development and testing of theory, whenever contradictions or inconsistencies arise, the challenge becomes one of recognition, elucidation, and explanation. For the immediate future, at least, our assumption is that this will be the most useful way to proceed. The testing of two or more contradictory hypotheses or partial theories within the lateral pressure framework, for example, may force conceptual or theoretical reformulation, enrich the statement of generic processes, and lead step by step toward a more parsimonious synthesis. While fully aware that the indeterminacies of national, international, and global politics cannot be eliminated, we are persuaded that the lateral pressure approach goes a long way toward reducing their range and helping us and other theoreticians and practitioners in the field of global politics to assess what we do and do not understand.

Today's world is changing with extraordinary rapidity. To the extent that current rates of population growth and trends in technological applications and economic growth continue, human pressures on the earth and its resources will be exacerbated. If, concurrently, our technologies (civil and military) and economic transactions are increasingly globalized, and if multi-nation states continue their fragmentation, the world of tomorrow will be characterized by growing numbers of smaller states. With population, technology, and resource-access dimensions of grossly differentiated 'sizes,' ratios, growth rates, and basic capabilities, these many lesser 'sovereignties' will find themselves competing for security (economic, political, strategic) and survival in a 'world order' that originated and established its boundaries and enforced its sanctions in an age of a few vastly expanded empires.

In tomorrow's new world of transformed 'wholes,' 'parts,' and uncertain relationships, we may expect the challenges of environmental management and global peacekeeping, for better or worse, to become more and more interactive, interdependent, and, short of some unprecedented 'reconstitution,' potentially explosive.

Our hope and expectations are that the specification of a global framework of interactive wholes and parts will be a useful step toward the reduction of inconsistencies, and contradictions, in the theory and practice of international and interregional relations during the next few decades. These decades will show increasingly globalized growth, contending patterns of development, conflicting actions, and a wide range of possible outcomes.

Major sources of quantitative data

Coefficient name	Variable	Sources of data*
Prewar model		
β_{11}	Imports of raw materials	3, 5
β_{12}	Industrial labor force over total labor force	5, 6
β_{13}	Coal production	3, 5
β_{14}	Balance of trade ($t-1$)	3
β_{15}	Colonial imports over total imports	3, 16
β_{21}	Exports of finished goods	3
β_{22}	Colonial imports over total imports	5, 16
β_{23}	Population of Japan proper	3
β_{24}	Balance of trade ($t-1$)	3
β_{31}	Russian military expenditure	1, 13
β_{32}	Colonial area	3
β_{33}	Colonial imports over total imports	5, 16
β_{34}	Army expenditure ($t-1$)	6, 10, 12, 14
β_{35}	Government revenue	3
β_{41}	US navy expenditure	1, 13
β_{42}	British navy expenditure	1, 13
β_{43}	Imports of raw materials	3, 5
β_{44}	Colonial area	3
β_{45}	Colonial imports over total imports	5, 16
β_{46}	Navy expenditure ($t-1$)	6, 10, 12, 14
β_{47}	Government revenue	3, 5
β_{51}	Military expenditure	6, 10, 12, 14
β_{52}	Imports of raw materials	3, 5
β_{53}	Food imports	3, 5
β_{54}	Population of Japan proper	3, 5
β_{61}	Merchant marine tonnage	3, 5
β_{62}	National income	3, 5
β_{63}	Military expenditure	6, 10, 12, 14
β_{64}	Colonial area	3
β_{65}	Food imports	3, 5
β_{71}	Government revenue	3, 5
β_{72}	Colonial imports over total imports	5, 16

* Entries refer to references listed at the end of this appendix.

Coefficient name	Variable	Sources of data*
β_{73}	Colonial area	3

Instrumental variables

	Steel production	3, 5
	Rice production	3, 5
	Wheat consumption	3, 5
	Government expenditure (general account)	3, 5
	Government expenditure (special account)	3, 5
	Length of railway	3

Deflator

	Wholesale price index	3, 8, 9, 11

Postwar model

β_{11}	Industrial labor force over total labor force	4, 5, 6
β_{12}	Foreign direct investment in Japan	4, 5, 6, 7
β_{13}	Japan's foreign direct investment abroad	4, 5, 6, 7
β_{14}	Exports of technology	2
β_{15}	Imports of nonfuel commodities	5, 6
β_{21}	Population	5, 6
β_{22}	Wheat consumption	5
β_{23}	Capital stock	5, 10, 11
β_{24}	Copper consumption	6
β_{25}	Merchant marine tonnage	5, 6
β_{26}	Total exports	5, 6
β_{31}	Domestic energy supply	5, 15
β_{32}	Population	5, 6
β_{33}	Gross national product	5, 6
β_{41}	Merchant marine tonnage	5, 6
β_{42}	Exports of technology	2
β_{43}	Gross national product	5, 6
β_{44}	Energy imports	2, 15
β_{45}	Japan's foreign direct investment	4, 5, 6, 7
β_{51}	Exports of technology	2
β_{52}	Gross national product	5, 6

Instrumental variables

	Steel production	3, 5
	Copper consumption	6
	National income	3, 5
	Gross domestic capital formation	3, 5, 10
	Total imports	3, 5
	Imports of raw materials	3, 5
	Merchant marine tonnage	3, 5
	Foreign direct investment in Japan	4, 5, 6, 7
	Exports of technology	2
	Index of productive capacity	3, 5, 10

Deflator

	Wholesale price index	3, 8, 9

REFERENCES: APPENDIX I

1 *Almanach de Gotha: Annuaire Généalogique Diplomatique et Statistique.* Gotha, Germany: Justus Perthes, various editions.
2 The Bank of Japan, *Economic Statistics Annual.* Tokyo, various editions.
3 The Bank of Japan, *Hundred-Year Statistics of the Japanese Economy.* Tokyo, 1966.
4 The Bank of Japan, *Monthly Statistics of Japan.* Tokyo, various editions.
5 The Bureau of Statistics, Prime Minister's Office (Japan), *Japan Statistical Yearbook.* Tokyo, various editions.
6 The Bureau of Statistics, Prime Minister's Office (Japan), *Monthly Statistics of Japan.* Tokyo, various editions.
7 International Monetary Fund (IMF), *Balance of Payments Yearbook.* Paris, various editions.
8 International Monetary Fund (IMF), *International Financial Statistics Yearbook.* Paris, various editions.
9 Metallgesellschaft Aktiengesellschaft, *Metal Statistics.* Frankfurt: Metallgesellschaft AG, various editions.
10 Ministry of Finance (Japan), *Meiji Taisho Zaiseishi* (Financial History of Meiji and Taisho Eras), Vol. 3. Tokyo: Meiji Zaisei-shi Hakkosho, 1926.
11 Ministry of Finance (Japan), *Monthly Financial Review.* Tokyo, various editions.
12 Ministry of Finance (Japan), *Showa, Zaisei-shi* (Financial History of the Showa Era), Vols 3 and 4. Tokyo: Toyo-Keizai Shimpo-sha, 1955.
13 *The Statesman's Yearbook.* London: Macmillan, various editions.
14 Toyo-Keizai Shimpo-sha, *Meiji Taisho Zaisei Shoran* (Detailed Financial Statistics of the Meiji and Showa Eras), 2nd edn. Tokyo: Toyo-Keizai Shimpo-sha, 1929.
15 United Nations (Department of Economic and Social Affairs), *World Energy Supplies.* New York: United Nations, various editions.
16 Wright, P. G., *Trade and Trade Barriers in the Pacific.* Stanford, Calif.: Stanford University Press, 1935.

Pre-World War II model estimation (for Chapter 6)

EXPORTS OF FINISHED GOODS: ESTIMATION

Independent variable	Name of coefficient	Estimated value of coefficient		
		1878–1941	1878–1914	1915–41
Constant[b]	α_1	13.1303 (20.8862)	−7.52703 (4.23275)	1,095.5000 (62.7284)
Imports of raw materials	β_{11}	77.82 (10.60)	22.30 (12.02)	69.76 (15.92)
Percentage of labor of secondary industry to total labor[c]	β_{12}	−2.31628 (2.33246)	1.32408 (0.580529)	−3.65172 (4.82641)
Production of coal	β_{13}	984.00 (726.56)	428.19 (544.01)	1,862.70 (1,230.76)
Balance of trade $(t-1)$	β_{14}	14.99 (5.23)	−2.65 (2.92)	14.28 (9.34)
Imports from colonies[d]	β_{15}	45.5649 (42.6440)	−9.82310 (33.8704)	48.9971 (59.9897)
$\bar{R}^2$		0.71	0.88	0.67

[a]A commonly used measure of the goodness of fit of a linear model is R^2 (R square), also called the coefficient of determination. $\bar{R}^2$ (adjusted R^2) is the statistic that corrects R^2 to more closely reflect the goodness of fit of the model in the population. $\bar{R}^2$ is given by:

$$\bar{R}^2 = R^2 - \frac{p(1-R^2)}{N-p-1}$$

where p = the number of independent variables in the equation.
[b]Millions.
[c]Millions.
[d]Billions.

IMPORTS OF RAW MATERIALS: ESTIMATION

Independent variable	Name of coefficient	Estimated value of coefficient		
		1878–1941	1878–1914	1915–41
Constant[a]	α_2	−1.412600 (0.676241)	−1.446970 (0.528566)	−.00750349 (1.34610000)
Exports of finished goods	β_{21}	0.005 (0.002)	0.007 (0.004)	0.006 (0.003)
Imports from colonies[b]	β_{22}	−.753938 (0.701517)	−.447445 (0.622962)	−1.8977 (0.849254)
Home population	β_{23}	37.27 (16.71)	37.57 (13.18)	29.29 (28.14)
Balance of trade (t–1)	β_{24}	0.18 (0.05)	0.09 (0.06)	−0.06 (0.11)
$\bar{R}^2$		0.81	0.51	0.70

[a]Millions.
[b]Billions.

ARMY EXPENDITURES: ESTIMATION

Independent variable	Name of coefficient	Estimated value of coefficient		
		1878–1941	1878–1914	1915–41
Constant	α_3	−164,800.0 (57,063.4)	148,101. (55,611.3)	−192,068.0 (124,371.0)
Russian military expenditures × Russia as potential enemy	β_{31}	1.14 (0.30)	1.06 (0.05)	2.07 (0.34)
Colonial area	β_{32}	−1.17 (0.49)	3.49 (5.93)	−0.47 (0.34)
Imports from colonies[a]	β_{33}	−2.03830 (1.01755)	6.72926 (3.40581)	2.75522 (1.09324)
Army expenditures (t–1)	β_{34}	0.46 (0.14)	1.07 (0.43)	0.70 (0.10)
Government revenue	β_{35}	161.09 (44.25)	−502.65 (183.33)	−57.61 (41.17)
$\bar{R}^2$		0.93	0.74	0.94

[a] Billions.

NAVY EXPENDITURES: ESTIMATION

Independent variable	Name of coefficient	Estimated value of coefficient		
		1878–1941	1878–1914	1915–41
Constant	α_4	−456.59 (14,654.40)	10,368.40 (7,880.69)	83,473.7 (83,589.1)
US navy expenditures × US as potential enemy	β_{41}	0.31 (0.08)	−0.69 (0.36)	0.28 (0.10)
Britain's navy expenditures × Britain as potential enemy	β_{42}	0.17 (0.15)	n.a. n.a.	0.26 (0.21)
Imports of raw materials	β_{43}	−0.15 (0.04)	0.06 (0.11)	−0.20 (0.06)
Colonial area	β_{44}	−0.23 (0.13)	0.38 (0.34)	−0.08 (0.11)
Imports from colonies[a]	β_{45}	−1.06347 (0.274008)	0.507539 (0.516908)	−1.05757 (0.394184)
Navy expenditures $(t-_1)$	β_{46}	0.46 (0.13)	0.80 (0.22)	0.30 (0.22)
Government revenue	β_{47}	92.73 (10.57)	−7.33 (20.26)	94.19 (18.25)
$\bar{R}^2$		0.98	0.98	0.99

[a]Billions.

JAPAN'S COLONIAL AREA: ESTIMATION

Independent variable	Name of coefficient	Estimated value of coefficient		
		1878–1941	1878–1914	1915–41
Constant[a]	α_5	−0.0349279 (0.311748)	−0.0261568 (0.183902)	−1.140670 (0.802517)
Military expenditures	β_{51}	0.11 (0.02)	0.03 (0.02)	0.09 (0.03)
Imports of raw materials	β_{52}	0.24 (0.12)	0.20 (0.10)	0.15 (0.16)
Imports of raw materials/home population	β_{53}	−12,653.80 (9,623.61)	−4,387.28 (3,164.42)	−23,690.9 (21,947.4)
Home population	β_{54}	0.33 (7.72)	0.79 (4.81)	20.76 (16.05)
$\bar{R}^2$		0.69	0.47	0.74

[a]Millions.

IMPORTS FROM COLONIES: ESTIMATION

Independent variable	Name of coefficient	Estimated value of coefficient		
		1878–1941	1878–1914	1915–41
Constant	α_6	-5.91140×10^{-5} (2.09294×10^{-5})	-1.04673×10^{-5} (9.57955×10^{-6})	1.26997×10^{-5} (2.96034×10^{-5})
Merchant marine	β_{61}	3.56622×10^{-8} (1.25589×10^{-8})	1.05545×10^{-7} (1.73857×10^{-8})	-1.75079×10^{-9} (2.89051×10^{-8})
National income	β_{62}	1.91239×10^{-8} (4.91911×10^{-9})	2.26219×10^{-9} (2.44976×10^{-9})	2.34016×10^{-8} (5.22079×10^{-9})
Military expenditures	β_{63}	3.01129×10^{-12} (6.72387×10^{-12})	-4.38363×10^{-11} (1.19742×10^{-11})	7.40396×10^{-13} (6.69004×10^{-12})
Colonial area	β_{64}	-1.67873×10^{-10} (7.52577×10^{-11})	-1.62726×10^{-10} (1.22036×10^{-10})	$-1.18306 = 10^{-10}$ (4.83433×10^{-11})
Imports of foodstuffs/ home population	β_{65}	-1.37957×10^{-5} (3.17263×10^{-6})	-3.14436×10^{-6} (1.53301×10^{-6})	-1.75561×10^{-5} (6.38475×10^{-6})
$\bar{R}^2$		0.90	0.95	0.89

GOVERNMENT EXPENDITURES FOR COLONIAL ADMINISTRATION: ESTIMATION

Independent variable	Name of coefficient	Estimated value of coefficient		
		1878–1941	1878–1914	1915–41
Constant	α_7	$-3,973.83$ (19,229.0)	$-18,611.9$ (12,559.1)	$-122,903.0$ (47,533.3)
Government revenues	β_{71}	20.26 (6.06)	35.53 (9.30)	30.54 (7.23)
Percentage of imports from colonies to total imports[a]	β_{72}	0.753457 (0.169097)	0.332230 (0.321794)	1.308570 (0.271739)
Colonial area	β_{73}	0.14 (0.11)	0.33 (0.25)	0.03 (0.11)
$\bar{R}^2$		0.90	0.65	0.96

[a]Billions.

Appendix III

Post-World War II model estimation (for Chapter 15)

GROSS NATIONAL PRODUCT: ESTIMATION

Independent variable	Name of coefficient	Estimated value of coefficient 1946–76	Standard error
Constant	α_1	1,826.02	738.64
Industrial labor force	β_{11}	253.5	755.75
Foreign direct investment in Japan	β_{12}	45.83	35.60
Japan's foreign direct investment	β_{13}	129.34	21.88
Exports of technology	β_{14}	597.29	198.41
Imports of nonfuel commodities	β_{15}	−6.43	2.39
$\bar{R}^2$		0.66	

NONFUEL IMPORTS: ESTIMATION

Independent variable	Name of coefficient	Estimated value of coefficient 1946–76	Standard error
Constant	α_2	−25.12	215.67
Population	β_{21}	−19.61	159.63
Wheat consumption	β_{22}	0.06	0.19
Capital stock	β_{23}	37.54	36.86
Copper consumption	β_{24}	3.12	0.84
Merchant marine tonnage	β_{25}	−0.17	0.12
Total exports	β_{26}	0.52	0.34
$\bar{R}^2$		0.33	

ENERGY IMPORTS: ESTIMATION

Independent variable	Name of coefficient	Estimated value of coefficient 1946–76	Standard error
Constant	α_3	10.87	8.80
Domestic energy supply	β_{31}	−1.37	0.80
Population	β_{32}	−1.40	6.41
Gross national product	β_{33}	0.003	0.001
$\bar{R}^2$		0.47	

TOTAL EXPORTS: ESTIMATION

Independent variable	Name of coefficient	Estimated value of coefficient 1946–76	Standard error
Constant	α_4	−20.30	91.31
Merchant marine tonnage	β_{41}	0.22	0.10
Exports of technology	β_{42}	−26.58	42.62
Gross national product	β_{43}	−0.04	0.03
Energy imports	β_{44}	29.40	10.40
Japan's foreign direct investment	β_{45}	−12.94	4.28
$\bar{R}^2$		0.65	

JAPAN'S FOREIGN DIRECT INVESTMENT: ESTIMATION

Independent variable	Name of coefficient	Estimated value of coefficient 1946–76	Standard error
Constant	α_5	−2.71	10.66
Exports of technology	β_{51}	−9.24	3.85
Gross national product	β_{52}	0.01	0.002
$\bar{R}^2$		0.20	

Simulation summary statistics post-World War II (for Chapter 16)

	GNP	Simulated	Simulation error	Percent simulation error
Mean	2,927.79	2,927.78	−0.010286	320.197
RMS[a]	5,153.27	8,049.51	5,347.65	1,465.62
Std dev.	4,313.28	7,626.36	5,439.07	1,454.67
	Nonfuel imports	Simulated	Sim. error	Perc. sim. error
Mean	215.061	215.06	−0.00317	92.3115
RMS	465.777	270.41	352.514	569.999
Std dev.	420.219	166.726	358.54	572.09
	Total exports	Simulated	Sim. error	Perc. sim. error
Mean	398.975	398.973	−0.000439	−460.758
RMS	651.902	596.141	469.95	2,900.57
Std Dev.	524.367	450.521	477.984	2,912.69
	Foreign dir. inv.	Simulated	Sim. error	Perc. sim. error
Mean	11.7906	11.7905	−6.001789E−05	−1242.24
RMS	52.6073	55.7941	42.6387	3,983.28
Std Dev.	52.1455	55.4663	43.3676	3,862.66
	Energy imports	Simulated	Sim. error	Perc. sim. error
Mean	16.3186	16.3185	−4.425048E−05	404.578
RMS	25.7068	27.7805	16.6411	2,937.43
Std Dev.	20.2027	22.8668	16.9256	2,959.17

[a] The root mean square (RMS) of the error is the most important summary statistic in indicating how well the simulated model tracks empirical observations:

$$\text{RMS}_{error} = \frac{\displaystyle\sum_{i=1}^{n}(A_i - P_i)^2}{n}$$

where n = number of periods simulated, A_i = historical (known empirical) values for an endogenous variable, P_i = simulated values for the endogenous variable. Other important summary statistics include the mean of the forecast and the mean of the simulation and the percentage error for each. See *Troll/1 User's Guide* (June 1972).

Notes

2 THE PROFILE AND CAPABILITIES OF JAPAN: A CRITICAL CENTURY

1 The profile of Japan described in this chapter draws upon the Bank of Japan (1966). This source provides the data for the quantitative analysis in subsequent chapters. Wherever appropriate, we make reference to alternative estimates presented by other scholars and by more recent sources.
2 The census counted the subject alone, and excluded the samurai, the nobles, and the untouchables. Those uncounted are estimated to be as many as 15% to 20% of those counted. Hence, the total population may have been over 30 million at the time.
3 During the first ten years of the Meiji era (1870–80) the population rate of increase was about 5.0 per million, and thereafter the rate increased to 7.6, 10.0, 12.0, and 13.0 to 17.0 between 1920 and 1930. By then, Japan was adding approximately 10 million people to the population every decade.
4 Emigration during the same period amounted to about 600,000.
5 We have chosen 1906 to enable comparison with the results in *Nations in Conflict*.
6 See especially Minami (1986) for an analysis of Japanese development in a comparative context.
7 Whereas the land area involved in rice production increased by only about 17 percent between the 1890s and the 1960s, improved methods of production led to substantial improvements in annual harvests. With traditional farming methods, the average rice harvest had amounted to one metric ton per hectare (0.445 short tons per acre). After World War II, a maximum of land – some 3,300,000 hectares – was brought under rice cultivation, and improved techniques contributed to a quadrupling of average yield to over 4 metric tons per hectare, illustrating the role of technology in relaxing critical constraints. Partly because of crop failures, however, and partly because of changes in Japanese diet, rice production began to decline significantly in the late 1960s.
8 The first steel ship was built in the 1890s, and about that time shipbuilding subsidies were made available on a regular basis. By 1909 the industry included six major shipyards and employed 26,000 workers, and the average gross annual gross tonnage of ships launched had reached 50,000 metric tons (Allen 1981: 84).
9 The rate of real income growth declined from the latter half of 1979 through the first half of 1980 (Japan Institute of International Affairs 1982: 54).

10 Owing to steep increases in the national oil bill, which rose some $29 billion (or approximately 2.9 percent of GNP) above the 1978 bill, and to the appreciation of the yen, Japan's current account incurred a deficit of $13.9 billion in 1979.

11 The influence of this factor (i.e. military allocations at t-1) relative to other influences on the military budget is examined quantitatively in later chapters.

12 For example, precious metals for the Spanish in Central and South America, spices for the Portuguese and Dutch in the East Indies, furs for the French in Canada and (along with timber and, later, minerals) for the Russians in Siberia, tobacco and sugar lands for the British in Virginia and the West Indies, fibres for various European powers in Africa, India, and elsewhere, and furs, minerals, timber, and agricultural land for the United States in Indian territories and Mexico north of Baja California and the Rio Grande. The more successful empires of the past have been those which acquired valuable resources early and at relatively low cost. Thereafter the growth and development of major empires has tended to follow a logistic curve – accelerating rapidly for decades, perhaps generations or centuries, then tapering off as costs have risen relative to returns. By the middle decades of the twentieth century, the costs of acquiring and maintaining colonies had risen so high that the established empires disintegrated rapidly.

13 According to Itoh and Kiyono (1986: 66–7) the distribution of foreign direct investments for the period in question (in $100 million) is as follows:

(a) Asia: mining, 4813.
(b) North America: transportation machinery, 339.
(c) North America: commerce, 2590.
(d) Asia: iron and metal, 1305.
(e) North America: finance and insurance, 1250.
(f) Europe: commerce, 1071.
(g) Latin America: mining, 1066.

14 General trading companies not only deal with final products made by Japanese firms, including small firms, but organize exports of large-scale plants, including petrochemicals, power plants, and airports, to developing countries.

15 The semiconductor industry has come to symbolize this collision and to assume a reality of its own in strengthening a conflict that has no signs of abating. The semiconductor industry is now emerging as a noted indicator of leadership in the world economy. Although the United States remains dominant in most technological areas and in manufacturing and finance, Japan is rapidly closing the gap (Okimoto 1984).

16 At the turn of the century, Taiwan had a density of 78 persons per square kilometer, Korea between 37 and 75 depending on population estimates, and Manchuria 23, as compared with 116 for Japan.

5 COMPARISONS OF PROFILES: JAPAN AND THE MAJOR POWERS

1 These general comparisons are important for three reasons. First, they enable us to assess national capabilities and demands, domestic pressures, and the directions in which each nation was pressing its interests and influence; second, they suggest conditions that gave rise to competitions and conflicts that led to World War I; third, they illustrate the dynamic nature of the international system. (Nations do not simply 'stand still' relative to each other in terms of population, technology, access to resources, or military capabilities.)

2 In 1870 the British output of iron and steel was almost three times the German output; by 1913, however, the volume of German production had increased by a factor of more than eight. Nonetheless, Britain continued to maintain a somewhat narrow lead over German production until around 1900, when Germany overtook Britain and then continuously increased its lead.

3 The number of ships is an unreliable comparison, since the minimum tonnage required for a craft to be counted differed among the nations in our study.

4 By 1885 a newly established *Kolonialzeitung* had contributed to the establishment of a central organization which attracted 10,000 members in a year and began coordinating various previously scattered efforts at colonial expansion which had already led to the acquisition of New Britain, New Ireland, and New Guinea in the Pacific. Soon thereafter, a series of treaties of 'protection and friendship' were concluded with back-country chiefs in Africa and elsewhere. These and subsequent acquisitions were hailed by Bismarck as leading to expanded trade, the winning of new markets for German industry, and the provision of new fields for German capital, activity, and civilization (Aydelotte 1937: 18, 23–24).

6 A MODEL OF LATERAL PRESSURE: FROM THE MEIJI RESTORATION TO WORLD WAR I

1 Other scholars have argued that Japan represents a norm rather than a distinctive case in its developmental path (Minami 1986). Our purpose is not to resolve this issue but rather to highlight the developmental path and profile of this particular case.

2 The similarities all converge around the use of quantitative data, econometric techniques, and attendant simulation and counterfactual forecasting. The differences pertain to theory, to the primary domain of interest, and to the conceptual framework underlying analysis. Ours is not a theory of economic growth or development; it is a theory of expansion and conflict. Driving expansion, however, is the phenomenon of growth.

3 On theoretical grounds it is relevant to stress that these objectives differ from those of Kelley and Williamson (1974: 4) or Minami (1986).

4 A tradition of modeling Meiji Japan's economic development provides a counterpart for our approach (e.g. Kelley and Williamson 1971; Kelley *et al.* 1972).

5 The process of formulating the equations shown in Table 6.2 reflected four types of initial probes. First, the World War I study provided relevant background – at the level of theory development and formal representation (seeking the proverbial 'parsimony without oversimplification'). Second, extensive analysis of Japanese history (1868–1976) guided the effort in both 'fitting to facts' and 'parsimony without oversimplification.' In particular, although shortened in the text for reasons of space, a detailed and painstaking chronicle of Japanese expansion – troop deployment overseas, territorial acquisitions, casualties inflicted and incurred, campaign strategies, and so forth – provided valuable guidelines and reference points. Third, experimentation and the search for model accuracy for each question were undertaken in order to modify the equations so that more accurate specification, higher explanatory power, and a more theoretically persuasive 'fit' were obtained. Fourth, by drawing upon the rich literature in quantitative international politics, it was possible to draw upon the insights of others without generating undue replication.

6 Implicit therein is a theory of economic growth that infers the significance of

inputs into productive processes by focusing on the output variable critical to the Japan case.

7 In addition, two other factors are included in this equation: a constant term (α) and an error term (μ). The constant term, α, represents the intercept of the regression function. The constant, like all coefficients in these equations, is an unknown parameter, the value of which is estimated from empirical data. This term can be interpreted substantively as the value of the dependent variable when the values of all independent variables are zero. In many cases the constant may be interpreted as the inertia of the dependent variable, set during the period *before* the initial point of our analysis. The disturbance term, μ, represents the errors encountered in analysis. There are three major sources of error: (a) misspecification of the functional and structural nature of the equation; (b) systematic measurement error in the data; and (c) random factors or chance. Error may also come from data *sources*. Even the standard sources of demographic, production, budgetary, and other data are often inconsistent, and errors and inconsistencies within single sources are not uncommon. The base and criteria for the definition, selection, and compilation of data in one source often change from year to year, sometimes without explanation or even adequate indication.

8 Population here is to be interpreted as a demographic 'pressure' variable, placing claims on the country's resources. It is also to be viewed in a 'consumption mode,' consistent with neoclassical formulation of demand. The intercept and the error terms are included as well, each providing additional (but unspecified) information about the broader resource demand process.

9 This process, representing the interactive nature of great power activities, is modeled by a 'dummy variable' indicating adversaries' expenditures. In equation (3) the dummy variable in the army expenditure equation (set either at 1 or 0) depends on the existence or absence of the Japanese government's perception of Russia/USSR or the United States (or both) as potential threats – a consideration which preceding chapters have shown to be a source of uncertainty and debate in the months preceding the attack on Pearl Harbor. In equation (4), the navy equation, Great Britain is also included as a potential 'enemy' for the Japanese navy – even though, as we have seen, the leadership as a whole found difficulty in assessing the implications of Britain's navy in conjunction with that of the US.

10 An intercept term is also included, to be interpreted as indicating the level of the hypothesized dependent variable in the absence of the explanatory variables, i.e. what it would have been without the influence of the independent variables.

11 As in the other equations, an intercept term and an error term are included.

12 Again, intercept and error terms are included in the equation.

13 Since ordinary least squares (OLS) is inappropriate where there are simultaneities among the relationships as well as lagged endogenous variables, alternative estimation procedures are used. Possible parameter distortions are corrected by employing the generalized least square (GLS) method in conjunction with the two-stage least square (2SLS) method. These techniques are discussed in standard econometric texts and summarized in *Nations in Conflict*, appendix B. (The computation system, provided by the TROLL system developed by the National Bureau of Economic Research, embeds these algorithms.) As noted earlier, we used the OLS system in an initial probe during the stage of model development. This probe assisted us in making the transition from the known system of the World War I case to

the more complex dynamic (less known) system of Japan over a period of more than 100 years.

14 In it, arms expenditures, colonial areas, and other variables were tracked and simulated for individual countries in terms of single equations in a complex system. In the Japan model, by contrast, considered respecification was undertaken allowing for more detailed formulation. For example, military expenditures are composed of two equations, and, similarly, colonial expansion is represented by two equations. Also, in *Nations in Conflict* the trade factor was specified in capsule form, whereas for the Japan case the process of imports was specified separately from the export process, and connections were made between them as an interactive process.

15 While we do agree with economic and diplomatic historians as to the salience of the 1941 break, thereby requiring distinct specification, we are less certain of the 'system-change' impacts of World War I. For this reason we use the *same* analytical model for 1878–1914 and 1915–41, and then compare the results. (The distribution of residuals and their characteristics provide insights into underlying differences prevailing in the two periods.)

16 The identification of nations as potential 'enemies' was based on the Teikoku Kokubo Hoshin (Imperial Defense Guideline) prepared in 1907 and revised from time to time thereafter. This document incorporates the imperial government's formal and official prescription of its position and that of other major powers, and was used as the basis for the raw data for these variables. We literally derived the variables as 'enemy' or 'adversary' based on this account.

17 In all equations, autoregression in the error term was detected, its form identified, and the appropriate adjustments made accordingly.

18 William Stanley collaborated in the writing of this section.

19 As noted in *Nations in Conflict*, in countries whose military expenditures are expanding largely for domestic reasons, the primary importance of domestic factors in army and navy spending does not preclude the reality of arms competition, which is likely to be exacerbated to the extent that such powers become aware of each other's rising arms spending.

7 GAINS FROM WORLD WAR I: JAPAN AS AN EMERGING POWER

1 As a rough measure of Japan's military capabilities and leverage, at this time, the nation's military expenditures per capita were roughly assessed at $3.24 as compared with $14.00 for Britain and $25.00 for the United States (in 1906 dollars).

8 JAPANESE EXPANSION, CONFLICT AND ESCALATION

1 The US Tariff Act of 1930 had included a 'flexible tariff' clause under which duties were imposed on Japanese 'tuna fish packed in oil, canned clams (other than razor clams), frozen swordfish and wool knit gloves valued at not more than $1.75 per dozen pairs.' The act raised rates but also imposed specific duties which increased in ad valorem terms as the price of Japanese goods in dollar terms fell during the depression. Duty charges were set at 111 per cent on Japanese china and porcelain, 139 percent on toothbrushes with cellulose

handles, 197 percent on thermos bottles, 255 percent on 'stamped' pencils, and so forth. Beginning in 1933, further new US import restrictions were placed on Japanese commodities (Lockwood 1936: 33–4).

2 In the wake of the Bolshevik seizure of power in 1917, the new Soviet government had renounced without compensation the claim to the Chinese Eastern Railway in Manchuria, which had been built with Tsarist Russian capital, together with 'all the mining concessions, forestry, gold mines, and all the other things which had been seized' from China 'by the government of the Tsars, that of [Alexander] Kerensky, and the Brigands, Horvat, Seminoff, Koltchak, the Russian ex-generals, merchants, and capitalists' (Woodhead 1925: 868–972). Soviet spokesmen soon denounced this text, however, and denied that their government had made any such offer (Degras 1951: 151–61; Whiting 1954: 355–64).

3 With allowance for the Japan Production Party, we would be in error to label as fascist the right-leaning and militaristic tendencies in Japan leading up to the invasion of China and the country's entry into World War II. The country did not produce anything comparable to the Italian Fascist Party or the Nazi Party, nor a dictator like Mussolini or Hitler.

4 There were clear indications of sensitivity and vulnerability interdependence as defined by Choucri (1976) and Keohane and Nye (1977).

5 As early as four months prior to the Lukouchiao Incident of July, US Ambassador Joseph E. Davies reported from Moscow that relations between the USSR and the Chiang Kai-shek government had improved 'immeasurably' within a few days. Later, in November, Davies reported a Soviet credit of 100 million Chinese dollars extended to Chiang Kai-shek for the purchase of military supplies and deliveries of Soviet bombers and pursuit planes, accompanied by 40 Soviet instructors, all estimated at a total value generously exceeding the announced credit. More than 200 trucks were said to be providing caravan transport between the Soviet Union and Nationalist China. The Chinese Nationalist ambassador to Moscow was reported by Davies to have asked for more direct military support for the Nationalist government through active participation by the USSR (Davies 1941: 134, 241). Subsequently, the total of Soviet aid to the Chinese Nationalists between 1938 and 1939 was thought to be about $250 million (US) – a sum falling far short of the loans granted by the United States later on, but coming at a time when it was desperately needed. The USSR was also championing the Chinese cause in the League of Nations (League of Nations 1937: 43, 79). All of these activities could be assessed as part of Soviet willingness to support Chiang Kai-shek, however temporarily, in his efforts to expel the Japanese (and other 'imperialists') from Chinese territories.

6 For a detailed study on the Nomonhan Incident, see Coox (1985).

9 TOWARD THE PEARL HARBOR DECISION

1 The imperial decision on 2 July and subsequent operation plans were leaked to Moscow through intelligence agents close to Konoye (Fujimura 1981: 220).

10 MODELING JAPAN'S LATERAL PRESSURE TO WORLD WAR II

1 Individual links, viewed piecemeal, are negative; however, the entire loop is positive, strong, and statistically significant.

2 In other words, certain dampening influences (or negative links) operating from the trade sector to the military allocations sector served to constrain the conflict spiral, but these were not sufficiently robust to prevail over the entire 65 years.

3 These results remain entirely consistent with recent analysis of Japanese economic history, stressing the crucial role of imports and exports (Minami 1986: 253).

4 Parenthetically, there is a seeming anomaly, namely, the negative effect of imports of food per capita on imports from the colonies. It is explained, however, by the fact that food imports per capita were declining between 1927 or thereabouts and 1938 (when they increased slightly until the outbreak of war in 1941, whereas, by contrast, imports from the colonies were growing rapidly – in an uninterrupted upward trend from the turn of the century through Pearl Harbor).

5 Colonial area and government revenue appear to be negatively associated with army spending, but treated individually, they are not statistically significant.

6 A feedback relationship may be operating here which is not fully specified in the model.

11 COMPARING LATERAL PRESSURE PROCESSES: WORLD WAR I AND WORLD WAR II

1 Recall that each arrow represents the direction of the influence between two variables. Some are direct; others are related through each other only because of the intervening links. These intervening links, or steps, referred to as 'indirect,' are often important in generating the total impact between any two variables. In the convention of statistical and econometric analysis, the magnitude of each of the factors contributing to Japan's lateral pressure is indicated by the estimated coefficient. Since comparing the values of the causal factors is something like comparing apples and oranges, it is always a challenge to determine the relative influence of individual factors. This chapter is based on the beta coefficients and path analysis, a slightly different inference framework than in econometrics, although in essence the database and quantitative computations are the same. Beta coefficients are used to determine the *total*, direct as well as indirect, impact of each variable on other variables. Because of interdependence among the various measures for Japan's growth and expansion, the impact of a particular variable (such as population) can be felt by almost all the other variables in the system.

2 The military expenditures of the United States, the USSR, and the United Kingdom were included in the model as indicators of potential enemy threat. Japanese historical documents show that the then top-secret Japan experienced changing perceptions of enemy threat. For example, according to Teikoku Kokubo Hoshin (Imperial Defense Guideline), the second edition (1918) has listed Russia, the USA, and China as the greatest potential enemies, and the fourth edition (1936) registered the USA, the Soviet Union, China, and Great Britain as the greatest potential enemies.

3 We have found that interconnections among the endogenous variables in the model are more influential in the earlier period than in the later one. In particular, interactions between the military and colonial subsystem dynamics are conspicuous in the earlier period – a finding that seems to contradict the earlier observation that statistically significant feedback loops were more conspicuous in the later period. Both explanations are correct. A statistically

significant link is not necessarily influential, and an influential link is not necessarily statistically significant. This means that although there is clearly an impact, the impact is not sufficiently strong to be statistically significant – an important distinction inasmuch as some relations can be influential but latent. Only when they become more powerful do they become statistically significant. By latent we mean that the impacts were there but not strong; when they become stronger, they became more observable (and statistically identifiable).

4 The coefficients indicating the *total* impact of population on raw materials imports assume a value of 1.08 for the 1878–1914 period and 0.84 for the 1915–41 period. And the total impact of population on colonial area assumes a coefficient of 1.02 for the pre-World War I years and 0.43 for the later period.

5 When we consider the total (direct and indirect) effects of national income, we see that there are no significant positive or negative impacts prior to 1915; after that, there are strong and positive influences on the colonial variables and negative impacts on imports of raw materials and, to a lesser extent, on army expenditures.

6 This chapter focuses entirely on beta or standardized coefficients.

12 SIMULATING GROWTH AND EXPANSION: PATHS TO WAR

1 Simulation entails the reproduction or replication of processes designed to represent or approximate an underlying reality. The model of growth and expansion developed in earlier chapters is now used as a vehicle for simulating lateral pressure, as captured by the process of the model developed. The equations are part of an integrated framework (and model) indicating specific interconnections among endogenous variables; however, it is not at all obvious how these variables interact dynamically within the entire system. Methods used here represent an improvement on the basic approach used in *Nations in Conflict*.

2 As an illustration, for the following model

$$Y_t = a_1 + b_{11}A_t + b_{12}Z_{t-1} + u_1$$
$$Z_t = a_2 + b_{21}X_t + b_{22}B_t + u_2$$

where Y and Z are endogenous variables and A, B and X are exogenous variables, and a_1, a_2, b_{11}, and b_{12} are the coefficients (estimated from the previous regressions on the simultaneous system), simulation would proceed as follows. For the first time point (year) Y_t and Z_t are calculated using exogenous values for A_t, B_t, and X_t, and an exogenous starting variable Z_{t-1}. For the second year $(t + 1)$, Y_{t+1} and Z_{t+1} are computed using exogenous values for A_{t+1}, B_{t+1}, and X_{t+1} and simulated endogenous value for Z_t from the previous period.

Historical values for the endogenous variables are then no longer employed. This procedure is repeated for each succeeding year, calculating the endogenous variables from their simulated values for the previous period and the current values of the exogenous variables. At each time point subsequent to the initial t, known values for the exogenous variables must be provided.

3 Three common reasons for failure to simulate are: first, the system may have diverged because (a) parameter coefficients were weak; (b) the theoretical specification of the functional form of the equation was incomplete; and/or (c) the structural form of the equation was erroneous. If the object is short-term

forecasts, multicollinearity need not be a drawback, but if some of the independent variables are multicollinear, the prediction interval obtained will be large. By eliminating some collinear variables, one can reduce the prediction interval for any given value of the independent variables included while altering the actual outcome only minimally. Pragmatic forecasts and simulation are indifferent to the extent of collinearity, whereas sophisticated ones are not. But both will make similar forecasts and the errors will be very similar. Variability in the success of a simulation may be explained by discontinuities in the data series employed – notably when 'soft' (metricized) measures have been used rather than the generally monotonic series of 'hard' variables. Since regression generally captures 'trends' rather than discrete points, a trendless series would be expected to yield a much greater degree of error in the behavior of the entire system and to explore the effects with what would have happened if conditions had been different. These 'conditions' are essentially our hypotheses; for example, how different would have been the historical record if Japan had made different levels of military allocation, or different decisions about expenditures?

4 The TROLL/1 system which we used for simulation calculates values of the jointly dependent variables in the model over a period for which data for the exogenous variables are available, or for any subperiod therein.

5 Basically the solution for a variable for any given period is a function of a series of iterations in which all the equations are solved and iteration values of the endogenous variables produced. Convergence criteria are established by default (or changed by the investigator), and identify the point at which the iteration has reached a solution. A common procedure for checking the performance of the simulation, once convergence is attained, is to examine the summary statistics and compare the simulated values of the endogenous variables with historical or known values.

6 In order to test the validity of the Japan model, the most rigorous simulation technique was applied. The observed data for the exogenous variables were utilized as initial inputs and the values of the endogenous variables obtained from simulation were utilized as the basis for replicating the system as a whole. Unlike techniques which forecast individual equations separately, with explanatory variables exogenously supplied, the simulation approaches employed here would be vulnerable to the accumulation distortion of error terms as the entire system of equations was simulated simultaneously. Because simulated variables (the values obtained from simulation) were used wherever endogenous variables appeared as lagged independent variables, we would expect the simulation error to accumulate as the simulation proceeded. This means that the output data generated could deviate increasingly from historical reality as the simulation unfolded. If, on the other hand, the initial simulation period approximates historical reality well, it is probable that an initial 'fit' would persist if the system were simulated further. In this procedure, the simulated values are based on the endogenous variables that, themselves, are simulated, as opposed to actual. Throughout, the simulation's time frame is affected by the data base for estimation. The choice of time frame for estimates is dictated by data availability.

7 After the Russo-Japanese War, Korea had become a protectorate of Japan in 1905, but it was not formally annexed, and not recorded as such, until 1910.

8 Because of the simultaneities in the system, and its highly interactive nature, we cannot simply expect proportional responses to the 10 percent adjustments posited.

9 A word of caution is required. Because of the highly interactive nature of these relationships, an unresolved programming difficulty necessitated that Japanese navy simulation be undertaken on a single equation basis (the navy) rather than on the basis of the entire system (all seven equations). Note that even in the single equation case the coefficients are derived from the full system of simultaneous equations. There are two bases for confidence in these results, however. First, a comparison of the entire system simulation generating the navy expenditures with the single equation forecasts for Japan's navy expenditures yields the *same* path (and nearly identical values of navy expenditures). Thus, exploring the impacts of the USA for the single equation case is essentially no different than for the entire system case. Second, in *Nations in Conflict* we found that the counterfactual simulations for army and navy expenditures, and for other aspects as well, usually approximated closely the results obtained from the simulation of full multivariate equation systems.

10 The interpretations of these two techniques are somewhat different; altering coefficient values postulates a change in the relationships between variables, whereas changing the values of variables assumes that the inputs differ while the basic relationship between the variables remains constant.

11 When the coefficient for military expenditures ($t - 1$) in the military expenditures equation was increased to near 1, the effect on the level of military expenditures, alliances, and colonial area was explosively positive, whereas violence behavior and the intensity of intersections decreased disproportionately. Decreasing the coefficient for military expenditures ($t - 1$), by contrast, had relatively little impact on the simulated outcomes.

13 LATERAL PRESSURE AFTER WORLD WAR II

1 The first atomic bomb, named Little Boy, dropped on Hiroshima, was made with ^{235}U. The second bomb, named Fat Man, used ^{239}Pu. The two fission-type nuclear weapons were experimented with at intervals of only a few days.

14 ECONOMIC GROWTH AND VULNERABILITY

1 Because the name of the bill might be considered potentially threatening, the Japanese government changed it to the Bill for the Promotion of Designated Industries when it was submitted to the Diet by the government.

2 For a more detailed discussion, see Yasutomo (1983).

3 Indonesia at the time was still in transition from pro-Communist to pro-Western regime, and in the following year a pro-Western government under General Suharto joined the MCEDSEA.

4 For detailed analyses of these issues, see e.g. Destler (1976), among others.

5 The Smithsonian Agreement was the agreement among the so-called G-10 held at the Smithsonian Institution in Washington, DC, on 17–18 December 1971. It had collapsed by early 1973, failing to enter the float system.

6 For more detailed discussion on this issue, see Yoshitsu (1984: ch. 1).

15 POSTWAR JAPAN: NEW MODEL OF LATERAL PRESSURE

1 *The Economist* referred to these facts somewhat irreverently, e.g. that 'Japan has an unenviable reputation as a technological leech,' and noting also that Japan spends four times more per year importing American technology than

the United States is able to 'winkle out' of Japan (*The Economist*, 28 May 1986: 84).

2 The immediate postwar period revealed difficulties in data reliability which required some estimation of missing observations. By contrast, the data availability after 1950 was very high. The variables and their labels are listed in Appendix I.

3 In the interpretation of results, it should be borne in mind that we are now dealing with *changes* in the key variables. This transformation is both a detrending technique, tending to reduce the extent of collinearity, as well as a theoretically based response to the dominance of change in the postwar period.

4 The generalized least squares estimation undertaken for the prewar Japan model was not necessary because the first-order difference transformation substantially eliminated the autocorrelation in the error term.

5 Interestingly, changes in the country's industrial labor force were not significant (indeed, were remarkably unimportant) in determining changes in economic activity. (See Appendix III for the results of estimation for the post-World War II equations.)

6 The impact of merchant marine tonnage is negative. Population, wheat consumption, and capital stock appear to have no statistically significant impacts on nonfuel imports.

7 The influence of the population factor is weak in the imports of energy equation, as it is for nonfuel imports.

8 The significant push on energy comes from GNP, where economic growth has necessitated greater energy imports, revealed by a strong, significant impact of GNP on energy imports.

9 This direct comparison is made by comparing the size of the respective beta coefficients.

10 To explain the variance of *changes* in the dependent variables is much more difficult than to explain absolute values of these levels, since a clear de-trending is imposed on the variables. The model's statistical successes mean that the independent (explanatory) variables were generally the right ones, and in the right combination, to explain the process of growth, resource demand, and economic expansion, and to explain their interconnections.

11 In the analysis of Japan before World War II, the total impact of the variables (direct impact plus indirect impact) on each other was calculated based on beta coefficients. In the post-World War II model, however, the total impact cannot be ascertained because the endogenous variables are too highly interdependent, making such total estimations infeasible.

12 Two positive upwardly spiraling feedback relationships are apparent and also statistically significant (at the 5 percent level of confidence). One feedback linkage relates changes in GNP, total exports, and nonfuel imports; the other feedback loop connects changes in GNP, changes in foreign direct investment, in total exports, and in nonfuel imports. The least significant effects (in terms of beta coefficients) relative to the other variables and relationships in the model are the food (wheat) consumption and population variables.

13 Note that the change in copper consumption is the only exogenous variable with a beta coefficient in excess of 0.50.

14 See Chapter 1 for the theoretical foundation of these profiles.

16 SIMULATING JAPAN'S POST-WORLD WAR II EXPANSION

1 Note, again, that we are still dealing with *changes* in the key variables, not absolute levels.

2 This means that for the 1947–60 period or so we were not able to depict accurately the degree and direction of change in the GNP, because our explanatory variables captured these changes imperfectly for those years and partly because the coefficients for those variables incorporated were estimated lower than their 'true' value.

3 The simulation does capture successfully the sharp swings during the later period, which means that, limitations of methods aside, we are still on the right track; this is an important consideration, given the centrality of energy imports to Japan.

4 Recall that the equation to estimate change in GNP accounted for 66 percent of the variance. The model fails to account for the remainder, however, and the underestimate of the level of GNP simulated reflects this missing element.

5 The equation accounted for 33 percent of the variance, leaving scope for additional explanation.

6 Two technical reasons account for this discrepancy; (a) the equation accounted for only 20 percent of the variance in changes of Japanese foreign investment, thus (b) simulation of changes in Japanese investment abroad diverged from the historical record until the early 1960s, precisely the period in which the two levels (simulated and actual) also diverge.

7 Two factors explain these results technically; (a) the model explained 65 percent of the variance in changes in Japan's exports over time, and (b) the simulation diverged from actual changes before 1960.

8 In other words, the initial level of the simulation for each variable was set at the actual value for the first year in the period – 1946 – and the first differences were 'undone' by adding to the transformed increments the value between the points in such a way as to obtain the absolute level.

17 ADAPTATION TO A NEW INTERNATIONAL ENVIRONMENT

1 A tight financial policy later on shrank the Tokyo stock market by nearly half in 1990. Then the market began to recover at a slow rate.

2 For example, the government sent officials to the United Nations Peacekeeping Offices in Afghanistan and participated in the UN management of Namibia's independence election. In 1989 Tokyo's development assistance exceeded that of the United States. Also, the government finally gained international agreement to increase Japan's contribution to the IMF and the World Bank, attaining the largest share after the United States, and the same as Germany.

18 RETROSPECTION AND THOUGHTS FOR THE FUTURE

1 It should be noted that there are difficulties in defining foreign direct investments to allow for consistent measurement across countries. There are differences also in national treatment of intercompany borrowing and repatriation of dividends.

2 By 1988, beyond the scope of our quantitative analysis, Japan's flow of net equity investments abroad was twice the rate two years earlier (to $17 billion, two-thirds of which went into the United States) (*The Economist*, 23 April

1988: 82). And at the time of writing Japan is 'the world's largest exporter of long-term capital' (Economist Intelligence Unit 1984). In the banking sphere, a sector of the economy not included in our quantitative analysis, it bears noting that the world's ten largest banks (based on size of total assets) are Japanese.

3 For historical trends of military expenditures, see e.g. *The Military Balance*, published by the International Institute for Strategic Studies.

4 The portion of those aged 65 and over is expected to double by 2000 by 9.8 percent. In 1983 life expectancy is already among the highest in the world and continues to rise (Economist Intelligence Unit 1988: 6). By 2020 over one in five Japanese will be 65 and over (*The Economist*, survey, 10 December 1988: 4) with attendant implication for welfare expenditures as a percentage of government allocation and as a share of GNP. There is also the new issue of illegal immigration to buttress the labor force, officially estimated at 20,000 and unofficially at closer to 100,000 and growing. Citing Ministry of Justice records of foreign labor, it is expected that legal in-migration will also be on the rise (*The Economist*, 16 April 1988:42).

5 For example, forecasts by *The Economist* toward the end of the 1980s stressed that Japan's population will be aging much faster than that of the United States (see 21 November 1987). World Bank analysis had already explored the macroeconomic implications of relative 'aging' (Horioka, 1986).

6 The projections were as follows, with all the qualifications that such a method may imply the average of the mean percent increase change over five-year intervals (1970, 1975, 1980, 1985) was used as the base to forecast the value of each variable (for each country) from 1985 to 2010. Sources include the Central Intelligence Agency (1988), the U.S. Arms Control and Disarmament Agency (various years), and the Organization for Economic Cooperation and Development (various years).

7 Projections are always contingent on some theory of foreign exchange rates, and there are a variety of contending theories. The foreign exchange measure most consistent with actual economic performance is a measure based on the concept of purchasing power parity (PPP). Analysts in Japan believe that if the difference in the annual rate of growth between the United States and Japan continues to be 3 percent, the yen will be appreciated by the same percentage each year. By such calculation, the yen would be projected to appreciate by 80 percent by the year 2010. (In terms of purchasing power comparison, if one US dollar is equivalent to 200 yen, then the exchange rate will be 110 yen per dollar in 2010.)

8 Because native American populations invaded by Britain and France were sparsely distributed, insufficiently organized, and relatively easily dispossessed of their territorial bases, Canada (aside from the Quebec issue) and the United States (with allowance for its record in the Philippines, Guam, Hawaii, Puerto Rico, Cuba, *et al.*) have been relatively successful in absorbing their multinational (and multiethnic) components – although not without resistance.

19 EPILOGUE: A CRITICAL ASSESSMENT

1 For an example of this type of critique see Zuk (1985). For a thoughtful and thorough review see Levy (1989).

References*

Akaneya, Tatsuo 1985. *Saikeikoku Taigu wo Motomete* [Longing for Most-Favored Nation Treatment]. In Watanabe 1985, pp. 108–34.

Allen, George C. 1940. *Japanese Industry: Its Recent Development and Present Condition*. New York: Institute of Pacific Relations.

Allen, George C. 1965. *Japan's Economic Expansion*. London: Oxford University Press.

Allen, George C. 1967. *Japan as a Market and Source of Supply*. London: Pergamon Press.

Allen, George C. 1981. *A Short Economic History of Modern Japan*, 4th edn. New York: St Martin's Press.

Almond, Gabriel A. and Powell Jr, G. Bingham 1966. *Comparative Politics: A Developmental Approach*. Boston, Mass.: Little, Brown.

Anchordoguy, Marie 1988. Mastering the market: Japanese government targeting of the computer industry. *International Organization* 42 (3): 509–44.

Angell, Norman 1936. *Raw Materials, Population Pressure and War*. Boston, Mass.: World Peace Foundation.

Apter, David and Sawa, Nagayo 1984. *Against the State: Politics and Social Protest in Japan*. Cambridge, Mass.: Harvard University Press.

Aron, R. 1967. *Peace and War*. New York: Praeger.

Arrow, Kenneth J., Karlin, Samuel and Suppes, Patrick 1960. *Mathematical Methods in the Social Sciences, 1959: Proceedings of the First Stanford Symposium*. Stanford, California: Stanford University Press.

Asahi, Isoshi 1934. *The Secret of Japan's Trade Expansion*. Tokyo: International Association of Japan.

Asakawa, K. 1904. *The Russo-Japanese Conflict: Its Causes and Issues*. Boston, Mass.: Houghton, Mifflin.

Ashley, Richard K. 1980. *The Political Economy of War and Peace: The Sino-Soviet-American Triangle and the Modern Security Problematique*. New York: Nichols.

Aydelotte, William O. 1937. *Bismarck and British Colonial Policy*. Philadelphia, Pa: University of Pennsylvania Press.

Axelrod, Robert M. 1972 *Framework for a General Theory of Cognition and Choice*. Berkeley, Calif.: Institute of International Studies.

Axelrod, Robert M. 1978. *Framework for a General Theory of Cognition and Choice*. Berkeley, Calif.: University of California Press.

* These references do not include data sources. See Appendix I (p. 321–3) for data-related sources.

Bank of Japan 1966. *One Hundred Year Statistics of the Japanese Economy*. Tokyo: Statistics Department.

Barraclough, Geoffrey (ed.) 1978. *The Times Atlas of World History*. Maplewood, NJ: Hammond.

Beckman, George 1962. *The Modernization of China and Japan*. New York: Harper & Row.

Beer, Francis A. 1981. *Peace against War: The Ecology of International Violence*. San Francisco: W. H. Freeman.

Bergsten, C. Fred 1975. *The Dilemmas of the Dollar*. New York: New York University Press.

Berton, Peter A. 1980. Introduction: northern defense. In Morley 1980, pp. 3–12.

Boltho, Andrea 1975. *Japan: An Economic Survey 1953–1973*. Oxford: Oxford University Press.

Borg, Dorothy and Okamoto, Shumpei 1940. *Japan since 1931, its Social and Political Development*. New York: Institute of Pacific Relations.

Borg, Dorthy and Okamoto Shumpei, (eds) 1973. *Pearl Harbor as History: Japanese American Relations, 1931–1941*. New York: Columbia University Press.

Borton, Hugh 1955. *Japan's Modern Century*. New York: Ronald Press.

Boulding, Kenneth D. and Gleason, Alan H. 1965. War as an investment: the strange case of Japan. *Peace Research Society (International)*. III: 1–17.

Brecher, Michael with Geist, Benjamin 1960. *Decisions in Crisis: Israel, 1967 and 1973*. Berkeley, Calif.: University of California Press.

British State Papers 1902. *Accounts and Papers,* Dispatch to His Majesty's Minister at Tokyo, 3 January 1902. London.

Brown, Seyom 1974. *New Forces in World Politics*. Washington, DC: Brookings Institution.

Bueno de Mesquita, Bruce 1981. *The War Trap*. New Haven, Conn.: Yale University Press.

Bullock, Alan 1959. *Hitler: A Study in Tyranny*. London: Odhams.

Butow, Robert J. 1961. *Tojo and the Coming of the War*. Princeton, NJ: Princeton University Press.

Buzbee, B. L., Ewald, R. H., and Worlton, W. J. 1982. Japanese supercomputer technology. *Science* 218: 1189–93.

Byas, Hugh 1942. *Government by Assassination*. New York: Knopf.

Campbell, John C. 1977. *Contemporary Japanese Budget Politics*. Berkeley, Calif.: University of California Press.

Carneiro, Robert L. 1970. A theory of the origin of the state. *Science* 169: 733–8.

Central Intelligence Agency (1988). *Handbook of Economic Statistics*. Washington, DC: US Government Printing Office.

Chen, Edward I-te 1984. The attempt to intergrate the empire. In Myers and Peattie 1984, pp. 240–74.

Chenery, Hollis B., Shishido, Shuntaro, and Watanabe, Tsunehiko, 1977. The pattern of Japanese economic growth, 1914–1954. In Kosobud and Minami 1977, pp. 276–337.

Ch'ien Tuan-sheng (ed.) 1950. *The Environment and Politics of China*. Cambridge, Mass.: International Secretariat of the Institute of Pacific Relations.

Choucri, Nazli 1974. *Population Dynamics and International Violence: Propositions, Insights, and Evidence*. Lexington, Mass.: Lexington Books.

Choucri, Nazli (ed.) 1984. *Multidisciplinary Perspectives on Population and Conflict*. Syracuse, NY: Syracuse University Press.

Choucri, Nazli and Bousfield, M. 1978. Alternative futures: an exercise in forecasting. In N. Choucri and T. W. Robinson (eds), *Forecasting in International Relations: Theory, Methods, Problems, Prospects*, pp. 308–26. San Francisco: W. H. Freeman.

Choucri, Nazli with Ferraro, Vincent 1976. *The International Politics of Energy Interdependence*. Lexington, Mass.: D C. Heath.

Choucri, Nazli with the collaboration of North Robert C., 1972. In search of peace systems: Scandinavia and the Netherlands, 1870–1970. In B. Russett (ed.), *Peace, War, and Numbers*. San Francisco: Sage, pp. 239–74.

Choucri, Nazli and North, Robert C. 1972. Dynamics of international conflict: some policy implications of population, resources, and technology. In Tanter and Ullman 1972, pp. 80–122.

Choucri, Nazli and North, Robert C. 1975. *Nations in Conflict: National Growth and International Violence*. San Francisco: W. H. Freeman.

Choucri, Nazli and North, Robert C. 1989. Lateral Pressure in international relations: concept and theory. In Midlarsky 1989, pp. 289–326.

Choucri, Nazli with Ross David Scott, 1981. *International Energy Futures: Petroleum Prices, Power, and Payments*, Cambridge, Mass.: MIT Press.

Chugai Shogyo Shimpo 1936. *Industrial Expansion of Japan*. Tokyo.

Claude, Inis L. 1962. *Power and International Relations*. New York: Random House.

Cohen, Jerome B. 1949a. *The Japanese War Economy: 1937–1945*. Minneapolis, Minn.: University of Minnesota Press.

Cohen, Jerome B. 1949b. *Japan's Economy in War and Reconstruction*. Minneapolis, Minn.: University of Minnesota Press.

Conroy, F. Hilary 1960. *The Japanese Seizure of Korea, 1968–1910: A Study of Realism and Idealism in International Relations*. Philadelphia, Pa: University of Pennsylvania Press.

Coox, Alvin D. 1985. Introduction: the Japanese–Soviet confrontation, 1935–1939. In James Morley 1976, pp. 115–27.

Coox, Alvin D. 1985 *Nomonhan: Japan Against Russia, 1939*. Stanford, Calif.: Stanford University Press. 2 volumes.

Craig, Albert M. 1968. Fukuzawa Yukichi: the philosophical foundation of Meiji nationalism. In Ward 1968, pp. 99–148.

Craig, Gordon A. and Gilbert, Felix 1953. *The Diplomats, 1919–1930*. Princeton, NJ: Princeton University Press.

Craig, William 1967. *The Fall of Japan*. New York: Dial Press.

Crowley, James B. 1966. *Japan's Quest for Autonomy: National Security and Foreign Policy, 1930–1938*. Princeton, NJ: Princeton University Press.

Crowley, James R. 1971. Intellectuals as visionaries of the new Asian order. In Morley 1971, pp. 319–73.

Crowley, James R. 1974. Japan's military foreign policies. In Morley 1974, pp. 3–117.

Cyert, Richard M. and March, James G. 1963 *A Behavioral Theory of the Firm*. Englewood Cliffs, NJ: Prentice-Hall.

Dallin, David J. 1950. *The Rise of Russia in Asia*. London: World Affairs Book Club.

Davies, Joseph E. 1941. *Mission to Moscow*. New York: Simon & Schuster.

Degras, Jane (ed.) 1951. *Soviet Documents on Foreign Policy*. London: Royal Institute of International Affairs.

Dell, Burnham N. and Luthringer, George F. 1938. *Population, Resources and Trade*. Boston, Mass.: Little, Brown.

Dempster, Prue 1969. *Japan Advances*. London: Methuen.

Denison, Edward F. and Chung, William K. 1976. *How Japan's Economy Grew So Fast: The Sources of Postwar Expansion*. Washington, DC: Brookings Institution.

Destler, I. M. 1976. *Managing An Alliance*. Washington, DC: Brookings Institution.

Destler, I. M. 1982. *Coping with US–Japanese Economics Conflicts*. Lexington, Mass.: Lexington Books.

Deyo, Frederic C. (ed.) 1987. *The Political Economy of East Asian Industrialism*. Ithaca, NY: Cornell University Press.

Dore, Ronald 1986. *Flexible Rigidities: Industrial Policy and Structural Adjustment in the Japanese Economy 1970–80*. London: Athlone Press.

Duus, Peter 1971. Oyama Ikua and the search for democracy. In Morley 1971, pp. 423–58.

Duus, Peter 1984. Economic dimensions of Meiji imperialism: the case of Korea, 1895–1910. In Myers and Peattie 1984, pp. 128–63.

Duus, Peter (ed.) 1988. *The Cambridge History of Japan*. Vol. 6: *The Twentieth Century*. Cambridge: Cambridge University Press.

Duus, Peter, Myers, Ramon H., and Peattie, Mark R. (eds) 1989. *The Japanese Informal Empire in China, 1895–1937*. Princeton, NJ: Princeton University Press.

Easton, David 1965. *A Systems Analysis of Political Life*. New York: Wiley.

Economic Planning Agency 1981. *Economic Survey of Japan, 1980–81*. Tokyo.

Executive Committee of the Communist International 1935. *International Press Correspondence*. 2 December, 1935. London, pp. 971–2.

Economist Intelligence Unit 1988. *Japan: Country Profile 1987/88*. London.

Economist, The. London (various issues).

Eudin, Xenia J. and North, Robert C. 1957. *Soviet Russia and the East, 1920–27*. Stanford, Calif.: Stanford University Press.

Farley, Miriam S. 1940. *Problem of Japanese Trade Expansion in the Post-War Situation*. London: Allen & Unwin.

Fei, John C. H. and Ranis, Gustav 1964. *Development of the Labor Surplus Economy: Theory and Policy*. Homewood, Ill.: Irwin.

Feis, Herbert 1950. *Road to Pearl Harbor: The Coming of the War between the United States and Japan*. Princeton, NJ: Princeton University Press.

Fitzgerald, Charles P. 1966. *A Concise History of East Asia*. New York: Praeger.

Frank, Isaiah and Hirono, Ryokichi 1974. *How the United States and Japan See Each Other's Economy*. New York: Committee for Economic Development.

Friedman, David 1988. *The Misunderstood Miracle: Industrial Development and Political Change in Japan*. Ithaca, NY: Cornell University Press.

Frost, Ellen L. 1987. *For Richer, for Poorer: The New US–Japan Relationship*. New York: Council on Foreign Relations.

Fujimura, Michio 1981. *Sekai Gendaishi 1: Nihon Gendaishi* [Contemporary History of the World. Vol. 1: Contemporary History of Japan]. Tokyo: Yamakawa Shuppansha.

Fujino, Shozaburo 1966. Business cycles in Japan, 1868–1962. *Hitotsubashi Journal of Economics* 74: 56–78.

Fukui, Haruhiro 1988. Postwar politics, 1945–1973. In Duus 1988, pp. 154–213.

Gann, Lewis H. 1984. Western and Japanese colonialism. In Myers and Peattie 1984, pp. 497–525.

George, A.L. and Smoke, R. 1974. *Deterrence in American Foreign Policy: Theory and Practice*. New York: Columbia University Press.

George, A. L., Hall, D. K. and Simons, W. E. 1971. *The Limits of Coercive Diplomacy: Laos, Cuba, Vietnam*. Boston, Mass.: Little Brown.

Gershenkron, Alexander 1962. *Economic Backwardness in Historical Perspective*. Cambridge, Mass.: Harvard University Press.

Gilpin, Robert 1975. *US Power and the Multinational Corporation*. New York: Basic Books.

Gilpin, Robert 1981. *War and Change in World Politics*. New York: Cambridge University Press.

Gilpin, Robert 1987. *The Political Economy of International Relations.* Princeton, NJ: Princeton University Press.

Gooch, G. P. and Temperley, Harold, (eds) 1926–38. *British Documents on the Origins of the War, 1898–1914,* 11 vols. London: His Majesty's Stationery Office.

Great Britain, Foreign Office 1936. *Accounts and Papers* XXVII, treaty series no. 2. London.

Great Britain, Foreign Office 1937. *Accounts and Papers* XXXI, treaty series nos 41, 50, 61. London.

Haas, Ernst B. 1971. The balance of power: prescription, concept or propaganda? In Quester 1971, pp. 250–83.

Hadley, Eleanor M. 1970. *Antitrust in Japan.* Princeton, NJ: Princeton University Press.

Hadley, Eleanor M. 1982. Industrial policy for competitiveness. *Journal of Japanese Trade and Industry* 5: 45–50.

Hanley, Susan B. 1983. A high standard of living in nineteenth-century Japan: fact or fantasy? *Journal of Economic History* XLIII (1): 183–92.

Hanley, Susan B. and Yamamura, Kozo 1977. *Economic and Demographic Change in Preindustrial Japan, 1600–1868.* Princeton, NJ: Princeton University Press.

Hata, Ikuhiko 1976. The Japanese–Soviet confrontation, 1935–1939. In Morley 1976, pp. 129–78.

Hata, Ikuhiko 1983a. The army's move into northern Indochina. In Morley 1980, pp. 155–208.

Hata, Ikuhiko 1983b. The Marlo Polo Bridge Incident, 1937. In Morely 1983, pp. 243–307.

Hayashi, Kentaro 1971. Japan and Germany in the interwar period. In Morley 1971, pp. 461–88.

Heckscher, Eli F. 1935. *Mercantilism,* trans. Mendel Shapiro. London: Allen & Unwin.

Hellmann, Donald C. 1972. *Japan and East Asia.* New York: Praeger.

Hermann, Charles F. 1969. *Crises in Foreign Policy: A Simulation Analysis.* Indianapolis, Ind.: Bobbs-Merrill.

Hermann, Charles F. (ed.) 1972. *International Crises: Insights from Behavioral Research.* New York: Free Press.

Hershey, Amos S. and Hershey, Susanne W. 1919. *Modern Japan: Social–Industrial–Political.* Indianapolis, Ind.: Bobbs-Merrill.

Hirschman, Albert O. 1945. *National Power and the Structure of Foreign Trade.* Berkeley, Calif.: University of California Press.

Ho, Samuel Pao-san 1984. Colonialism and development: Korea, Taiwan and Kwangtung. In Myers and Peattie 1984, pp. 347–86.

Hobson, J. A. 1902. *Imperialism: A Study.* London: Allen & Unwin.

Holsti, Ole R. 1972. *Crisis, Escalation, War.* Montreal: The McGill-Queens University Press.

Horioka, Charles Xuji 1986. Why is Japan's private savings rate so high? *Finance & Developement* (December), pp. 22–3.

Hosoya, Chihiro 1971. Retrogression in Japan's foreign policy decision-making process. In Morley 1971, pp. 81–105.

Hosoya, Chihiro 1974. Japan's policies toward Russia. In Morley 1974, pp. 340–406.

Hosoya, Chihiro 1976. The Tripartite Pact. In Morley 1976, pp. 191–257.

Hosoya, Chihiro 1980. The Japanese–Soviet neutrality pact. In Morley, 1980, pp. 13–114.

Huh, Kyong-Mo 1966. *Japan's Trade in Asia.* New York: Praeger.

Hunsberger, Warren S. 1964. *Japan and the United States in World Trade.* New York: Harper & Row.

Hymer, Stephen H. 1976. *The International Operations of National Firms: A Study of Direct Foreign Investment*. Cambridge, Mass.: MIT Press.

Ike, Nobutaka 1967. *Japan's Decision for War: Records of the 1941 Policy Conferences*. Stanford, Calif.: Stanford University Press.

Iklé, Fred. C. 1964. *How Nations Negotiate*. New York: Harper & Row.

Iklé, Frank W. 1974. Japan's policies toward Germany. In Morley 1974, pp. 265–339.

Inada, Juichi 1985. Hatentojo-koku to Nihon [Developing countries and Japan]. In Watanabe 1985, pp. 285–314.

Inoguchi, Takashi and Okomoto, Daniel I. (eds) 1988. *The Political Economy of Japan*. Vol 2: *The Changing International Context*. Stanford, Calif.: Stanford University Press.

Institute of Pacific Relations 1950. *The Government and Politics of China*, ed. Ch'ien Tuan-sheng. Cambridge, Mass.

International Institute for Strategic Studies (various years). *The Military Balance*. London.

Iriye, Akira 1971. The failure of military expansionism. In Morley 1971, pp. 107–138.

Iriye, Akira 1974. Japan's policies toward the United States. In Morley 1974, pp. 407–59.

Iriye, Akira 1984. Introduction: the extension of hostilities, 1931–2. In Morley 1984, pp. 233–40.

Ishida, Takeshi 1968. The development of interest groups and the pattern of political modernization in Japan. In Ward 1968, pp. 293–336.

Itami, Hiroyuki 1988. *Jinponshugi Kigyo* [Humanism Enterprise]. Tokyo: Chikuma Shoten.

Itoh, Takashi 1976. *Nihon no Rekishi 30: 15-nen Senso* [History of Japan. Vol. 30: The Fifteen-Years War]. Tokyo: Shogakukan.

Itoh, Motoshige and Kiyono, Kazuharu 1986. Japanese foreign direct investment. In Michele Schmiegelow (ed.), *Japan's Response to Crisis and Challenge in the World Economy*, pp. 63–84. London: M. E. Sharpe.

Jansen, Marius B. (ed.) 1968a. *Changing Japanese Attitudes toward Modernization*. Princeton, NJ: Princeton University Press.

Jansen, Marius 1968b. Modernization and foreign policy in Meiji Japan. In Ward 1968, pp. 149–88.

Jansen, Marius 1984a Japanese: late Meiji perspectives. In Myers and Peattie 1984, pp. 61–79.

Jansen, Marius 1984b. Introduction: the Manchurian Incident, 1931. In Morley 1984, pp. 119–37.

Japan Institute of International Affairs various years. *White Papers of Japan*. Tokyo.

Jervis, Robert 1971. Hypthesis on misperception. In George M. Questor (ed.) *Power, Action, and Interaction*, pp. 104–32. Boston: Little, Brown.

Johnson, Chalmers 1978. *The Japanese Public Companies*. Washington, DC: American Enterprise Institute.

Johnson, Chalmers 1982. *MITI and the Japanese Miracle: The Growth of Industrial Policy, 1925–1975*. Stanford, Calif.: Stanford University Press.

Jones, Samuel Shephard and Myers, Denys (eds) 1941. *Documents in American Foreign Relations*. Boston, Mass.: World Peace Foundation.

Jorgenson, Dale W. 1961. The development of a dual economy. *Economic Journal* (June) 71: 309–34.

Kaigun Daijin Kanbo (Navy Ministerial Secretariat) (ed.) 1921, 1934. *Kaigun Gunbi Enkaku* [A History of Naval Armament], reprint 1970. Tokyo: Gannan Do.

Kaplan, Eugene J. 1972. *Japan: The Government–Business Relationship*. Washington, DC: US Department of Commerce.

Karol, K. S. 1967. *China: The Other Communism*. New York: Hill & Wang.

Kase, Toshikazu 1950. *Journey to the Missouri*. New Haven, Conn.: Yale University Press.

Katzenstein, Peter J. 1988. Japan, Switzerland of the Far East? In Inoguchi and Okomoto 1988, pp. 275–304.

Kelley, Allen C. and Williamson, Jeffrey G. 1971. Writing history backwards: Meiji Japan revisited. *Journal of Economic History* (December) 31 (4): 729–76.

Kelley, Allen C. and Williamson, Jeffrey G. 1974. *Lessons from Japanese Development: An Analytical Economic History*. Chicago: University of Chicago Press.

Kelley, Allen C., Williamson, Jeffrey G., Cheetham, Russel J. 1972. *Dualistic Economic Development: Theory and History*. Chicago: University of Chicago Press.

Kennedy, Paul N. 1987. *The Rise and Fall of the Great Powers: Economic Change and Military Conflict from 1500 to 2000*. New York: Random House.

Keohane, Robert O. (ed.) 1986. *Neorealism and its Critics*. New York: Columbia University Press.

Keohane, Robert O. and Nye, Joseph S. 1977. *Power and Interdependence: World Politics in Transition*. Boston, Mass.: Little, Brown.

Keynes, John Maynard 1936. *General Theory of Employment, Interest and Money*. New York: Harcourt Brace.

Kindleberger, Charles P. 1969. *American Business Abroad: Six Lectures on Direct Investment*. New Haven, Conn.: Yale University Press.

Kito, Hiroshi 1983. *Nihon 2000-nen no Jinko-shi* [Japan's Demographic History over 2000 Years]. Tokyo: PHP Kenkusho.

Koh, T. T. B. 1974. An overview and commentary on *Japan as an Economic Power and its Implications for Southeast Asia*. In Sandhu and Tang 1974, pp. 106–14.

Kojima, Koyoshi 1973a. A macroeconomic approach to foreign direct investment. *Hitotshubashi Journal of Economics* 14 (1): 1–21.

Kojima, Koyoshi 1973b. Reorganization of North–South trade: Japan's foreign economic policy for the 1970s. *Hitotshubashi Journal of Economics* (February).

Kojima, Koyoshi 1977a. Transfer of technology to developing countries: Japanese type versus American type. *Hitotshubashi Journal of Economics* 17 (2): 1–14.

Kojima, Koyoshi 1977b. *Japan and a New World Economic Order*. Boulder, Colo. Westview Press.

Kojima, Koyoshi 1978. *Direct Foreign Investment: A Japanese Model of Multinational Business Operations*. New York: Praeger.

Kojima, Koyoshi 1985. Japanese and American direct investment in Asia: a comparative analysis. *Hitotshubashi Journal of Economics* 26 (1): 1–35.

Komiya, Ryutaro, Okuno, Masahiro and Suzumura, Kotaro. (eds) 1984. *Nihon no Sangyo Seisaku* [Japan's Industrial Policy]. Tokyo: Tokyo Daigaku Shuppankai.

Kosai, Yutaka 1988. The postwar Japanese economy, 1945–1973. In Duus 1988. pp. 494–537.

Kosobud, Richard and Minami, Ryoshin (eds) 1977. *Econometric Studies of Japan*. Urbana, Ill.: University of Illinois Press.

Krasner, Stephen S. 1978. *Defending the National Interest: Raw Materials Investments and US Foreign Policy*. Princeton, NJ: Princeton University Press.

Krasner, Stephen S. 1986. Trade conflicts and the common defense: the United States and Japan. *Political Science Quarterly* 101 (5): 787–806.

Kravis, I. B., Heston, A., and Summers, R. 1978. *International Comparisons of Real Product and Purchasing Power*. Baltimore, Md: Johns Hopkins University Press.

Kume, Ikuo 1988. Changing relations among the government, labor, and business in Japan after the oil crisis. *International Organization* 42 (4): 659–88.

Kuznets, Simon 1966. *Modern Economic Growth: Rate, Structure and Spread*. New Haven, Conn.: Yale University Press.

Lambelet, J.-C., Luterbacher, U., and Allan, P. 1979. Dynamics of arms races: mutual stimulation vs self-stimulation. *Journal of Peace Science* 4: 49–66.

Langer, William L. 1950. *The Diplomacy of Imperialism, 1890–1902*. New York: Knopf.

Langer, William L. 1956. *European Alliances and Alignments: 1871–1890*. New York: Knopf.

Langer, William L. 1969. The origin of the Russo-Japanese War. In W. L. Langer (ed.), *Exploration in Crisis*, Cambridge, Mass.: Harvard University/Belknap Press.

League of Nations 1937. *League of Nations Official Journal*, special supplements pp. 43, 79. Geneva.

Lederer, Ivo J., (ed.) 1962. *Russian Foreign Policy: Essays in Historical Perspective*. New Haven, Conn.: Yale University Press.

Lederman, Leonard L. 1987. Science and technology policies and priorities: a comparative analysis. *Science* 237: 1125–1133.

Lenin, V. I. 1939. *Imperialism, the Highest Stage of Capitalism*. New York: International Publishers.

Lensen, George A. 1959. *The Russian Push toward Japan: Russo-Japanese Relations 1097–1875*. Princeton, NJ: Princeton University Press.

Lessard, Donald and Antonelli Cristiano (eds) 1990. *Managing Globalization of Business: Proceedings of the 1988 Sloan School – STOA Conference*. Naples, Italy: Editoriale Scientifica s.r.l.

Levy, Jack S. 1989. The cause of war: a review of theory and evidence. In Phillip E. Tetlock, Joe L. Husbands, Robert Jervis, Paul C. Stein and Charles Tilley (eds), *Behavior, Society and Nuclear War*, Vol. I. Oxford: Oxford University Press, pp. 202–333.

Lewis, W. Arthur 1954. Economic development with unlimited supplies of labour. *Manchester School of Economic Development and Social Studies* (May) 22: 139–91.

Lobanov-Rostovsky, Nikita D. 1933. *Russia and Asia*. New York: Macmillan.

Lobanov-Rostovsky, Nikita D. 1935. *Grinding Mill: Reminiscences of War and Revolution in Russia, 1913–1920*. Toronto: Macmillan.

Lockwood, William W. 1936. *Trade and Trade Rivalry between the United States and Japan*. New York: Institute of Pacific Relations.

Lockwood, William W. 1954. *The Economic Development of Japan: Growth and Structural Change, 1868–1938*. Princeton, NJ: Princeton University Press.

Lockwood, William W. 1968. *The Economic Development of Japan: Growth and Structural Change*, expanded edn. Princeton, NJ: Princeton University Press.

Louis, William R. 1967. *Great Britain and Germany's Lost Colonies, 1914–19*. New York: Oxford University Press.

Luterbacher, U. 1975. Arms race models: where do we stand? *European Journal of Political Research* 3: 199–217.

MacMurray, John V. 1921. *Treaties and Agreements with and concerning China. 1894–1919*, Vols I and II. Oxford: Oxford University Press.

Maddison, Angus 1964. *Economic Growth in the West*. New York: Twentieth Century Fund.

Maddison, Angus 1969. *Economic Growth in Japan and the USSR*. London: Allen & Unwin.

Maddison, Angus 1977. The twentieth century–2. In Carlo M. Cippola (ed.),

The Fontana Economic History of Europe, Vol. 5, pp. 442–508. New York: Harvest Press.

Maddison, Angus 1982. *Phases of Capitalist Development*. Oxford: Oxford University Press.

Mahan, Alfred T. 1900. *The Problem of Asia and its Effect upon International Policies*. Boston, Mass.: Little, Brown.

Malozemoff, Andrew 1958. *Russian Far Eastern Policy 1881–1904*. Los Angeles, Calif.: University of California Press.

Masamura, Kimihiro 1988. *Zusetsu Sengoshi* [An Illustrated History of Post-War Japan]. Tokyo: Chikuma Shobo.

Maslow, A. 1970. *Motivation and Personality*, revised edn. New York: Harper & Row.

Matsushita, Yoshio 1956. *Meiji Gunsei Shiron* [A History of the Military System in the Meiji Era] 2 vols. Tokyo: Yuhikaku.

McClelland, Charles A. 1961. The acute international crisis. *World Politics* (October) 14 (1): 182–204.

McNelly, Theodore 1986. The renunciation of war in the Japanese constitution. *Armed Forces and Society* 13 (1): 81–106.

Mendel, Douglas 1961. *The Japanese People and Foreign Policy*. Berkeley, Calif.: University of California Press.

Mendel, Douglas 1968. Japanese policy and views toward Formosa. *Journal of Asian Studies* 28 (3):513–84.

Meyer, Stephen M. 1984. *The Dynamics of Nuclear Proliferation*. Chicago: University of Chicago Press.

Midlarsky, Manus I. 1969. Equilibria in the nineteenth-century balance-of-power system. *American Journal of Political Science* 25: 270–96.

Midlarsky, Manus I. 1984. Preventing systemic war. *Journal of Conflict Resolution* 26: 563–84.

Midlarsky, Manus I. 1988. *The Onset of World War*. Boston, Mass.: Unwin Hyman.

Midlarsky, Manus I. 1989. *Handbook of War Studies*. Boston, Mass.: Unwin Hyman.

Minami, Ryoshin 1986. *The Economic Development of Japan: A Quantitative Study*. New York: St Martin's Press.

Mitchell, B. R. 1980. *European Historical Statistics 1750–1975*. New York: Macmillan.

Modelski, George 1972. *Principles of World Politics*. New York: Free Press.

Morgenthau, Hans J. 1967. *Politics among Nations: The Struggle for Power and Peace*, 4th edn. New York: Knopf.

Morishima, Michio 1982. *Why Japan Has 'Succeeded': Western Technology and the Japanese Ethos*. Cambridge University Press.

Morley, James W. 1957. *The Japanese Thrust into Siberia*. New York: Columbia University Press.

Morley, James W. (ed.) 1971. *Dilemmas of Growth in Prewar Japan*. Princeton, NJ: Princeton University Press.

Morley James W. (ed.) 1974. *Japan's Foreign Policy 1868–1941: A Research Guide*. New York: Columbia University Press.

Morley, James W. (ed.) 1976. *Deterrent Diplomacy: Japan, Germany and the USSR, 1935–1940*. New York: Columbia University Press.

Morley, James W. (ed.) 1980. *The Fateful Choice: Japan's Advance into Southeast Asia 1939–1941*. New York: Columbia University Press.

Morley, James W. (ed.) 1983. *The China Quagmire: Japan's Expansion on the Asian Continent, 1933–1941*. New York: Columbia University Press.

Morley, James W. (ed.) 1984. *Japan Erupts: The London Naval Conference and the Manchurian Incident, 1928–1932*. New York: Columbia University Press.

Morse, Hosea B. 1910. *The International Relations of the Chinese Empire*. Vol. I. London: Longmans, Green.

Moulton, Harold G. 1931. *Japan, an Economic and Financial Appraisal*. Washington, DC: Brookings Institution.

Murakami, Yasusuke 1987. The Japanese model of political economy. In Yamamura and Yasuba 1987, pp. 33–90.

Muroyama, Yoshimasa 1984. *Kindai Nihon no Gunji to Zaisei* [Military and Fiscal Policy of Modern Japan] Tokyo: Tokyo Daigaku Shuppankai.

Myers, Ramon H. 1984. Post-World War II Japanese historiography of Japan's formal colonial empire. In Myers and Peattie 1984, pp. 455–477.

Myers, Ramon H. and Peattie, Mark R. (eds) 1984. *The Japanese Colonial Empire, 1895–1945*. Princeton, NJ: Princeton University Press.

Myers, Ramon H. and Saburo, Yamada 1984. Agricultural development in the empire. In Myers and Peattie 1984, pp. 420–52.

Nagaoka, Shinjiro 1980. Economic demands on the Dutch East Indies; and the drive into southern Indochina and Thailand. In Morley 1980, pp. 125–53, 209–40.

Nakamura, Takafusa 1983. *Economic Growth in Prewar Japan*. New Haven, Conn.: Yale University Press.

Nakamura, Takafusa 1985. *Economic Development of Modern Japan*. Tokyo: Ministry of Foreign Affairs.

Nakamura, Takafusa 1986. *Showa Keizaishi* [Economic History of Showa Japan]. Tokyo: Iwanami Shoten.

Nakamura, Takafusa 1989. *Makuro keizai to sengo keiei* [Macroeconomy and post-war economic policy]. In Nishikawa and Yamamoto 1989 pp. 1–36.

Nish, Ian H. 1974. Japan's policies toward Britain. In Morley 1974, pp. 184–235.

Nishikawa, Shunsaku, and Abe, Takeshi (1989a). *Nihon Keizaishi 4: Sangyoka no Jidai, Jo* Economic History of Japan. Vol. 4: The Age of Industrialization, Part I. Tokyo: Iwanami Shoten.

Nishikawa, Shunsaku, and Yamamoto, Yuzo 1989b. *Nihon Keizaishi 4: Sangyoka no Jidai, Ge* Economic History of Japan. Vol. 5: The Age of Industrialization Part II Tokyo: Iwanami Shoten.

Nomikos, Eugenia V. and North, Robert C. 1976. *International Crisis: The Outbreak of World War I*. Montreal: McGill-Queens University Press.

Nomura, Minoru 1983. *Taiheiyo Senso to Nihon Gunbu* [The Pacific War and the Japanese Military]. Tokyo: Yamakawa Shuppansha.

Norman, E. Herbert 1940. *Japan's Emergence as a Modern State*. New York: JPR.

North, Douglass C. 1981. *Structure and Change in Economic History*. New York: Norton.

North, Robert C. 1990. *War, Peace, Survival: Global Politics and Conceptual Synthesis*. Boulder, Colo.: Westview Press.

North, Robert C. and Choucri Nazli, 1983. Economic and political factors in international conflict and integration. *International Studies Quarterly* 27: 443–61.

Ohata, Tokushiro 1976. The Anti-Comintern Pact, 1935–1939. In Morley 1976, pp. 9–111.

Ohkawa, Kazushi 1979. Aggregate growth and product allocation. In K. Ohkawa and M. Shinohara (eds), *Patterns of Japanese Economic Development: A Quantitative Appraisal* New Haven, Conn.: Yale University Press.

Ohkawa, Kazushi and Yujiro, Hayami (eds) 1978. *Papers and Proceedings of the Conference on Japan's Development Experience and the Contemporary Developing Countries*. Tokyo: International Development Center of Japan.

Ohkawa, Kazushi and Rosovsky, Henry 1960. The role of agriculture in modern Japanese economic development. *Economic Development and Cultural Change* (October) 9 (1) pt II: 43–68.

Ohkawa, Kazushi and Rosovsky, Henry 1968. Postwar Japanese economic growth in historical perspective: a second look. In Lawrence R. Klein and Kazushi Ohkawa (eds), *Economic Growth: The Japanese Experience*. Homewood, Ill.: R. D. Irwin.

Ohkawa, Kazushi and Rosovsky, Henry, 1973. *Japanese Economic Growth: Trend Acceleration in the Twentieth Century*. Stanford, Calif.: Stanford University Press.

Okimoto, Daniel I. 1984. *Competitive Edge*. Stanford, Calif.: Stanford University Press.

Okimoto, Daniel I. 1986. Regime characteristics of Japanese industrial policy. In Patrick 1986, pp. 35–96.

Okimoto, Daniel I. and Saxonhouse, Gary R. 1987. Technology and the future of the economy. In Yamamura and Yasuba 1987, pp. 385–419.

Okimoto, Daniel I., Sugano, Takuo and Weinstein, Franklin B. (eds) 1984. *Competitive Edge: The Semiconductor Industry in the US and Japan*. Stanford, Calif.: Stanford University Press.

Okita, Saburo 1975. *Japan's High Dependence on Natural Resource Imports and its Implications*. Canberra: Australia National University.

Olsen, Edward A. 1978. *Japan: Economic Growth, Resource Scarcity and Environmental Constraints*. Boulder, Colo.: Westview Press.

Ono, Giichi 1922. *War and Armament Expenditures of Japan*. New York: Oxford University Press.

Organization for Economic Cooperation and Development (various years). *Economic Outlook: Historical Statistics*. Paris.

Organski, A. F. K. and Kugler, Jacek 1980. *The War Ledger*. Chicago: University of Chicago Press.

Ozawa, Terutomo 1975. The emergence of Japan's multinationalism: patterns and competitiveness. *Asian Survey* 15 (12): 1036–53.

Ozawa, Terutomo 1979. *Multinationalism, Japanese Style: The Political Economy of Outward Dependency*. Princeton, NJ: Princeton University Press.

Packard, George 1966. *Protests in Tokyo: The Security Treaty Crisis of 1860*. Princeton, NJ: Princeton University Press.

Panglaykim, J. 1974. Business relations between Indonesia and Japan. In Sandhu and Tang 1974, pp. 19–49.

Passin, Herbert, (ed.) 1975. *The United States and Japan*. Washington, DC: Columbia Books.

Patrick, Hugh 1971. The economic muddle in the 1920s. In Morley 1971, pp. 211–66.

Patrick, Hugh (ed.) 1976. *Japanese Industrialization and its Social Consequences*. Berkeley Calif.: University of California Press.

Patrick, Hugh (ed.) 1986. *Japan's High Technology Industries: Lessons and Limitations of Industrial Policy*. Seattle, Wash.: University of Washington Press.

Patrick, Hugh and Rosovsky, Henry (eds) 1976. *Asia's New Giant: How the Japanese Economy Works*. Washington, DC: Brookings Institution.

Patterson, Gardner 1966. *Discrimination in International Trade: The Policy Issues. 1945–1965*. Princeton, NJ: Princeton University Press.

Peattie, Mark R. 1984. Japanese attitudes toward colonialism, 1895–1945. In Myers and Peattie 1984, pp. 80–127.

Pempel, T. J. 1982. *Policy and Politics in Japan: Creative Conservatism*. Philadelphia, Pa: Temple University Press.

Pinson, Koppel S. 1954. *Modern Germany: Its History and Civilization*. New York: Macmillan.

Pooley, A. M. (ed.) 1915. *The Secret Memoirs of Count Tadasu Hayashi*. New York and London: Putnam.

Popper, Karl 1972. *Objective Knowledge: An Evolutionary Approach*. London: Oxford University Press.

Price, Ernst B. 1933. *The Russo-Japanese Treaties of 1907–16 concerning Manchuria and Mongolia*. Baltimore, Md: John Hopkins University Press.

Quester, George H. 1971. *Power, Action and Interaction*. Boston, Mass.: Little, Brown.

Rasler, K. A. and Thompson, W. R. 1989. *War and State Making: The Shaping of the Global Powers*, Boston, Mass.: Unwin Hyman.

Reischauer, Edwin O. 1950. *The United States and Japan*. Cambridge, Mass.: Harvard University Press.

Reischauer, Edwin O. 1953. *Japan, Past and Present*, 2nd edn, revised. New York: Knopf.

Reischauer, Edwin O. 1964. *Japan, Past and Present*, 3rd edn, revised. New York: Knopf.

Reischauer, Edwin O. 1970. *Japan: The Story of a Nation*. New York: Knopf.

Reischauer, Edwin O. 1971. What went wrong? In Morley 1971, pp. 489–519.

Richardson, Bradley M. 1974. *The Political Culture of Japan*. Berkeley, Calif.: University of California Press.

Richardson, Bradley M. and Flanagan, Scott C. 1984. *Politics in Japan*. Boston, Mass.: Little, Brown.

Richardson, Lewis F. 1960a. *Arms and Insecurity: A Mathematical Study of the Causes and Origins of War*. Pittsburgh, Pa: Boxwood Press.

Richardson, Lewis F. 1960b. *Statistics of Deadly Quarrels*. Pittsburgh, Pa.: Boxwood Press.

Riker, William H. 1962. *The Theory of Political Coalitions*. New Haven, Conn.: Yale University Press.

Robinson, Ronald K. and Gallagher, John 1961. *Africa and the Victorians: The Climax of Imperialism in the Dark Continent*. New York: St Martin's Press.

Rosen, Baron 1922. *Forty Years of Diplomacy*. New York: Knopf.

Rosenau, James N. (ed.) 1969a. *International Politics and Foreign Policy: A Reader in Research and Theory*, revised ed. New York: Free Press.

Rosenau, James N. (ed.) 1969b. *Linkage Politics*. New York: Free Press.

Rosovsky, Henry 1961. *Quantitative Japanese Economic History*. Berkeley, Calif.: University of California Press.

Royal Institute of International Affairs 1929. *Survey of International Affairs, 1929*. London.

Russett, Bruce M. 1967. Pearl Harbor: deterrence theory and decision theory. *Journal of Peace Research* 4: 89–106.

Russett, Bruce M. 1972. *No Clear and Present Danger: A Skeptical View of the US Entry into World War II*. New York: Harper & Row.

Russett, B. 1985. The mysterious case of vanishing hegemony. *International Organization* 39: 207–31.

Salvatori, Carlos 1990, A look at the impact of internationalization on corporate finance. In Lessard and Cristiano 1990, pp. 241–8.

Samson, George 1950. *The Western World and Japan*. New York: Knopf.

Samuels, Richard J. 1987. *Business of the Japanese State: Energy Markets in Comparative and Historical Perspective*. Ithaca 5 NY: Cornell University Press.

Sandhu, K. S. and Tang, Eileen P. T. (eds.) 1974. *Japan as an Economic Power and its Implications for Southeast Asia*. Singapore: Singapore University Press.

Sawai, Minoru 1989. Kikai kogyo [Machine industry]. In Nishikawa and Abe 1989, pp. 213–53.

Saxonhouse, Gary 1986. Industrial policy and factor markets: biotechnology in Japan and the United States. In Patrick 1986, pp. 97–136.

Scalapino, Robert A. 1980. Introduction: southern advance. In Morley 1980, pp. 116–122.

Scalapino, Robert R. 1984. Election and political modernization in prewar Japan. In Morley 1984, pp. 249–91.

Scalapino, Robert A. and Masumi, Junnosuke 1962. *Parties and Politics in Contemporary Japan*. Berkeley, Calif.: University of California Press.

Schelling, Thomas C. 1960. *The Strategy of Conflict*. Cambridge, Mass.: Harvard University Press.

Schelling, Thomas C. 1966. *Arms and Influence*. New Haven, Conn.: Yale University Press.

Schelling, Thomas C. 1978. *Micromotives and Macrobehavior*. New York: Norton.

Schumpeter, Elizabeth B. (ed.) 1940. *The Industrialization of Japan and Manchukuo. 1930–1940: Population, Raw Materials and Industry*. New York: Macmillan.

Seki, Hiroharu 1984. The Manchurian Incident, 1931. In Morley 1984, pp. 139–230.

Shilling, David 1976. A reassessment of Japan's naval defense needs. *Asian Survey* 16 (3): 216–29.

Shimada, Toshihiko 1983. Designs on North China, 1933–1937. In Morley 1983, pp. 11–230.

Shinohara, Miyohei 1979. Manufacturing. In K. Ohkawa and M. Shinohara (eds), *Patterns of Japanese Economic Development: A Quantitative Appraisal*, pp. 104–21. New Haven, Conn.: Yale University Press.

Shishido, Toshio 1983. Japanese industrial development and policies for science and technology. *Science* 219: 259–64.

Simon, Herbert A. 1955. *Administrative Organization*. New York: Macmillan.

Singer, J. D. and Small, M. 1966. The composition and status ordering of the international system, 1815–1940. *World Politics* 18: 236–82.

Sites, Paul 1973. *Control: The Basis of Social Order*. New York: Dunellen.

Smith, Guy H. and Good, Dorothy 1943. *Japan: A Geographical View*. New York: American Geographical Society.

Smith, Thomas C. 1955. *Political Change and Industrial Development in Japan: Government Enterprise, 1868–80*. Stanford Calif.: Stanford University Press.

Smoke, R. 1977. *War: Controlling Escalation*. Cambridge, Mass.: Harvard University Press.

Snyder, Glenn H. and Diesing, P. 1977. *Conflict among Nations: Bargaining, Decision Making, and System Structure in International Crises*. Princeton, NJ: Princeton University Press.

Sogo Enerugi Chosakai (Energy Commission, the Ministry of International Trade and Industry) 1990. *Chikyu-kibo no Enerugi Shin-choryu heno Chosen – chuskan-hokoku soron*. [The Challenge to a New Energy Trend on a Global Scale – Interim Report, Overview]. mimeo.

Solow, Robert M. 1960. Investment and technical progress. In Arrow, Karlin and Suppes, pp. 89–104.

Sorensen, Theodore C. 1965. *Kennedy*. New York: Harper & Row.

Sprout, Harold and Sprout, Margaret T. 1965. *The Ecological Perspective on Human Affairs, with Special Reference to International Politics*. Princeton, NJ: Princeton University Press.

Staley, Eugene 1935. *War and the Private Investor*. Garden City, NY: Doubleday.

Staley, Eugene 1937. *Raw Materials in Peace and War*. New York: Council on Foreign Relations.

Staley, Eugene 1939. *World Economy in Transition: Technology vs, Politics, Laissez-faire vs, Planning, Power vs, Welfare*. New York: Council on Foreign Relations.

Steinberg, Michael, (ed.) 1990. *The Technical Challenges and Opportunities of a United Europe*. London: Pinter.

Storry, George R. 1960. *A History of Modern Japan*. New York: Penguin.

Tanaka, Akihiko 1985. Bei-Chu-So no Aida-de [Between the USA, the PRC, and the USSR]. In Watanabe 1985, pp. 220–53.

Tanter, Raymond and Ullman, Richard H. (eds) 1972. *Theory and Policy in International Relations*. Princeton, NJ: Princeton University Press.

Teng, Ssu-Yu and Fairbank, John K. 1961. *China's Response to the West: A Documentary Survey, 1839–23*. Cambridge, Mass.: Harvard University Press.

Thompson, W. R., and Rasler K. A. 1988. War and systemic capability reconcentration. *Journal of Conflict Resolution* 32: 61–86.

Thompson, Warren S. 1946. *Population and Peace in the Pacific*. Chicago: University of Chicago Press.

Thompson, Warren S. 1959. *Population and Progress in the Far East*. Chicago: University of Chicago Press.

Thucydides 1954. *History of the Peloponnesian War*, trans. R. Warner. Baltimore, Md: Penguin.

Tickner, J. Ann 1986. *Self-Reliance versus Power Politics: The American and Indian Experiences*. New York: Columbia University Press.

Tiedemann, Arthur E. 1955. *Modern Japan: A Brief History*. London: Macmillan.

Tiedemann, Arthur E. 1971. Big business and politics in prewar Japan. In Morley 1971, pp. 267–316.

Tiedemann, Arthur E. 1974. Japan's economic foreign policies, 1868–1893. In Morley 1974, pp. 118–52.

Tiedemann, Arthur E. 1984. Introduction: the London Naval Treaty, 1930. In Morley 1984, pp. 3–10.

Treadgold, Donald W. 1962. Russia and the Far East. In Lederer 1962, pp. 531–74.

TROLL/1 User's Guide various years. Cambridge, Mass.: Computer Research Center for Economics and Management Science, National Bureau of Economic Research Inc.

Tsunoda, Jun 1967. *Manshu Mondai to Kokubo Hoshin* [The Manchurian Question and Defense Policy], Tokyo: Hara Shobo.

Tsunoda, Jun 1980. The navy's role in the southern strategy. In Morley, 1980, pp. 241–95.

Umemura, Mataji, and Yamamoto, Yuzo 1989. *Nihon Keizaishi 3: Kaiko to Ishin*: Economic History of Japan, Vol. 3: The Opening of Ports and the Restoration] Tokyo: Iwanami Shoten.

US Arms Control and Disarmament Agency (various years). *World Military Expenditures and Arms Transfers*. Washington, DC: US Government Printing Office.

US Department of Defense 1971. *United States–Vietnam Relations, 1971*. Washington, DC: US Government Printing Office.

US Department of State 1914. *Foreign Relations of the United States*. Washington, DC: US Government Printing Office.

US Department of State 1915. *Foreign Relations of the United States*. Washington, DC: US Government Printing Office.

US Department of State 1922. *Foreign Relations of the United States*. Washington, DC. US Government Printing Office.

US Department of State 1924. *Foreign Relations of the United States*. Washington, DC. US Government Printing Office.

US Department of State 1940. *Papers Relating to the Foreign Relations of the United States, Vol. IV*. Washington, DC: US Government Printing Office.

US Department of State 1949. *United States Relations with China*. Washington, DC: US Government Printing Office.

US House, Committee on Armed Services 1971. *United States–Vietnam Relations, 1945–67*, Vol. 8. Washington, DC.: US Government Printing Office.

US Senate, Committee on the Judiciary 1952. *Institute of Pacific Relations, Hearings before the Sub-Committee to Investigate the Administration of the Internal Security Act and Other Security Laws*, 7A, appendix II. Washington, DC: US Government Printing Office.

US Tariff Commission 1936. *Report 105*. Washington, DC: US Government Printing Office.

US Tariff Commission 1937. *Report 119*, second series. Washington, DC: US Government Printing Office.

US War Department, Military Intelligence 1945. *Chinese Communist Movement: Hearings before the Senate Sub-Committee*, 7A, appendix II. Washington, DC: US Government Printing Office.

Usui, Katsumi 1983. The politics of war, 1937–41. In Morley 1983, pp. 309–435.

Uyehara, Shigeru 1936. *Industry and Trade of Japan*, 2nd edn, revised. New York: Alfred H. King.

Vernon, Raymond 1966. International investment and the product life cycle. *Quarterly Journal of Economics* 80: 190–207.

Vogel, Ezra F. 1979. *Japan as Number One: Lessons for America*. Cambridge, Mass.: Harvard University Press.

Von Laue, Theorore H. 1963. *Sergei Witte and the Industrialization of Russia*. New York: Columbia University Press.

Waltz, Kenneth N. 1959. *Man, the State, and War: A Theoretical Analysis*. New York: Columbia University Press.

Waltz, Kenneth N. 1979. *Theory of International Politics*. Reading, Mass.: Addison-Wesley.

Waltz, Kenneth N. 1986. Anarchic orders and balances of power. In Keohane, 1986, pp. 98–130.

Ward, Robert E. (ed.) 1968. *Political Development in Modern Japan*. Princeton, NJ: Princeton University Press.

Watanabe, Akio (ed.) 1985. *Sengo-Nihon no Taigai Seisaku* [Postwar Japan's Foreign Policy]. Tokyo: Yuhikaku.

Weatherford, M. Stephan and Fukui, Haruhiro 1989. Domestic adjustment to international shocks in Japan and the United States. *International Organization* 43 (4): 585–625.

Weber, Max. *Economy and Society: An Outline of Interpretive Sociology*. New York: Bedminster Press.

White, John A. 1950. *The Siberian Intervention*. Princeton, NJ: Princeton University Press.

White, John A. 1964. *The Diplomacy of the Russo-Japanese War*. Princeton, NJ: Princeton University Press.

White, Nathan 1976. Japan's security interests in Korea. *Asian Survey* 16 (4): 299–318.

Whiting, Allen S. 1954. *Soviet Policies in China, 1917–24*. New York: Columbia University Press.

Witte, Sergiei J. 1921. *Memoirs*, trans. and ed. Abraham Yarmolinsky. Garden City, NY: Doubleday, Page.

Wohlstetter, Roberta 1962. *Pearl Harbor: Warning and Decision*. Stanford, Calif.: Stanford University Press.

Woodhead, H. G. W. (ed.) 1925. *The China Yearbook, 1924*. Chicago: University of Chicago Press.

Woodhead, H. G. W. (ed.) 1929. *The China Yearbook, 1928*. Chicago: University of Chicago Press.

Woodhead, H. G. W. (ed.) 1930. *The China Yearbook, 1929–30*. Chicago: University of Chicago Press.

Woodhead, H. G. W. (ed.) 1940. *The China Yearbook, 1939*. Shanghai: North China Daily News.

Wright, P. G. 1935. *Trade and Trade Barriers in the Pacific*. Stanford, Calif.: Stanford University Press.

Wright, Quincy 1955. *The Study of International Relations*. New York: Appleton-Century-Crofts.

Yamakage, Susumu 1985. Ajia-Taiheiyo to Nihon [The Asia-Pacific and Japan]. In Watanabe 1985, pp. 135–61.

Yamakage, Susumu 1990. Will Japan seek regionalism? In Steinberg, 1990. pp. 147–63.

Yamamura, Kozo 1986. Caveat emptor: the industrial policy of Japan. In Paul R. Krugman (ed.), *Strategic Trade Policy and the New International Economics*, pp. 169–210. Cambridge, Mass.: MIT Press.

Yamamura, Kozo (ed.) 1990. *Japan's Economic Structure: Should It Change?* Seattle, WA: Society for Japanese Studies, University of Washington.

Yamamura, Kozo and Yasuba, Yasukichi (eds) 1987. *The Political Economy of Japan*. Vol. 1: *The Domestic Transformation*. Stanford, Calif.: Stanford University Press.

Yanaga, Chitoshi 1949. *Japan since Perry*. New York: McGraw-Hill.

Yasuba, Yasukichi 1986. Standard of living in Japan before industrialization: from what level did Japan begin? A comment. *Journal of Economic Risks* XLVI (1): 217–24.

Yasutomo, Dennis T. 1983. *Japan and the Asian Development Bank*. New York: Praeger.

Yoshitsu, Michael M. 1984. *Caught in the Middle East*. Lexington, Mass.: Lexington Books.

Young, Oran 1968. *The Politics of Force-Bargaining during International Crises*. Princeton, NJ: Princeton University Press.

Zinnes, Dina A. 1967. An analytical study of the balance of power theories. *Journal of Peace Research* 4: 270–87.

Zuk, G. 1985. National growth and international conflict: a reevaluation of Choucri and North's thesis. *Journal of Politics* 47: 269–81.

Index*

---

* Note that this index is selective in that
only the significant entries of each term are
indexed.